T2-CSE-076

LATER LIFE
The Realities of Aging

HAROLD COX

Indiana State University

PRENTICE-HALL, INC., Englewood Cliffs, New Jersey 07632

Library of Congress Cataloging in Publication Data

Cox, Harold.
    Later life.

    Includes bibliographies and index.
    1. Aged—United States—Social conditions. 2. Geron-
tology—United States. 3. Aged—United States—Psychology.
1. Title. [DNLM: 1. Aged. 2. Aging. WT 100 C877L]
HQ1064.U5C64 1984   305.2'6'0973   83-19106
ISBN 0-13-524157-X

Editorial/production supervision: Colleen Brosnan
Cover design: Ben Santora
Manufacturing buyer: John Hall

Acknowledgments of Excerpts

p. 57, from Ralph Linton, *The Cultural Background of Personality* (New York: Appleton-Century-Croft, 1945).

p. 107, from W. Somerset Maugham, *The Summing Up.* ©1954 by W. Somerset Maugham. Reprinted by permission of Doubleday & Co., Inc., and William Heinemann Limited and The Executors of the Estate of W. Somerset Maugham.

p. 227, from Shura Saul, *Aging* (New York: John Wiley, 1974). ©1974 by John Wiley.

p. 291, from "The Elderly: Prisoners of Fear," *Time,* November 29, 1976. ©1976 by Time Inc. All rights reserved. Reprinted by permission of *Time.*

p. 307, from Robert Frost, *The Poetry of Robert Frost,* ed. Edward Connery Lathem (New York: Holt, Rinehart & Winston, 1974). ©1964 by Lesley Frost Ballantine. ©1969 by Holt, Rinehart & Winston. Reprinted by permission of Holt, Rinehart & Winston, Publishers, and Jonathan Cape Ltd.

Printed in the United States of America

10 9 8 7 6 5 4 3 2 1

ISBN 0-13-524157-X

Prentice-Hall International, Inc., *London*
Prentice-Hall of Australia Pty. Limited, *Sydney*
Editora Prentice-Hall do Brasil, Ltda., *Rio de Janeiro*
Prentice-Hall Canada Inc., *Toronto*
Prentice-Hall of India Private Limited, *New Delhi*
Prentice-Hall of Japan, Inc., *Tokyo*
Prentice-Hall of Southeast Asia Pte. Ltd., *Singapore*
Whitehall Books Limited, *Wellington, New Zealand*

CONTENTS

II
THE INDIVIDUAL AND THE SOCIAL SYSTEM

IV
SOCIETAL ISSUES CONFRONTING OLDER AMERICANS

PREFACE

The demographic revolution which has taken place in modern industrial nations seems to have occurred because of a decline in the crude birth rate combined with an improved medical technology's ability to save and prolong life. The result, in all of the industrially developed nations, has been the same—a growing number and percentage of these nation's populations living to age 65 and beyond. Barring any unforeseen demographic changes in the near future the number of older persons in Western Europe and the United States will continue to grow and constitute an ever larger percent of these populations. The elderly in the United States have grown from approximately 3,000,000 in 1965, comprising less than 4 percent of the population, to 25,544,000 in 1980, comprising approximately 11 percent of the population. This shift in the age composition of the American population has resulted in a growing public awareness of the problem, potentials, and realities of aging. Persons in their middle years almost uniformly expect to live to retirement age and beyond. There is widespread interest in the quality of life of older Americans, expressed both by those approaching retirement and those who are already there. This widespread interest and concern about the lives of older Americans has produced innumerable articles and editorials from the popular press, the growth of interest and research on the part of the scientific community, and the implementation of numerous government-sponsored service delivery programs for older Americans.

This book attempts to synthesize and integrate material from the vast proliferation of research and writing on the subject of aging into a meaningful discussion of the major trends and developments in the field. It reflects the interdisciplinary nature of subject matter and includes material from psychology, sociology, social work, anthropology, the biological sciences, medicine, and psychiatry. A serious attempt was made to favor neither the medical model which sees old age as a process of deterioration, disease, and progressive decline nor the more recent and popular human development model which sees old age as a period of further growth, development, and new experiences. While the later years are a further development of the individual's life history and offer opportunities for growth and new experiences, ultimately all people suffer certain health losses and die. Thus, considerable effort was made to present the later phase of the life cycle as realistically as possible.

The interdisciplinary nature of gerontology tends to make texts eclectic in nature. While this is true, an attempt was made in the chapters in this book—written from a social science perspective—to utilize a symbolic interaction frame of reference. Thus, it was hoped that the reader would be provided with a single theoretical approach to view the behavioral aspects of aging.

Writing a text, much like teaching a class, involved the synthesizing and organizing of a variety of diverse materials into an understandable, interesting, and challenging presentation of the facts. In the case of the textbook, the finished product should be interesting, understandable, intellectually challenging, and applicable to one's own life and personal experiences. Hopefully this was achieved in this text. Only you, the reader, can judge the quality of the product. Inevitably, writing a text is a process in which the author learns much more than any future reader of the material. His attempts to synthesize, organize, and present the material to the reader inevitably begin with his clear understanding of it. In this way, I have already gained much in this process since it has increased my knowledge, sensitivity, and comprehension of the realities of later life.

I would like to thank all of my colleagues and friends at Indiana State University who provided me assistance and support as I prepared this manuscript; my students who raised questions, challenged my ideas, and thereby increased my understanding of the subject matter; Joyce Sanders, for her careful and diligent work in preparing the manuscript; C. Ray Wingrove of the University of Richmond and Vern L. Bengtson of the University of Southern California, for reviewing the manuscript; and my wife who is always supportive and understanding of my work, however successful or unsuccessful it might be.

H. C.

1

EMERGENCE
AND SCOPE
OF GERONTOLOGY

The year grows rich as it groweth old,
and life's latest sands are its sands of gold!

Julia C. R. Dorr
To the "Bouquet Club"

THE ADVENT OF GERONTOLOGY

During the past twenty years aging and the field of gerontology have become the
focus of extensive concern, discussion, editorializing, and political action. Aging
has arrived as an issue and object of study; people are examining what it means
to be old in America.

What accounts for this burst of interest? A number of factors might explain it—factors stemming both from individual experience and from the experience of society as a whole. The increasing number of people and percentage of
our total population living to age 65 and beyond have made the problems of
aging more widespread, visible, and ultimately more widely known. And because
of this increased longevity, almost all of us at one time or another have had the
experience of helping an aging relative adjust and survive under changing life
circumstances.

When only a small proportion of older people experience poverty, illness, or social isolation, we may not be aware of their problems. But as the number of older people living under these conditions grows, a challenge is directly
posed to our social service systems, and the problem "takes off"—it becomes
acute enough to be discussed and debated by politicians, the media, and other
concerned individuals and groups. One definite effect emerges: a growing consciousness of—and sensitivity to—the problems of older people.

As the number of older persons has grown and public awareness of
problems of the aged has increased, government "delivery systems" for older

Americans have developed, providing services such as food, employment, information, homemaking, and counseling. New paraprofessional and professional occupations deal with the problems of older people, and political action and legislation have been initiated on their behalf. Significantly, the academic community has recognized aging as a legitimate area of study.

Before this surge of interest, physicians, health practitioners, and behavioral scientists often avoided the study of aging. Perhaps concern with the illnesses and problems of younger persons seemed more directly related to a humane cause: Young people have all their lives before them, and those who help them rightly feel that they are contributing to the future of society.

Older people, on the other hand, have most of their mortal lives behind them. Their medical, psychiatric, and social problems are often more difficult to deal with because they are frequently complex and interrelated. Medically, the communicable diseases of the young can often be entirely cured, whereas many of the chronic medical problems of later life cannot be. At best, the illnesses of the aged can be controlled, and a bad situation will not get worse; at worst, illnesses may resist treatment, resulting in disability and death. It is easy to understand why doctors would find more satisfaction in curing a disease than in stopping it from accelerating. But whatever the reason, older people have not received as much attention from health and other professionals as have younger people.

In much the same way, psychology, sociology, and social work have not devoted as much research and attention to the problems of older persons as they have to younger people. Since scientists are subject to the same latent fears about aging and death as those that trouble the general population, they frequently find the study of aging uncongenial, if not depressing. Paying attention to aging processes reminds researchers that someday they too will grow old and die. As a result, the subject of aging has not received the attention it demands of scientists.

This neglect of the problems related to aging appears to be over. Aging has become a legitimate subject of study, and the relevant professions as well as the general public are becoming increasingly sensitive to the issues and problems of the later part of the life cycle.

The remainder of this chapter will provide you with an overview of the demographic trends which reveal the dramatic rise in the number of persons 65 years and older in the population; additionally, we will introduce some of the major problems of this group, as well as common public perceptions of the lives of older persons.

DEMOGRAPHIC TRENDS

In 1900 there were three million Americans over age 65, comprising approximately 4 percent (one in 25) of the total population. In 1970, 20 million Americans were over age 65, and they comprised approximately 10 percent (one in

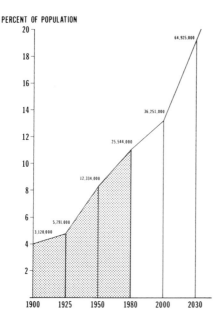

PERCENT OF POPULATION

Figure 1–1
U.S. Population Age 65 and Older, 1900–2030
1985–2030 figures are projections

Source: Bureau of the Census, Social Security Administration

ten) of the total population.[1] In 1980 there were 25,544,000 Americans over 65, comprising approximately 11 percent (one in nine) of the total population. Demographers estimate that by the year 2000, 36 million Americans will be over age 65; they may comprise as much as 13 percent of the total population (Figure 1–1).

These figures are based on the current birthrate. Should the birthrate suddenly rise, the percentage of the total population over age 65 would drop slightly. The long-range trend in the birthrate has been downward, however, and no one is predicting any dramatic reversals in the next thirty years. Any further drop in the birthrate would make the 65+ group comprise an even larger percentage of the total population.

Population figures for the 65+ age group have grown by three million to four million per decade since 1940. Growth during the 1970s exceeded earlier projections; it climbed at an annual increment of 460,000. Every day approximately 5000 persons reach their sixty-fifth birthday. Every day 3600 persons in the same age group die. This means an increase of 1400 persons in the 65+ group each day. Figure 1–2 reveals how much more rapidly the 65+ group is growing compared to the total population since 1900.

Not only are more people living to age 65 but once they reach that age they live longer. In 1900 fewer than one million Americans were 75 and older and approximately 100,000 were 85 and older. In 1980 there were 9.5 million persons 75 and older and 2.3 million persons 85 and older. While the 65 and older group has increased approximately eightfold since 1900, the population

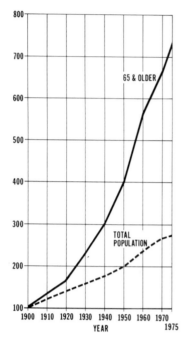

Figure 1–2
Rate of Increase 65 and Older vs. Total U.S. Population
1900–1975
1900 = 100
Source: Bureau of the Census

85 and older has grown 22 times its size in the same period. Moreover, the 85+ group is projected to grow more rapidly than the 65+ age group until about 2010 when cohorts born in the baby boom of the 1940s and 1950s begin to retire (see Figure 1–3).[2] Since it is the 85+ group which makes the greatest demand

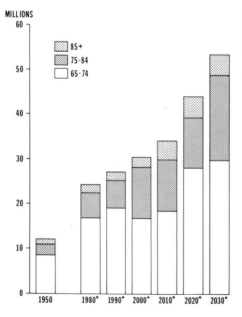

Figure 1–3
Distribution of the Older Population by Age
Group, 1950 and 1980 to 2030
*Projections

Source: Bureau of the Census

for services one can easily see the implication of the growth of this age group for the resources of federal, state, and local governments.

Louis Harris and Associates believe that there are three basic reasons for the current growth of America's older population. First, the large number of people born when the birthrate was high are now reaching age 65. Second, a high rate of immigration of younger adults during World War II further added to the number of people now reaching 65. Finally, improvements in medical technology have created a dramatic increase in life expectancy.

Since 1900 life expectancy at birth has increased, and a greater differential in life expectancy has arisen between men and women. In 1900 the life expectancy for women in the United States was just under 51 years; for men, 48 years. By 1978 the life expectancy for women had increased to 77.2 years; for men, to 69.5 years. While life expectancy had generally increased by 25 years, the sex difference in life expectancy had increased from 3 to 7.7 in favor of female longevity. White females have the highest life expectancy: 77.8 years, followed by 73.6 years for females of other races. White males can expect to live to age 70.2; other males to 65.0 (see Figure 1–4).

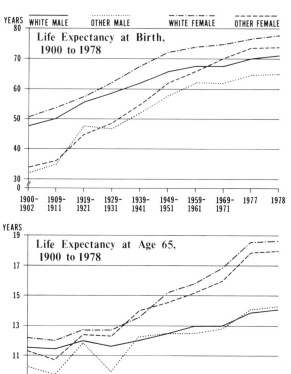

Figure 1–4

Source: National Center for Health Statistics

Life expectancy at birth is determined by finding the average number of years a person can expect to live from the time of birth. For every child that dies in the first few months of life, others must live to very advanced age in order to give the entire population an average life expectancy of approximately 73.3 years. Since a person could die at any age in life, those who arrive at age 65 are a select group who have presumably experienced and survived many health problems and other obstacles along the way. Currently, those arriving at age 65 can expect to live approximately 16.3 years beyond that time.

Between 1900 and 1950 the increase in life expectancy came about primarily because of a decrease in mortality among the younger age groups. Stated simply, larger numbers of persons reached the older ages, but once there they did not live much longer than the previous generation. Since 1950, however, life expectancy at the older ages has increased more rapidly than at birth. Between 1950 and 1978 life expectancy for the 65+ group increased by 2.4 years, more than it had increased between 1900 and 1950.[3] Moreover, a major medical breakthrough in the control of heart disease or cancer could extend life expectancy even longer. If retirement age remains the same, the current generation of younger Americans may well spend almost as many years in retirement as they did during their working careers.

Formerly, the diseases that took large numbers of younger people's lives were "communicable" diseases, traced to viruses or bacteria. Medical science, in working to immunize the population against such diseases as smallpox, diphtheria, measles, and mumps, has come a long way toward controlling the kinds of diseases that kill younger people. Older Americans are less affected by acute communicable diseases; they more often experience problems with chronic conditions and the deterioration of vital organs. The biggest single health problem experienced by older persons is a failure of the circulatory system. This can include anything from heart attacks to hardening of the arteries. A second major cause of death in the older population is cancerous growths. These are characterized as a breakdown in body chemistry in which cancerous cells divide and redivide at abnormally fast speeds. Both heart trouble and cancer have been more serious for men than for women.

Rheumatism, arthritis, stiffening joints, and brittle bones tend to be the kind of chronic conditions that many older people eventually experience. Medical science has made little headway in dealing with these conditions. When they are treated by medicine, the goal is most often to stabilize the condition and keep it from getting worse; a cure is seldom likely.

George L. Maddox is critical of medicine's neglect of the problems of aging; he contends that the United States spends much more money on spectacular medical achievements such as heart transplants and artificial kidney treatment than on preventive care, especially for older people. He argues that we do not care for older Americans until they are so sick that they require hospitalization, which only raises the cost of treatment.[4]

Gerontologists believe that there are two general strategies for increasing life expectancy. One is the effort to conquer disease. They believe that if death from cardiovascular disease and malignancy were eliminated, life expectancy could be increased by five to fifteen years. The second strategy is to alter biological processes that are regarded as promotive of aging yet independent of disease. This would require research into the biochemistry of the aging individual to discover the factors controlling the rate of aging. It is hoped that rather than controlling disease medicine could control the rate at which the individual ages.[5]

Pressure from such critics as Maddox may encourage medical science to attempt to control the diseases of later life as well as the rate at which the individual ages. Once the resources of the medical profession are harnessed and directed toward the problems of aging, the results could be impressive. Although no fountain of youth would spring up, it might not be unreasonable to anticipate a further increase in the life expectancy of older Americans.

While the number of persons arriving at age 65 is expected to increase for the foreseeable future, the increase should prove gradual rather than dramatic between now and the year 2010. The reason for this is that the 1930s was a period of low birthrate. Since these people will be retiring between now and the year 2010, the increase will be gradual. Also, the *dependency ratio* will probably not change appreciably in the next thirty years (see Figure 1–5). The dependency ratio is calculated by comparing those in the work force with those out of the work force. Thus most people under 18 and over 65 are out of the work

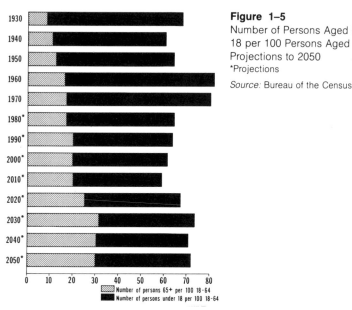

Figure 1–5
Number of Persons Aged 65 and Older and Under 18 per 100 Persons Aged 18–64, 1930–1980 and Projections to 2050
*Projections

Source: Bureau of the Census

force and depend on those between 19 and 64 to produce the goods and services that they need. Since those born in the baby boom following World War II are now entering the labor force, they have the effect of keeping the dependency ratio lower than it would otherwise be. This high birthrate after 1945 is presently creating difficulties for many because jobs must be found for a large group of younger people. The major problem, however, is expected to come in the year 2010 and thereafter, when the postwar baby boom begins to retire and is followed by fewer people who must support them. The dependency ratio should increase dramatically at that time. One can only imagine what changes may be necessary in production, taxation, and the support system for older Americans. And there is an additional question: Will taxpayers in their working years be willing to be taxed heavily to support this large group of retirees?

SEX RATIO

According to Louis Harris and his research associates, in 1900 there were 102 males for every 100 females at age 65. Currently, there are only 69 males for every 100 females at age 65+; for age 75+ this figure drops to 58 males for every 100 females. The projection for 1990 reveals a further drop, with only 54 males for every 100 females in the 75+ population.

Table 1–1, showing the sex differences in mortality from heart disease and cancer, indicates part of the reason for the shortage of men in the later years. Heart disease and cancer, two of the major diseases and killers of older Americans, are considerably more prevalent among men than among women. While the mortality rate for both sexes has been declining in recent years, it has

Table 1–1   Death Rates by Major Causes at Age 65, by Sex, for Selected Years

CAUSE OF DEATH	65 TO 74 YEARS			75 to 84 YEARS			85 YEARS AND OVER		
	1940	*1954*	*1973*	*1940*	*1954*	*1973*	*1940*	*1954*	*1973*
All Causes	4.8	3.8	3.4	11.2	8.6	7.9	23.6	18.2	17.4
Male	5.5	4.7	4.7	12.1	9.8	10.1	24.6	18.7	19.8
Female	4.2	3.0	2.4	10.3	7.6	6.6	22.8	17.7	16.2
Diseases of the Heart									
Male	2.1	2.1	2.1	5.0	4.4	4.5	10.3	8.3	9.3
Female	1.5	1.3	1.0	4.2	3.5	3.0	9.7	8.1	7.9
Malignant Neo-plasms									
Male	0.7	0.8	1.0	1.3	1.3	1.7	1.5	1.7	2.0
Female	0.6	0.6	0.6	1.0	1.0	0.9	1.3	1.3	1.1

(Rates per 1000 population)

Source: National Center for Health Statistics, *Vital Statistics Rates in the United States, 1940–1960; Vital Statistics of the United States, Mortality, Part A; 1973* (Washington, D.C.: U.S. Public Health Service, 1973).

been declining much more rapidly for females. In the case of cancer, the mortality rates for males have actually increased in recent years.

The fact that women at any age in life are less likely to die than men, coupled with their low mortality from the two major diseases of older Americans, helps to explain the imbalance in the sex ratio at age 65.

AGING BLACK AMERICANS

In comparing blacks and whites, the 1980 census data indicates that 11.2 percent of the total white population is 65 and over while only 7.8 percent of the black population is in this age group.

The 1980 census indicated that of the 23 million persons aged 65 and over, 90 percent were white, 8.2 percent were black, and 2 percent were "other races."

One factor that explains the lower percentage of blacks is their higher birthrate, which keeps the percentage of the 65+ group lower than might be expected. Another factor is that life expectancy for blacks is lower than that for whites. This may in part be explained by the fact that discrimination has kept blacks in the lower class—burdened with a poor diet and less-than-adequate medical attention. And discrimination may force blacks into high-risk occupations.

Comparisons of the sex ratios of blacks and whites find the black sex ratio a little more balanced. Whites currently have 69 men per 100 women at age 65. Blacks, on the other hand, have 73 men per 100 women. It could be argued that racial discrimination causes black women to experience poorer diet and less adequate health and medical attention than white women enjoy, thereby bringing their numbers into closer correspondence with those of black men.

MARITAL STATUS

As a result of the fact that women outlive men by approximately 7.7 years the older the woman becomes the more likely she is to be a widow. Carole Allen and Herman Brotman point out that:

> At ages 55–64 over 70 percent of women are married, at ages 65–74 the figure drops to less than 50 percent and beyond 75 it drops to a little more than 20 percent. Thus, a remarkable seven out of every ten women age 75 and older are widows. By contrast, the percentage of men who are married declines relatively slowly with age. At ages 55–64, 87 percent of all men are married, at ages 65–74 the figure is 81 percent and at 75+, 69 percent of the men are still married.[6]

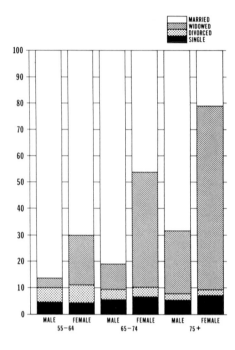

Figure 1–6

Percent Distribution of Persons Aged 55 and Older by Age Group and Marital Status, 1979

Source: Bureau of the Census

(See Figure 1–6.) In addition to the longer life expectancy of women, two factors tend to explain the disparity in these figures. First, the tendency is for men to marry younger women at any age in life, and these age differences become wider as the men reach middle and older age. It has been argued that men in middle and older age with secure incomes have generally been able to find younger women who are willing to marry them. At age 65 the wives were on the average seven years younger than their husbands.

Another explanation for the surplus of widows is the relatively short supply of available men from whom to choose a second marital partner. The surplus of women after age 65 makes it easy for a man to remarry but relatively difficult for a woman.

The result of the different sex ratio and remarriage rates of men and women is that more than three-fourths of the men 65 and above live in a family setting while less than half of the women do. By age 75 most women are heads of their own households, living alone or with a nonrelative. Less than one-fourth of the men, on the other hand, are single householders after the age of 75.

As age increases, the percentage of older persons living alone or in institutions increases. Women are therefore both more likely to be living alone and more likely to be institutionalized (see Figure 1–7).

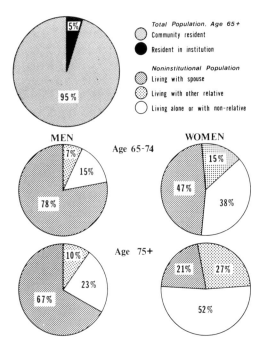

Figure 1–7
Living Arrangements of the 65+ Population
by Sex and Age Group, 1979
Source: Bureau of the Census

AGING: WHAT THE PROBLEMS ARE

Now that we have reviewed the demographic trends toward the rise in the number of persons arriving at age 65 and the tendency for this age group to live longer than their predecessors, let's examine some of the major problems that confront them.

Aging is experienced as an inevitable and lifelong process. During the time it took you to read the first sentence in this paragraph, you have aged. Being "old," "aged," a "senior citizen" is a stage in the process of aging. In 1935 the United States government set age 65 as the age at which one was allowed to begin drawing social security checks, effectively making this the age of retirement. Sixty-five, however, was an arbitrary choice. It could just as easily have been 60 or 70. Realistically, aging is a continuum, with conception at one end and death at the other. However, for the purposes of much of this text, we will think of 65 as the beginning of older age, while realizing, of course, that this is essentially a social definition.

Social Problems

At age 65, older Americans are often confronted with a series of developmental and adjustment problems. Most companies provide strong inducements for their workers to retire at 65 or before. With retirement comes less income and the loss of status, privilege, and power associated with one's position in the occupational hierarchy. A major reorganization of one's life activities is required, since the nine to five workday is now meaningless. Those who have come to shape their identities and personalities to the demands of their occupational roles can expect a changing definition of self. And there can be a considerable degree of social isolation if new activities are not found to replace work-related activities. Finally, there is often a search for new identity, meaning, and value for one's life.

The major reorganization of one's life that must take place at the time of retirement entails numerous adjustments for those who must negotiate the change. This reorganization can be viewed in the light both of *gerontology* and of *geriatrics*. Gerontology studies the social, economic, political, and related social aspects of aging; geriatrics is a branch of medicine that deals with the problems and diseases of old age.

Like certain philosophers, students of aging have difficulty with the dualism of the "mind-body" problem. Events in one's social life, such as the loss of a lifelong marital partner, can lead to loss of the will to live and the onset of a series of physical and medical problems. Conversely, certain physical disabilities, such as diabetes, prostate trouble, and arthritis may diminish one's capabilities as husband or wife and so alter one's social world. The physical and social adjustments of older Americans are often interrelated and difficult to separate.

Growing older is physiologically inevitable and is commonly experienced as a progressive decline in organic functions, and psychologically as a progressive loss of sensory and cognitive capacities. These losses, however, are quite different for each individual, and there is no predictable pattern by which all individuals will progress through them. For one person, aging may bring with it the development of a form of diabetes (for example, excessive amounts of blood sugar) which if not curbed can lead to the loss of limbs or blindness. For another person, aging may bring hardening of the arteries, with slowing of the blood flow to the brain accompanied by the experience of occasional forgetfulness and the onset of senility.

While the pattern is not predictable, as a general rule older people require more medical attention than do younger people because they experience greater vulnerability to ill health. However, it should not go unnoticed that many older persons live healthy lives into extreme age, and some remain in good health almost until death. *Old age is not inevitably a period of poor health.* According to studies by Richard Kalish, variability in the aging process can be seen by comparing three-year-olds with 75-year-olds. Biologically, three-year-olds are all likely to be going through approximately the same stage of development at approximately the same speed. At age 75, individuals vary much more in biological and behavioral functioning than do three-year-olds or even young adults.[7]

Medical Problems

Leslie Libow, medical director and chief of geriatric medicine at the Jewish Institute for Geriatric Care, has summarized what he considers are some of the most common medical problems of older Americans.

1. Mobility problems: Twenty percent of persons over 65 have some problem in walking. Although only 5 percent of these are homebound, most use canes, walkers, or wheelchairs in order to get about.
2. Brain: From 5 to 15 percent of the population over 65 experience serious problems in thinking—most often identified as senility.
3. Stroke: The most common physical reason for older persons to be placed in nursing homes. Approximately two-thirds of older people suffering from strokes are expected to have complete or partial recovery; the remaining one-third will survive but not be ambulatory.
4. Heart: Fifty percent of older people in nursing homes have a serious heart problem. The figures for the total population are not known.
5. Prostate: A disease very common among older men. Fortunately, it is operable with less than 1 percent mortality from surgery. There is much confusion about this operation, and patients should understand that it does not entail the loss of sexual functioning.
6. Bowels: Changes and constipation are common in later life. Time for excessive self-concern can result in an obsession with this problem. It is a problem easily avoided; doctors recommend a proper diet, including fruits and fibrous foods.
7. Bones: In aging, bones weaken and break more easily. As a rule, blacks experience fewer fractures than whites, and men fewer than women. Increasing physical activity (walking, dancing, jogging, bicycling) is believed to be the best way to reduce fractures. Dietary changes are also held to reduce the risks.
8. Breast problems: Cancer of the breast is a concern of women, with older women usually faring better than women in the middle years.
9. Eyes: Cataracts are a common eye problem but are almost always surgically treatable. Glaucoma, which is not as treatable, is usually manageable. The only eye change considered normal is a tendency to farsightedness as a part of the aging process.
10. Arthritis: One of the most common problems of later life, with no known medical cure.
11. Nutrition: Signs of malnutrition in older people may include cracked lips, which indicate a vitamin-B deficiency, excessively dry skin, and some anemia. Obesity caused by high-calorie diets is a common problem, and heavy consumption of fats is held to contribute to hardening of the arteries. Malnutrition may result from poverty, inaccessibility of grocery stores, or lack of incentive to eat.[8]

That the experience of physiological decline is a problem for older people can be seen in a study done by Harold Cox and others in western Indiana. Cox asked a random sample of persons aged 65 and above about the degree of difficulty experienced in performing daily activities.

As Table 1–2 indicates, by their own admission 40 percent of the people in this study had difficulty getting up and down stairs; 20 percent had difficulty washing and bathing; 15 percent had difficulty dressing; 19 percent had difficulty getting out of the house; 6 percent had difficulty watching TV; 25 percent had difficulty using the telephone; 19 percent had difficulty cooking; 30 percent had difficulty cleaning; 45 percent had difficulty maintaining their own home; 20 percent had difficulty getting around the house; and 30 percent had difficulty doing the laundry.

Psychological Problems

Professionals are often challenged in the diagnosis of the psychological problems of aging; it is difficult to distinguish whether problems are the result of a physical condition, such as hardening of the arteries (with related malfunction of the brain, perhaps occasioning bizarre behavior), or the result of psychological depression.

Mrs. Jones retired at age 65 in good health and with no particular physical or emotional problems. By age 75, however, she had begun to experience a hearing loss and a heart problem accompanied by poor circulation which resulted in her having considerably less energy. These combined factors became her reason for staying at home most of the time, interacting with others much less frequently than in the past; she began experiencing periodic depression. Thus, a route can sometimes be traced from biological problems to social or emotional difficulties.

Table 1–2 Limitations in Daily Activities of Persons Aged 65+

DIFFICULTY	YES	NO
Getting up and down stairs	40%	60%
Washing and bathing	20	80
Dressing	15	85
Getting out of the house	19	81
Watching TV	6	94
Using the telephone	25	75
Cooking	19	81
Cleaning your house	30	70
Maintaining your house	45	55
Getting around the house	20	80
Doing the laundry	30	70

Source: Cox, Sekhon, and Norman, *Social Characteristics of the Elderly in Indiana* (Terre Haute: Indiana Academy of Social Sciences, 1978), p. 190.

Paranoia in old age is not uncommon, according to Frederick Charatan. Those experiencing this disorder believe that they are the object of hostile attention from others. Older people suffering from paranoia, although perfectly normal in every other way, have gone so far as to believe they were being spied on by the FBI or Communists.

Undue depression is another common problem of older people, according to Charatan. They have often experienced a series of losses in their lives and feel that they can only look forward to still further losses. Depression in older age is twice as common in women as in men and usually follows immediately upon some loss. The most difficult loss for older persons is that of a spouse, and statistics show that bereavement in later years increases survivor mortality, often labeled the "broken heart syndrome." Men especially experience depression following retirement. The "retirement syndrome" is a depressive illness identified and labeled by psychiatrists.

The physiological, psychological, and social problems of older people are real experiences that must ultimately be dealt with in some fashion. Although we regard aging as a lifelong process for all of us, the problems confronted at the later end of the life cycle seem somehow more serious and foreboding than those of earlier life. Unfortunately, for older persons these problems sometimes occur one after another, thus becoming intertwined and complex to untangle; often, too, they occur when people seem to have the fewest resources with which to cope with them. Yet despite the fact that over three-fourths of the older population suffer from at least one long-term deteriorating condition, most learn to live with their disabilities and to adjust in ways allowing them to find continual satisfaction in life.

PUBLIC PERCEPTIONS OF OLDER PERSONS

Perhaps the major social problem confronting older Americans today is how they are viewed by the general population. Students of symbolic interactions have long argued that at any age in life the most crucial determinant of our well-being is how we are defined and categorized by others in our social environment. Once categorized by others as handsome or ugly, intelligent or stupid, bold or timid, or any other label, it takes a very strong and determined person to resist the social definition placed on him or her by others and to carve out a new image. Most often people behave the way others in their social world expect them to behave. The problem for older persons is that they are often seen in negative and stereotypic terms by other age groups in society.

The word *stereotype* comes from a Greek word meaning "hardcore." Today, the world has come to mean *the most frequent combination of traits assigned by one group to another.* As a perception of an individual or a group, it is f·-··'·ently rigid and biased, as well as negative if not derogatory. Categor· stereotyping those around us—with attendant expectations concer·

motives and future behavior—is a social perception process that allows one to live in a complex world without having to deal with the wealth of details and particulars that characterize each individual. Thus, one who reduces all older people to a stereotype saves the time and energy it would take to respond to each of them on an individual basis. While this process may allow us to coexist with large numbers of other persons with a minimum of effort, it is most often unfair to the individual or group that is stereotyped. Very frequently, stereotypes of any group different from ourselves tend to establish the norm for that group on the basis of the least desirable traits possessed by some members of the group. Stereotypes of older persons are no different; they are often thought of as feeble, senile, and destitute, since this is the plight of the least fortunate members of this group.

Gerontologists have coined the term *ageism* to refer to a pejorative concept of someone based on his or her advanced chronological age. Like racism or sexism, ageism is an unduly negative view attached to all older persons. Hendricks and Hendricks observe that part of the myth implicit in ageism is the view that older persons are somehow different from our present and future selves and therefore not subject to the same desires, fears, and concerns we have. We might also consider whether we do not share many of their fears, desires, and concerns ourselves.

Perhaps the most stereotypic view of the 65+ group in America is that all old people are alike; indeed, this kind of thinking lies at the heart of all stereotypes. But in fact, there is considerable difference in the health of two 65-year-olds. Illness, lifestyle, and previous occupational pressures may result in quite different states of health for persons the same age. Mrs. Jones, for example, regularly volunteers to help older people at the community senior-citizen center, most of whom are younger than she. E. Grant Youmans speaks frequently in his work of the different problems experienced by the "young old" and the "old old."

Similarly, older Americans retire as members of the working class, middle class, or upper class. Retirement incomes, previous experiences, and preferred lifestyles of the different social classes vary greatly, to say the least. Having a winter home in Florida and a summer cottage on a lake in Canada, which middle-class and upper-class older people may well have, is quite different from living in a small slum-district apartment in the heart of Detroit. We should be careful to keep these distinctions in mind when talking about the problems of older people.

Another stereotypic view of older persons is that they are isolated. For some older Americans this is true, but for the majority it is not. The current social security and welfare systems have given older people some degree of independence. Most of them can now maintain their own homes rather than having to move in with their children or into government housing. This condition of independence and continuity, in which older persons remain in familiar neighborhoods, socially intact with past friends and associates, is desired by both older and younger people. Family sociologists have also found much higher degrees of inter-generational family interaction than was expected. Telephone calling, frequent visiting, and vacations are used to maintain considerable contact and involvement between different generations of the same family. Irving Rosow, in his study of older apartment-dwellers in Cleveland, and Bruce Lemon and others, in their study of retirement communities, found considerable social interaction and involvement among older Americans. Although some older Americans do find themselves isolated, this is not the most common pattern; the majority are socially active and involved.

Stereotypic Views of Retirement

A third stereotype commonly entertained of older people is that retirement is a period of crisis and adjustment. Rosamonde Boyd and Charles Oakes observe that many blue-collar workers not only look forward to retirement but, if guaranteed an adequate income, will retire early. Herbert Parnes found that about half of the retirees he interviewed retired voluntarily and seven out of ten of these had retired before age 65.[9] Even for white-collar workers who find some meaning in their work, there is no evidence that retirement precipitates a lengthy crisis.

Related to the view that retirement is a crisis is the commonly held belief that society forces able-bodied older persons to retire. It is true that less than 5 percent of those over age 65 continue to work but, as we have just noted, the majority of older workers choose to retire early if they are granted retirement income sufficient for living comfortably. Although in 1978 Congress raised the legal mandatory retirement age from 65 to 70, there is no evidence that any significant number of older people will necessarily choose to work longer. James Schulz found that of every 1000 retirees, only 70 were forced to retire. The remaining 930 apparently chose their retirement voluntarily. Sometimes poor health is the reason for retiring. However, retirees in good health look forward to the freedom to choose and do what they want.

Another myth about retirement is that it undermines the physical health of the retiree and often leads to death. Many, upon observing an acquaintance, friend, or relative die shortly after retirement, presume that retirement shortens life. What they may be overlooking is that at any age, some persons will die, whether working or not. Longitudinal studies have found that most retirees show a slight *improvement* in their overall health following retirement and that there is no difference in the mortality rate for this group and those remaining in the labor force. *Retirement simply does not precipitate death.*[10]

Still another view is that retirement is highly disruptive of family relations, since it alters the balance of power and division of labor between husbands and wives. Richard Kalish and others observed that the retired male has time to dedicate to the roles of husband, father, grandfather—roles that in the past were often slighted in favor of occupational demands. Thus retirement may actually improve family relations by allowing one more opportunity to assume previously neglected roles. Many couples find that they have more time to spend together—almost a second courtship period. Of course, retirement *can* be experienced as the alteration of a "power balance," with negative consequences for family relations. Even so, conflict is often managed within families and as such does not necessarily show up in an increase in divorce.

Further complicating the view that retirement is a time of crisis is the common belief that retirement plunges people into poverty because it is often accompanied by a 50 percent decline in income. Gordon Streib and Clement Schneider in one study and James Schulz in another found that while retirees often experienced a sharp drop in income, most of them said that they were getting along well enough. Research findings indicate that older people are apparently able to exist on smaller amounts of money and feel no decline in status or class position.

Another complication is the myth that retirees are denied a normal role in the community and are forced into geriatric ghettos. Journalists often see the older people as victims whom society assigns to segregated communities. In reality, many middle-class older Americans have voluntarily moved to retirement communities. Irving Rosow's work indicates that social interaction increases among older persons in these segregated communities. It is perhaps a legitimate question to ask whether society provides desirable environments for its older population. A collateral question is whether society should provide older people with protective environments to shield them from any loss of status. While researchers may well examine these questions, it is currently a misconception to believe that all older persons are forced into geriatric ghettos. Most often those who move to retirement communities and segregated housing do so freely. A few are pressured by their children to move to nursing homes, but this is the exception rather than the rule.

Misconceptions of the Plight of Older People

Louis Harris and Associates were commissioned by the National Council on Aging to study attitudes toward older Americans. Their report, following 4250 interviews, reveals some interesting misconceptions among the younger population concerning the experiences of older Americans. Collectively, only 2 percent of a sample of Americans of all ages considered the years after 60 as the best of a person's life. Simultaneously, nearly one-third of the 18-to-64-year-olds—and a larger percent of those over 65—saw those years as the least desirable.

Table 1–3 indicates that younger adults perceive the problems of older people as actually greater than they are. While only 25 percent of older subjects report fear of crime as a serious concern of older Americans, fully 50 percent of the public believes that it is. While only 12 percent of the older population reports loneliness as a serious problem, 60 percent of the public perceive it as such. The pattern is the same for every one of a series of variables, ranging from not

Table 1–3 Public Perceptions and Problems of Older Persons

	VERY SERIOUS PROBLEMS ACTUALLY EXPERIENCED BY OLDER PEOPLE	VERY SERIOUS PROBLEMS PUBLIC EXPECTS OLDER PEOPLE TO EXPERIENCE	NET DIFFERENCE
Fear of crime	23%	50%	+27
Poor health	21	51	+30
Not having enough money to live on	15	62	+47
Loneliness	12	60	+48
Not having enough medical care	10	44	+34
Not having enough education	8	20	+12
Not feeling needed	7	54	+47
Not having enough to do to keep busy	6	37	+31
Not having enough friends	5	28	+23
Not having enough job opportunities	5	45	+40
Poor housing	4	35	+31
Not having enough clothing	3	16	+13

Source: L. Harris and Associates, *The Myth and Reality of Aging in America* (Washington, D.C.: The National Council on the Aging, Inc., 1975), p. 31.

feeling needed to poor housing: *The general public perceives the problem to be considerably greater than what older Americans actually experience.*

This discrepancy may in part be explained by the fact that in a youth-oriented society, most people are not conditioned to looking forward to old age. Another part of the discrepancy may be explained by the mass media's presentation of the elderly, a presentation that tends to focus on the less fortunate cases. In addition, most people associate aging with death. Since medical science has dedicated itself to such a degree to saving the lives of the younger population, it is principally older people who die in our society. The result is that the social psychology of Americans is often conditioned to view the older years negatively and Americans tend to exaggerate the problems that accompany the aging process. Many look for examples to confirm their biases. Upon seeing four older persons, three of whom are well dressed and one poorly dressed, many, if not most, will remember the poorly dressed person. Though an attempt has been made in this chapter to present an overview of some of the problems confronting older persons, one must constantly guard against too negative a view of the later phase of the life cycle. When Leslie Libow observes that 20 percent of persons 65 and over have some trouble walking, we fail to recognize the fact that this means 80 percent of older people are ambulatory and have no trouble getting around. Similarly, while Libow finds that from 5 to 15 percent experience some problems in thinking this means that from 85 to 95 percent are rational and can think clearly. In the Cox and other studies of limitations of daily activities of older persons (Table 1–2) less than half of the subjects experienced any of these limitations. Depending on the variable examined, from 60 to 90 percent of the sample had no limitation at all. Thus, while the problems confronted by older persons are real and must be dealt with, let us not be unduly pessimistic in our view of the lives of older Americans. The majority of older Americans believe themselves to be in reasonably good health, think that they have adequate incomes, and are convinced that they are living their lives just about the way they would like to.

Our discussion of ageism—the myths and stereotypes of aging—should not imply that older Americans do not have problems, but rather should show that their problems are often exaggerated in the thinking of the general public. The intent of government planners and service providers is realistically to identify the problems of aging and to work for their solution. Thus, since the myths surrounding the subject of aging require careful investigation, it becomes critical for professionals in the field to examine these with scientific objectivity. The gerontologist, prepared with scientific training in one of the behavioral sciences, is likely to perceive his or her role as that of a detached observer. The public-service worker in programs for older Americans, on the other hand, is likely to perceive himself or herself as an advocate.

Detached observers attempt to carefully describe how people think, feel, and act. Moreover, they attempt periodically to offer solutions to problems confronted by a particular group of people. Advocates are likely to be politically active and vocal in an effort to improve the situation of the people they serve, or whose cause they espouse. Advocacy often involves exaggeration of the conditions confronted by older Americans, as well as propagandizing, lobbying, and moralizing for the desired improvements in these conditions. Advocates may use, and even create, stereotypic views in order to further their cause. This text aims at filling the role of the unbiased observer attempting to present the reality of aging in America.

CONCLUSION

From the moment of conception to the moment of death, aging is experienced by the human organism. Throughout the early years of life, aging involves physiological growth and development; it is therefore generally viewed favorably by the individual and by significant others in his or her environment. Adult life and middle age tend to be periods of physiological stability and increasing social power and privilege, but parts, nevertheless, of the lifelong aging process. Old age may be seen as a period of physical decline as well as of declining social prestige. All of these are parts of the life course of the individual, but it is not difficult to understand why older age is often negatively labeled by the general population and regarded with considerable aversion by those entering the later years. Research findings indicate, however, that the lives of older persons are not nearly as foreboding nor as unhappy as the general public believes they are. Most older persons are leading reasonably healthy, happy and fulfilling lives just as do all other age groups. Moreover, older persons have the same opportunity for growth, development, learning, and new experiences that one finds at any age in life. *v*

Joan Arehart Treichel distinguishes between chronological aging, primary aging, and secondary aging. *Chronological aging* refers to the time that elapses from birth, providing others with some clue to the roles and patterns of behavior that are to be expected of us as members of a particular age group. The behavior of a five-year-old child is quite different from that of a 45-year-old. Thus, chronological age assumes importance in the human life cycle. Since old age is negatively defined, many Americans invest large sums of money and go to great lengths to look young. Jack Benny made a lifetime joke of always being 39 and thus avoiding the problems of old age.

Primary aging, according to Treichel, refers to biochemical changes that accompany chronological aging. These are considered to include the daily loss of thousands of cells in the individual brain, a tendency for facial skin to dry out by age 30, and gradual deterioration of parts of the body, until finally death occurs. Primary aging is considered to be to some extent genetically determined.

Secondary aging, according to Treichel, is primary aging that has been accelerated as a result of a lifetime of stresses—emotional tension, physical trauma, disease, or other insults to the body.

While we cannot slow down chronological aging, scientific knowledge may allow us to better understand the processes of aging and, by suggesting changes in lifestyle, prevent various kinds of secondary aging and perhaps in the process slow down primary aging.

Many younger people feel that aging is simply not relevant to them, that older people have their best years behind them, that there is at most a hopeless gap in lifestyles and aspirations between younger and older people, and that the contemplation or mere thought of getting old and dying is depressing. Thus, younger people often avoid studying problems of aging.

Richard Kalish argues that anyone concerned with the maintenance of human dignity must understand the *entire* life cycle, including the later years. He argues that there are a number of reasons why the study of the later part of life should be important to each of us. Among these are

1. To participate in providing resources for those who are old today and for those who will be old tomorrow (that's us, you and me) so that they—and we—can lead a more satisfactory life during the later years.
2. To enable us to better understand the aging process so that we can lead a more satisfactory life ourselves today.
3. To place the earlier years of the life span in proper perspective and to perceive individual development as a lifelong process.[11]

The chapters that follow will examine some of the basic developments, problems, and adjustments of aging. The lives of older Americans will be viewed from the context of the entire life cycle and as much pertinent information presented as space will allow. Gerontology, perhaps more than any other subject matter, utilizes an interdisciplinary approach in explaining the lifestyles and behavior patterns of older persons. While the perspective of this text may be slightly biased in favor of the sociological view, research findings from biological, psychological, economic, political, and anthropological studies will also be included. Hopefully, they are presented in such a way as to enhance the reader's understanding of the roles and lives of older Americans.

KEY TERMS

ageism	gerontology
aging	primary aging
dependency ratio	secondary aging
ethnocentric	stereotype
geriatrics	

SUGGESTED READINGS

ALLEN, CAROLE, AND HERMAN BROTMAN, *Charts on Aging in America.* The 1981 White House Conference on Aging.

ANDERSON, J. E., "Summary and Interpretation," in *Psychological Aspects of Aging,* ed. J. C. Anderson, pp. 267–89. Washington, D.C.: American Psychological Association, 1966.

BENGTSON, VERN L., *The Social Psychology of Aging.* Indianapolis: Bobbs-Merrill, 1973.

BLACKMAN, ANNE, "Over 65 Set Growing 1,600 a Day in U.S." in Harold Cox, *Focus Aging* (2nd ed.), pp. 12–15. Guilford, Ct.: Dushkin Publishing Group, Inc., 1980.

BOTWINICK, J., AND L. W. THOMPSON, "Individual Differences in Reaction Time in Relation to Age," *Journal of Genetic Psychology,* 112 (1968), 73–75.

BOYD, ROSAMONDE R., AND CHARLES G. OAKES, *Foundations of Practical Gerontology.* Columbia: University of South Carolina Press, 1973.

CARLSON, A. J., AND E. J. STIEGLITZ, "Physiological Changes in Aging," *American Academy of Political and Social Science,* 279 (1952), 18–31.

CHARATAN, FREDERICK, "Psychological and Psychiatric Aspects of Aging," in *What Do We Really Know About Aging,* ed. Antoinette Bosco and Jane Porcino. Stony Brook: State University of New York at Stony Brook, 1977.

COX, HAROLD, GURMEET SEKHON, AND CHARLES NORMAN, "Social Characteristics of the Elderly in Indiana," *Proceedings of the Indiana Academy of Social Sciences* (1978), pp. 186–97.

EISENSTADT, S. N., *From Generation to Generation: Age Groups and Social Structure.* New York: Free Press, 1956.

HARRIS, CHARLES, *Fact Book on Aging: A Profile of America's Older Population,* pp. 1–30. National Council on the Aging, 1978.

HENDRICKS, JON, AND C. DAVIS HENDRICKS, *Aging in Mass Society: Myths and Realities.* Cambridge, Mass.: Winthrop, 1981.

"Issue Paper on the Minority Aging." Urban Resources Consultants Incorporated, June, 1978.

JANSEN, CLIFFORD, "Some Sociological Aspects of Migration," in *Migration,* ed. J. A. Jackson, pp. 60–73. New York: Cambridge University Press, 1969.

KALISH, RICHARD, *Late Adulthood: Perspectives on Human Development.* Monterey, Ca.: Brooks/Cole, 1975.

LEMON, BRUCE W., VERN L. BENGTSON, AND JAMES A. PETERSON, "Activity Types and Life Satisfaction in a Retirement Community," *Journal of Gerontology,* 4, no. 27 (1972), 511–23.

LIBOW, LESLIE, "Medical Problems of Older People," in *What Do We Really Know About Aging,* ed. Antoinette Bosco and Jane Porcino. Stony Brook: State University of New York at Stony Brook, 1977.

MADDOX: See Anne Blackman

MILLER, SHEILA J., "Segregation of the Aged in American Cities." Unpublished paper, Wichita State University, 1967.

PARK, ROBERT E., *Human Communities.* Glencoe, Ill.: Free Press, 1952 .

PARK, R. E., AND E. W. BURGESS, *The City.* Chicago: The University of Chicago Press, 1925.

POLLACK, O., *Social Adjustment in Old Age.* New York: Social Science Research Council, 1948.

ROSOW, IRVING, *The Social Integration of the Aged.* Glencoe, Ill.: Free Press, 1967.

SCHOCK, N. W., "Biology of Aging," in *Problems of America's Aging Population,* ed. T. L. Smith, pp. 37–46. Gainesville: University of Florida Press, 1951.

SCHULZ, JAMES, *The Economics of Aging.* Belmont, Calif.: Wadsworth, 1980.

STREIB, GORDON F., AND CLEMENT J. SCHNEIDER, *Retirement in American Society.* Ithaca and London: Cornell University Press, 1971.

TREICHEL, JOAN AREHART, "It's Never Too Late to Start Living Longer," in *Focus Aging,* ed. Harold Cox, pp. 17–19. Guilford, Ct.: Dushkin Publishing Group, Inc., 1980.

YOUMANS, GRAM E., "Attitudes: Young Old and Old Old," *The Gerontologist,* 17, no. 2 (April 1977), 175–86.

2

THEORETICAL
PERSPECTIVES
ON THE AGING PROCESS

*All sorts of allowances are made for the illusions of youth, and
none, or almost none, for the disenchantments of age.*

R. L. Stevenson
Virginibus Puerisque: Crabbed Age and Youth

THEORY AND RESEARCH

The goal of any scientific enterprise is to explain some aspect of the natural or
social world in a logical and understandable manner. Science is often defined as
the development of knowledge in an empirical, validated and replicable manner.
The three defining features of science are: (1) the development of a general
theory, (2) the testing and empirical validation of the theory, and (3) the replication of tests of the theory.

Science is the activity of gaining knowledge in a particular way. The scientific community is a group of people who have accepted a certain set of values
in the acquisition of knowledge. These values include the beliefs (1) that there is
order to social and physical phenomena, (2) that we come to know the world
through our senses, (3) that knowledge is better than ignorance, (4) that skepti-
cism is worthwhile, and negative evidence contributes to knowledge.

All scientific explanations are grounded in theory; they attempt to account for a given set of phenomena with the development of a model that is pre-
dictive and that can be empirically demonstrated. A *theory* is a set of logically interrelated propositions that account for some set of phenomena. Scientific
theory differs from other forms of theory in that it must (1) generate propositions that are capable of being rejected, (2) explain why the propositions are related, and (3) be empirical and subject to test.

The process that the scientist goes through in developing a theory includes (1) the establishment of precise definitions for the variables he or she deals with, (2) the framing of propositions which assert that two or more phenomena are logically related, and (3) the development of a theory which is a set of interrelated propositions that account for the phenomena in question. The sequence of the development of a theory is represented in Figure 2–1. Inductively, the scientist goes from definitions of the variables to propositions relating two or more variables to the development of a theory; a set of logically interconnected propositions then account for the phenomenon in question.

Scientists never entirely prove or disprove a theory. They merely develop a greater or lesser degree of confidence in the theory. This is because a theory does not rest on a single proposition but on a series of propositions, any one of which may be partly in error. The empiricist derives hypotheses from a theory that states that if the theory is true, we should expect to find a predicted relationship between the variables. Sometimes the hypotheses are proved; sometimes they are disproved. Research findings always contribute to the theory by either (1) supporting the theory when the hypothesized relations are proved valid, (2) reshaping the theory, should part of the hypotheses be proved but other parts disproved, (3) refuting the theory should the hypotheses be all disproved, or (4) initiating a new theory should unanticipated findings lead the research in an entirely new direction.

Research Techniques

Since any scientific theory must be capable of being empirically tested, scientists have developed a variety of research techniques which can be utilized for this purpose. Cross-sectional studies, longitudinal studies, and cohort analysis are three techniques which are frequently used by gerontologists.

CROSS-SECTIONAL STUDIES.   In *cross-sectional* studies the researcher takes a sample of people at one point in time and attempts to identify their basic attitudes, beliefs, values, or behavior patterns. The most common of the cross-sectional studies are the public opinion polls of Gallup, Lubel, and others regarding national politicians and political issues. Thus in September 1984 the pollsters might find that 51 percent of the population believe President Reagan is doing a good job as president and 49 percent believe he is not. This does not indicate what the American public will believe about the President's performance a month or a year later. What it does say is that as of September 1984, this is

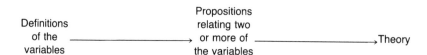

Figure 2–1   Theory Development

what a cross section of the American public thinks about President Reagan's performance.

LONGITUDINAL STUDIES.   Longitudinal studies, on the other hand, follow a sample of respondents over a period of time ranging from a few months to a lifetime. A sample of subjects could be chosen in 1980 and then interviewed in 1985, 1990, 1995, and 2000 to see how their attitudes regarding the leading political figures or political issues changed over time. Thus 60 percent of the sample may favor unrestricted abortions for American women in 1980, but only 40 percent of the sample may favor them in 1985. The researchers would ask, "Why are the attitudes of the public on this issue changing over time?" Longitudinal studies establish trends and patterns of change on the part of the respondents.

Longitudinal studies that take a sample of cohorts and follow them over a long period of time have proven most fruitful in studies of the life cycle. Many previous errors made by scientists regarding human behavior have been a result of cross-sectional studies of different age groups done at a single point in time. A tacit assumption of these studies is that all other characteristics of their subjects are the same, when in fact they are not. A classic example of this is studies of the relationship between age and intelligence.

An intelligence test was given to all age groups in a very short period of time. The result was a cross-sectional analysis of the intelligence of different age groups at a single point in time which indicated a decline in I.Q. scores for the older age groups. Knowing that a higher level of education leads to higher scores on intelligence tests raised some questions, however. Since the older cohorts as a group were not as well educated as their younger counterparts, was the difference in the I.Q. scores of the different age groups a result of age or education? Only longitudinal studies could answer this question.

Difference in education (a cohort effect) was found in later longitudinal studies to explain much of the decline in intelligence test scores for the older age groups. In addition K. W. Schaie found that a bias built into intelligence tests favored motor performance and skills more easily exercised by the young, and the peculiarities of the test situation tend to intimidate those who have not recently experienced testing and performance. Future research will undoubtedly further clarify which specific kinds of performance as measured by intelligence tests are most likely to improve or decline with the age of the respondent.

COHORT ANALYSIS.   That younger people scored higher on intelligence tests, at least in part because of their greater number of years of education, would be considered by gerontologists to be a cohort effect. Because they were born and grew up at a particular time they experienced something which was unique to their age group and that had not been experienced by the previous generation. In the context of human development time may be seen as a sequence of related biological, psychological, and sociological experiences.

Gerontologists often use the term cohort or generation to convey the sense of a common time in which a group of persons are born and experience certain events.

Cohort analysis is utilized by gerontologists to compare groups of people born during specific time periods (usually separated by five-year to ten-year intervals) as they move through the life cycle. These people usually experience particular historical events at approximately the same time in their biological, psychological, and sociological development, so they are imprinted or affected by these events in a very similar fashion. Leonard Cain's research on age cohorts finds considerable differences between cohorts (i.e. different age groups) in such characteristics as attitudes toward labor-force participation, fertility rates, education, and sex.

Douglas Kimmel observes the effect of different historical events on cohorts:

> Persons age 65 in 1975 were born in 1910 during a period in the United States of peace and isolation from world conflcts. They were at the forefront of industrial expansion and westward migration. Obviously a great deal has changed since then. Average length of education has increased by several years, and the task of living in society has become more and more complex . . . . If you are a college student today, your parents were probably born between the end of World War I and the years of the Great Depression . . . . They learned that economic security and material possessions may evaporate for reasons beyond their control. Your parents probably went to school during the Depression and their early socialization experiences, which influenced later attitudes and values, took place during this period of inadequate material resources.[1]

The fact that such historical events can have prolonged effects on the attitudes, beliefs, and values of cohorts born in a given time span is apparent. Vern Bengtson, moreover, holds that there is a complex interplay between the historical events that cohorts experience and their own stage of development. Thus the individual's life should be viewed as the product of dynamic interaction between the social system and the personality system, each of which reflects both stability and change over time.

Biological events that a person commonly experiences over time include achievement and loss of reproductive capacity, growth and decline in physical vigor, and an increasing probability of disease in organs. Psychologically the individual experiences the growth and development of motor skills, perceptive and cognitive ability, and the development of personality. Sociological events include the entrance and exit from major social institutions, marriage, work, social organizations, and a commensurate growth and decline in responsibility and power.

The ability of a person to cope with these biological, psychological, and sociological changes in life is related to several factors, not the least of which are such dramatic events as wars and depression. Obviously, someone who is approaching the end of educational training and who seeks employment during an economic recession can be set back by a condition over which he or she may have no control. Similarly, persons who during the Vietnam war were considering the advantages and disadvantages of seeking a college education may suddenly have found themselves drafted and as a result may have never completely returned to their previous educational plans. Historical events, then, interact in complex ways with a person's development and *life-chances* (the probability of a person of specified status achieving a specified goal or suffering a specified disadvantage). Cohort analysis is useful to gerontologists because it allows them to study the effects of these events on a broad group of individuals, all of whom experienced the same historical event at a similar stage of development. In this way it can be a useful research tool for those interested in testing some of the assumptions of the theories of human development.

DISENGAGEMENT THEORY

Theories in the social sciences can be more or less complex. What gerontologists have described as the earliest theories in the field seem to be less complex, and more philosophical than theoretical in nature. Disengagement and activity theory appear to be as much philosophical recommendations as to how to live one's life during the later years as they are theories that explain human behavior. One can, however, derive hypotheses from these perspectives and test these to determine their accuracy. Therefore, the disengagement and activity perspectives can be classified as theories. We recognize they are more narrow in focus and more prescriptive than many of the more general theories in the behavioral sciences.

One of the earliest and most influential theories in gerontology was called *disengagement.* In its simplest form, and as originally described by Elaine Cumming and William Henry, this theory stated that aging involves an inevitable withdrawal or disengagement, resulting in decreased interaction between the aging person and others in the social milieu to which he or she belongs. The process may be initiated by the individual or by others in his or her social system. Disengagement theory implies that society and the individual prepare in advance—by an inevitable, gradual, and personally satisfying process of disengagement from society—for the ultimate withdrawal of the individual (who is expected to experience an incurable, incapacitating disease and then death).

A basic assumption of the theory is that both the individual and society are gratified by the process. For the individual, the withdrawal brings a release from societal pressures for continued high-level productivity and performance. For society, the withdrawal of the older members presumably allows younger, more energetic, competent, and recently trained persons to assume the roles that must be filled in the social system.

The assertion that disengagement of the older members of society is necessary for survival of the social system is an example of *sociological functionalism,* which views the elements and members of society as functionally interdependent. Specific behavior patterns within a social system can be regarded as either functional or dysfunctional. Functional patterns help to maintain and integrate social elements; dysfunctional patterns tend toward social breakdown or disintegration. Thus, many would argue that the disengagement of the older Americans is functional, or useful, for society, since it allows a smooth transfer of power to younger people. However, there is no *proof* that the withdrawal of older persons from employment and other useful roles is necessarily good for society. It might just as well be argued that the disengagement process is bad, since some of the most knowledgeable, capable, and experienced performers in society are being removed, either voluntarily or by mandatory policies.

At the heart of the disengagement process is the forfeiting of the individual's major life role; for the female, this has in the past meant the parental role and for the male the occupational role. On the whole, men are seen as making an abrupt transition from engaged to disengaged state, while women are seen as having a gradual and smooth withdrawal from previous roles and patterns of activity.

Disengagement for men was seen as abrupt since their careers, which were expected to be the central focus of their lives, were suddenly terminated by retirement. Women, on the other hand, even when employed, were seen as principally concerned with family matters. Homemaking and household duties continued during periods of employment and followed women into the retirement years. Substitute roles following retirement, which brought the respect of others and thereby self-esteem, were always readily available to women, but not to men. This is not to say that men could not find alternative roles to assume following retirement, but rather that they were not nearly so apparent and accessible as they were for women, given the social milieu in which they found themselves.

Accompanying role losses both at the launching of offspring into the adult world and at retirement is the diminished interaction—both qualitative and quantitative—between aging persons and others in the social system to which they belong. In this case, disengagement theory, if followed to its logical conclusion, would predict the individual's withdrawal from previous activities, followed by preoccupation with self and ultimate death.

The following brief work history of a steelworker perhaps best illustrates the rationale of disengagement theorists. Samuel Y. was a manual laborer all his life; he had begun working at age 12 in a coal mine. Each subsequent job involved heavy labor only, whether it was pushing a wheelbarrow loaded with coal or later stacking beams of steel weighing up to one hundred pounds. Long before retirement at age 65, he began looking forward to the time when he would not have to strain his muscles in the daily work grind.

For Mr. Y., disengagement came some time before mandatory retirement. He had been a foreman during his 40s and early 50s, but after he slipped one day and fell, suffering a broken ankle, his job as foreman was taken by a younger man who could move easily throughout the plant. He was then relegated back to the paint rack, an assignment that required little walking but considerable strain on his shoulders and arms as he wielded a paint gun the whole day, spraying large sheets of steel.

Having gladly accepted mandatory retirement at age 65, Samuel now has time to enjoy his family, including children and grandchildren, whom he regularly visits. Although his eyesight is failing slightly he is still able to do many of the things he enjoys, such as hunting, fishing, and gardening. Disengaging from the seven to four work routine seems to have considerably enriched his life.

Vern Bengtson argues that the disengagement theory implies a dramatic shift from middle to older age marked by an entirely new balance of forces between the personality and the social systems of the individual. The manner in which the individual has organized the diverse roles that he or she is currently assuming into an organized and consistent view of self is called personality. Social systems refer to the variety of social groups that the individual identifies as his or hers and with whose members he or she regularly interacts (i.e. family, fellow workers, members of the Lions Club, etc.). The extent to which social norms impinge on the individual would be greatly reduced in older age, and the sources of psychological well-being in older age would be considerably different from those of middle age. Whether in fact this much of a shift in the personality system actually occurs is highly debatable.

Richard Kalish believes that the theory of disengagement must be evaluated on three different levels, each of which should be carefully analyzed in terms of whether it refers to psychological disengagement or social disengagement. The levels of evaluation as he sees them are (1) disengagement as a process, (2) disengagement as inevitable, and (3) disengagement as adaptive.[2]

Disengagement is often viewed as a process, since for most people it does not occur all at once but gradually over a period of time. The last child may leave home when the couple are in their early 50s; parental responsibilities are thereby withdrawn. The wife may decide to give up her job after the expenses of putting children through college are no longer pressing. The husband may decide not to serve another term on the county council. Later, he may decide to take early retirement at age 62 rather than wait until 65. As a process, disengagement is always selective in that the individual chooses to withdraw from some roles and not from others, and the process takes place over a number of years rather than all at once.

Disengagement is presumed to be inevitable since almost everyone considers at some point that he or she will die. If increasing age brings with it an increasing probability of sickness and death, then disengagement is inevitable. The individual is considered ready to disengage upon recognizing that the length of life or amount of life space available is shrinking and that his or her energy level is declining. Life space refers to the area of the world, community, neighborhood, and home which the individual considers his or her environment. Sometimes older persons may give up driving, travel out of the neighborhood less frequently, and spend greater amounts of time in their home or apartment. Thus the life space in which they exist and travel begins to shrink as they become less mobile and feel less capable of coping with broader and more diverse environments.

Disengagement is regarded as adaptive from both the individual and the societal point of view. Disengagement presumably allows the individual to withdraw from previous work roles and from competition with younger counterparts as his or her energy presumably declines. Thus the individual adapts to aging and the loss of energy and the capability to compete with others by withdrawing from the social situation that demands competition. From the societal point of view, disengagement permits younger employees to assume critical positions as the older ones become less efficient, thereby allowing for the smooth transition of power and control from one generation to the next.

The proponents of disengagement believe that it is both inevitable and adaptive. In the later years of declining energy and health, disengagement is believed by some gerontologists to allow the retention of meaningful family relationships at a relatively undiminished level as long as possible. This, in their opinion, requires the sacrifice of other kinds of engagement, such as work.

Proponents of this theory believe that gradual withdrawal from the social system and declining involvement in activities are an inevitable part of the aging process. Howard Kaplan observes that people are too often evaluated not in terms of where in the life cycle they are, but rather in terms of where they are going or where they have been. To require older persons to be measured by the same criteria by which we measure younger persons is, in the view of disengagement theorists, unfair.

The critics of disengagement theory have been numerous, adamant, and persistent. They were quick to question the presumed inevitability of the disengagement process. Many gerontologists questioned whether the process was functional for either the individual or the social system. George Maddox pointed out that different personality factors might make the individual more or less amenable to disengagement. Since there is social pressure to disengage, gerontologists who focused on personality factors felt that those who throughout their lives had dealt with stress by turning inward and insulating themselves from the world would probably continue to manifest a pattern of withdrawal. On the other hand, those who were inclined to remain engaged had probably been so inclined over the course of their lives. For this group, the kind of activities engaged in might change, but they would seek relationships allowing them to resist general disengagement patterns.

In responding to the critics, Elaine Cumming distinguished between "impingers" and "selectors." *Impingers* were seen as taking an assertive stance in human interaction, being more anxious and apprehensive about the disengagement process. *Selectors* were viewed as more passive interactors in social relations, primarily waiting for others to confirm their own preexisting assumptions about themselves, while being sensitive only to cues tending to reinforce their views.

Thus selectors were felt to be able, by selective perception of social cues, to insulate themselves from the negative connotations of disengagement. Developmental psychologists have argued that there is a gradual turning inward by individuals over the course of life. Thus one might expect people as they age to be less attentive to external events and more attuned to their own inner states. In Cumming's defense and restatement of the theory, she argues that personal coping mechanisms derived from previous experiences will determine the level of engagement and disengagement during subsequent stages of the life cycle. Each individual develops ways of defending himself or herself from negative or inconsistent communications from others regarding their self and personality. Some use selective perception and hear only those things that they want to hear in the communication with others, while ignoring other parts of the communication which would be threatening. Others withdraw and thus avoid any communication with others which in any way might be negative or critical. These are just two of a variety of coping mechanism used to protect the individual's ego and view of self from contradictory information.

ACTIVITY THEORY

In direct opposition to disengagement theory is *activity theory;* Robert Havighurst and other proponents maintain that normal aging involves maintaining as long as possible the activities and attitudes of middle age. This implies that for those activities and roles which the individual is forced to give up at the time of retirement, substitutes should be found.

Our understanding of *dis*engagement can only be as great as our understanding of what *engagement* means to middle-class Americans. Middle-class values generally maintain that being active and productive is desirable for a successful life. Early in life the children of middle-class families are encouraged to become involved in as many activities as possible. Little League baseball, music lessons, Girl Scouts, the YMCA, and similar activities can consume the spare time of these children. Adult life for this group is a continuation of the pattern, with serious dedication to career, the Elks, country club, church, ladies auxiliary, etc., consuming most of the hours of the day.

One can easily see, then, why this group is likely to view retirement and disengagement with considerable ambivalence, since their lives have centered on the so-called Protestant ethic, with positive orientation toward work, activity, and social responsibilities. Similarly, activity theory most reflects these common attitudes and is frequently expressed in the writings and philosophy of the Golden Age magazines. Many older Americans insist that they would "rather wear out than rust out."

The assumptions of activity theory are in direct conflict with those of the disengagement theorists, according to Havighurst.

Activity theory assumes that the relationship between the social system and the personality system remains fairly stable as an individual passes from the status of middle age to that of old age. It holds that the norms for old age are the same as those for middle age, and that the older person should be judged in terms of middle-age criteria of success.[3]

According to activity theorists, any exhibition of behavior by older persons that would not be appropriate in middle-aged persons is considered maladjustment. Fred Cottrell and Robert Atchley found in their sample of retired women that very few described themselves as old, preferring "middle-aged" or "just past middle age."[4] This tendency was found even among women who had passed their seventieth birthday. Thus it would appear that older people themselves view middle-age patterns of behavior as desirable for themselves. In all likelihood this reflects their acceptance of the dominant values in American society and something of age discrimination as well.

The inability of Dr. Maura K., a university professor, to adjust to the retirement years perhaps best illustrates the beliefs of the activity theorists. Dr. K. retired from academic life after twenty-five years of a university-oriented existence. A philosophy professor throughout her career, she had been active in almost every committee and council, both departmental and campus-wide. She was active in off-campus civic activities as well. Suddenly, after twenty-five years of days crammed with action as she moved from classes to committee meetings and then to civic responsibilities in the after-work hours, she found herself with the ample free time she had always complained about not having.

Instead of enjoying relief from responsibilities, however, she found that time lay heavily on her hands. No classes; no committee meetings; her colleagues weren't quite as eager to talk to her as they had previously been. She could not seem to adapt to spending her time puttering around her yard and garden. She started haunting her old department, trying to keep up with what was going on, both departmentally and at the university in general. She was confronted, however, with the usual questions directed at retirees—"What are you doing here?" "Why aren't you in Florida basking in the sun?" "Why don't you learn to enjoy life?" Dr. K.'s mandatory retirement was not pleasant, because she could find few activities to substitute for work-related roles and none that gave her the same satisfaction.

Activity theory emphasizes the stability of personality-system orientations as an individual ages and ignores any need for societal-structured alternatives to compensate for losses that the individual experiences as part of the aging process. One obvious difficulty of the theory is that it does not seriously consider what happens to the person who cannot maintain the standards of middle age in the later years. If the individual accepts the belief that he or she must remain active while experiencing physiological losses as part of aging, the result could be considerable frustration, anxiety, and guilt about one's inability to handle the behavioral expectations of activity.

Bruce Lemon, Vern Bengtson, and James Peterson isolated what appear to be two fundamental propositions of activity theory: (1) that there is a positive relation between social activity and life satisfaction in old age, and (2) that role losses such as widowhood and retirement are inversely related to life satisfaction. Their findings from a study of people moving to a retirement community did not support these propositions. Only social activity with friends was in any way related to life satisfaction. This study therefore raised questions about the validity of the basic propositions of activity theory and so cast doubts on the theory itself. On the other hand, studies by Erdman Palmore, Robert Havighurst and others—to name only two—have repeatedly found positive associations between morale, personal adjustment, and activity levels.

HUMAN DEVELOPMENTAL THEORIES

The criticism of both the disengagement and activity theories has led to alternative ways of looking at the problems of aging. Some gerontologists have argued that in order to understand the experiences of older persons you must understand what has happened to them at earlier stages in the life cycle. Certainly few would disagree that the experiences of an entire life are going to shape the individual's perceptions, attitudes, and means of adjusting to the later years. Thus some gerontologists argue human developmental theories may be fruitfully utilized to explain the adjustments of old age.

Freud

Freud emphasized the importance of the development of the sexual function in the human animal. Some of his basic premises were

1. Sexual development manifests itself after birth.
2. Sexual life comprises the function of obtaining pleasure from zones of the body.
3. The development of the sexual function has two phases. The early phase increases steadily until the end of the fifth year and is followed by a lull, in which progress is at a standstill (the latency period). The second phase begins at puberty.[5]

How the sexual function is developed in the early period is thought to have important implications for later adult life. Freud believed that personality development begins with the oral phase—the earliest developmental period, beginning soon after the birth of the child. The first organ to make libidinal demands upon the mind is the mouth. The mouth, as an erotogenic zone (zones in which sexual feelings can be aroused), is the means through which nourishment is provided and physiological needs for the survival of the child are satisfied. Beyond this, however, the child's persistent sucking tendency is an indication of the need to obtain pleasure through the mouth, independent of nourishment. Freud labeled this need sexual.[6]

The stage following the oral Freud characterized as the sadistic anal. Although sadistic impulses are said to occur during the oral phase, their extent increases greatly during the anal. Satisfaction is sought in aggression and in the excretory function. Mastery of bowel and bladder functions is achieved in this stage.

The phallic phase, according to Freud, follows the sadistic phase and is the period in which the Oedipus complex develops. The boy begins to manipulate his penis and desires to have sexual relations with his mother.[7] As he realizes that he is in competition with the father for the mother's attention, he fears that he will be castrated by the father. Moreover, he finally realizes that women do not have penises, and he represses his earlier desires. During the phallic phase his efforts are in the pursuit of pleasure derived from the sexual function.

The fourth of the Freudian phases of development is the period of latency. Freud argues that after the early developmental stages there is a period of a few years in which very little personal development takes place. This lasts until the onset of puberty, which introduces the fifth—the genital—phase, in which normal heterosexual interests occur. The organization of the individual's instinctual drives around the sexual function is then completed.

Thus for Freud there is a close relationship between the adult personality and the sexual life of the child. Adjustment and personality formation are largely biological and the result of instinct.

Charlotte Buhler, Carl Jung, and Erik Erikson have all attempted to trace human development through the entire life cycle rather than merely through the child and adolescent phases.

Erikson

Erik Erikson's "eight stages of life" is perhaps the most complete of these theories. There is some similarity between the first five of these stages and stages of the Freudian model. Erikson's stages of development are set in terms of paradoxical demands placed on the child at each stage of development.[8]

According to Erikson, the first of these stages centers on a conflict, in the infant, between developing feelings of trust and a sense of distrust. Erikson believes that the infant's first social achievement is a willingness to let the mother out of sight without undue anxiety or rage, because she has become an "inner certainty" as well as an "outer predictability." The general state of trust, furthermore, implies not only that one has learned to rely on the sameness and continuity of the outer providers but also that one may trust oneself and the capacity of one's own organs to cope with urges.

Erikson's next stage occurs in later infancy, when anal muscular maturation has occurred, and is focused on a growing sense of autonomy versus a sense of shame and doubt. Parental firmness must protect the child against the potential anarchy of his as yet untrained sense of discrimination, his inability to know when to hold on and let go of parents' support and other support objects. As the child's home environment encourages him to stand on his own feet, it must protect him against meaningless and arbitrary experiences of shame and early doubt.

The third stage, the period of greatest locomotor development, focuses on a developing sense of initiative versus a sense of guilt. Erikson believes that the child's need for that autonomy concentrates on keeping out potential rivals and is to no small extent an expression of jealous rage most often directed against encroachments by younger siblings. Initiative brings with it the anticipation of rivalry with those who have preceded one in some area or endeavor and who presumably are better fitted for the thing to which one's initiative is directed. Infantile sexuality and the incest taboo unite here to bring about the specific development problem in which the child must turn from an exclusive attachment to parents to the slow process of becoming a parent, a carrier of tradition.

The fourth developmental stage, Erikson asserts, comes in the middle years of childhood, during which there is a struggle between the sense of industry and a sense of inferiority. The child recognizes as a finality that there is no workable future within the boundaries of his or her family. The child is now ready to approach skills and tasks that go far beyond the pleasurable functioning of the limbs. The individual develops industry to bring a productive situation to completion, an aim that gradually replaces the whims and wishes of the autonomous organism.

The fifth stage occurs in adolescence and involves a sense of ego identity (certainty of self and a sense of continuity and belonging regarding career, sex role, and a system of values) versus role confusion. The central developmental task is to find one's position in life as a productive and responsible adult with a consistent set of attitudes about oneself including an integrated sexuality. This stage is resolved when one's education is completed, an occupation begun, and a marriage partner secured.

The sixth stage, according to Erikson, is the capacity for sexual intimacy versus isolation. A youth does not become capable of a fully intimate relationship until his or her identity crisis is fairly well resolved. One prerequisite is a clear concept of self, thus resolving any identity crisis before one can fuse that identity with another in full appreciation of the other's uniqueness. Many early attempts at intimacy, according to Erikson, are attempts to find one's identity through a romantic relationship with another.

Erikson's seventh stage relates to a perceived conflict between generativity and stagnation. This occurs in one's productive years, extending from young adulthood into old age. This stage is critical to the individual's sense of achievement and fulfillment in life. Unsuccessful attempts to cope with this developmental stage are likely to result in stagnation, bitterness, and physiological and emotional decline.

Erikson describes the final stage as integrity versus despair. One's awareness of this stage is precipitated by the awareness of the finitude of life and of one's closeness to death. A feeling of integrity is the ultimate fulfillment of the previous seven stages along with the recognition that one's offspring provide a continuity of life with the newborn generations. The negative resolution of this developmental stage is one of meaninglessness, despair, and a feeling of the uselessness of one's life.

Most developmental theorists believe that each stage of life presents different developmental tasks that must be met and mastered before one can enter the next stage of life, for failure at any level implies inability to move on in the expected pattern.

The developmental theories, much like the disengagement and activity theories, offer a unique way of looking at individual's adaptation to the later years of life. They encourage the gerontologist to connect any explanation of the individual's current behavior to his or her earlier history and thereby perceive a developmental progression throughout the individual's life. They do not posit a desired pattern of behavior in the later years such as disengagement or activity but rather expect a variety of different adjustment patterns based on the individual's personality and previous experiences.

One problem with the developmental theories is that they tend to be general and abstract while offering little hope for those people who have arrived at old age and have not mastered the developmental tasks of the earlier phases of life. What happens to the individual who experiences stagnation instead of generativity in a later phase of the life cycle? Is bitterness inevitable, as Erikson suggests? Is there nothing the individual can do to put his life in order given the fact that he may have made earlier mistakes? Viewed from this perspective the developmental theories seem unduly pessimistic.

CONTINUITY THEORY

While gerontologists who were psychologically oriented were inclined to turn to human developmental theories to compensate for their dissatisfaction with disengagement and activity theory, those who were sociologically oriented were inclined to turn to continuity theory. Building on the well-established sociological concept of continuity of socialization and on the developmental psychologists' views on the stages of life, the theory is based on the continuity of behavior patterns through the different phases of life.

Sociologists have long argued that the experiences a person has at a given point in life are often preparing that person for the roles that he or she must assume at the next stage of life. The little girl playing doctor, the boy building a model rocket ship, the young woman working as camp counselor, and the apprentice imitating the master craftsman are all developing skills at one stage of life, that they can use in a later stage. Formally, by advising, encouraging, and sending children to school to acquire the desired skills, the parent attempts to socialize them into adult roles. Informally, by the games they are taught to play, the gifts they receive, and the model of adult behavior provided to them by the parent, they learn the proper attitudes and values required for assuming adult responsibilities. Thus both formally and informally childrearing practices contribute continuity to the socialization process by which the individual is prepared for the next stage of life. Similarly, there is considerable *anticipatory socialization,* by which a person imagines, so to speak, what it will be like to assume the roles and responsibilities of the next period of life.

Each successive grade in school is predicated on what is taught in a previous grade. Education builds knowledge and skills in increments, so that the high school graduate is presumed to be considerably more informed than a fourth-grader, who is herself superior in this respect to those in grades below her. During the life course, movement into adult status in the early twenties presumes successful handling of adjustment problems in the teen years. Life cycles thus have patterns in which there is considerable continuity from one stage to the next, with each succeeding age built on the experiences and skills of the previous period.

Having in mind a logical development of the individual life course and the different tasks and skills mastered at each stage in life, one can appreciate why retirement might be attended with problems, since nothing in the previous years in any way prepares one for the retirement years. Retirement poses considerable discontinuity from all of the previous stages of life: Career and occupational skills are no longer needed; work is not expected to be a vital part of one's life; leisure time is now ample; and the constant drive for achievement and success no longer dominates one's life.

Continuity theory—building on the sociologists' ideas of continuities in socialization and on the developmental psychologists' views of continuity and change between different phases of the life cycle—holds that, in the course of growing older, the individual is predisposed toward maintaining stability in the habits, associations, preferences, and lifestyle that he or she has developed over the years. This theory asserts that the individual's reaction to aging can be understood only by examining the complex interrelationships among biological, psychological, and social changes in the individual's life and the previous behavior patterns. Exponents of the theory believe that a person's habits, preferences, associations, state of health, and actual experiences will in large part determine that person's ability to maintain his or her lifestyle while retiring from full-time employment and perhaps having to adjust to the death of a loved one. The person's lifelong experiences thus create dispositions to a certain lifestyle that he or she will attempt to maintain if at all possible.

Disengagement and activity theory both posit a single direction that they believe is most appropriate for successful adaptation to the aging process. Continuity theory, on the other hand, starts with the single premise that the individual will try to maintain as long as possible his or her preferred lifestyle, and then holds that adaptation can go in several different directions depending on how the individual perceives his or her changing status and attempts to adjust to this change. Continuity theory does not assert that one must be disengaged or active in order to be well adjusted in the later years but rather that the decision regarding which roles are to be discarded and which maintained will in large part be determined by the individual's past history and preferred style of life.

Warren Peterson seems to approach the perspective of continuity theory in arguing that when disengagement occurs, it is a very selective process. The individual, in Peterson's view, always maintains the roles that conferred the greatest status and relinquishes those that were of less value. Thus the individual maintains as long as possible his or her previous self-concept by continuing in those activities and roles that are most directly related to this ideal self and by discarding those less directly related. Like the proponents of continuity theory, Peterson believes that you can predict retirement adjustment patterns only by knowing the individual's past history as well as by having some understanding of his or her ideal self and the relation of past roles to this ideal.

Two case histories may give some clue to the selective relinquishing of the roles in life to which Peterson refers. Claudius S. was a professor of political science at a well-known university. During his career he had written innumerable articles and several books in his field and was a nationally recognized scholar. Dr. S. had never been extremely effective as a teacher since he was not a particularly good public speaker and did not enjoy this responsibility. Upon his retirement, he was given an office at the university and spent the next two years writing a book on social movements. Relinquishing the teaching role, which he never really enjoyed, in favor of total dedication to writing—which he enjoyed very much and which brought him considerable prestige—is easily understandable.

By way of contrast, Clarissa J., a professor of political science at a neighboring college, was an excellent teacher and recognized as such by both colleagues and students. During her academic career, however, she did very little writing and did not seem to enjoy this aspect of her work. Upon retiring, she spent the next several years lecturing at various universities and public gatherings throughout the Midwest. In these two case histories one can easily see Peterson's pattern of retirees giving up those roles that brought them the least status and maintaining those that conferred the greatest status.

Continuity theory has the advantage of offering a multiplicity of adjustment patterns—rather than just one—from which the older individual can choose. The "disadvantage" of continuity as theory is the difficulty encountered in trying to test it empirically. Each individual's pattern of adjustment in retirement must become a case study in which the researcher attempts to determine to what degree that individual was able to continue in his or her previous pattern of living. Sociologically, some test of the theory could be developed based on what we know about the lifestyles of those occupying different social-class positions and how aging affects these patterns. Still, we could anticipate considerable individual variation.

AGE STRATIFICATION THEORY

A theory that is particularly attractive to social gerontologists is known as *age stratification*. Matilda Riley and others were primarily responsible for introducing this perspective. A stratified society is one that is divided or arranged on the basis of classes, castes, or social strata. Age is the basis on which the stratification of society occurs from this perspective. Thus children, teenagers, young adults, mature adults, and older persons can be identified as distinct status groups in any society. Age becomes almost universally a basis for acquiring different roles, status, and varying amounts of deference from others in any society. Older people, for example, vary in status from industrial societies, where they are generally accorded a low status and the less important roles, to traditional Asian societies, where they are often given high status and the more important roles.

Persons of different age categories are differentially viewed and treated in all societies. Age tends to qualify and disqualify people for desired roles and privileged positions. In the United States, one most often cannot obtain a driver's license until age 16; marry, without parents' consent, until age 18; become a senator until age 30. You are not likely to become the president of General Electric at 25. In the 1980 U.S. presidential election, one of the campaign issues was whether Ronald Reagan was too old to be president. Age is a significant variable in social stratification and is used to qualify and disqualify individuals for different roles.

It is apparent that much can be inferred about a person's social position and status by looking at his or her age. Moreover, members of a cohort (people born during a given time period), in passing through various stages, share similar historical events and experiences and therefore—whether they realize it or not—have much in common. Family and social gatherings often find older persons drawn together to talk about the "good old days" and what they remember about them.

Age stratification is a theory that allows the social scientist to look at any age group in terms of its distinctive demographic characteristics (i.e., size, racial composition, sex ratio) and history as well as its relationship to other age groups in the same society. Stratification theory allows us to view a particular age group as a member of a particular status group in a structured social system and as an active participant in a changing society. Consideration of generational differences in experiences, attitudes, and behavior in part helps us to understand and explain generational conflict. While this theory may have limited value in the explanation of any single individual's behavior, it does lend itself to historical and sociological explanations of the attitudes and behavior of age cohorts.

Age stratification theory has so far yielded few empirical studies. It remains to be seen whether it will become more widely accepted, leading to a variety of research approaches designed to help scientists understand and explain the behavior of older persons.

OLDER AMERICANS AS A MINORITY GROUP

Many would argue that the best way to study the problems of older Americans is to view them as a minority group faced with the same difficulties that other minority groups have confronted. Like blacks, Native Americans, and Asian Americans, older people are discriminated against because they share a common biological characteristic. As with racial discrimination, the discrimination against older people is promoted by the relative ease with which the undesirable characteristic trait is observed. Proponents of this view argue that older people are like other minority groups in that they usually have low incomes, low status, and unequal opportunity, and they are generally viewed by others as inferior.

Arnold Rose, while not going so far as to define older Americans as a minority group, did argue that they could be considered a subculture of American society. He believes that a subculture among age groups emerges when the group members interact with each other significantly more than they interact with persons in other age categories. This, he asserts, occurs when the members (1) have a positive affinity for each other due to such factors as long-standing friendship or common problems, interests, or concerns, and (2) are excluded from interaction with other groups in the population to some significant extent. Both sets of circumstances, according to Rose, could readily apply to older Americans, who are most often not actively involved in an occupation or career, are dependent on others for their income, and are generally excluded from the mainstream of American life.

The weaknesses of both the minority-group and subculture theories is that they do not universally apply to all situations or all older persons. In the United States Congress, the seniority system favors older representatives and senators, delegating considerable prestige and power to them. In reality, not all older Americans are living on low incomes. Middle- and upper-class senior citizens may have considerable retirement incomes and lead a quite comfortable life. While studies by Donald Cowgill, and Harold Cox and Albert Bhak indicate that older people are found predominantly in certain sections of large cities, less than five percent are moving to the totally segregated sun cities of California, Arizona, and Florida. By far the great majority still live in age-integrated neighborhoods; and their social interactions are often with family members, cutting across generation lines. Therefore, the heterogeneity, variable lifestyles, diverse family ties, and social interaction patterns of older Americans simply do not seem to support the subculture or minority-group status suggested by Rose and others. Gordon Streib, in attacking what he believes is the minority-group myth, says:

> The aged do not share a distinct, and separate culture: membership in the group defined as "aged" is not exclusive and permanent, but awaits all members of our society who live long enough. As a result, age is a less distinguishing group characteristic than others such as sex, occupation, social class, and the like. . . . The aged are not organized to advance their own interests and are not particularly attracted to such organizations. Nor are they systematically deprived of power and privilege.[9]

Perhaps the most realistic way to view older people is to see them as a status group similar to other such groups in society. Leonard Cain noted that every society has established means of grouping persons of approximately the same age into what have been called *age sets*. These include (1) age status system, the differentiation of status on the basis of age; (2) socialization, the formalized means by which individuals are prepared for subsequent age statuses; (3) rites of passage, formalized means by which individual members are transferred from one age status to another; (4) age grading, identification of persons of comparable ages as distinctive categories; and (5) generational phenomenon, establishment of intergenerational patterns among those of different age sets.

That age does serve as a basis of grouping people in society seems in little doubt. S. N. Eisenstadt observed that age differences are among the most basic and crucial aspects of human life and destiny. All societies are confronted with age-related role changes and the progression of power and capacities connected with age changes. Thus the transition from youth to older age is subject to social and cultural definitions. Age factors differentially integrate individuals into the community. Whether older age is viewed as a desirable or undesirable status in current American society, it must be recognized that those 65 and older are a distinct group of individuals who have survived many of life's obstacles in the course of arriving at this age stratum. Even if this age group is generally little valued by society, living to age 65 and beyond is considered by almost everyone to be more desirable than the alternative.

AGING AS EXCHANGE

James Dowd, in criticizing the basic assumptions of both disengagement and activity theory, states:

> Neither theory, however, while focusing for the most part on descriptive accounts of the peculiar relationship between the social psychological variables of social interaction and life satisfaction, attempts to offer anything but the most perfunctory of explanations for the decreased social interaction itself. Rather this phenomenon is given the status of a sociological 'given,' that is, it is treated as something requiring no additional explanation.[10]

Dowd believes that the methodological difficulty (difficulty in finding the appropriate research technique to either prove or disprove theory) of disengagement theory precludes answers to the question of why social interaction decreases in older age; untestable assumptions are so effortlessly produced as to preclude any search for alternative answers. Thus, older persons are seen as suffering from lower income and poorer health than their younger counterparts and therefore are unable to remain engaged in social life to the extent that they were when younger.[11] In Dowd's view, the overemphasis of disengagement and activity perspectives has retarded the development of alternative theoretical perspectives in gerontology.

Dowd believes the decreased social interaction in older age can perhaps best be explained in terms of an intricate process of exchange between society and its older population resulting from the older people's power-dependent relationship. The basic premises on which exchange theory rests are that:

1. Society is made up of social actors in pursuit of common goals.
2. Pursuing these goals, actors enter into social relations with other actors; these entail some costs in the form of time, energy, effort, and wealth.
3. Actors expect to reap as their reward the achievement of desired goals; for this they are willing to assume the necessary costs.
4. Regardless of the nature of the exchange relationship, each actor will attempt to maximize rewards and minimize costs.
5. Exchange processes are more than an economic transaction, since they involve intrinsic psychological satisfaction and need-gratification.
6. Only those activities that are economical will be repeated.

Power enters the exchange relationship when one of the participants in the exchange values the rewards gained in the relationship more than the other participant does. The exchange theorist's view of power is that it is derived from imbalances in the social exchange. From Peter Blau's perspective, much of social life is an intricate exchange in which every participant in social interaction approaches and withdraws in patterns that add to or subtract from his or her store of power and prestige.

Sue McIntire and Tim Pierce are college students who have been dating each other for the last two months and their relationship could be used as an example of an exchange relationship. The question that an exchange theorist would immediately ask is what is each party getting out of the relationship. Sue, an attractive young coed, chooses to be seen dating Tim, who is the star of the university basketball team, in order to prove to others how desirable a date she is and thus improve her fellow students' opinion of her. Tim, on the other hand, by dating the most attractive coed on campus may be able to show how his popularity in athletics can become a valuable resource in other areas of life (i.e., attracting members of the opposite sex). Thus, we can see a balanced exchange relationship in which each person involved wants to continue the relationship because of the benefits they are deriving.

Power would enter this relationship if Tim wanted to continue the relationship and Sue wanted to terminate it. In any kind of interpersonal exchange Sue would be able to bargain more effectively with Tim because she is willing, at any point, to terminate the relationship. Tim, who wants to continue the relationship more than Sue, would have to make concessions to her demands in order to persuade her to continue to date him. Thus we would have an imbalanced exchange relationship in which Sue can exercise more power and thereby more easily control Tim because she is not as committed to continuing the relationship as he is.

In viewing aging as exchange, Dowd argues that decreased social interaction is the eventual result of a series of exchange relationships in which the power of older persons relative to their social environment is gradually diminished until all that remains of their power resources is the humble capacity to comply. Where the worker was once able to exchange skill, knowledge, or expertise for needed wages, the final exchange becomes one of compliance with mandatory retirement in return for sustenance in the form of social security, retirement pensions, and medicare. Table 2–1 sets forth Dowd's concept that the probability of continued engagement in social relationships is principally a function of the already existing power relationships between the aging person and the society. The skills of many aging workers may rapidly become outmoded, resulting in an unfavorable power balance. The danger for the less powerful party—the older person—is that, once established, this unbalanced exchange relationship becomes institutionalized and thereby provides a normative basis for future unbalanced exchanges.

Blau notes that in any complex work organization, there are limited resources. Therefore it is possible for management to balance one exchange relationship only by unbalancing others. As one group gains a relative advantage, another group is threatened. Younger workers exchange their labor for wages and the implicit promise of job security and promotion. The longer the older worker remains on the job, the more he or she is blocking the career path of younger workers.

From the perspective of exchange theory, then, aging workers primarily face a problem of decreasing power resources. As their particular skill or expertise becomes outmoded or its value reduced in any way, they have little to exchange that is of critical value. One answer, therefore, to the question why older persons disengage is not that it is mutually satisfying for the individual and society, but rather that in the exchange relationship between older persons and society, society enjoys a distinct advantage.

The exchange theory offers a new perspective from which to view the process of aging and the interaction between the individual and the social system. Because the introduction of this theory to the field of gerontology is very recent, there have been few attempts to test it. Dowd believes that one of the advantages of the exchange perspective is that it rejects the functionalist disen-

Table 2–1 Disengagement and Power Relationships

INDIVIDUAL READINESS TO DISENGAGE	SOCIETY	
	Positive	*Negative*
Positive	Power Balance (Mutually satisfying exchange)	Power Imbalance (The individual with critical expertise is forced to remain engaged)
Negative	Power Imbalance (The individual with little critical expertise is forced to retire? Disengage?)	Power Balance (Continued role incumbency is institutionally sanctioned, e.g., religious and political leaders)

gagement notion of reciprocity between the individual and the social system (in which both the individual and society are seen as benefiting from the disengagement process) and requires an explicit analysis of both sides of each social transaction (exchange) in order to determine who is benefiting most and why. Only future research will be able to determine the value of exchange theory as an explanation of the aging process.

THE SYMBOLIC INTERACTION PERSPECTIVE

Symbolic interaction theory as developed by George Mead, Charles Cooley, William Thomas, and other social thinkers is one of the basic theoretical perspectives of sociologists. The acquisition of language by human beings makes them distinctly different from any other form of life, according to the symbolic interactionists. Through language, humans live in a symbolic environment as well as a physical environment and can be stimulated to act by symbols as well as by physical stimuli. Through language (symbols), humans have the capacity to stimulate others in ways other than those in which they themselves are stimulated. Thus, the sergeant may tell his soldiers that it is their patriotic duty to fight and risk their lives saving a hill in order that the sergeant might be seen as an effective leader and thereby be promoted to lieutenant. The symbolic interactionists assume that the individual communicates to others in order to evolve meanings and values in others. In the above illustration the sergeant believed that the soldiers' sense of patriotic duty would make them willing to risk their lives.

The exponents of symbolic interaction maintain that through the communication of symbols, human beings can learn huge numbers of meanings and values and hence ways of acting from other persons. Thus it is assumed that most of adult behavior is learned specifically in symbolic communication rather than through trial and error conditioning.

Thinking is seen by the symbolic interactionists as a process by which possible solutions and other future courses of action are examined, assessed for their relative advantages and disadvantages in terms of the values of the individual, and one option is then chosen for action. Thinking is a symbolic process of deductive trial and error.

Sheldon Stryker outlined what he considered to be the basic assumptions of the theory:

1. Humankind must be studied at its own level. Valid principles of human social psychological behavior cannot be inferred from the study of nonhuman forms, since humans are qualitatively and quantitatively different from their predecessors in the evolutionary process. Thus, principles derived from other forms of life cannot completely account for human behavior.

2. The most fruitful approach to human social behavior is through the analysis of society. Interaction is the basic building block of society from which both individual and societal patterns of behavior are derived. Utilizing this block, sociology builds in the direction of collective behavior; social psychology builds in the direction of the behavior of individuals.

3. A baby is neither social nor antisocial but rather asocial, with potentialities for social development. A baby has impulses, but these impulses must be channeled in a given direction.

4. In the interaction process, the human being is an actor as well as a reactor, and does not simply respond to external stimuli. What constitutes a stimulus depends on the activity in which a human being is involved. A human's environment is a selected segment of the "real world," the selection having been made in the interest of behavior initiated by that human being. Thus, through the learning of a culture (including specialized cultures found in particular segments of society), we are able to predict each other's behavior most of the time and adjust our own behavior to the predicted behavior of others.

LABELING THEORY

One of the current social psychological perspectives on human behavior is that known as *labeling*, a derivation of symbolic interaction theory. The basic assertion of labeling theory is that one derives a concept of self from interaction with other people in one's social milieu. We tend to think of ourselves in terms of how other people define us and react to us. The behavioral corollary of labeling theory is that once others have defined us into distinct categories, they react to us on the basis of these categories; and as a result, our self concept and behavior changes. As we observed in Chapter 1, most people behave the way others in their social world expect them to.

Thus from the labeling perspective, the behavior of older persons may largely depend on the reactions of significant others in their immediate social milieu. The reactions of these significant others depend on how they define and categorize older Americans. The behavior of older Americans therefore is in large measure socially determined by the norms of the social group to which they belong, according to labeling theory.

Building on the concepts of the labeling perspectives, Jack Zusman has constructed a social breakdown syndrome, and Joseph Kuypers and Vern Bengtson have constructed a social reconstruction model that they believe offers considerable promise for explaining, and intervening in, the behavior of older Americans in order to help them remain independent as long as possible.

Zusman proposes a multistage cycle of social breakdown that is consistent with the pattern illustrated in Figure 2–2. Among the steps that Zusman suggests are

1. The individual's precondition or susceptibility to psychological breakdown (having problems with identity or inappropriate standards concerning social relationships);
2. The labeling of the individual by others as incompetent or deficient in some respect;
3. The individual's induction into a sick dependent role, learning the behavior associated with that role, and the atrophy of previous skills;
4. The individual's identification with the "sick-role," with self-identification as inadequate. The malignant cycle begins again, for the individual is even more susceptible to stages in the cycle of psychological breakdown.

Joseph Kuypers and Vern Bengtson, applying the Zusman model to older Americans, state that

1. The elderly are likely to be susceptible to and dependent on social labeling because of the nature of social reorganization in later life. That is, role loss, vague and inappropriate normative information, and lack of reference groups all serve to deprive the individual of feedback concerning who he is.
2. Second, this feedback vacuum creates a vulnerability to, and dependence on, external sources of self-labeling, many of which communicate a stereotypic portrayal of the elderly as useless and obsolete.
3. Third, the individual who accepts such negative labeling is then inducted into the negative, dependent position—learning to act like old people are supposed to act—and previous skills of independence atrophy.
4. Fourth, he accepts the external labeling and identifies himself as inadequate, setting the stage for another vicious spiral.[12]

We see how the complex interplay between the older person and his or her social milieu can largely determine that person's self-concept and behavior.

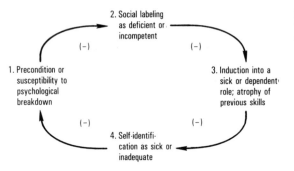

2. Social labeling as deficient or incompetent
(-)
(-)
1. Precondition or susceptibility to psychological breakdown
3. Induction into a sick or dependent role; atrophy of previous skills
(-)
(-)
4. Self-identification as sick or inadequate

Figure 2–2
The Social Breakdown Syndrome (A vicious cycle of increasing incompetence)

Source: Vern L. Bengtson, *The Social Psychology of Aging* (Indianapolis, Indiana: Bobbs-Merrill Co.), p. 47.
©1973, The Bobbs-Merrill Company, Inc.

Kuypers and Bengtson suggest that assistance to the aging individual who may be experiencing various stages of the social breakdown syndrome can easily be suggested and might result in an entirely different outcome for the individual. This assistance can result in a reversal of the social breakdown syndrome which Kuypers and Bengtson illustrate in their social reconstruction syndrome which

1. Characterizes the dynamic interaction between the individual and the individual's social system as he or she moves through time.
2. Portrays some inputs that can be made to assist older people (Figure 2–3).

These inputs include

1. Efforts made to liberate the individual from an age-inappropriate view of status; the functionalist work ethic, which suggests self-worth, is contingent on performance in economic or "productive" social positions and is particularly inappropriate to old age. Consequently, a more humanitarian frame of self-judgment needs to be developed.
2. The improvement of social services to older persons. Their capacity for adapting to their new circumstances can be enhanced by reduction or elimination of the debilitating environmental conditions that most older people face, such as poor housing, poor health, and poverty. This improvement would facilitate their ability to cope.
3. Assisting older persons to develop greater self-confidence in their ability to manage their own life. Those serving older people could delegate

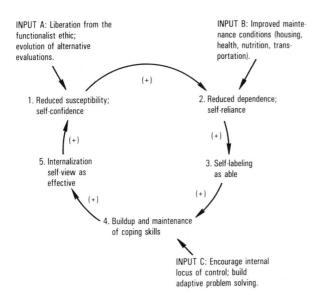

Figure 2–3

The Social Reconstruction Syndrome (A benign cycle of increasing competence through social-system inputs)

Source: Vern L. Bengtson, *The Social Psychology of Aging* (Indianapolis, Indiana: Bobbs-Merrill, 1973), p. 48. ©1973, The Bobbs-Merrill Company, Inc.

some of their power and control over service programs to the older people themselves, thereby allowing them some measure of self-determination in the areas of policy, administration, and involvement in these programs.

The symbolic interaction theory seems to offer a number of advantages over other theoretical perspectives on aging. First, it views aging as a dynamic process revolving around the interaction between the individual and the individual's social world rather than as a process governed by any single deterministic or functionalist imperative. Second, it offers no philosophical mandate to disengage or remain active in the later years and thus is value-free. Third, it suggests the social-psychological effect of negative labeling and the vague and often inappropriate behavioral expectations that older Americans find themselves confronted with. Finally, to counter the effect of negative labeling of older Americans, the social reconstruction model suggests realistic solutions that practitioners could easily implement in their attempt to intervene in behalf of this group.

CONCLUSION

Research in the field of gerontology has often been of an applied rather than a theoretical nature. This is largely due to the fact that older Americans were daily experiencing so many problems demanding immediate solutions that researchers invested much of their time in seeking these solutions, often leaving aside the broader theoretical questions.

The 1950s and 1960s saw the emergence of both disengagement and activity theory. Empirical examination of these theories led researchers to conclude that neither adequately explained the life course of older Americans. Neither disengagement nor activity theory was found to be highly correlated with life satisfaction for older Americans.

The 1970s saw the proliferation of other theoretical perspectives directed to the aging process. Many of these were broader theories of human behavior which had been developed much earlier but which could be easily utilized in explaining the behavior patterns of older Americans. Among these human development, continuity, exchange, age stratification and symbolic interaction seem to offer considerable promise for future research and testing.

Continuity theory, the most direct spin-off from disengagement and activity theory, would seem to be the most difficult to support or refute. Hypotheses derived from this theory are often tied to the researcher's knowledge of the individual's previous lifestyle. Support for the theory based on a series of case histories may be exceedingly long in developing.

Age stratification, exchange, and symbolic interaction theories, on the other hand, can lead to innumerable hypotheses that can be easily tested by traditional research tools and are therefore likely to appear more frequently in future research reports. Symbolic interaction seems somewhat broader, more sociologically grounded, and therefore more useful.

No matter which of the theories eventually proves most valuable to gerontologists, there seems to be little doubt that these new perspectives offer alternative explanations of the aging process as well as a more value-free approach and a multiplicity of new directions for future research in the field.

KEY TERMS

theories of aging:
   disengagement
   activity
   continuity
   developmental
   exchange
   symbolic interaction
   stratification

cohort
sociological functionalism
impingers
selectors

SUGGESTED READINGS

ATCHLEY, R., *Social Forces in Later Life*. Belmont, Calif.: Wadsworth, 1980.

BARRON, M. L., "Minority Group Characteristics of the Aged in American Society," *Journal of Gerontology*, 8 (1953), 477–82.

BENGTSON, VERN L., *The Social Psychology of Aging*. Indianapolis: Bobbs-Merrill, 1973.

BENGTSON, VERN L., "Adult Socialization and Personality Differentiation: The Social-Psychology of Aging," in *Contemporary Gerontology: Issues and Concepts*, ed. J. Barren. Los Angeles: Los Angeles Geronotology Center, 1969.

BENGTSON, VERN L., AND D. D. BLACK, "Inter-generational Relations and Continuities in Socialization," in *Life Span Developmental Psychology: Personality and Socialization*, ed. P. Baltes and W. Schaie. New York: Academic Press, 1973.

BLACK, D. W., AND K. J. GERGEN, "Cognitive and Motivational Factors in Aging and Disengagement," in *Social Aspects of Aging*, ed. Ida H. Simpson and John C. McKinney, pp. 289–95. Durham, N.C.: Duke University Press, 1966.

BLAU, PETER M., *Exchange and Power in Social Life*. New York: John Wiley, 1964.

BLAU, ZENA, *Old Age in a Changing Society*. New York: New Viewpoints, 1973.

BLOOM, MARTIN, "Life Span Analysis: A Theoretical Framework for Behavioral Science Research," *Journal of Human Relations*, 12 (1964), 538–54.

BUHLER, CHARLOTTE, "The Developmental Structure and Goal Setting in Group and Individual Studies," in *The Course of Human Life*, ed. Charlotte Buhler and Fred Massarick. New York: Springer, 1968.

BUHLER, CHARLOTTE, AND FRED MASSARIK, *The Course of Human Life*. New York: Springer, 1968.

BULTENA, GORDON L., "Life Continuity and Morale in Old Age," *The Gerontologist*, 9, no. 4, pt. 1 (1969), 251–53.

CAIN, LEONARD D., "Life Course and Social Structure," in *Handbook of Modern Sociology*, ed. R.E.L. Faris. Chicago: Rand McNally, 1964.

CAIN, LEONARD D., JR., "Age Status and Generations Phenomena: The New Old in Contemporary America," *The Gerontologist*, 7, no. 2 (1969), 83–92.

CARP, FRANCES M., "Some Components of Disengagement," *Journal of Gerontology*, 23 (1968), 382–86.

CAVAN, RUTH S., R. J. HAVIGHURST, AND H. GOLDHAMER, *Personal Adjustment in Old Age*. Chicago: Science Research Associates, 1949.

COTTRELL, FRED, AND ROBERT C. ATCHLEY, *Women in Retirement: A Preliminary Report*. Oxford, Ohio: Scripps Foundation, 1969.

COWGILL, DONALD J., "Segregation Scores for Metropolitan Areas," *American Sociological Review*, 27 (June 1962), 400–402.

COX, HAROLD, AND ALBERT BHAK, "Determinants of Age Based Residential Segregation," *Sociological Symposium*, no. 29 (Winter 1980), 27–41.

CUMMING, ELAINE, "Further Thoughts on the Theory of Disengagement," *UNESCO International Social Science Bulletin IS* (1963), 377–93.

CUMMING, ELAINE, AND OTHERS, "Disengagement: A Tentative Theory of Aging," *Sociometry*, 23 (1960), 23–35.

CUMMING, ELAINE, AND WILLIAM H. HENRY, *Growing Old*. New York: Basic Books, 1961.

DEROCHES, H. F., AND B. D. KAIMAN, "Stability of Activity Participation in an Aged Population," *Journal of Gerontology*, 19 (1964), 211–14.

DEROCHES, H. F., AND B. D. KAIMAN, "Disengagement Potential: Replication and Use as an Explanatory Variable," *Journal of Gerontology*, 23 (1971), 76–80.

DEROCHES, H. F., AND B. D. KAIMAN, "Disengagement Theory in Sociocultural Perspective," *International Journal of Psychiatry*, 6, no. 1 (1968), 69–76.

DOWD, JAMES J., "Aging as Exchange: A Preface to Theory," *Journal of Gerontology*, 30 (1975), 584–94.

EISENSTADT, S. N., *From Generation to Generation: Age Groups and Social Structure*. New York: Free Press, 1965.

ERIKSON, ERIK H., *Child and Society* (rev. ed.). New York: W. W. Norton & Co., Inc., 1964.

FREUD, SIGMUND, *An Outline of Psychoanalysis*. New York: W. W. Norton & Co., Inc., 1949.

HAVIGHURST, ROBERT J., "Successful Aging," in *Process of Aging*, ed. Richard H. Williams, Clark Tibbit, and Wilma Donahue, p. 299. New York: Lieber-Atherton, 1963.

HAVIGHURST, ROBERT J., BERNICE L. NEUGARTEN, AND VERN L. BENGTSON, "A Cross-National Study of Adjustment to Retirement," *Gerontologist*, 6 (1966), 137–38.

HENRY, WILLIAM E., "The Theory of Intrinsic Disengagement," in *Age with a Future*, ed. P. Form Hansen, pp. 415–18. Copenhagen: Munksgaard, 1964.

HENRY, WILLIAM E., "Engagement and Disengagement: Toward a Theory of Adult Development," in *Psychobiology of Aging*, ed. R. Kastenbaum, pp. 19–35. New York: Springer, 1965.

JUNG, CARL G., *The Stages of Life*, trans. R.F.C. Hull, in *The Portable Jung*, ed. Joseph Campbell. New York: Viking Press, 1971.

KALISH, R. A. "Of Social Values and the Dying: A Defense of Disengagement," *The Family Coordinator*, 21 (1972), 81–94.

KAPLAN, HOWARD B., "Age-Related Correlates of Self-Derogation: Contemporary Life Space Characteristics," *Aging and Human Development*, 2 (1971), 305–13.

KIMMEL, DOUGLAS, C., *Adulthood and Aging.* New York: John Wiley, 1974.

KUTNER, B., "The Social Nature of Aging," *Gerontologist*, 2, no. 1 (1962), 5–9.

KUYPERS, JOSEPH A., AND VERN L. BENGTSON, "Competence and Social Breakdown: A Social-Psychological View of Aging," *Human Development*, 16, no. 2 (1973), 37–49.

LEBO, D., "Some Factors Said to Make for Happiness in Old Age," *Journal of Clinical Psychology*, 9 (1953), 385–90.

LEMON, BRUCE W., VERN L. BENGTSON, AND JAMES A. PETERSON, "Activity Types and Life Satisfaction in a Retirement Community," *Journal of Gerontology*, 27, no. 4 (1972), 511–23.

LIPMAN, A., "Role Conceptions and Morale of Couples in Retirement," *Journal of Gerontology*, 16 (1961), 276–81.

LIPMAN, A., AND K. J. SMITH, "Functionality of Disengagement in Old Age," *Journal of Gerontology*, 23 (1968), 517–21.

LOETHER, H. J., *Problems of Aging.* Encino, Calif.: Dickenson, 1967.

MADDOX, G., "Activity and Morale: A Longitudinal Study of Selected Elderly Subjects," *Social Forces*, 42 (1963), 195–204.

MADDOX, G., "Disengagement Theory: A Critical Evaluation," *Gerontologist*, 4 (1964), 80–82.

MADDOX, G., in *Older People and Their Social World: The Subculture of the Aging*, ed. A. Rose and W. A. Peterson. Philadelphia: F. A. Davis, 1965.

MADDOX, G., "Fact and Artifact: Evidence Bearing on Disengagement Theory," in *Normal Aging*, ed. Edman Palmore, pp. 318–28. Durham, N.C.: Duke University Press, 1970.

MADDOX, G., "Persistence of Life Style Among the Elderly," in *Normal Aging*, ed. Edman Palmore, pp. 329–31. Durham, N.C.: Duke University Press, 1970.

MADDOX, G., "Themes and Issues in Sociological Theories of Human Aging," *Human Development*, 13 (1970), 17–27.

MANIS, JEROME G., AND BERNARD N. MELTZER, *Symbolic Interaction: A Reader in Social Psychology.* Boston: Allyn and Bacon, 1972.

MARTIN, W. C., "Activity and Disengagement: Life Satisfaction of In-Movers into a Retirement Community," *Gerontologist*, 13, no. 2 (Summer 1973), 224–27.

MEAD, GEORGE G., ed., *Mind, Self and Society.* Chicago: University of Chicago Press, 1934.

NEUGARTEN, B. L., *Personality in Middle and Late Life.* New York: Lieber-Atherton, 1964.

NEUGARTEN, B. L., "New Thoughts on the Theory of Disengagement," in *New Thoughts on Old Age*, ed. R. Kastenbaum, pp. 3–18. New York: Springer, 1964.

NEUGARTEN, B. L., R. T. HAVIGHURST, AND S. TOBIN, "The Measurement of Life Satisfaction," *Journal of Gerontology*, 16 (1961), 134–43.

NEUGARTEN, B. L., AND J. MOORE, "The Changing Status System," in *Middle Age and Aging,* ed. B. L. Neugarten. Chicago: The University of Chicago Press, 1968.

NEUGARTEN, B. L., J. W. MOORE, AND J. C. LOWE, "Age Norms, Age Constraints, and Adult Socialization," *American Journal of Sociology,* 70, no. 6 (1965), 710–17.

PALMORE, ERDMAN B., "Differences in the Retirement Patterns of Men and Women," *Gerontologist,* 5 (1965), 4–8.

PECK, R., "Psychology Developments in the Second Half of Life," in *Psychological Aspects of Aging,* ed. J. E. Anderson, pp. 42–53. Washington, D.C.: American Psychological Association, 1956.

PETERSON, JAMES, VERN BENGTSON, AND BRUCE LEMON, "An Exploration of the Activity Theory of Aging: Activity Types and Life Satisfaction Among In-Movers to a Retirement Community," *Journal of Gerontology,* 27 (1972), 511–23.

PETERSON, WARREN, Lecture given at the Indiana State University workshop, "Critical Problems of Aging," June 1976.

PHILLIPS, B. S., "A Role Theory Approach to Adjustment in Old Age," *American Sociological Review,* 22 (1957), 212–17.

PRASAD, S. B., "The Retirement Postulate of the Disengagement Theory," *Gerontologist,* 4 (1964), 20–23.

RILEY, M. W., M. JOHNSON, AND A. FONER, "Aging and Society," *A Sociology of Age Stratification,* Vol. 3. New York: Russell Sage Foundation, 1972.

ROMAN, P., AND P. TAIETZ, "Organizational Structure and Disengagement: The Professor Emeritus," *Gerontologist,* 7, no. 3 (1967), 147–52.

ROSE, A., "A Current Theoretical Issue in Social Gerontology," *Gerontologist,* 4 (1964), 25–29.

ROSE, ARNOLD M., AND WARREN H. PETERSON, *Older People and Their Social World: The Sub-Culture of Aging.* Philadelphia: F. A. Davis, 1965.

ROSE, ARNOLD M., AND WARREN H. PETERSON, "The Impact of Aging on Voluntary Associations," in *Handbook of Social Gerontology,* ed. C. Tibbetts. Chicago: The University of Chicago Press, 1960.

ROSOW, I., *Social Integration of the Aged.* New York: Free Press, 1967.

SCHAIE, K. W., "Translations in Gerontology: From Lab to Life," *American Psychologist,* 29, no. 11 (1974), 802–7.

SIMPSON, IDA, *Social Aspects of Aging* (2nd ed.). Durham, N.C.: The Duke University Press, 1972.

STRACHEY, JAMES, ED., AND W. D. ROBSON, TRANS., *Sigmund Freud: The Future of an Illusion.* Garden City, N.Y.: Doubleday, 1961.

STREIB, GORDON F., "Are the Aged a Minority Group in Middle Age and Aging," ed. Bernice Neugarten. Chicago: The University of Chicago Press, 1968.

STRYKER, SHELDON, "Symbolic Interaction as an Approach to Family Research," *Marriage and Family Living,* 21 (1959), 111–19.

TALLMER, M., AND B. KUTNER, "Disengagement and the Stresses of Aging," *Journal of Gerontology,* 24 (1969), 70–75.

THOMPSON, W. E., AND G. STREIB, "Personal and Social Adjustments in Retirement," in *The New Frontiers of Aging,* ed. W. Donahue and C. Tibbett. Ann Arbor: University of Michigan Press, 1957.

TOBIN, S., AND B. L. NEUGARTEN, "Life Satisfaction and Social Interaction in the Aging," *Journal of Gerontology,* 16 (1961), 344–46.

WILLIAMS, R. H., C. TIBBETTS, AND W. DONAHUE, eds., *Processes of Aging,* Vol. II. New York: Prentice Hall-Atherton Press, 1963.

YARROW, M. R., AND O. W. QUINN, "Social Psychological Aspects of Aging." Paper read at the annual meeting of the Midwest Psychological Association, Chicago, 1957.

YOUMANS, E. G., "Some Perspectives of Disengagement Theory," *Gerontologist,* 9 (1969), 254–58.

ZUSMAN, JACK, "Some Explanations of the Changing Appearance of Psychotic Patients: Antecedents of the Social Breakdown Syndrome Concept," *The Millbank Memorial Fund Quarterly,* 64, no. 1 (January 1966), 2.

3

HISTORICAL AND CROSS-CULTURAL COMPARISONS IN THE AGING PROCESS

Although any individual is rarely of great importance to the survival and functioning of the society to which he belongs or the culture in which he participates, the individual, his needs and potentialities, lies at the foundations of all social and cultural phenomena. Societies are organized groups of individuals and cultures are, in the last analysis, nothing more than the organized repetitive responses of a society's members.

Ralph Linton
The Cultural Background of Personality

INTRODUCTION

While sociologists are likely to examine in great detail the older person's roles, status, functional utility and style of life in a particular culture at one point in time, anthropologists most often compare and contrast these variables and their interrelationships in a variety of different cultures. In comparing the relative position and status of older persons in different cultures, a number of patterns have emerged depending on the type of culture and the perceived role of older persons in these cultures.

Every society has a group of persons who are defined as old. Age grading seems to be a universal phenomenon in all societies. Anthropologists maintain that without exception every society has divided its people into categories based on age. At different points in history, however, the age at which one was considered to be old has varied considerably. Forty-year-olds in many primitive societies would have been considered very old persons, having for the most part outlived the great majority of their cohorts.

Table 3–1   Percent of Prehistoric Population
Deceased by Age

	AGE 30	AGE 40	AGE 50
Neanderthal	80.0%	95.0%	100.0%
Cro-Magnon	61.7	88.2	90.0
Mesolithic	86.3	95.5	97.0

Source: Shelburne Cook, "Aging of and in Populations," in *Developmental Physiology and Aging,* ed. P. S. Timiras (Berkeley: University of California Press, 1972), p. 595.

According to Thomlinson the potential lifespan of humans is about 120 years, if deaths from all causes except degenerative diseases were eliminated.[1] However, life expectancy, defined as the age at which the average person can expect to live to, has varied considerably over time. Archeologists have studied the age at death of our prehistoric ancestors and concluded that about 95 percent of them died before they reached the age of 40. It is estimated that 75 percent of them did not reach the age of 30.

High mortality rates in the prehistoric period are presumed most often to be the result of periodic famine and frequent malnutrition, each a characteristic of unstable food supplies.

Shelburne Cook has estimated that less than half the Greek population in the Hellenistic and Roman eras reached what we would today consider young adulthood. Those who survived the precarious early years of life might have expected to live a little longer than average since many babies died during childbirth and early childhood.[2] Figure 3–1 indicates life expectancy at age 15 in various historical periods.

Cook observed that at birth the ancient Egyptian male could have expected to live approximately 22 years. Those who survived the early childhood years could have expected to live to be 25 and those who reached age 25 could probably have expected to live to the age of 48.[3]

Estimates of life expectancy during the Middle Ages indicate that the average male at birth would have lived to be approximately 33 years of age.[4] David Fischer observes that the first census in the United States was taken in 1790 and at that time less than 20 percent of the American population survived from birth to the age of seventy. Today, more than 80 percent can expect to do so.

In the early historical period the old were most often valued because their experience and knowledge were useful for the survival of the entire culture. They held the culture's customs and traditions. Only the advent of senility could diminish the esteem in which they were held, and then they were sometimes given special statuses.

While the old were generally accorded a much higher status in primitive societies than they are in modern industrial nations, there is, of course, considerable disparity in how they were treated. Fischer traces the statements of Herodotus which indicated that at one extreme the Issedones who gilded the

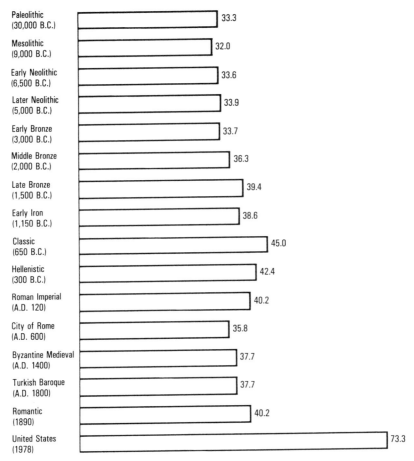

Figure 3–1 Life Expectancy at Age 15 for Different Historical Periods

Source: Adapted from J. Lawrence Angel, "Paleoecology, Paleodemography, and Health," in *Population, Ecology and Social Evolution,* ed. Steven Polgar (Chicago: Aldine, 1975), pp. 167–90.

heads of their aged parents and offered sacrifices before them. They seemed to worship their oldest tribal members. At the opposite extreme were the people of Bactria who disposed of their old folk by feeding them to flesh-eating dogs. Similarly, the Sardinians hurled their elders from a high cliff and shouted with laughter as they fell on the rocks.[5]

One difficulty anthropologists have in comparing the roles, status, and general position of older persons in a culture is the fact that some form of stratification exists in every society, and not all older persons are treated alike. Simone de Beauvoir observes that the role of the aged in any historical study is taken from the male point of view. Simone de Beauvoir notes it is men who express themselves in laws, books, and legends, essentially because the struggle for power has in the past been considered the concern of the "stronger sex." Among the apes, young males wrest power from the old males; they alone are killed, not the aged females.

In traditional China the old men were granted a privileged position. This was a value of the prevalent Confucian ideology. In politics and in the family the aged men occupied the top positions of power in hierarchical society that lasted for thousands of years. In the family, everyone gave deference to the oldest man. The wife was expected to be obedient to her husband; the son obeyed the father; and the younger son was obedient to the older son. The older man literally had the power of life or death over his children. He arranged their marriages and supervised both his children and their children throughout his life. The oldest male's wife also occupied a role of respect over both the younger males and females of the family. At fifty the man gained in importance; at approximately seventy he turned the household over to the oldest son while he began to be honored and worshipped as an ancestor.

Fischer makes reference to the stratification system among the aged, observing that for slaves and servants old age was probably so cruel that an early death was a kind of blessing. But for the elites, old age delivered the protection of power and property. Fischer points out that old men were so important to the government of Rome that Cicero argued that they were indispensable. Without old men Cicero felt there would be no civilized states at all.

Thus we find a wide variety of patterns regarding the treatment of the older members of different cultures, some being treated with a reverent respect and some being very cruelly put to death.

CRITICAL VARIABLES DETERMINING THE STATUS OF THE AGED

There are a number of variables, often interrelated, which either separately or in some combination seem to relate to the status accorded older persons in various cultures. These include: family form, religion, knowledge base of the culture, harshness of the environment, the means of production, and the speed of social changes.

In the consideration of cultural type and status of the aged, the general rule has been that in the nonindustrial, settled, agricultural societies the aged exercise considerable power and are granted a high status. In industrial societies, on the other hand, the aged exercise relatively little power and are granted less status. Cowgill and Holmes, in their work on aging and modernization, found an inverse relationship between the degree of modernization and the status accorded older persons in the system. In other words, the more industrialized the system became, the lower the status of the older person. While this is generally the case, a closer look reveals differential treatment of the elders even in the traditional societies. Sheehan, in a study of 47 traditional societies, found three different patterns of treatment of the aged. Approximately one-fifth of the traditional societies were geographically unstable, as semipermanent bands of people periodically relocating their villages or, in some cases, perpetually mobile. The lowest esteem for seniors was often found in these small and nomadic societies. They have the fewest material resources for seniors to accumulate, thereby gaining respect in the eyes of the younger persons; they are usually located in harsh environments which favor youth and vigor. Moreover, food is often in short supply and individual existence is precarious. The elderly may have to be sacrificed in order to insure the survival of the entire group. Among the societies studied, a plurality were comprised of various forms of tribes which were basically permanently settled, inhabiting fairly large villages and governed according to a belief in their common ancestry or kinship. Another group of the traditional societies was comprised of small peasant communities whose economic base was centered around agriculture or animal husbandry. The most highly developed social organizations of these traditional societies were the ones with large landed peasantries; there, the highest esteem was enjoyed by older persons.

It appears that once traditional societies became located in a permanent place with stated residence and property rights, the old began to exercise considerable power over the young by the ownership of the property and the ability to pass it on to their children. Where property is the only means of production, by controlling the property the aged are able to control the younger generations. The future occupations and chances for success of the younger generation are tied to seeking the favor of their elders, who control all the resources. While one's parents are alive they are of critical importance because they provide employment and the means of survival in the form of resources. After they die, the heirs inherit shares of their lands and thus control of these resources for themselves and their children. Therefore, in traditional societies that are permanently located, the individual is directly dependent upon his own senior generation for the acquisition of the means of production. The anticipated transfer of the property at the death of the parent to the children provides an incentive that encourages the young to respect their older family members. It is easy to see why the young defer to their elders and attempt to seek their special favor. Similarly, it is easy to understand how the old, by the development of stable institutions and the control of property, are able to maintain their power and privilege in the social system. This may also explain the higher value placed on the family in rural America where the transmission of land to the next generation may secure that generation a livelihood and a secure position in the social structure.

Thus, rather than Cowgill and Holmes's prediction of an inverse relationship between the degree of modernization and the status accorded older persons, we find a curvilinear one in which the old are accorded a low status in simple nomadic societies, a high status in settled agricultural communities, and a low status in modern industrial nations.

Tom Sheehan equates what happens to older persons in the nomadic tribes to what happens to them in modern industrial societies. Sheehan believes that with the development of modern technology, social and geographic mobility become goals, and individual autonomy reemerges as a primary value. The young forfeit the security of the village or family to work in factories and offices. They attain financial and social separation from many traditional restraints. Lifestyles turn away from extended family ties. There is now no special reason for younger family members to secure the favor of their parents and grandparents. The older family members lose their status, decision-making power, and the security they once had in earlier cultural settings.

The result is that the old are considered much less valuable in the modern contemporary states. In both of these cultural settings the old become quickly dependent on the young for their well-being and survival.

The form of the family is often related to the kind of culture and structural relations among institutions in a particular society. In traditional societies that are primarily agricultural in nature, the extended form of the family (most often comprised of mother, father, their sons and their wives and children) is often the prevalent one. The extended family is most often patriarchial, which means that power and lineage are traced through the male sides of the family. The wife, upon marriage, moves in with the husband's family, and when their children are old enough to marry, the parents arrange for their marriages and expect the wives of their sons to move into their household and their daughters to move into the households of their husbands. This family arrangement is one in which the oldest male member of the family exercises the greatest power, privilege, and authority. Individualism is discouraged. The individual is always subserviant to the demands of the group. The concept of romantic love (strong, intense emotional attachment between members of the opposite sex) is nonexistent and the criterion for the success of the marriage is the amount of family disruption caused by the entrance of the new bride. If she gets along well with her in-laws and does not cause difficulty in the family setting, it is considered a good marriage. The son's happiness is secondary to the good of the group. The extended family works best in stable cultures which are primarily agriculturally based. This culture is the one in which the older members exercise the greatest power and maintain the highest status.

The advent of industrialization leads to the breakup of the extended family. One no longer depends upon land as the principle means of production. New jobs, careers, resources, and opportunities become available. Modern industry requires mobile labor which can be moved from place to place as it is needed. Extended family ties are broken in order to move the labor force where it is most needed; if not, the industrial system itself would break down. The nuclear family—husband, wife, and children—is dominant. The influence of the father and mother over adult children is weakened. The size of the family declines as children themselves become units of consumption rather than of production and thereby become less desirable.

The difference between extended and nuclear families for the status of the aged can perhaps best be seen in Israel. Weihl observes that the older people among the migrants from the Orient are given a relatively high status in comparison to the relatively low status accorded older immigrants from the Western countries. The migrants from the Orient evidence considerable commitment to the concept of the extended family in contrast with the commitment to nuclear family evidenced by migrants from the West.

The religions of the Far East have generally supported the extended family and the higher status of its elder members by the moral and ethical codes that they espouse. The Confucian concept is one in which the aged are to be given tender loving care. They are to be exempt from certain responsibilities when they reach old age. Pre–World War II families in China and Japan were ones in which children cared for their elders, and older family members exercised the most authority. This meant also that the elders were the most respected members of the family.

While Christianity clearly admonishes the individual to honor his father and mother, this religious principle has probably had less impact in the Western world than one might expect. The pressure of industrialization results in the educational functions being gradually removed from the family socialization process to formal training outside the home. The nature of wealth changes from land to tangible property. The emphasis shifts to productivity. The young are always seen as more productive and the old as less productive. Degradation generally occurs for the older, and supposedly slower, workers.

Another aspect of modern industrial society is the location of knowledge. In traditional agricultural societies, the old are the reservoirs of knowledge—of past problems and their solutions, of old customs and the appropriate religious rituals. In industrial societies, books, libraries, universities, and current research enterprises are a base for the generation and transmittal of knowledge. The freshly trained college student is often more valuable in the business and industrial world than the older and more experienced employee whose knowledge and expertise may have become obsolete. The inability to maintain control of critical knowledge in modern society has been another factor that has contributed to the general loss of status of older persons.

American society has a well-developed and sophisticated educational system which prepares young people to enter an occupation, but it is ill equipped to retrain older workers when new technologies require workers' additional schooling.

The harshness of the environment in which the culture is found and the amount of physical labor required for survival are also factors that can reduce the usefulness and thereby the status of the older members of a culture. Holmberg notes that among the Sirono of the Bolivian rain forest, it is the general belief that

> Actually the aged are quite a burden; they eat but are unable to hunt, fish or collect food; they sometimes hoard a young spouse, but are unable to beget children; they move at a snail's pace and hinder the mobility of the group. When a person becomes too ill or infirm to follow the fortunes of the band, he is abandoned to shift for himself.[6]

Cowgill and Holmes note that there is some difficulty in adjusting to reduced activity in old age in a society which is so strongly dedicated to hard physical labor. Kibbutz society in Israel is one example; there, older persons may arrive at an ambiguous status because of their inability to keep up physically with younger counterparts.

Related to the changing knowledge base in modern society is the speed with which social change occurs within the system itself. Cowgill and Holmes believe that rapid social change in modern societies tends to undermine the status of older persons. Change renders many of the skills of older Americans obsolete. Not only can they no longer ply their trade but, simultaneously, there is no reason for them to teach it to others. In a rapidly changing society the younger people are nearly always better educated and possess more knowledge of recent technology than their elders; thus, the latter lose their utility and the basis of their authority.

Referring to both the speed of social change in modern society and the location of the knowledge base in the system, William Watson and Robert Maxwell hypothesize that societies can be arranged along a continuum whose basis is the amount of useful information controlled by the aged. They believe the greater the elders are in control of critical information, the greater is their participation in community affairs; their participation is, in turn, directly related to the degree of esteem in which they are held by other members of the community. Watson and Maxwell believe this control of information and consequent social participation declines with industrialization and its rapid sociocultural change.[7]

Watson and Maxwell argue that one of the most fruitful models developed for the investigation of human societies has relied heavily on the information storage and exchange model and is described as systems theory.[8] Goffman has demonstrated that groups which share secret information will tend to be more integrated and unified than those which do not. All stored information, according to Goffman, involves a stated arrangement of elements in the sense that they are a record of past events.[9]

In traditional societies, one of the main functions of old people is to remember legends, myths, ethical principles, and the appropriate relations that should be arranged with the supernatural, and they are frequently asked about these matters.

Elliott described this pattern among the Aleuts in northern Russia:

Before the advent of Russian priests, every village had one or two old men at least, who considered it their special business to educate the children, thereupon, in the morning or evening when all were home these aged teachers would seat themselves in the center of one of the largest village courts or oolagumuh; the young folks surrounded them and listened attentively to what they said.[10]

Watson and Maxwell believe that the printing press was to end this kind of arrangement in the social system. In industrialized societies the information that is important is written down, printed, and sold in bookstores.[11]

Some historians have argued that economically, politically, and socially older people are more conservative than younger people and tend to have a stabilizing effect on any social system. The young, being much more changeable in their view, offer adaptability and in some ways may increase the chances for survival in the social system.

One final factor which may in some way explain the declining status of the aged in modern industrial countries is the relative proportion of the entire population that they comprise. In most of the ancient and traditional societies they comprised less than 3 percent of the total population. It is easy to reserve a special status for a group of people that comprise a very small percent of the total population. In modern society the old have come to comprise between 8 to 15 percent of the total population (as Table 3–2 indicates). It may become increasingly difficult to preserve a privileged status for a group that comprises such a large percentage of a total population.

THEORETICAL VIEWS ON THE CHANGING STATUS OF THE ELDERLY

Functionalists have always maintained that a society is much like a human organism; all the parts fit together in a cooperative interdependent manner in order to keep the system operating. The job of the social scientist is to find and trace the pattern of interdependent relationship among the various institutions in a particular system. It is generally considered that family, religion, education, economic, and political systems represent five basic institutions existing in every society. The beliefs, behavior patterns, and normative expectations which emerge from these institutions are complementary and overlapping. The cooperative interdependence of these institutions are what make the survival of the socio-cultural system possible. Much of the material presented by the archeologist, anthropologist, and sociologist to explain the power, privilege, and status obtained by older people in different societies has been from a functionalist perspective.

Table 3–2 Percent of Total Population 65 and Over

COUNTRY	PERCENT
Thailand	3.0
Mexico	3.7
Japan	6.2
Union of Soviet Socialist Republics	7.1
Austria	13.6
Israel	6.4
Norway	11.8
Ireland	11.8
United States	9.3

Source: United Nations Demographic Yearbook (1966). Copyright 1966 by United Nations. Reproduced by permission.

The material thus far presented indicates that in the premodern sociocultural systems there are basically two broad categories: the first, nomadic tribes, and the second, permanently settled agrarian societies. Nomadic tribes frequently live under harsh environmental conditions in which the very survival of the group is often in doubt. Under those conditions the old exercise little power and are accorded a relatively low status. Their low status is related to the fact that as they aged they could not move as quickly as the tribe needed nor did they have the skill to provide for their own sustenance, let alone that of other tribesmen. At some point they become a detriment to the group's chance for survival and have to be discarded. In other words, if the tribe attempts to feed and transport some of its oldest members, the survival of the entire group might be in doubt.

As the sociocultural system becomes permanently settled, it is likely that agriculture is the main business, and land the principle means of production. Stable institutions and the established right to own land considerably change the power, privilege, and status of older persons. By control of the means of production in the form of land ownership, the aged maintain their status long after their physical dexterity begins to wane. Moreover, in the family and religious values and in the knowledge base of the system they are in an advantaged position. They are the reservoirs of knowledge, customs, the past, and religious rituals. They become functionally important to the sociocultural system's chance for survival and are accorded a high status.

The advent of industrialization changes the family structure, knowledge base, educational institutions, economy, religious and governmental structure of the sociocultural system. The nuclear family comprised of husband, wife, and children becomes the norm and there is considerably less commitment to extended family members. The industrial economy demands a mobile labor force in which extended family ties must be broken. The knowledge base of the system shifts from its senior members to bookstores, libraries, colleges, and research enterprises. Productivity is of prime value. The old are seen as less productive and therefore generally devalued; simultaneously, the knowledge base is transferred to universities, and rapid social change makes much of the knowledge and many of the skills of old persons obsolete. Thus, modern industrial nations find their older members to be of less functional utility to the survival of the system and accord them low status and less of the sociocultural system's wealth and resources.

The functionalist school of thought in the social sciences is often challenged by different theoretical perspectives. Symbolic interactionism is one of the alternative perspectives which can be utilized in analyzing the status of the elders in a society.

Symbolic interactionists have tended to rely heavily on the concept of social roles in explaining the behavior of individuals and the relationship among individuals in the group. Rather than raising the question of the functional importance of older persons' roles to the survival of the system, they want to know

(1) what roles older persons are expected to assume, and (2) what value is attached to these roles by others in society. It may well be that the role of religious leader, whether priest or Brahmin, is not crucial to the survival of the system since it could survive in the absence of the role. What is important is how valuable others in society believe the role of religious leaders to be. Thus, in the extended family we find that the role of grandparent is highly valued and respected. In the conjugal family, on the other hand, we find the role of grandparent reduced to babysitting. In terms of the functional utility to the sociocultural system, the grandparent role is probably about equally important in different cultures but it is accorded considerably more importance and thereby status in one culture than it is in another.

From the symbolic interaction perspective, the factors anthropologists and sociologists should pay close attention to in examining the position of the aged in any sociocultural system are

1. What roles the aged assume in the society;
2. What value is attached to these roles by other persons in the society;
3. Whether the roles performed by elders represent role continuity (the roles that someone is involved in at one stage of life prepare him or her for the skills he or she will need at the next stage of life) from previous roles they have assumed, or role discontinuity (the roles that someone is involved in at this stage of life are not preparing him or her with the skills that will be required at the next stage of life) from previous roles they have occupied.

In order to evaluate the positions of older persons in different sociocultural systems, it is necessary to look in some detail at three different cultures: One in which the old experience role continuity, and there is little difference in what tasks they perform in the later years in comparison to the middle years; and two in which they experience role discontinuity. In one case of role discontinuity, the role shifts in later life give them the less desirable roles and a loss of status in the eyes of others. In the other the role shift is to a much more highly prized role, and they are given a considerably more highly valued status.

THE ABKASIANS: ROLE CONTINUITY IN LATER LIFE

Sula Benet, in a 1971 edition of *The New York Times Magazine,* wrote an article entitled, "Why They Live to be 100, or Even Older, in Abkasia." While some would question whether the Abkasians are as old as they claim, Professor Benet's account of Abkasian life provides an example of a group of people in which role continuity from one stage of life to the next is the expected and practiced pattern. In addition, the Abkasians have secure roles and statuses in extended family groups which are relatively constant throughout the life cycle. Unlike the Americans who lose status during the later years and many Oriental cultures whose people gain status during the later years, other Abkasian's status changes very little in later life.

The Abkasians live in a mountainous region north of the Black Sea in southern Russia. Members of this society were believed to regularly live to be 120 years or older. Benet writes:

> In the village of Dylgerda, where I visited last summer, there were 71 men and 110 women between 81 and 90 and 19 people over 91—15 percent of the village population of 1200. . . . In 1954, the last year for which overall figures are available, 2.58 percent of the Abkasians were over 90. The roughly comparable figures for the entire Soviet Union and the United States were 0.1 percent and 0.4 percent, respectively.[12]

Abkasia, a very rough mountainous region, is described as a very hard land to scrape a living out of. Abkasians, recognizing the harshness of their environment, say that it is one of God's afterthoughts but that it is a beautiful one.

A large portion of the Abkasian population are between the ages of 80 and 120 and still go to work every day. A Russian scientist writes:

> After spending months with them, I still find it impossible to judge the age of older Abkasians. Their general appearance does not provide a clue. You know they are old because of their gray hair and the lines on their faces but are they 70 or 107? There is no way to tell.[13]

At 120 years of age, according to the reports of the Russian scientists who visited them, most work regularly, are still blessed with good eyesight, and have most of their own teeth. Most of them take walks of more than two miles a day and swim in the mountain streams.

For centuries the Abkasians have been horsemen, and they believe it is very important to be lightweight. According to Benet, there is a saying among the Abkasians which asserts that when one lies on his side he should be so small around the middle that a dog can pass beneath him.

Since 1932 the Russian government has sent medical doctors, psychologists, sociologists, and other scientists to study the reasons for the Abkasian longevity.

The findings of the Russian scientists indicate that 40 percent of the men and 30 percent of the women have vision good enough that they may thread a needle without wearing glasses. Forty percent still had not experienced any loss in hearing. In a nine-year study of people over 100 in Abkasia there were no reported cases of either mental illness or cancer. According to the Russian scientists, all showed clear and logical thinking, and most correctly estimated their physical and mental capacities. Abkasians are hospitalized only rarely, excepting stomach disorders and childbirth. They apparently set their own broken bones and practice an elaborate system of folk medicine using more than 200 indigenous plants to cure a wide variety of ills. When all else fails they are taken to the hospital but with the full expectation that they will get well.

The Abkasians do not have a phrase for old people. Those over 100 are called "long-living" people.

Benet described some of the explanations for their longevity that the Russian scientists considered. One possible explanation explored by the scientists concerned genetic selection. In any war or conflict situation the Abkasians have always been cavalrymen. Some scientists felt that repeated hand-to-hand combat during the centuries of Abkasian existence may have eliminated those with poor eyesight, obesity, and other principal shortcomings, thus producing a healthier group of Abkasians in each succeeding generation. There are no existing records which would make it possible to substantiate this, however.

Some scientists are inclined to believe that the Abkasians live so long because of their diet and the positive value that is attached to remaining slim. Benet reports that overeating "is considered dangerous in Abkasians and fat people are regarded as ill." Their diet consists of fruits, vegetables and meat. Cholesterol content in the blood of Abkasians is considerably lower than for industrial workers. Heart attacks and circulatory problems are much less common in this group of people. Thus, the conclusion is that much of their longevity is due to their diet.

The Abkasians themselves, according to Benet, believe that their longevity is due to their sex practices and work habits. Their values are strongly ingrained with a doctrine of self-discipline. This applies to work and sexual matters as well. Thus, an Abkasian should conserve his or her sexual energies rather than grasping at whatever sweetness is available at the moment. The norms of the culture call for sexual relations to be postponed until after the age of 30—the traditional age of marriage. It was once even considered unmanly for the new husband to exercise his sexual rights on the wedding night. Abkasian men have been known to father children at the age of 100. Sex, to the Abkasians, is a pleasure to be regulated for the sake of one's health—like a good wine it becomes better with age.

The Abkasians, in explaining their longevity, also attach much importance to their work habits, according to Benet. From the beginning of life until its end, the individual does what he or she is capable of doing because he or she and those around him or her consider work vital to their lives. He or she makes demands on himself or herself that he or she can meet. During the growing years the demands are increased gradually over time. During the later years the demands are decreased gradually over time. Those individuals over the age of 100 had decreased their work loads to about four hours a day, but they lost no status in the eyes of their families and tribal members by doing so. Both the Abkasians and the medical doctors agree that their work habits have a great deal to do with their longevity. Abkasians candidly state that work helps vital organs to function optimally.

Sociologists and psychologists are likely to view the stability and consistency of the Abkasians' status throughout the life cycle as well as the degree of social integration in their lives as important factors in the longevity. They are born into a family group in which their status is ascribed and secure. Their family group is a work group as well as social group of which they are a part throughout their entire lives. Group identity gives each individual an unshaken feeling of personal security and continuity, according to those who have studied these people. They seem to maintain or gain status throughout the life cycle, and there are no abrupt changes in their lives. A 99-year-old Abkasian writes:

> It isn't time to die yet. I am needed by my children and grandchildren, and it isn't bad in this world—except that I can't turn the earth over and it has become difficult to climb trees.[14]

Another possible explanation for Abkasian longevity is that physical exercise and exertion are a regular part of their lives. They live in a mountainous region and walk daily. They maintain themselves by being herdsmen and farmers. They are outdoors daily. They work at physical labor daily. They tend to be what the gerontologist would refer to as activity theorists. The Abkasians say that it is better to move without purpose than it is to sit still.

THE WESTERN MODEL: ROLE DISCONTINUITY IN LATER LIFE

The Abkasian culture structures work as a daily part of life while gradually increasing the assigned tasks and the amount of skill required to complete them. There is considerable role preparation for the next task a person is expected to master. Thus, the Abkasian way of life stresses a gradual transition from one stage of life to the next and much role continuity. Western industrial nations, by comparison, are more typically characterized by considerable role discontinuity, by long periods of life in which not much is expected out of the individual, and by periods, such as retirement, in which not only is the work role removed but simultaneously the individual experiences a loss of status.

Considering work activities over the life cycle in the U.S., we find the disjointed pattern. From birth to somewhere between the ages of 18–22 (depending on whether the individual attends college), not much is expected of the individual in the way of work. He or she is encouraged to attend school, participate in social and recreational activities, and discouraged from assuming adult responsibilities. If he or she works at all, it is usually a part-time job primarily for the purpose of having a little spending money. Upon the completion of education, Americans are expected to acquire jobs, be totally dedicated to careers and upward mobility, to get married, settle down and raise families, as well as become responsible and respected members of the community. Sociologists are quick to observe that there is considerable role discontinuity in this pattern and considerable lack of preparation of youth for the responsibilities of adulthood. For the next 40 to 50 years adults are expected to be almost totally dedicated to their careers with little time or energy left over for leisure pursuits and sometimes not even adequate time left for family responsibilities.

During the final phase of the life cycle, industrial nations usually require their employees to retire at a given age. In the United States the retirement age has been considered to be 65. While Congress recently passed a law allowing persons to work until they are 70, less than 5 percent of the population actually works beyond the age of 65. Thus, upon retirement the individual is expected to cease his or her ambitious striving for success and upward mobility, forget about the last 40 years of overriding commitment to work, sit back and relax during his or her remaining years. Simultaneously, he or she also experiences a considerable drop in status in the eyes of peers and community. Thus industrial nations are often characterized by sudden role shifts and inadequate preparation for the new positions that individuals assume.

Cowgill and Holmes, in discussing this problem, state:

> Austria, Norway, and the United States, where individualism is more pronounced, where the work role is largely divorced from the family, particularly the extended family, and where success is mainly through individual effort and failure is viewed as the individual's responsibility, the status of the aged appears to suffer most; it is here that people feel useless, dread feeling dependent, and play empty roles.[15]

Cowgill and Holmes believe that disengagement is to be expected in modern industrial nations. The current values in the United States and other industrial nations are such that the older one becomes, the more likely he or she is to experience a loss of status, prestige, and power.

Table 3–3 was developed to make a comparison of the Abkasian culture, whose members live to very old ages (over 100), and the United States culture, where the life expectancy is shorter and an 80-year-old person is considered very old.

First, as the Russian scientists have argued, it may have been possible for the Abkasians to experience an evolutionary process by which wars and battles over the centuries had a tendency to kill off their weaker members. The short history of the United States would not allow for any similar comparisons. The United States has not been in existence long enough for any long-range evolutionary process to have killed off the weaker persons. Historians tell us the early immigrants to this century were both the strong and the weak. On the one hand, the early American immigrants were the nobility of Europe who had been deeded large tracts of land by the English or French kings. Simultaneously, however, we had the debtors, vagrants, and criminals who were given free passage to the United States to keep them from overcrowding European jails.

The diet of Abkasians in comparison to that of U.S. citizens offers a marked contrast. As observed earlier, the Abkasians believe it is very important

Table 3-3 Comparison of the Abkasian and U.S. Cultures

CATEGORY	ABKASIAN	U.S.
Evolution	Hand-to-hand combat may have killed off the weak creating a stronger group of people.	No long evolutionary process. Early ancestors both the strong and weak.
Medically	Believe it important to be slim. Eat a higher protein diet.	Tend to overeat. Eat a lot of carbohydrates and fatty foods.
Work (roles)	Work throughout the entire life cycle.	Don't work until around 20. Don't work after 65.
Retirement (roles)	Never retire.	Most often forced to retire.
Social Integration	Are part of family and work group throughout their entire life.	Are encouraged to break family ties early. Must be mobile. Move from place to place.
Feeling of Usefulness	Feel useful and needed throughout their entire life.	Often feel a burden on their friends and relatives in old age.
Ascribed vs. Achieved Status	Status throughout life is ascribed.	Outside of sex and age, most status is achieved.
View of Old People	Have no negative feeling or word for old. Speak of certain individuals being "long-living."	Old is considered bad. Use a variety of cosmetics and dyes to make themselves look young.
Power and Privileges in Old Age	Do not retire nor lose status in the later years.	At retirement lose power and privileges.
Kind of Economy	Agricultural.	Industrial.

Source: Adapted from Sula Benet, "Why They Live to Be 100 and Even Older in Abkasia," *New York Times Magazine,* December 26, 1971. © 1971 by The New York Times Company. Reprinted by permission.

to remain slim. Any Abkasian who is even slightly overweight is questioned about his health. His companions will want to know if he has been sick lately. Being overweight is equivalent to being sick to an Abkasian. The caloric intake is 23 percent lower in the Abkasian diet than in industrial workers. Citizens of the United States tend to overeat and their diet is rich in carbohydrates and fatty foods. Being overweight seems to be the norm rather than the exception, particularly for middle-aged and older Americans.

Abkasians work every single day of their lives at some task which is relative to their skill and ability. Thus, as Abkasian children grow and develop they are given increasingly more complex tasks. At a later stage in the life cycle the work responsibilities of those over a hundred years of age may be reduced to where they are only working four hours a day, but they do work every day. The work history of U.S. citizens is quite different. Young people don't work at all or work only at part-time jobs for approximately the first twenty years of their lives. Then they are expected to work very hard for the next 45 years, in most cases at complex tasks requiring considerable skill. When they arrive at age 65 they are expected to retire, engage in leisure pursuits, and do very little or no work activities of a productive nature. Compared to the work histories of Abkasians, in which smooth and gradual transitions are made from one stage of life to the next, the U.S. pattern is irregular and disjointed. There is no way of estimating the effect of these disparate work patterns on longevity, but one cannot help but wonder if the Abkasian pattern is one in which the individual finds it considerably easier to adjust. One additional difference in work life between these two cultures is that Abkasians, being in an agricultural economy, are always involved in work requiring considerable physical energy and exertion. A large percentage of the U.S. population works at office tasks, or the equivalent which are primarily sedentary, requiring little physical exercise and exertion. Most medical doctors believe that regular physical exercise contributes to health and longevity. There is often a psychological strain which accompanies work in American society; one is expected to be upwardly mobile. Thus, whatever current success and job security the individual might have he or she is expected to strive even harder for future promotions and new positions. A degree of psychological insecurity is produced in the individual by the demand for upward mobility.

In terms of the degree of social integration throughout the life cycle, the ledger clearly favors the Abkasian. The Abkasian family is a production unit which works together to produce needed foods and services. From birth to death one is tightly integrated into a close family group which is also a work group. The family is both a consumption and a production unit. The American family, by comparison, is a nuclear unit consisting of husband, wife, and children. The American family, while slightly patriarchal (in which the husband exercises greater authority), is moving in the direction of being more democratic, with shared responsibility between husband and wife. The family is neolocal, the young couple being expected upon marriage to establish a residence independent of either set of in-laws. Shortly after the completion of one's education or apprenticeship the individual is expected to break the tie with his or her family of origin, marry, and enter an occupation. Any strong emotional ties to one's parents or extended relatives would be seen as a threat to the industrial system which requires a mobile labor force. Strong extended family ties would discourage the individual from moving away from his or her home community. The family system is a small fragile nuclear unit which is broken frequently by divorce. Just as the parent was expected to break family ties early in life, so children twenty years later are expected to do likewise. There is considerably more insecurity, less certainty, and less of a tightly knit group of which one is a part throughout the entire life cycle.

The Abkasians, since they do work as part of a family unit throughout their lives, are likely to see their value to the production unit. They feel needed and useful throughout the entire life cycle. Americans, in contrast, are required to do nothing after their retirement. This creates lingering doubts on the part of many individuals of their usefulness during the later years. They are most likely to feel that their usefulness is over and that life has passed them by. Retired Americans frequently speak of themselves as being put out to pasture or on the shelf. Such slogans illustrate their self-doubt.

The Abkasians have an ascribed status throughout their entire lives. This ascription is most often based on the age and sex of the individual. Certain roles and the accompanying status are most often granted to them based on their age and sex. The effect of this is to reduce the pressure to compete for desired roles and status since they are automatically granted. American society has placed a high value on achieved status. Not all positions are granted on the basis of age and sex. Many roles and the status that they entail go only to a privileged few. Not everyone can become a doctor, senator, movie star, or astronaut. While highly valued, relatively few achieve these positions in the sociocultural system. Since all are encouraged by the values of the system to aspire to the more preferred roles, when in fact only a few will actually achieve them, the U.S. culture creates considerable strain and tension for the individual trying to prove his or her worth by achieving the preferred positions. Since many, regardless of their efforts, will not be able to do so, there is considerable feeling of guilt and lack of accomplishment on the part of many individuals in the system. An ascribed status system would seem to offer the individual a greater feeling of security.

The Abkasians have no negative feeling or derogatory terms for old persons. They speak of certain individuals as being long-living, but this carries no negative connotation. In the United States, old is considered bad. Americans invest great amounts of money in a variety of cosmetics from hair dye to facial creams to keep themselves from appearing old. If being old is defined and labeled as undesirable then one can escape this negative label by not appearing old.

In the Abkasian culture the old, as senior members of the family, are granted certain privileges and rights that younger members do not have. In the United States older persons lose considerable power and privilege upon retirement. The older they become the more of their former rights they are likely to lose. Self-devaluation during the later years seems unlikely in the Abkasian system and almost inevitable by comparison in the American system.

Many of the previously discussed differences in the two cultures may in part be explained by the fact that the Abkasians have an agricultural economy, and the U.S. has an industrial economy. The demands of these two productive systems are quite different and result in a considerably different arrangement of the basic social groupings, values, and institutions of the culture.

AGING IN A GERONTOCRATIC SOCIETY

Cowgill and Holmes's book *Aging and Modernization* contains a chapter by John Hamer on the Sidamo of southwest Ethiopia, who are described as a gerontocratic society.

While the society is patriarchal, with the males exercising ultimate power over the females, old age in both sexes is highly esteemed. For the males in this society Hamer lists a number of life-crisis periods which include birth, early childhood, initiation, marriage, promotion to elderhood, exalted old age, and death. These are generally viewed as progressive and bring greater status to the individual as he advances through the various stages of life.

For the males, the father-son relationship stresses respect for the father rather than friendship. The sons, if punishment is necessary, are punished by their fathers. The harshness of the punishment is based on the father's desire to raise the son properly and to keep him from becoming soft and dependent.

According to Hamer, grandfathers rarely, if ever, punish grandsons but are seen by the young as wise and knowledgeable persons to turn to in times of trouble. The relationship of the grandfather-grandson tends to be a warm one. Grandfathers are turned to for advice when their grandsons have difficult decisions to make.

Most of the young men marry between the ages of 18 and 20, and this may be the greatest period of tension between father and son. As Hamer describes the situation:

> The reason is that the father is the one who provides ego with the land, animals, and bridewealth which enable him to marry and begin to accumulate wealth. Fathers allocate a share of land to each son at marriage, with a slightly larger share going to the eldest. In addition, fathers often pick favorites, and though they cannot show partiality in the distribution of land, they may indulge one son at the other's expense by providing him with a larger share of animals and money.[16]

This system of land distribution results in considerable rivalry between the brothers and considerable resentment against the father on the part of the sons.

Promotion to the status of elderhood is considered by many to be the most important event in the lives of men and usually comes in middle age. Once promoted to this preferred status the elder ceases to do manual labor and is no longer expected to take part in military activities. His primary roles will be directing the work of the younger generation and resolving any conflicts that may arise. Elders often have many rituals to perform, such as cutting the throat of the animal, sprinkling blood over the gathering, and pronouncing his blessing on ceremonial occasions.

Hamer describes *Woma* as the most exalted stage of old age for the Sidamo men, granted about the age of 70. *Woma* is granted very old men who are believed to personify the highest ideals of culture such as courage, truth, justice, and moral strength. Persons granted *Woma* are seen as having greater wisdom than other men and the ability to predict the future.

As Hamer views it, death is the most sacred of all events in the Sidamo culture. All the deceased's relatives, regardless of the distance separating them, are expected to attend the funeral rites. Among the survivors performing the rites, age continues to take precedence over other factors. Thus, the eldest son is seen as assuming the authority of the dead father and is the first to place earth on the grave. The youngest sons are called upon to build a fence around the grave. Hamer states:

> Style, as well as artistry of fence construction, is dependent on the age of the deceased. For young men a circle of board is considered sufficient but for old men an elaborate bamboo enclosure is constructed, which entails a trip to the mountains for bamboo and long hours of work.[17]

Even in death the rigid status system based on age is thus apparent. The older members receive considerably more elaborate burials than the young.

While the female is always subordinate to the male, she does accrue certain privileges because of age. Both boys and girls are taught deference to their elders when at mealtime food is presented first to the elders, then young men, young women, and children. Early in their training, however, a division of labor emerges. Girls are taught to assist their mothers in food preparation while boys are directed to work with their fathers in food production. Upon marriage the wife must be subordinate not only to her husband but also to the elder men and women in his family.

During the middle years the wife reaps the first rewards that go with middle age. She becomes entitled to deference from a son-in-law based on avoidance taboos which are usually ended after her daughter's first child. Certain ceremonial rites eventually fall on elder women. The eldest woman initiates the gathering of other women for a housewarming. One of the privileges that come to very old women is described by Hamer:

She no longer keeps her eyes focused on the ground when approaching other men, and may speak casually with them without first obtaining permission from her husband. An old woman may be invited to eat and converse with old men.[18]

The Sidamo have established a male-dominated gerontocracy. The life cycle patterns of both men and women involve emphasis on old age and the prestige it brings to the individual. While the American culture and that of most industrial nations have been youth-oriented, the Sidamo are oriented to the old. For older women the senior roles involve the gradual increase in responsibility. Old age among the Sidamo is equated with prestigious positions, privilege, and power.

The Abkasian, American, and Sidamo societies were chosen for description because they represent three distinctly different ways older persons are treated. Among the Abkasians there is a continuation of the roles of the middle years being performed by older persons. While they are gradually relieved of the amount of time they invest in work activity, this involves no loss of status. Their roles and status remain relatively constant in old age. In the industrial nations like the United States, old age brings forced retirement and a loss of role and status. The older person in industrial nations is seen as being beyond his or her most productive years and experiences a loss of status. The United States tends to be a youth-oriented society. Aging among the Sidamo brings changing roles which involve greater responsibility, prestige, and status during the later years. The Sidamo is an old age oriented society where the aged exercise the greatest control and power in their social system.

Thus, the patterns of the Abkasian, American, and Sidamo cultures represent distinctly different treatments of their older members. From a symbolic interaction perspective the critical difference in how the old are regarded and treated in these systems is significantly connected to roles they assume and the values attached to these roles by others in the society. Aging can bring, then, a continuation of the same roles and status as among the Abkasians, a withdrawal of previous roles and status with forced retirement as in the United States and other industrial nations, and new roles and greater status as among the Sidamo. The desirability of these different patterns of dealing with the older members of society depends on one's values and beliefs about what the roles of the aged ought to be. From the perspective of the older person the pattern of the industrialized societies may be the one with which it is most difficult to cope.

CONCLUSION

Studies of aging in different cultural settings have revealed a number of observable characteristics. As a general rule older people will receive greater respect, status, and thereby more favorable treatment in societies which are agricultural, have extended families, have institutionalized land ownership systems (which allow the elderly to control the means of production), are found in less-harsh climates, have some form of ancestor worship as part of their religious beliefs, change very slowly, and where the more powerful and prestigious political and religious roles are reserved for the elderly.

Retirement, a modern invention of industrial nations, is perceived with some degree of ambivalence on the part of older persons. On the one hand, it is considered a well-deserved rest from the more strenuous competition of work and career. On the other hand, it is a forced disengagement in which older persons are removed from the mainstream of adult life and all the power, status, and privilege that is brought to the individual. There seems little doubt that retirement roles are not highly valued, so retired persons lose status in their later years.

Since cross-cultural studies of aging are at times contradictory and inconclusive, a number of hypotheses regarding the roles and status of older persons in a sociocultural system would seem in order. Among these are

1. Cultures which are mobile, either geographically or socially, tend to undermine the previous status of older persons.
2. The more older persons are socially integrated into the mainstream of the culture the more highly they will be regarded.
3. Retirement, since it tends to disengage and isolate older persons, will usually involve a loss of status on their part.
4. Rapid social change will always, regardless of the kind of society or historical period, tend to undermine the status of the old.
5. The moral and ethical values of all religions will tend to demand respect for one's elders.
6. Older persons in all societies will attempt to maintain their independence as long as possible.
7. Extended family ties or cultural values which stress family obligations will improve the status of the elderly.
8. Old persons will attempt as long as possible to maintain those roles that brought them the highest social esteem and discard the less valuable roles.

Many of the industrialized nations in Western Europe and North America appear to be entering the postindustrial phase of their development. This period seems to suggest that sustenance and survival needs of the people will be guaranteed and that there will be much greater concern for the quality of life. It should follow that human, emotional, and social aspects of life will receive greater attention than they have in the past. Whether the postindustrial period with its emphasis on the quality of life will mean an improvement in the lives of older members of these societies remains to be seen.

KEY TERMS

age grading	functionalism
lifespan	patriarchal
life expectancy	neolocal

SUGGESTED READINGS

ANGEL, J. L., "Human Biology, Health and History in Greece from the First Settlement until Now," *American Philosophical Society Yearbook* (1954), p. 171.

BEAUVOIR, SIMONE DE, *The Coming of Age.* New York: Putnam's, 1972.

BENET, SULA, "Why They Live to Be 100 and Even Older in Abkasia," *The New York Times Magazine,* December 26, 1971, pp. 3–34.

COOK, SHELBURNE, "Aging of and in Population," in *Developmental Physiology and Aging,* ed. P. S. Timiras, p. 595. New York: Macmillan, 1972.

COOK, S. F., "Survivorship in Aboriginal Populations," *Human Biology,* 19, no. 2 (1947), 83–89.

COWGILL, DONALD O., AND LOWELL D. HOLMES, *Aging and Modernization.* New York: Appleton-Century-Crofts, 1972.

ELLIOTT, H. W., *Our Arctic Province: Alaska and The Sea Islands,* pp. 170–71. New York: Scribner's, 1886.

FISCHER, DAVID H., *Growing Old in America,* p. 6. New York: Oxford University Press, 1978.

GOFFMAN, ERVING, *The Presentation of Self in Everyday Life,* p. 70. Garden City, NY: Doubleday, 1959.

HAMER, JOHN H., "Aging in a Gerontocratic Society: The Sidamo of Southwest Ethiopia," in *Aging and Modernization,* eds. D. Cowgill and L. Holmes, pp. 15–31. New York: Appleton-Century-Crofts, 1972.

HENDRICKS, JON, AND C. DAVIS HENDRICKS, *Aging in Mass Society: Myths and Realities.* Cambridge, MA: Winthrop, 1977.

HOLMBERG, A. R., *Nomads of the Long Bow,* pp. 224–25. Garden City, N.Y.: Natural History Press, 1969.

LINTON, RALPH, *The Cultural Background of Personality,* p. 5. New York: Appleton-Century-Crofts, 1945.

PALMORE, ERDMAN, "What Can the USA Learn from Japan About Aging?" *The Gerontologist,* 15 (February 1975), 64–88.

RILEY, M. W., AND OTHERS, "Socialization for the Middle and Later Years," *Handbook of Socialization Theory and Research,* ed. D. A. Goslin. Skokie, Ill.: Rand McNally, 1969.

RUSSEL, J. C. *British Medieval Population.* Albuquerque: University of New Mexico Press, 1948.

SHEEHAN, TOM, "Senior Esteem as a Factor of Socioeconomic Complexity," *The Gerontologist,* 16, no. 5, 433–40.

THOMLINSON, R., *Population Dynamics: Cause and Consequences of World Demographic Change.* New York: Random House, 1965.

WATSON, WILLIAM H., AND ROBERT T. MAXWELL, *Human Aging and Dying: A Study in Sociocultural Gerontology,* pp. 2–32. New York: St. Martin's Press, 1977.

WEIHL, HANNA, "Aging in Israel," in *Aging in Contemporary Society,* ed. Ethel Shanas, pp. 107–17. Beverly Hills, Calif.: Sage Publications, 1970.

4

BIOLOGICAL
AND HEALTH
CORRELATES
OF THE AGING PROCESS

Age is like love, it cannot be hid.

Thomas Dekker
Fortunatus, Act II, Sc. 1

INTRODUCTION*

While it is true that one ages from the moment of conception to the moment of death, we do not normally talk about an aging child. Aging for most of us carries some connotation of decline or deterioration of health and vitality. Marion Lamb believes that most biologists concerned with the problems of aging have accepted this assumption and focused their attention on what happens to the individual after maturity has been reached. Moreover, much of the research of biology and medicine dealing with the aging process has focused on the latter part of the mature adult's life cycle. Strehler defined senescence as

> the changes which occur generally in the post-reproductive period and which result in decreased survival capacity on the part of the individual organism.[1]

Lamb accepts Strehler's definition of senescence and delineates three types of deleterious changes that occur to individuals during the process of aging. First, aging involves a decrease in the ability of the animal to cope with its

*I wish to express my most heartfelt thanks to Dr. Joe Albright, Department of Life Sciences, Indiana State University, for reviewing and editing the biological aspects of this chapter.

environment. Second, Lamb argues that age-related changes are cumulative. Death is final and often occurs suddenly but it is a result of the progressive increase in the probability of dying for the aging individual. Lamb's third characteristic of aging and senescence is perhaps the most difficult for the biologists to prove. This one states that the processes of aging are common to all members of a species and are inescapable.[2]

This third characteristic of aging implies universality. In other words, that it must happen to all individuals. While it is true that all individuals will eventually die, the causes of their death are quite different. For one individual arteriosclerosis (hardening of the arteries) may slow down the flow of blood throughout the body to the point that the heart becomes overworked and a heart attack or stroke follows and ultimately results in death. But not all individuals suffer from arteriosclerosis and those who do may show considerable variation in the severity of the problem. Similarly some aging individuals will experience the growth of tumors because of lowered resistance to these kinds of growths. Some of these tumors will be malignant and result in the individual's death. Once again, however, the problem of universality is not met. Not all older persons will have tumors and of those who do, not all of the tumors will be malignant. Neither biologists nor medical doctors can find any characteristic of aging that happens to all individuals. The goal of the biologist according to Strehler is to identify the underlying basic aging processes which will occur in all older individuals of a species whether they result in death or not. It may be that all individuals experience a lowered resistance to the growth of tumors but some do not come in contact with the specific environmental factor that precipitates the growth of tumors. While biologists will be looking for the underlying aspects of aging that occur to all individuals over the course of time, the complex interplay between individuals and their environments makes the detection of common causes exceedingly difficult.

Ultimately the biologists' search for the universal characteristics of aging that are common to all members of a species and inescapable may have to be abandoned. They may have to be satisfied to describe the characteristics of aging, some of which will be experienced by all individuals at some point in life. Thus the speed of the aging process can be seen as varying from individual to individual and some aspects of the process may never be experienced by some individuals.

Adrian Verwoerdt believes that the maintenance of a dynamic equilibrium between oneself and one's environment is the hallmark of good health. She argues that disease develops when the biological or psychological mechanisms for coping with one's environment are taxed beyond capacity.

Lamb uses Figure 4–1 to illustrate the loss of vitality (the ability to sustain life) by the aging individual. The straight horizontal line at the bottom of the diagram represents the death threshold. When vitality falls below the threshold, death occurs. If environmental conditions are more severe, the threshold will be higher; length of life will become shorter. Lamb traces the time of death for four

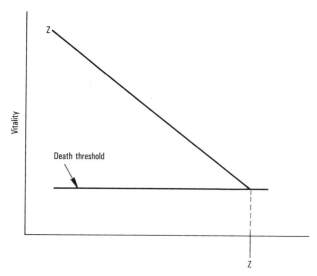

Times of Death

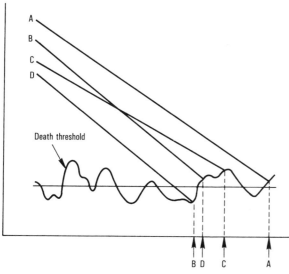

A,B,C,D, = Life course of four individuals
· · · · = Point at which individual would die

Figure 4–1
Diagrammatic Representation
of Aging

Source: Marion J. Lamb, *The
Biology of Aging* (New York:
John Wiley, 1977), p. 4.
Reprinted by permission of John
Wiley and The Blackie
Publishing Group.

individuals in order to indicate that individuals start life with different degrees
of vitality, age (lose vitality) at different rates, and thereby die at different points
in time depending on when their vitality drops below the death threshold. Since
there are genetic differences between people in either the rate of aging or vitality or both, in Lamb's opinion, we could not expect them all to die at the same

age. The wavy line on the bottom of the second diagram indicates that the environment is never completely constant for individuals, and therefore the point at which they will die is never completely predictable.[3]

The varying age at which any individual can display one of the characteristics attributed to older persons can be seen in such characteristics as graying hair and strength of handgrip. Lamb refers to an Australian study of Keogh and Walsh of the point at which one's hair turns gray. Keogh and Walsh assessed hair graying of Australian men and women in three categories which included complete graying, any graying, and no graying. Some people were completely gray prior to age 30 and others were not entirely gray when they were beyond 60. Thus the characteristics of aging vary considerably in terms of when they make their first appearance. (Figure 4–2.)

The rise and decline of handgrip strength over the life cycle can be seen in Figure 4–3. The midthirties appear to be the point at which handgrip strength is the greatest. Following this there is a gradual but regular decline in handgrip strength. The pattern apparent in terms of graying hair, handgrip strength, and any one of a number of other characteristics that one considers to be age-related seems to be very similar. There is considerable variation from individual to individual but over time most individuals will display some graying hair and some loss of handgrip strength.

Eventually, all persons will experience some of the following characteristics of aging: modest-to-complete graying of hair, some dryness and wrinkling of skin, some pigmentation and darker blotches on their skin, some loss of strength, a loss of height and a stooped appearance. (Figure 4–4.)

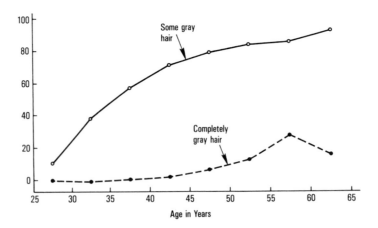

Figure 4–2 Rate of Hair Graying for 3872 Australian Men and Women with Medium Color Hair
Based on data of Keogh and Walsh, 1965.

Source: Marion J. Lamb, *The Biology of Aging* (New York: John Wiley, 1977), p. 10. Reprinted by permission of John Wiley and The Blackie Publishing Group.

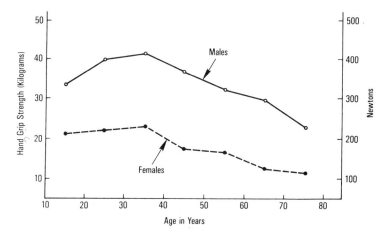

Figure 4–3   Changes in Handgrip Strength with Age
Based on data of Hollingsworth and others, 1965.

Source: Marion J. Lamb, *The Biology of Aging* (New York: John Wiley, 1977), p. 11. Reprinted by permission of John Wiley and The Blackie Publishing Group.

Figure 4–4

AGE-RELATED CHANGES IN HUMAN PHYSIOLOGY

Verwoerdt very carefully describes some of the most common and observable physiological characteristics of the elderly:

1. Skin changes in appearance, becoming darker, more pigmented, and more vulnerable to bruises and skin sores. The skin loses elasticity.

2. Joints stiffen and the bone structure becomes less firm which often results in a loss of height and stooped posture. There is also a loss of muscle strength. Thus the older person loses mobility and routine daily tasks become more difficult. Breathing, urination, and defecation can be negatively affected by these changes. Regular physical exercise and activity can reduce some of these deteriorating effects.

3. The heart muscle over time loses strength. Simultaneously, the hardening and shrinking of the arteries (arteriosclerosis) makes it more difficult for blood to flow freely throughout the body. The body may compensate by an increase in the systolic blood pressure. The increased work placed on the heart and circulatory system can lead to strokes and heart attacks.

4. The exchange of oxygen and carbon dioxide in the lungs may become more difficult as the respiratory system of the older person becomes less efficient. This loss of efficiency may be a result of a weakening of the muscles and changes in the joints of the ribs and chest. The fibers of the lung may lose their elasticity and the blood vessels may harden. The result is that it becomes more difficult for the older person to breathe.

5. The gastrointestinal system can change in the older person leading to different dietary demands. Loss of control of bowel and bladder movements may fluctuate between constipation and incontinence. Older persons often decrease fluid intake and increase the liking for sweets. With the decline in metabolic rate of the body, fewer calories are actually needed. Since eating is a social as well as a physiological event, old persons are often somewhat isolated and in the absence of others do not prepare and eat the right foods. The result can be loss of physical vigor and sometimes the signs of malnutrition. Other older persons may compensate for their loneliness by overeating which is the only pleasure they derive from an otherwise dreary existence. The result may be the unhealthy accumulation of fat.

6. A common urinary problem of older Americans is frequent urination. The enlargement of the prostate gland can cause the problem in men while infection in the urethra or bladder is often the source of the problem in women. The removal of the prostate gland usually eases the problem for men. The belief that the removal of the prostate negatively affects sexual performance is apparently inaccurate.[4]

Beyond the ones outlined by Verwoerdt there are additional changes in the human body which accompany the aging process. The nervous system is altered in part due to the loss of the total bulk of the brain substance. Brain weight diminishes to about 92 percent of age 30 value by age 75. The kidney filtration system shows a decline with age. The kidney filtration rate of a person age 75 is about two-thirds (60 percent) the rate of a 30-year-old. The sensations of touch or pain are reduced with age. Visual acuity diminishes. Less light reaches the retina in an aging eye and the lens often changes color, acquiring a yellow cast. Cataracts are found increasingly with age. Taste and smell become less sensitive. Reflexes and reaction time are slowed. The net effect is often that the individual feels less capable of mastering his or her environment, becomes increasingly defensive, and slowly begins to isolate himself or herself.

Aging often results in increased vulnerability to physiological, psychological, and sociological stress. The stresses of older persons may include disease, accidents, retirement, widowhood, economic insecurity, and loss of status. It may be that persons who live to very old age are those who are more able to deal with stress either because of genetic make-up or psychological and social skills.

The fact that each of us at any age in life can see the stress placed on our older friends and relatives leads to some anxiety on our part concerning what will happen to us when we get old. "Gerophobia" is a term coined by gerontologists to refer to the abnormal fear of old age, disease, disability, and death which some individuals display at any age in life.

MAJOR CAUSES OF ILLNESS AND DEATH IN OLD AGE

Strehler has characterized the human mortality rate by a number of different phases all related to the life span of the individual. The first of these is a period of a rapid decrease in the death rate during the first few years and months of the child's life. The longer the newborn infant survives, the better are his or her life chances. This is followed by a period between the ages of 10 and 30 years in which there is a low but slowly increasing mortality rate. The third period encompasses the years 35 to 100 in which the mortality rate climbs very rapidly and at an ever-increasing rate. (Figure 4–5.) The following descriptions of acute and

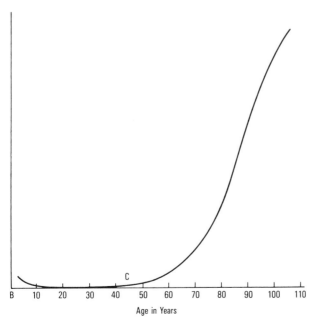

Figure 4–5
Percentage of Population Dying at Different Ages
Percent mortality rate, year vs. age.

Source: Adapted from Bernard Strehler, *Time, Cells and Aging* (New York: Academic Press, 1962), p. 106.

chronic health conditions will help explain the different causes of death in the younger and older populations.

Acute Conditions

Chapter 1 indicated that the major reason for the advances in life expectancy at birth has been the success of the medical sciences in dealing with the acute conditions which were more likely to take the lives of young people. Acute conditions are those which are expected to be temporary. Thus, most of the diseases caused by viruses or germs tend to be acute. The individual is exposed to the disease, either resists the infection or does not. If he or she is not strong enough to resist the infection, illness occurs. In some of the less serious acute conditions like measles or chicken pox, illness lasts usually for a few days and recovery is rapid. Most often convalescence requires a week or two. In the case of persons who become ill with the more serious illnesses such as scarlet fever, bubonic plague, and smallpox, death could easily result if the patient were not strong and carefully nurtured back to good health.

The acute conditions have most often been communicable and thus passed from person to person. In attacking these diseases, medical scientists have often devised some system by which persons could be immunized so that even if they came in contact with the disease agents they would not become sick. They have in essence built on the body's immune system by developing the immunity to these particular diseases.

Acute conditions are more likely to take young people's lives and less likely to take older person's lives. (Figure 4–6.) Older persons, having come in

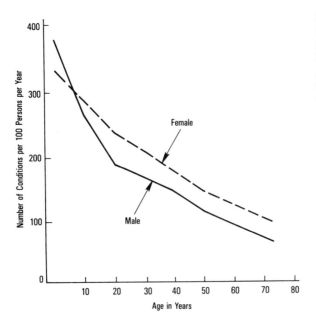

Figure 4–6
Incidence of Acute Conditions per 100 Persons per Year by Sex and Age, 1974–75

Source: National Center for Health Statistics, Series 10, No. 114 (February 1977).

Table 4–1 Incidence of Selected Acute Conditions per 1000 Persons by Age, U.S., 1973

	ALL ACUTE CONDITIONS	INFECTIVE & PARASITIC	RESPIRATORY	INJURIES
17–44 years	172.8	15.7	89.2	33.8
45–64 years	102.3	7.3	55.1	20.0
65+ years	88.2	4.9	42.1	19.4

Source: National Center for Health Statistics, *Health United States* (Washington, D.C.: U.S. Department of H.E.W., 1975), pp. 479, 555. Using health interview survey data. Figure does not meet NCHS standards of reliability and precision.

contact and survived a variety of acute conditions during their younger years, have developed immunity to the point that they are much less often affected by acute conditions. Table 4–1 indicates the likelihood of contracting an acute condition by various age groups in the population.

Chronic Conditions

Chronic conditions are long-term conditions that are either permanent, or that can leave residual disability. Chronic conditions include such illnesses as rheumatism, arthritis, diabetes, heart and circulatory problems, emphysema, blindness, deafness, mental retardation, prolonged mental illness, and others.

The five most prevalent chronic conditions of older Americans, according to Charles Harris, are arthritis, found in 38 percent of this age group; hearing impairments, found in 29 percent; visual impairments, found in 20 percent; hypertension, found in 20 percent; and heart conditions, found in 20 percent. Women are generally less likely to die from acute conditions and simultaneously are able to take better advantage of medical advances dealing with acute conditions, thereby surviving longer, but may not be any better off than men in resisting chronic conditions. Harris reports that women are more prone to be afflicted by arthritis and hypertension than men, are slightly more prone to visual disorders but have lower rates of hearing difficulties, and are about equally vulnerable to heart conditions.[7] Table 4–2 indicates the incidence of chronic conditions by various age, race, and sexual groups in the population.

The older one becomes the more likely he or she is to experience one or more chronic conditions. Among 45- to 65-year-olds about 72 percent have one or more chronic conditions. Among the population 65 and over, 86 percent have one or more chronic conditions. Multiple chronic conditions are a common problem among older Americans.[8]

Visual and auditory conditions sooner or later seem to afflict practically all older Americans. Within the 75–79 age group only 15 per 100 persons have 20/20 vision even with correction.[9] Between the ages of 45 and 54 nineteen percent of the population evidence some hearing loss. Beyond the age of 75, approximately 75 percent of the population have hearing impairments.[10]

There can be considerable variability in the seriousness of some of the

Table 4–2 Prevalence of Selected Chronic Conditions per 1000 Persons by Age, Sex, and Race, U.S.

	ARTHRITIS (1969)	HEARING (1971)	VISION (1971)	HYPERTENSION (1972)	HEART CONDITION (1972)
17–44 years	40	42	32	38	25
45–64 years	204	114	63	127	89
65+ years					
total	380	294	205	199	199
males	287	338	183	141	199
females	450	262	220	241	198
white	376	299	201	195	200
all other races	425	238	246	249	185

Source: National Center for Health Statistics, *Health United States* (Washington, D.C.: U.S. Department of H.E.W., 1975), pp. 481, 487, 557. Using health interview survey data.

chronic health conditions which older persons experience. The least severe health conditions are ones in which the older persons are aware of their problem but it does not limit their daily activities or at most it restricts only a few minor activities. The more severe health conditions are those that are serious enough to require medical care; they do disrupt older persons in their work and daily activities. The most severe health conditions are those that make it impossible for older persons to care for themselves; they require hospital or nursing home care.

The most serious chronic condition of the elderly in terms of their being able to remain independent is any condition that interferes with their mobility. Approximately 18 percent of the elderly report some limitation of mobility. This is in contrast to the 1 percent of the 17–44 age group and 5 percent of the 45–65 age group. The major causes of mobility limitation among the elderly are arthritis and rheumatism, impairments of the lower extremities, heart conditions and strokes.[11]

The three most common causes of death among older persons are heart disease, strokes, and cancer; these account for 65 percent of all deaths among this age group. The leading cause of death for both sexes for those over 65 is heart trouble.

In summary the acute conditions of the young are primarily caused by infectious organisms coming from outside the body. The illness tends to be short lived and the recovery period usually requires only a few days. The chronic conditions of older persons originate inside the body and are usually a result of a breakdown in body chemistry or a deterioration of some of the body's vital organs. Cancerous growth resulting from an abnormal division of cells represents a breakdown in chemistry. Heart trouble is an example of a deterioration of a vital organ. The diseases of old age often come on gradually and frequently result in permanent damage and limitation of activity. Undoubtedly, the doctor can derive greater satisfaction from curing the acute conditions of the young than from controlling the chronic conditions of the old. Robert Butler has been critical of the medical profession for not investing more research and effort on the chronic diseases of older persons which may be less spectacular but more far-reaching than those diseases that have received intensive medical research.

BIOLOGICAL THEORIES OF AGING

Over time there have been a wide variety of biological theories of aging developed by scientists. These range in scope from the more simple, basic, and down-to-earth perspectives to the most complex. While many of these theories are interesting and intriguing, none have been able to totally convince the scientific community of their validity.

The *"wear and tear" theory* of aging is one of the oldest and can be traced back to such thinkers as Aristotle and Descartes. This theory asserts that man is like a machine; after prolonged use the parts wear out. Thus while most persons believe that vigorous activity helps the body's vital organs function efficiently, this theory suggests that it might wear them out. Realistically, reasonable amounts of exercise and activity do seem to keep the individual conditioned and healthy. Excessive exercise and use could at some point begin to negatively affect the person's health. Perhaps it is the excessive use and strain on the body that the "wear and tear" theorists believe occurs over time.

Biologically the aging body is seen as one that has accumulated more and more damage due to minor diseases and injury. Most biologists do not accept, however, that senescence is caused by the accumulation of previous injury and infection. They are more likely to believe senescence is an innate process which would occur regardless of any previous injuries or disease.[12] Curtis, in attempting to discredit the "wear and tear" theory, imposed repeated doses of nitrogen mustard and tetanus toxin to mice. When the stress was removed, they found that the animals lived as long as those which had never been treated. Scientists, therefore, doubt that senescence is entirely a result of wear and tear. Environment undoubtedly has something to do with aging and senescence but how big a part it plays is highly debatable.

A popular but much too general theory of aging is that each individual has a "fixed amount of time" to live and the faster he or she uses it, the quicker it is gone. Thus those who lead vigorous lives would be expected to die young. The evidence indicates, however, that regular exercise prolongs life and that those who lead vigorous lives do not necessarily live any shorter or longer lives than those who do not.

Very similar to the fixed amount of time view of aging is that of the *declining energy theory*. The basic belief of this theory is that each individual has a fixed amount of energy or vitality (somewhat like a battery that cannot be recharged). Aging brings with it a decline in energy and vigor. Thus aging results in a lower ability to deal with outside forces (lessened resistance and tolerance of environmental stress). This view is similar to a philosophy of vitalism which was popular in the Middle Ages. The vital principle which this group of thinkers espoused was thought to use the physical apparatus of the body, such as the nerves, muscles, and specialized organs, as a means to act on the natural world.[13]

The conclusion of this particular school of thought was that the gradual loss of energy over time and finally its ultimate disappearance is what brings about old age and death. Marcella Weiner and others note, in discussing this theory, that a similar notion was implicit in Freud's theory of libido—an innate instinctual energy that conceivably dissipates with age.[14]

The belief in declining energy would be most amenable to the disengagement theorists' assertion that successful aging involves a gradual withdrawal from the mainstream of life on the part of aging individuals. The aging individual should welcome this withdrawal as a result of his or her declining energy. This implies also that the normal individual is at the mercy of social and environmental factors in later life. Neugarten, Havighurst, and Tobin argue, however, that the individual makes choices that can alter both the biological and social pressures he or she may be experiencing. He or she is inclined to select from the environment in accordance with his or her long-established needs and in so doing, to make a strong imprint on his or her future life course.[15] Regular exercise supplemented with proper diet can revitalize the energy and vitality of older persons. Choices can be made by individuals as to which social roles they will occupy during their later years and thus considerable energy and vitality previously utilized in other activities can be directed to the chosen roles. It would thus appear that neither energy nor vitality are given to the individual in fixed and unalterable amounts.

The *collagen theory* relates the aging process to the connective tissues of the body. Connective tissues are made up of cells, fibers, collagen, and elastin. Collagen is found in most organs, tendons, skin, blood vessels, and other parts of the body. Some biologists have argued that most of the aging changes seen in mammals can be related to changes in collagen. As they are, the connective tissues show increasing stiffness, at least in part, as a result of the changes in collagen. Collagen stiffens with age and tissues containing collagen lose elasticity. Lamb reports that as animals get older the amount of readily soluble collagen present in their body decreases. Change in amount and quality of the collagen component of the body's connective tissues apparently accompanies aging but is not believed to be a basic cause of senescence.

Frequently scientists have been led to believe that the cause of aging can be found in relation to the ability of cells to reproduce themselves (i.e., "divide"). One crucial question as to whether aging is linked to the vitality of the cells is whether cells have a finite lifespan. Hayflick has done research which seems to indicate that cells do have a lifespan. His studies indicate that cells grown in laboratory cultures die out after 50 doublings.[16]

Bierman and Hazzard also indicate that human cells grown in tissue culture do not divide indefinitely but instead show a decreasing capacity for divi-

Table 4–3   The Finite Lifetime of Cultured Normal Embryonic Human and Animal Fibroblasts*

SPECIES	RANGE OF POPULATION DOUBLINGS FOR CULTURED NORMAL EMBRYO FIBROBLASTS (CELLS)	MEAN MAXIMUM LIFE SPAN IN YEARS
Galapagos tortoise	90–125	175 (?)
Human being	40–60	110
Mink	30–34	10
Chicken	15–35	30 (?)
Mouse	14–28	3.5

*A fibroblast is an undifferentiated cell giving rise to connective tissue.

Source: Adapted from L. Hayflick, "Why Grow Old?" *The Stanford Magazine,* 3, no. 1 (1975), 36–43. Published by the Stanford Alumni Association.

sion with age. They observed that cells from an embryo divide about 50 times in a culture. Those taken from a 28-year-old duplicate about 30 times and those taken from older persons divide about 20 times. Table 4–3 indicates the relationship between cell division and lifespan of man in comparison to other animals. The Galapagos tortoise, interestingly, lives approximately 175 years and experiences 90–235 cell divisions. Unfortunately, there is no general age-associable loss in the cell's ability to divide followed by the dying of cells. Neither can scientists be sure that cells in the living organism function the same way they do in the laboratory culture where these experiments were conducted.[17]

The proponents of "programmed aging" imply that there is a biological clock which keeps track of the amount of elapsed time and thus sets in motion the aging pattern when certain limits are reached. The advantage of this theory is that it can explain the differential rate of cell division in different animals and the consistency with which cell populations double their numbers from sample to sample. Since these factors vary considerably from species to species, one would like to think that the clock is controlled by genetic material. While this theoretical approach to aging is intriguing, there is at the present time very little evidence of support. At most it seems to be speculative.

Related to the changes in cell division as one ages are the *error theory* and *mutation theory.* The basic argument is that in the course of cell division errors occur. The potential errors that can occur are mutations, cross linkages, and incorrect transcription in the formation of RNA from DNA synthesis in the cells. Thus an error could produce two new faulty cells which would then divide creating four faulty cells which would then divide producing eight faulty cells, and so on. The result could be a progressive loss of function and vitality in those parts of the organism where the error occurred. Similarly any mutations occurring in cells over time or numerous cell divisions could spread throughout the organ or body tissue. It is generally believed that mutated cells are less efficient than the original cells. Scientists, however, cannot fully accept the argument that genetic mutations are necessarily directly linked to senescence. Genetic mutations can increase many times over, with only a small reduction in life expectancy. Apparently some mediating factor minimizes the effects of genetic mutations in these cases. Thus mutation or error theory remains highly speculative at the present time. Lamb argues that for the more general error theory to be accepted one must explain why different species have different characteristic life spans. Lamb states:

> It is necessary to postulate either (1) that the molecules in the cells and tissues of some species are less likely to suffer from damage than those of other species, or (2) that species differ in their abilities to repair damage or (3) that some species are more able to tolerate damage than others.[18]

The *immune theory* of aging is advocated by some biologists. Over time, children gradually build up immunity to a variety of different diseases especially those caused by infectious agents which are present in one's environment. Control of the acute communicable diseases frequently is based on giving persons a vaccination with small amounts of the potential disease-causing organism to allow the body time to build up its resistance to such organisms. As the individual grows and develops, he or she inevitably comes in contact with an increasing number of potential disease-causing organisms which stimulate the immune system thus maintaining the immunity initiated by vaccination. The development of the human immune system apparently peaks about age 40. After that age the immune system begins to decline in effectiveness, and this decline speeds up as age increases.

Lamb observes that the immune response is a very complex one which is dependent on a number of different cells and tissues and the complex interactions between them. Therefore, while it is difficult to explain aging in terms of the immune system, since it is so complex, it is easy to imagine the opportunities for error and inefficiency in such a system. Immunities established during an earlier age may never entirely disappear; however, they may decline below some threshold level of effectiveness. Lamb points out that allergic reactions tend to be less common in the elderly and old people are considerably less likely to be hypersensitive to antigens such as tuberculin which they had probably encountered early in life.

One facet of the immune theory of aging is concerned with autoimmunity. This theory suggests that as age increases, cell mutations or other changes may lead to proteins that are not recognizable as part of "self" and are thus responded to as if they were foreign substances. The immune reaction occurs when the body responds to foreign substances, that is, those that are "not-self." When antibodies are produced in response to altered proteins (or certain other substances) no longer recognizable as self, the result is an autoimmune reaction. Thus the body is reacting against itself. The autoimmune reaction can explain some unexpected research findings. Past studies have indicated that restricted food intake in youth extends the life span. Restricting food intake is known to delay the maturation of immune responses and, therefore, could delay the onset of autoimmune reactions. Experiments have also shown the life span of fish to be increased by keeping them at low temperatures. Because low temperatures slow the immune reactions, the longer life span of the fish can be explained by the delaying of autoimmune reactions. The *autoimmune theory* appears to be one of the more promising in terms of explaining aging and mortality.

PSYCHOLOGICAL AND SOCIOLOGICAL ASPECTS OF ILLNESS

There is a complex interplay between physical and psychosocial aspects of an individual's health which is difficult to untangle at any age in life and is particularly difficult to untangle among older persons. Many of the undesirable things happening to older persons are partly physical and partly social. Thus individuals are retired from a job which is basically a social event but an underlying assumption of this retirement may be that due to declining energy they are no longer able to compete with younger counterparts. A man experiences the death of a spouse, which is a physical event, but now finds that as a single person he no longer fits well in the group of friends which he and his deceased wife previously shared. An individual may experience a heart attack from which he or she adequately recovers but may not return to previous activities for fear that he or she will strain himself or herself and cause a recurrence of the heart attack. He or she may stay home more, go out less, and begin to socially isolate himself or herself from his or her former friends. He or she may avoid any kind of sexual relationship with his or her spouse out of the often-mistaken belief that his or her heart cannot stand the excitement of sexual stimulation. The spouse becomes concerned that he or she is no longer cared for.

The Cox, Sekhon, and Norman study found that 40 percent of their sample of older Americans were somewhat isolated; they frankly stated that they often felt the need for companionship. The difficulty in distinguishing the complex interplay between both the physical and social problems that older persons are confronted with is that of locating the primary source of the problem. A person may be behaving in what is an irrational manner because of an organic reason such as weakened heart or blocked arteries which is slowing the flow of blood to the brain resulting in behavior which a psychiatrist might label as neurotic or psychotic. On the other hand, the irrational behavior may be caused by the individual's inability to adjust to a variety of role changes and the loss of status that accompany the aging process. Or it may be caused by a combination of both these factors. The result for the individual will be the same, however, whatever the cause may be. The individual will find his or her friends and family avoiding him or her and progressively will find himself or herself more and more isolated. Lowenthal tried to determine among the three variables of physical illness, mental illness, and social isolation which were the independent and dependent variables. Physical illness might lead to social isolation which then produces mental problems. On the other hand, mental and emotional problems could lead to social isolation which are sometimes followed by physical decline. Social isolation could be more of a cause than a consequence of mental illness. Lowenthal was never able to totally resolve the issue.[19] For many older persons who are often experiencing both physical and emotional problems simultaneously, it is very difficult to identify the initial cause.

Related to the problem of distinguishing between physical and psychosocial causes of illness and social isolation in later life is the older person's willingness to seek help and find solutions to these problems. The evidence clearly indicates that as age increases there is a tendency to see doctors about physical illness more often and to see a doctor about mental and emotional problems less often. This seems unusual when many of the medical doctors who treat older people estimate that anywhere from 40 to 75 percent of the people they see have psychological or psychosomatic problems rather than physical ones. Sainsbury found that in his sample of older people, 30 percent of them could be classified as depressed. This study indicates that both psychosis and psychosomatic symptoms increase after age 65.[20] A study done in New York City found that among persons with impaired mental health, 34 percent of those between the ages of 20 and 29 had seen a doctor, while only 21 percent of those between the ages 50 and 54 had done so.[21]

In attempting to explain why older people seem to shy away from professional attention to their mental health needs, Cousert borrowed from the symbolic interactionist perspective and utilized Zusman's social breakdown model and the social reconstruction model of Kuypers and Bengtson (discussed in Chapter 2). The advantage of these models is that they recognize the interaction between psychological, physiological, and sociological factors in developing the individual's self-concept and pattern of behavior.

There are a variety of reasons why the older person might shy away from any visitation to a mental health professional:

1. Family, friends, and physicians may be quick to label the older person mentally ill or senile long before the actual event. A visit to a psychiatrist would provide validation to the label.
2. Some more aggressive family members may be anxious to have a person committed to a nursing home or mental hospital. The psychiatric visit might then precipitate the very action that the older person is trying to avoid.
3. The psychiatrist or psychologist is likely to be able to find what would be considered a treatable emotional problem thus requiring further visits and further threats to the loss of independence on the part of the individual.
4. The individuals themselves might begin to have self-doubts and become further confused about their identity as a result of the visit to the psychiatrist.[22]

Cousert's basic position was that older persons avoid visits to mental health professionals because it could precipitate them being negatively labeled by family and friends, the mental health personnel, perhaps, and ultimately themselves. Being labeled mentally ill is difficult at any age in life but it has particularly dire consequences for older persons who at best will be treated as though they are senile and at worse could be institutionalized by their family. Moreover, it is likely to shake an already uncertain self-concept on the part of the individual.

Cousert's basic argument was that the way the individual perceives the responses of others toward him or her will heavily influence his or her behavior. Thus treating a person as though he or she is feeble and senile may encourage the individual to behave this way even if he or she is perfectly healthy and rational. Work on reference groups and their effect on behavior indicates that as a person identifies with a group, such as the group of aged, he or she takes on some of the significant characteristics of the group. It is generally agreed among social psychologists that a person seeks maximum congruency among (1) his or her self-concept, (2) his or her perception of his or her own behavior toward other persons, and (3) his or her perception of the behavior of others toward him or her.

The older person may avoid seeing a mental health professional partly because of the negative label he or she would receive from significant others following such a visit as well as the fact that they themselves may hold a negative view of psychiatrists. Their fear of being labeled as senile or mentally ill is a strong deterrent to visiting a psychiatrist. Simultaneously, their undesirable view of the psychiatrist and the mental health treatment process is a further deterrent to seeking help with their emotional problems. The older person may have a negative view of the mental health professional based on what he or she has heard from significant others, or seen or heard through the media. The individual may have had contact with a mental health professional or have had a close friend who has visited a mental health professional. This experience may reinforce the negative label. Finally, the individual himself or herself comes to accept the negative definition of the psychiatrist.

Figure 4–7a-b follows Zusman's social breakdown model and the Kuypers and Bengtson social reconstruction model in explaining the difference in the interaction between the medical doctor and the older person (with the potential support to identity) and the interaction of the older person and the mental health professional (with the potential threats to identity).

In Figure 4–7a we see that the older person with a shaken self-confidence and uncertain identity visits a medical doctor with a health problem (Step 1 on diagram). The doctor, after examining the patient, tells him that he is not seriously ill and will get well if he follows the doctor's instructions. The doctor often gives the patient a mild tranquilizer or perhaps something to lower his blood pressure (Input A). The patient's uncertainty is eased and self-confidence returns (Step 2 on the diagram). The patient feels no further need to visit a doctor for that particular symptom and routinely gets the medicine refilled (Input

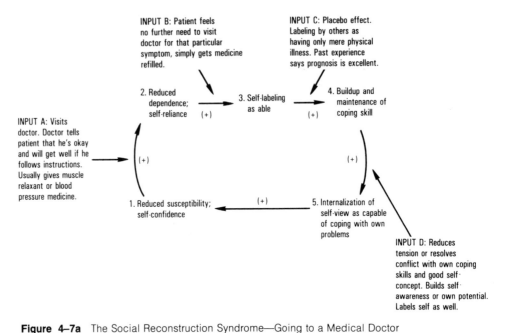

INPUT B: Patient feels no further need to visit doctor for that particular symptom, simply gets medicine refilled.

INPUT C: Placebo effect. Labeling by others as having only mere physical illness. Past experience says prognosis is excellent.

2. Reduced dependence; self-reliance (+)

3. Self-labeling as able (+)

4. Buildup and maintenance of coping skill

INPUT A: Visits doctor. Doctor tells patient that he's okay and will get well if he follows instructions. Usually gives muscle relaxant or blood pressure medicine.

(+)

(+)

1. Reduced susceptibility; self-confidence

(+)

5. Internalization of self-view as capable of coping with own problems

INPUT D: Reduces tension or resolves conflict with own coping skills and good self-concept. Builds self-awareness or own potential. Labels self as well.

Figure 4–7a The Social Reconstruction Syndrome—Going to a Medical Doctor

Source: Adapted from David Cousert, "Symbolic Interactionist Approach to Attitudes of Older People Toward Psychiatrists versus Medical Doctors." Unpublished paper, Indiana State University, 1977.

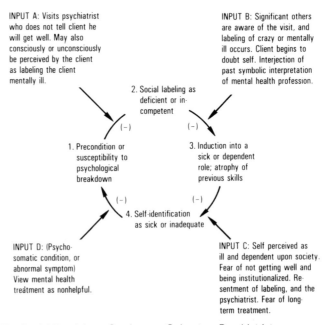

INPUT A: Visits psychiatrist who does not tell client he will get well. May also consciously or unconsciously be perceived by the client as labeling the client mentally ill.

INPUT B: Significant others are aware of the visit, and labeling of crazy or mentally ill occurs. Client begins to doubt self. Interjection of past symbolic interpretation of mental health profession.

2. Social labeling as deficient or in-competent

1. Precondition or susceptibility to psychological breakdown

(−)

(−)

3. Induction into a sick or dependent role; atrophy of previous skills

(−)

(−)

4. Self-identification as sick or inadequate

INPUT D: (Psycho-somatic condition, or abnormal symptom) View mental health treatment as nonhelpful.

INPUT C: Self perceived as ill and dependent upon society. Fear of not getting well and being institutionalized. Resentment of labeling, and the psychiatrist. Fear of long-term treatment.

Figure 4–7b The Social Breakdown Syndrome—Going to a Psychiatrist

Source: Adapted from David Cousert, "The Attitude of Older People Toward Visiting a Psychiatrist," Unpublished paper, Indiana State University, 1977.

B). The individual gains confidence in his ability to handle his problem. Significant others, in hearing the doctor's report, now define the older person as having only a minor physical illness. Prognosis for recovery is excellent. The individual is treated as normal by significant others (Input C). This tends to bolster the individual's self-confidence, thus building maintenance and coping skills (Step 4 on the diagram). The individual can now internalize a view of himself as capable of dealing with his problems. If the need arises he will return to the doctor who so capably helped him past the crisis.

Cousert sees negative rather than positive results occurring when the older person visits the mental health professional. Once again we begin at the point in which the individual's self-confidence is shaken because he is currently experiencing some problem (Step 1 in Figure 4–7b). He visits a psychiatrist who does not immediately assure him that he will get well but tells him that his problem may require further diagnosis and office visits (Input A). This may be perceived by the client as proof that he is mentally ill and has a serious problem (Step 2 on the diagram). Friends and family come to know that the individual has visited a psychiatrist and is going to have to make other visits. They begin to define the individual as senile or losing his mind, thus labeling him as incompetent (Input B). The person is encouraged by those around him to act sick and previous interpersonal skills begin to deteriorate. The patient now becomes increasingly frightened. He is now afraid of not getting well or of perhaps being institutionalized (Input C). He begins to think of himself and act as though he were sick. Thus a further deterioration of self-confidence and further changes in behavior occur.

Cousert thus perceives a considerably different sequence of events for older persons who visit a psychiatrist than for older persons who visit a medical doctor. He believes the older person is likely to receive reassurance and a reduction of his anxiety about his health from the medical doctor but may inadvertently receive information from the psychiatrist that leads to further anxiety and a loss of self-confidence. If Cousert is correct, this would in part explain the very low number of older persons who seek out the services of mental health professionals.

Parsons outlined what he considered to be the characteristics of the sick role at any age in life which includes:

1. The patient is exempt from his normal role responsibilities such as working or supporting his family.
2. The person is exempt from any responsibility for himself. He is not expected to pull himself together nor is he blamed for acting sick because he is sick. Nurses or other family members will see that he is bathed, shaved, etc.
3. The patient is obliged to seek professional help.
4. The patient is obliged to want to and try to get well.[23]

The first two of the aspects of the sick role which Parsons describes may be considered the privileges of the role. Not having to be responsible for one's job, family, and community obligations is a privilege only granted to the sick. Similarly, not having to be responsible for one's body and personal hygiene is a privilege only granted to the sick. Being obliged to seek professional help and get well can be seen as obligations of the sick role.

The problem for older Americans is that they are often granted the privileges of the sick role without the commensurate obligation to get well. Often their family and friends as well as the doctors and nurses expect them to die. Thus they may be socially dead long before they are physically dead.

Older persons often fear being committed to a nursing home. First they fear it because it represents a loss of independence for them. They are no longer masters of their own fate and destiny but are at the mercy of others in the form of the nursing home staff. Second, they believe that it is a place where they have been sent to die. Most would be correct in this assumption, unfortunately.

The nursing home is a place where the patients are expected to adopt the sick role. The nursing home staff expects the person to act sick, the fellow patients at the nursing home believe he or she should act sick, the family and friends expect it of the person. It takes a very strong-willed person under these conditions not to act sick.

Figure 4–8 indicates a few of the different patterns of response on the part of the patient, his or her family, and the nursing home staff to the possibility of the patient's recovery. The person who is the least likely to recover and who may be defined as socially dead is the one who doesn't expect to get well, his or her family and close friends do not expect him or her to get well, and the nursing home staff do not expect him or her to get well. Recovery from an illness seems highly unlikely under this set of circumstances.

Patients who want to get well while their family and the nursing home staff do not expect them to get well find themselves in a difficult situation. Significant others are pressuring them to behave in a way they do not believe is appropriate. If they act well, they are in essence deviants from the socially expected sick role that patients in a nursing home are supposed to adopt. Thus, while the nursing home staff want a patient to remain quiet and act sick he or she is up roaming throughout the nursing home. He or she may quickly be defined as an administrative problem and negative sanctions imposed on his or her behavior

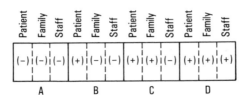

Figure 4–8
Possible Patterns of Positive and Negative Attitudes toward the Patient's Recovery on the Part of the Patient, Family, and Nursing Home Staff

by the staff. The staff may solicit the support of the family to pressure the pa-tient to behave in the institutionally expected manner. The patient is expe-riencing pressures from both the nursing home staff and his or her family to behave in a manner contrary to how he or she would like to act.

Another possible pattern for the older nursing home resident is the one in which the patient and his or her family expect the person to get well while the nursing home staff does not. The patient in this case could be seen as under less pressure to behave in a manner he or she does not prefer since it is only the staff that stands in opposition to his or her future image of self and desire for recovery.

Patients with the best possible chance of recovery are the ones who want to get well, the family wants and expects them to get well, and the nursing home staff is working for their recovery. Unfortunately for the older persons, any one of these four patterns of response to their illness is possible.

CONCLUSION

Today, more than ever before in the history of our country, a higher number and percentage of our population are living to the age of 65 and beyond. This is largely a result of the fact that medical science has been successful in eliminating the acute diseases of the very young, thus allowing more persons to live through the entire life cycle. The older population are more likely to suffer from and ultimately die of chronic conditions more than they are of acute conditions. It is in the areas of such chronic conditions as arthritis, diabetes, heart and circula-tory problems, emphysema, etc., that medical science has made the fewest ad-vances. Despite the presence of one or more chronic conditions, approximately 80 percent of older Americans are not seriously handicapped in leading full lives and pursuing normal daily activities. Approximately 20 percent have chronic conditions which impair their ability to get out and around their communities and neighborhoods. While this is true, 86 percent of older Americans do have one or more chronic conditions which make normal routine daily activities a lit-tle more difficult for them than it is for the average citizen. Despite these limit-ing factors, a majority of older Americans, when asked to compare their health with others their age, believe they are in as good or better health than most of their friends and are not prevented from doing most of the things they want to do.

In terms of physiological changes which often happen to persons as they age, the skin tends to lose elasticity, to become darker and more pigmented and to bruise more easily, joints stiffen and the bone structure becomes less firm, there is a loss of muscle strength, the respiratory system becomes less efficient, changes in metabolism result in different dietary demands, the individual finds it more difficult to regulate bowel and bladder movements, visual acuity diminishes, hearing declines, and the system is less able to resist environmental stresses and strains.

Scientists, in attempting to explain the aging process, have come up with a host of ingenious ideas and theories, none of which have been proven at this time. The major problem for biologists in determining the causes of aging is their demand that whatever the characteristic or attribute of aging, it eventually must happen to all individuals. Most, but not all, of the characteristics of aging will be experienced by any one person at some point in time. Moreover, of those characteristics of aging experienced by any one individual, there is considerable variation when any one of the characteristics will first be noticed. The only thing the biologist can say for sure is that ultimately all living organisms will die. The causes and patterns of aging leading to individual death vary considerably.

Lamb, in her book on the biology of aging, developed Figure 4–9 to illustrate the changes that occur in the body's cells over time which result in the organism's reduced vitality and ultimate death.

In Lamb's view it is inevitable that in the process of cell division accidents will occur which include cross linkages, errors in the DNA synthesis and errors in the transcription and translation of genetic information. Once errors are made, further cell divisions perpetuate these errors. The result is less efficient cells and a loss of vitality. These errors over time may accumulate, creating changes in the body's tissues; for example collagen may stiffen the joints. Temporarily, the decline in cell efficiency can negatively alter tissues, organs, and the organ systems. These changes can thus result in a deterioration in the body's tissues and organs which ultimately result in death. Lamb recognizes (on the right side of Figure 4–9) all the corrective mechanisms that try to prevent the errors from becoming dangerous to the survival of the system. Over time, however, the errors overpower the body's ability to correct the mistakes and the system's vitality deteriorates ultimately to the point of death.

One factor in the aging process which appears to have not been carefully examined at this time is the social psychology of sickness. The symbolic interactionists maintain that at any age in life much of people's behavior and self-concept are determined by the roles that they assume and the expectations of others regarding how occupants of a particular role are to behave. To some extent one problem for older Americans is that they are often expected to assume the role of a sick, senile, and feeble elder long before they have physiologically arrived at that stage. Similarly for those persons in the later years who do become sick, the family, the medical personnel, and ultimately the individual himself or herself may not really expect recovery. The family may anticipate prolonged sickness and accelerating medical costs if the person recovers, the medical personnel may see the prolongation of life accompanied by several chronic and debilitating conditions, and the individual may see that she or he is a burden to others. Thus the person may be socially dead long before she or he is physically dead.

The effect that future medical discoveries will have on the prolongation

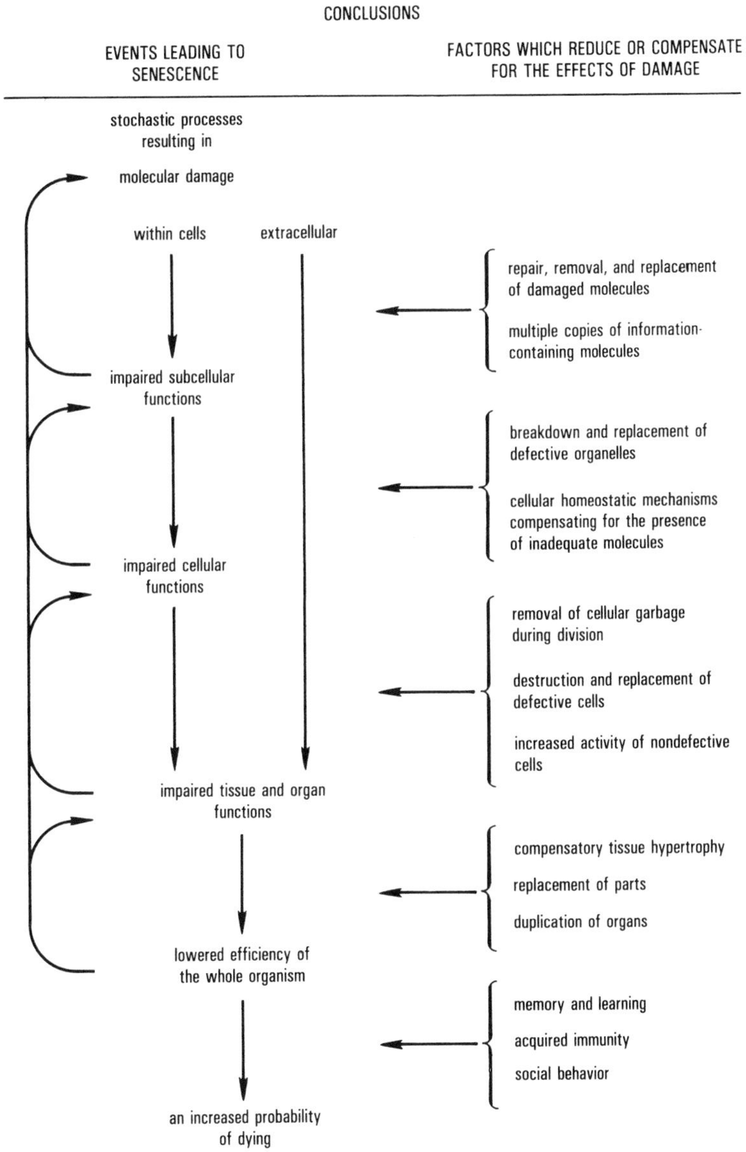

CONCLUSIONS

Figure 4-9 The Events Leading to Senescence and Death

Source: Marion J. Lamb, *The Biology of Aging* (New York: John Wiley, 1977), p. 164. Reprinted by permission of John Wiley and The Blackie Publishing Group.

of life is difficult to discern at this time. Some believe there is a limit to how far one can extend the life expectancy beyond age 65, regardless of how many of the chronic conditions of older Americans are brought under control. Others see adding a considerable number of additional years to each person's life will be a result of future medical advances. There is considerable evidence that preventive medicine has been an ignored field which is now coming into its own. To what degree some of the chronic health problems of older persons can be avoided or controlled by preventive medicine is highly speculative. There seems little doubt, however, that medical technology will improve and some of the chronic conditions of old age will be brought under control, thus extending and improving the individual's life during the later years. It remains to be seen how much the life expectancy can be extended by future medical breakthroughs.

KEY TERMS

biological theories of aging	acute illness
autoimmune	arteriosclerosis
collagen	chronic illness
declining energy	gerophobia
error or mutation	senescence
immune	
wear and tear	
fixed amount of time	
programmed aging	

SUGGESTED READINGS

ATCHLEY, ROBERT C., *The Social Forces in Later Life: An Introduction to Social Gerontology* (2nd ed.), pp. 33–38. Belmont, Calif.: Wadsworth, 1977.

BIERMAN, E. L., AND W. R. HAZZARD, "Biology of Aging," in *The Biologic Ages of Man: From Conception through Old Age,* eds. D. W. Smith and E. L. Bierman. Philadelphia: Saunders, 1973.

BUTLER, ROBERT N., *Why Survive Being Old in America,* pp. 174–224. New York: Harper & Row, pub., 1975.

COX, HAROLD, GURMEET SEKHON, AND CHUCK NORMAN, "Social Characteristics of the Elderly in Indiana," *Proceedings of Indiana Academy of Social Sciences,* 8 (1978), 186.

COUSERT, DAVID, "Symbolic Interactionist Approach to Attitudes of Older People Toward Psychiatrists versus Medical Doctors." Unpublished paper, Indiana State University, 1977.

CURTIS, H. J., *Biological Mechanisms of Aging.* Chicago: Chas. C Thomas, 1966.

FONER, A., AND M. RILEY, *Aging and Society, Vol. I: An Inventory of Research Findings,*" p. 370. New York: Russel Sage, 1968.

HARRIS, CHARLES S., *Fact Book on Aging: A Profile of America's Older Population,* Washington D.C.: National Council on Aging, 1978.

HAYFLICK, L., "Why Grow Old?" *The Stanford Magazine,* 3 (1975), 36–43.

Keogh, E. V., and R. J. Walsh, "Rate of Graying of Human Hair," *Nature*, 207 (1965), 877–78.

Kuypers, J. A., and W. L. Bengtson, "Social Breakdown and Competence: A Model of Normal Aging," *Human Development*, 16, no. 2 (1973), 37–49.

Langer, S. K., *Mind: An Essay on Human Feelings*. Baltimore, Md.: Johns Hopkins, 1967.

Lamb, Marion J., *The Biology of Aging*. New York: John Wiley, 1977.

Lowenthal, Marjorie F., "Social Isolation and Mental Illness in Old Age," *American Sociological Review*, 29 (1964), 54–70.

Neugarten, B. L., R. J. Havighurst, and S. S. Tobin, "Personality and Patterns of Aging," in *Middle Age and Aging*, ed. B. L. Neugarten, pp. 173–77. Chicago: The University of Chicago Press, 1968.

Parsons, Talcott, *The Social System*, pp. 428–79. New York: Free Press, 1951.

Sainsbury, P., "Suicide and Depression" in *Recent Development in Affective Disorders*, eds. A. Coppen and A. Walk, British Journal of Psychiatry Special Publication, No. 2 (1968).

Strehler, B. L., *Time, Cells, and Aging*. New York: Academic Press, 1962.

Verwoerdt, Adrian, "Biological Characteristics of the Elderly," in *Foundations of Practical Gerontology*, eds. Rosamonde Boyd and Charles Oakes, pp. 51–67. Columbia: University of South Carolina Press, 1973.

Weiner, Marcella, Albert Brok, and Alvin Snadowsky, *Working with the Aged: Practical Approaches in the Institution and Community*. Englewood Cliffs, N.J.: Prentice-Hall, 1978.

Zusman, J., "Some Explanations of the Changing Appearance of Psychotic Patients: Antecedents of the Social Breakdown Syndrome Concept," *The Millbank Memorial Fund Quarterly*, 64 (January 1966), 1–2.

5

PSYCHOLOGICAL CHANGES IN LATER LIFE

For the complete life, the perfect pattern includes old age as well as youth and maturity. The beauty of the morning and the radiance of the noon are good, but it would be a very silly person who drew the curtains and turned out the light in order to shut out the tranquility of the evening. Old age has its pleasures, which though different, are not less than the pleasures of youth.

W. Somerset Maugham
The Summing Up

INTRODUCTION

The next two chapters of this text will deal either directly or indirectly with the changing personalities, roles, and lifestyles of older Americans. During much of the last three decades psychologists and sociologists have addressed the problems of personality development and changes from quite different perspectives. The early psychologists, following the Freudian thinking, tended to see personality as almost permanently formed by adulthood and changing very little, if at all, during the adult and later years of the life cycle.

The sociologists, in contrast, were much more likely to see personality development as a lifelong process. Using the "symbolic interaction" frame of reference, the sociologists believed that personality resulted from learning new roles and the patterns of behavior that were expected of those persons occupying a role. Thus, one was not expected as a six-year-old to behave the way an older brother or sister did as a teenager. Similarly, one would not be expected to behave as a father the same as he had as a son, because the role had changed. At a later point in time one would not be expected to behave in the same manner as a grandfather as he had as a father because these two roles also call for different patterns of behavior. Thus the sociologists very early saw personality development as a lifelong process.

There seems to be some convergence in the thinking of psychologists and sociologists at the present time on the subject of personality development. The psychologists are more frequently discussing the effect of assuming adult and later life roles on personality change and adaption. Psychologists such as Daniel Levinson and others have attempted to very carefully document the stages and crises in adult life for the individual.[1] Similarly you will find sociologists, such as Vern Bengtson, discussing personality changes over the life cycle, and attempting to take into account biological, psychological, and sociological events that may alter the person's pattern of behavior.[2]

Both psychologists and sociologists seem now to be arguing that personality development should be viewed as a lifelong process. Neugarten believes that child psychologists and gerontologists may too arbitrarily segment personality development into just the years that their specialties focus on, ignoring what may have gone on before and what may happen later. Neugarten states:

> The effect has been to speak metaphorically, that as psychologists seated under the same circus tent, some of us who are child psychologists remain seated too close to the entrance and are missing much of the action that is going on in the main ring. Others of us who are gerontologists remain seated too close to the exit. Both groups are missing a view of the whole show.[3]

While the individual's entire life history is important to understanding his or her behavior, shorter periods of time are easier for researchers to investigate.

Over the course of any ten-year period in a person's life there occurs a variety of different events that leave a strong imprint on personality. Kalish observes that a ten-year period for older Americans can bring changes in weight, hair color, stamina, sleep patterns, and health. As a gray-haired, overweight, sixty-year-old with slightly high blood pressure, you may find you cannot work as long, as hard, or as efficiently as you did as a fifty-year-old. This undoubtedly would have some effect on your self and personality.

In the social sphere you may be retired rather than employed, a widow or widower rather than married, no longer totally financially independent but living on retirement income along with some assistance from your children; thus biologically, psychologically, and sociologically your life is quite different now than it was ten years ago.

In the next two chapters, in this one focusing on psychological changes in later life, and in the following one looking at changing roles, norms, and age constraints during the later years, an attempt will be made to explain the changes in lifestyle and the concomitant adaptations that older Americans must make in order to adjust to the changes in self and the environment with which they are confronted.

PSYCHOLOGICAL AND PERFORMANCE
CHANGES IN LATER LIFE

In Chapter 4 we discussed the biological changes correlated with the aging process. In considering the changing abilities and performance potentials of older Americans there is inevitably some overlap between biological changes and losses in the ability to perform. While the behavioral scientists and the biologists may never completely agree on what are the primary causes of the changing abilities of older persons, ultimately, biological, psychological, and social changes will have to be included in the explanations of the adaptations that older persons must make.

The data presented in Chapter 4 indicated that older persons generally experience a loss in hand grip and muscular strength, are slower in reacting to different stimuli, take longer in moving, and are generally less well coordinated and less capable of performing athletic movements such as running, swimming, and boxing. Birren indicates that all behavior mediated by the central nervous system tends to be slow in the aging organism. This slowness results from a loss of cells and age-related changes in the physiological make-up of nerve cells and fibers.

In Chapter 2 the cross-sectional studies which indicated a gradual decline in intelligence with increasing age were discussed. The findings of later longitudinal studies indicated that if education was controlled there was no general drop in intelligence over the life cycle, the only exception being a sharp decline in intelligence in the last few weeks before death.

The problem in attempting to establish the performance changes that accompany the aging process is the fact that it is difficult to determine what losses are a result of aging and what losses are caused by illness and deterioration of the body's vital organs—changes which are not common to all aging individuals. Stated simply, it is difficult to determine what performance changes are directly linked to the aging process and what ones are a result of the poor health of the older persons being studied. Illness will impair the performance of the individual at any age in life.

Birren attempted to determine the effect of illness on I.Q. by comparing two groups:

1. One group consisted of 31 institutionalized patients who had been diagnosed as psychotic with cerebral arteriosclerosis or senile psychosis.
2. Another group was composed of 50 persons who were considered to be well and in good health.

Both groups were made up of individuals from 60–70 years of age who had received no less than four years of formal schooling.[5]

The I.Q. tests scores of the two groups were significantly different with the healthy group receiving the highest scores. Birren states:

It is interesting to note that the Digit symbol subtest which has been commonly found to decrease most with age, showed a smaller difference between the patient and control groups than did the information subtest which characteristically declines minimally with age. If deterioration in the senile psychosis were a process of accelerated aging the subtests such as the Digit Symbol, which show the largest difference with age might also be expected to show the largest difference between the patient and control groups. This leads to the suspicion that the process of normal aging and senile decline are rather different.[6]

Birren also found a large difference between the two groups on verbal tests. This seems to follow the pattern of an earlier study which found that a sample of healthy males over the age of 65 had higher verbal scores than a sample of younger respondents. This led Birren, Botwinick, Weiss, and Morrison to conclude that with advancing age one tends to accumulate stored information, particularly of a verbal character. In a follow-up study of the elderly men in this sample, conducted five years later, some showed no change in intelligence while others showed a considerable decline. The researchers concluded that mental functioning is not something that declines gradually in the later years but rather seems to drop precipitously as the health of the individual declines.

Classical conditioning is the process by which two stimuli, only one of which has previously led to a particular response, are presented close together so that ultimately the subject will respond to the second stimulus in the same way she or he does to the first. Schonfield found that the conditioning of older persons takes considerably longer than that of younger persons.

In reviewing and summarizing the relevant literature, Botwinick concluded that good health and a high measured intelligence reduce age-related differences in verbal learning, whereas greater task difficulty increases the difference.

Canestrari offers the following explanations of the decline in problem-solving ability with age:

1. Interference, perhaps based on earlier learning
2. Rigidity
3. Reduced ability to abstract
4. Greater difficulty in organizing complex materials
5. Loss of short-term memory capacity
6. Defects in ability to discriminate between stimuli
7. Inability to delay responses because of defects of inhibitory processes[7]

The results of all these studies seem to lead to the conclusion that the process of aging differentially affects intelligence and that intelligence is fairly stable and predictable throughout the adult's life. Losses in intelligence during later life seem to be most often associated with ill health. There may be a tendency for the person's response patterns to slow down slightly with age due to changes in the central nervous system. There may be also a slight reduction of the older person's ability to solve complex problems. Vocabulary and verbal ability tend to accumulate with age so that older subjects score better than younger ones. Kalish argues that the belief that older people diminish in capability with age may reflect

1. People's observations of the very old
2. The substantial number affected by terminal decline
3. Some modest decrements they may suffer
4. The prejudice and expectations of the perceiver[8]

In terms of the general tendency of the response time of younger respondents to be quicker than older respondents, Botwinick and Thompson conducted an interesting piece of research. They compared a group of younger persons from which athletes had been excluded with a group of older persons and found that the difference in response time had been greatly reduced. They concluded that lack of exercise may be a significant factor in reducing the response time of the older persons.

Another factor which mediates between differences in the response time of younger and older persons in crucial life situations is that a more cautious approach to problem situations by older persons minimizes the need for quick responses and actions. One would expect that due to a slower response time older drivers would have more accidents than younger drivers but they don't. Case, Hulbert, and Beers compared drivers under 50, over 50, and over 65, and found that the younger drivers tended to drive faster, to push the brake less frequently, and to take more chances. The older drivers, by comparison, changed their rate of speed more frequently, pushed the brake pedal more often, and were generally more careful. Thus, even with a slower response time, they were involved in fewer accidents because of their more cautious approach to driving.

Furry and Baltes argued that the individual's energy level and the amount of time it takes him or her to become weary may be a contributing factor to age differences in learning ability. They found that older people become fatigued much more quickly in experimental settings and that differences in learning ability may result from the length of time the studies require.

In studies of simple and immediate memory there are only slight differences between young and old respondents. Bromley found, however, if there is any interference with the simple act of memorizing, the younger respondents do better. Bromley found, for example, that reciting numbers backwards or sorting them into classes resulted in a considerable decline in performance on the part of older respondents.

Similarly, more complex tasks involving immediate memory clearly were carried out better by younger respondents. It may be that with the more complex tasks what is already known and stored in the minds of the older respondents will interfere with the new materials to be memorized.

Lehman, in studying several different fields of scientific and artistic endeavor, concluded that the major new discoveries or techniques are made in the younger years of the person's work. For the new technique or innovation to become widespread it must be carefully developed. If this development is not forthcoming the significance of the innovation may be lost. When the total life work of the scientist or artist is considered the most productive years appear to be in the fifties. Dennis found, moreover, that considerable productivity continues well into the sixties, seventies, and occasionally beyond.

Kalish summarizes in his book what he believes to be the effects of losses in performance and ability on the part of older persons. He believes most older persons continue to perform fairly well because

1. These decrements often occur very gradually, and the aging individuals can adapt to the slight changes almost without being aware that they are adapting.
2. Other people of their own age are also showing the same signs and this fact is communicable among them, sometimes openly but often more subtly.
3. Some evidence is available that older people (and, undoubtedly, younger people as well) can adjust to chronic problems and continue to enjoy life, even though the same problem might have appeared overwhelming when it was initially noticed.
4. These decrements and losses are only one aspect of life. If other aspects are satisfying the importance of the deficits probably lessens.
5. A form of rehearsal for later age roles often occurs.[9]

In summary, the results of much of the past work on performance losses of older persons seem to suggest older persons may experience slight losses in a number of areas in comparison to their younger counterparts, particularly where speed is required. Poor health is probably the single most important cause of the losses experienced by older persons. Most older individuals successfully adapt to these losses perhaps without even being aware that they have adapted. There is no gradual decline in mental ability. Unless there is a serious health problem, such as cerebral vascular disease or senile dementia, the great majority of older persons will experience no losses which would prevent them from continuing to lead normal and productive lives well into their eighties.

PERSONALITY

Douglas Kimmel believes that personality is an important variable in explaining the individual's behavior because it reveals differences in the ways people respond to situations, and it simultaneously provides a system within which each

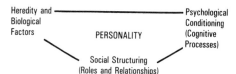

Figure 5–1

person's behavior remains fairly constant over a variety of different situations. Personality is the individual's adjustment to different environments with which he or she is confronted. Personality is a result of heredity and biological factors, psychological conditioning, and social structuring. (Figure 5–1.)

Behavioral scientists often ignore heredity as a factor in human behavior, probably because there are not any scientific tools for measuring and determining hereditary factors. The behavioral scientists must take them as a given. We know that the individual is born with certain biological needs which include such things as

1. nourishment
2. elimination of waste
3. activity
4. rest
5. growth
6. respiration
7. sexual gratification

Beyond these factors, however, it does appear that individuals are born with certain preprogrammed inclinations to behave in a certain manner. Selective breeding of animals has produced marked differences in the temperament of a species. A thoroughbred horse, for example, tends to be nervous, high-strung, and therefore can easily be trained to run for short distances at very high speeds. These are the horses that inhabit the racetracks of America. Quarter horses tend to be gentle, relaxed, and easygoing to the point at times of being considered lazy. These horses make excellent riding horses and family pets. Animal husbandry suggests that in animals, at least, there is a certain tempermental disposition that is acquired at birth. Daniel Freedman found this to be the case in studying dogs, and Broadhurst and Erpenck found this to be the case in rats. Kimmel argues, moreover, that such internal processes as psychological functioning, hormone balance, and activation levels are probably closely interrelated, both with the way in which the situation is perceived and with the individual's predisposition to respond. If heredity is a factor, as research with animals tends to suggest, then individuals at birth may be predisposed to have more or less nervous energy, to be calm or high-strung, or to be slim or heavy, or any of a variety of other factors that may affect their adjustment to the environment and ultimately their personality.

The psychological component of personality results from the cognitive processes that receive, interpret, and process information from the environment into a view of the world that allows one to adjust and react in a fairly stable and predictable manner over time. Kimmel speaks of the psychological aspect of personality as one that is similar to an internal gyroscope which, once it has been set in motion, moves in a given direction and resists pressure to change. Thus the individual's past experiences, cognitive processes, and current view of reality are fairly stable over time and tend to guide and direct his or her behavior through a variety of situations. Ultimately the individual develops a certain personality style which includes predispositions, traits, and fairly predictable patterns of behavior.

Examples of stability in patterns of behavior and personality can be found in the studies of internally/externally oriented persons and field-dependent/field-independent persons. Internally oriented persons believe that they are in control of themselves and their environment and believe that they determine their own life chances, successes, and failures. Externally oriented persons are individuals who believe that luck, chance, or fate determine what happens to them and that they are not in control of their own destiny. These patterns of response to the environment tend to become permanent and are carried by the individual from situation to situation. Over time individuals do tend to be internally or externally directed. Similarly, Walter Mischel argued that what psychologists refer to as field-dependent and field-independent persons are those who tend to react to the environment fairly consistently over time. Field-dependent persons tend to be group oriented and to want to go along as much as possible with what others in a particular social situation are doing—thus the term field dependent. Field-independent persons feel no compulsion to go along with what everyone else is doing and may independently go their own way or just not become involved in the group activity. These patterns of response were found by Mischel to be consistent over time and to follow the individual through a variety of different environments and circumstances.

Psychological traits and personality factors do not allow one to explain how personality changes over time. It is here that the social factors come into play, offering the best explanations of personality. A role is most often defined by sociologists as a set of norms and expectations placed on individuals who occupy a certain position in the social system. Thus one comes to expect that all doctors will behave very similarly, all ministers will behave similarly, and all teachers will behave in a similar fashion. Walking down the corridors of a public school one need not know the individual personality of the teacher to predict his or her behavior. All teachers will be standing in front of a class of students, leading a class discussion, or giving a lecture on some pertinent topic. Roles always carry with them the expectations of reciprocity or expected patterns of behavior from others in the social situation. The students in the classroom will be expected to be attentive to the teacher's comments, to be responsive to questions, and to act interested even if they are bored. The social view of roles and their effect on personality leads one to expect changes in personality due to the fact that roles change over time. The role of husband is different from that of father. Similarly the role of grandfather is different from that of father. Over time the roles change, resulting in changing expectations for one's behavior and ultimately changes in personality. Roles are learned in the socialization process, and new roles are constantly being prepared for and assumed by the individual as old roles are discarded over the life cycle.

Patrick Heine observes that the social model of personality more easily allows for and explains change. Moreover, consistency seems to vanish in this model into a collection of roles. Social roles are powerful explanations of personality change over time, as are other factors such as age, sex, and occupation.

In summary, the three critical factors determining personality appear to be heredity, psychological conditioning, and social structuring. Heredity provides the individual a range of biological drives (needs and urges which must be met in one way or another) and certain predispositions for being energetic, nervous, relaxed, or lethargic. These predispositions may be altered or accentuated by later environmental experiences. The psychological processes allow the individual to receive, interpret, and process experiences so that an appropriate adjustment or pattern of behavior can be adopted. Over time, personality traits and one's interpretation of environmental experiences allow a fairly stable and predictable behavior pattern to develop. These traits and behavior patterns that transcend situations become known as personality. Robert Carson maintains that individuals develop a personal style, that once established tends to be maintained. Over long periods of time personality is altered by the social structure and the roles one assumes at different ages of life. The personal style of the individual will somehow have to be shaped to fit the occupational demands of being a doctor, lawyer, or plumber.

STABILITY AND CHANGE IN PERSONALITY

In attempting to explain stability and change in personality, perhaps the symbolic interactionist view of the "I" and "me" concepts is most useful. The "I" is the individual's perception of himself or herself as a whole based on all of his or her past roles and experiences. The "I" is the response of the organism to the attitudes of others; the "me" is the organized set of attitudes of others which one assumes. The attitudes of others constitute the organized "me," then one reacts toward them as an "I." An individual may perceive of his or her various "me's" at once or in a hierarchy according to the degree of positive attitudes he or she holds toward them. This perception constitutes the "I" or self-concept. It can constitute purely personal and idiosyncratic aspects of personality. It is assigned by the individual to himself or herself. The "me" is the definition of the person as a specific role player in a given relationship. The "me" is the organized set of attitudes of others which one assumes when entering a role. These attitudes constitute the organized "me." Then one reacts toward them as an "I." The "I" is the impulsive tendency of the individual to act. It is the initial unorganized aspect of human behavior—the undirected other. The act begins as an "I" and usually ends in the form of the "me." The "me" brings the act under the control of societal expectation. The self mediates between the "I" and the "me."

Kimmel attempts to integrate both the psychological and sociological perspectives on personality into a dynamic model that can explain both stability and change in personality (Figure 5–2). Remembering that personality is the fit between the individual's self and the environment, Kimmel has shaded in the diagram what he believes to be the private aspects of personality. In the "I," memory, thinking, cognitive processes, physiological processes, and hereditary factors such as intelligence are included as the private individual aspect of personality.

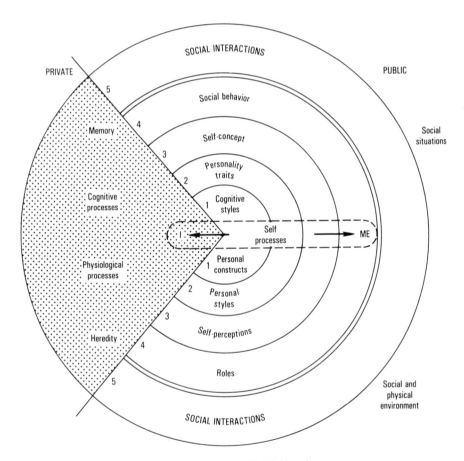

Figure 5–2 Conceptualization of Personality in Adulthood

Source: Douglas C. Kimmel, *Adulthood and Aging* (New York: John Wiley, 1974). © 1974 by John Wiley.

The unshaded part of the diagram represents the public aspects of the personality system. These represent the external environmental situations in which the individual finds himself or herself. Social behavior and social roles are a part of the external environment, largely determined by societal norms and expectations.

The diagram indicates that the individual's self-concept (Level 3) and personality traits (Level 2) are a mixture of public and private aspects of personality. The center of the model indicates the "self" as the interaction between the "I" and "me" aspects of personality. The "I" is seen as private and the "me" as public.

This model views personality as a dynamic system that simultaneously consists of relatively unchanging content aspects of personality (Levels 1–3) and relatively slowly changing process aspects of personality (Levels 3–5).[10]

From the time of birth to the time of death one may see considerable shifts in the central focus of the personality system in Kimmel's diagram. During the developing years, individual, family, and societal pressures tend to propel the person outward into the social world. The expectation is for the person to grow and develop, to assume new roles and responsibilities, and to move toward self-actualization. Adult life is then characterized by the assumption of a wide variety of different roles, and considerable responsibility for family, career, community. Adult life can be characterized by many role conflicts which demand more and more of the time, energy, and effort of the conscientious individual who attempts to successfully fulfill all the demands of the different roles that he or she is occupying. With advancing age the individual is allowed to withdraw from some roles. The external social situation becomes less crucial, and the internal processes become more important. The individual's focus often shifts from the outer world environments to inner thoughts and preoccupation with concerns of self. The disengagement theorists believe that this turning of attention inward by older Americans ultimately results in their almost total concern for self and finally death.

Carl Jung perhaps best describes the process when he states:

> Aging people should know that their lives are not mounting and expanding but that there are inexorable inner processes that enforce the contraction of life. For a young person it is almost a sin, or at least a danger to be too preoccupied with himself; but for the aging person it is a duty and a necessity to devote serious attention to himself. After having lavished its light upon the world, the sun withdraws its rays in order to illuminate itself.[11]

The young are seen by most behavioral scientists as in a period of maximum growth, development, and expansion. They are engaged in a process of developing new me's, as they learn new roles. In learning these new roles they must be considerably other-directed, meaning they are sensitive to the cues given them by others as they learn the rules of the game. Adulthood brings with it a growing self-confidence and a period of relative balance between internal orientation and external demands that are placed on the individual and increasing preoccupation with the self and internal processes. Buhler and Frenkel-Brunswik came to similar conclusions about this pattern of lifelong development. They saw the life course as a rising curve of growth and expansion culminating in the forties, followed by a period of turning inward and focusing one's attention on the self and finally an overall withdrawal from the community similar to the pattern described in disengagement. Marjorie Lowenthal and others made a study of people at four stages of life: high school seniors, newlyweds, parents of high school students, and older persons nearing retirement. They characterized the earlier stages of the life cycle as expansive in orientation, coupled with high expectations for achievement. Middle- and older-aged persons, they felt, were much more self-limited in orientation and apparently more concerned with minimizing frustrations by coping with life's problems and not setting one's goals too high.

Past studies that have attempted to determine the precise changes in personality that occur in old age have been somewhat inconclusive. Some of the findings indicate a considerable shift in personality in the later years, and others have found no change.

Riley, Foner, and associates reviewed several studies of personality change in old age and concluded that old people were more rigid and less adaptive to changing stimuli than their younger counterparts. Attitudinally they evidenced a high degree of dogmatism, a greater intolerance of ambiguity, and less concern about social pressure placed on them to conform. Moreover, they were found to be more passive, more conforming, and preoccupied with their own emotions and inner selves.

In one of a series of studies done in Kansas City in the 1950s researchers interviewed repeatedly a sample of older Americans over a seven-year-period. The results, interpreted by Bernice Neugarten indicate three age-related personality changes:

1. A shift in sex-role perceptions
2. A personality shift toward increased interiority
3. A shift in coping styles of personality.

Using the thematic apperception test, Bernice Neugarten and David Gutman asked the respondents to describe the old man and old lady in a picture. While younger respondents saw the man and woman in traditional sex roles, older respondents saw the old man as increasingly submissive. Older respondents saw the older women's role as increasingly authoritarian and less submissive. The old man and old woman were increasingly seen as playing reverse roles by older respondents. Neugarten found that a shift away from the outer world toward interiority and concern for self is consistent with other studies. Neugarten and associates found older subjects adopting a passive mastery style of dealing with the environment rather than an actual mastery style found in younger respondents. While these studies indicate considerable change in personality, others indicate considerable consistency.

A number of typologies have been developed by different researchers to describe the adjustment patterns of the persons to the later years of their lives. Suzanne Reichard and others developed a typology of five different types which included the mature, the rocking-chair men, the armored, the angry men, and the self-haters. They found no clear age differences among these personality types, indicating considerable consistency in the histories of the respondents in their sample. Kimmel believed that these findings indicate that the content aspects of personality in the form of personal styles and personal traits remain fairly consistent over time.

In a summary of the findings of the Kansas City Studies of Adult Life, Neugarten, Havighurst, and Tobin concluded that neither "activity" nor the "disengagement" theory seemed adequate. The findings indicated that those older persons who are highly engaged in various social roles generally have greater life satisfaction than those with lower levels of engagement. The relationship was not a consistent one, however. There were some older persons who were low in social role activity and who had high life satisfaction while others were high in activity but low in satisfaction. This led the researchers to believe that personality was the critical determinant of adjustment to the later years. They assumed that certain personality types, as they age, disengage with great discomfort and show a drop in life satisfaction. Others, they believed, will have shown low levels of role activity accompanied by high satisfaction and will show relatively little change as they age. Therefore, personality becomes the important variable, the focal point around which other variables are organized.

Neugarten and others developed a typology of adjustment patterns similar to the one developed by Reichard and others. The Neugarten typology included the following types:

1. Reorganizer
2. Focused
3. Disengaged
4. Holding on
5. Constricted
6. Succorance-seeker
7. Apathetic
8. Disorganized

In terms of the activity versus the disengagement model the "reorganizers" substitute new activities for lost ones, corresponding rather closely to the activity theory. The "focused" became selective in their activities, giving up some activities and at times picking up others, but being very selective about any new activities that were chosen. The "disengaged" voluntarily withdrew from former roles and responsibilities. All three of these patterns were found to be associated with high life satisfaction and secure personalities. The "holding on" and "constricted" which Neugarten describes seem to be defensive and protect themselves from anxiety about aging by clinging to middle age patterns in the "holding on" strategy or by avoiding any external threat by increasingly closing out the world in a constricted pattern. The "succorance-seekers" are satisfied with their lives as long as they can find someone to depend on. They need someone to look after and care for them. The "apathetic" are disengaged and have been so throughout much of their lives. They gave up on life early and never altered their self-defeating beliefs about their inability to cope with their environment. The "disorganized" were characterized as low in activity and poor in psychological functioning. The last three patterns were less satisfied with their lives in general.

The conclusion would seem to be that the broad external and observable adjustment patterns of persons to their environments are fairly stable, consistent, and independent of age. In terms of the more specific traits and characteristics of personality, aging, changes in health, and changing role and status precipitate considerable change over time in the coping mechanisms of the individual. Thus we find both consistency and change in personality over the life cycle.

SELF-ESTEEM

Since the behavioral scientists have assumed that a positive self-concept is crucial to a healthy personality, one question that frequently arises is: What is the effect of an aging body and deteriorating physical appearance on the individual's self-concept? Some individuals go so far as to not want to be seen in a bathing suit because they felt they would be embarrassed by their physical appearance.

Matilda Riley and others in their review of gerontological research found that older people compared to younger people were

1. Less likely to admit shortcomings
2. Less likely to consider themselves in good health
3. Less concerned about their weight
4. Among those still working, equally likely to view their job performance as adequate
5. Almost as likely to view their intelligence as being as good as others
6. More likely to consider themselves as having positive moral values
7. Somewhat more likely to feel adequate in their marriage or as parents[12]

Given the fact that looking in the mirror as an 80-year-old is a quite different experience than looking in the mirror as a 20-year-old, one wonders how older persons are able to maintain high self-esteem. Probably the understanding of reference groups can explain the phenomenon in question. Most of the friends and associates of old people are other old persons. Other than family members, their significant others are likely to be persons near their own age. Thus, they may compare themselves favorably to others in their reference groups. Many older persons take pride in the fact that they have outlived many of their friends. This then becomes a source of self-esteem.

Kalish found that economic status could also be a factor in the self-esteem of older Americans. Kalish reports that people living at, or higher than, the standard of living that they had anticipated earlier maintained high self-esteem after 60. For those persons whose standard of living was lower after age 60 than they had anticipated, self-esteem was considerably lower. Kalish also found those having a childhood fear of being left alone had low self-esteem after age 60. Kalish concludes:

> If the older people have a reasonably stable recent history, an antic-ipated standard of living, and no strong fears of being left alone, their self-esteem rises with age.[13]

Therefore, the deterioration of physical appearance and body image in old age does not necessarily lead to a loss of self-esteem when other factors are considered. The fact that one's friends and relatives are aging simultaneously, and the fact that the individual has outlived many of his or her cohorts tend to add to the person's feeling of pride and accomplishment. These factors coupled with reasonably good health and a secure income give considerable self-confidence to older persons.

ADJUSTMENT TO AGING

Successful adjustment to any age in life is difficult to define and even more diffi-cult to measure. Neugarten, Havighurst, and Tobin tried to develop a measure of life satisfaction which could be used in studying the adjustment of older Americans. The variables they included in the measurement of life satisfaction were:

1. Zest versus apathy—zest was defined as enthusiasm and ego-involvement in life's tasks. Apathy was seen as being listless or bored with life.
2. Resolution and fortitude—this was viewed as willingness to accept per-sonal responsibility for one's life in comparison to either blaming oneself too much or constantly blaming others.
3. Strong relationship between desired and achieved goals—the extent to which people accomplished the things in life that they set out to do.
4. Self-concept—holding a positive view of oneself.
5. Mood tone—described as happiness, optimism and spontaneity versus sadness, loneliness, and bitterness.[14]

Most often referred to as the Havighurst scale, it has become the most widely used scale in gerontological research. Many gerontologists have questioned the scale's validity. It is probably true that one of the major difficulties in research in the field of aging is the ability of the measurement to get at the precise concept that one is trying to measure. Whether a better measurement of life satisfaction will be forthcoming remains to be seen.

In attempting to define the variables that are correlated with successful adjustment to aging, Clark and Anderson outlined the following factors:

1. Sufficient autonomy to permit continued integrity of the self
2. Agreeable relationships with other people who are willing to provide help when needed without losing respect for the recipient of the help
3. A reasonable amount of personal comfort in body and mind and in one's physical environment
4. Stimulation of the mind and imagination in ways that do not overtax physical strength
5. Sufficient mobility to permit variety in one's surroundings
6. Some form of intense involvement with life, partly in order to escape preoccupation with death[15]

These, of course, represent ideal life circumstances for the elderly which very few probably achieve. They represent what the older person would like to have in terms of lifestyle and mastery of the environment. The loss of a spouse, the loss of one's good health, or the loss of an adequate income due to inflation mean that many, probably most, never achieve this desired state of affairs.

Clark and Anderson interviewed a sample of elderly people in San Francisco and attempted to identify the sources of high morale as well as the sources of low morale. Table 5–1 indicates the results of this study. As you can see "entertainment and diversion" tops the list of high morale factors while "dependency" tops the list of low morale factors.

Given the fact that many older persons will not live in the ideal set of circumstances in which they do have a positive outlook on life and are masters of their own destiny, what are the different possible adaptation patterns by which they adjust to their inevitable losses? Buhler outlined what she considered to be four accommodations to the aging process. These were

1. A desire to rest and relax now that the individual has completed his necessary life work.
2. A desire to remain active and the ability to do so.
3. The waning of strength, or determination to continue their work even if they may not be fully satisfied that they have accomplished everything they set out to do. This may involve considerable resignation and unhappiness on their part.
4. The feelings of frustration, anxiety, and guilt as a result of leading lives that they now find meaningless.[16]

Table 5–1

SOURCES OF HIGH MORALE	PERCENTAGE REPORTING THIS FACTOR
Entertainment and diversions	69
Socializing	57
Productive activity	54
Physical comfort (other than health)	52
Financial security	46
Mobility and movement	40
Health, stamina, survival	20

SOURCES OF LOW MORALE	PERCENTAGE REPORTING THIS FACTOR
Dependency (financial or physical)	60
Physical discomfort or sensory loss	57
Loneliness, bereavement, loss of nurturance	50
Boredom, inactivity, immobility, confinement	38
Mental discomfort or loss	18
Loss of prestige or respect	12
Fear of dying	10

Source: M. Clark and B. C. Anderson, *Culture and Aging* (Springfield, Ill.: Chas. C Thomas, 1967). Reprinted by permission.

Kalish in discussing this typology states that a fifth dimension should be added which states:

> People may, regardless of the degree of previous satisfaction they experience, find in their later years some meaningful activities or relationships that compensate for whatever old age has required of them.[17]

Kalish uses the example of a retired economics professor who has spent the last twenty years developing new hybrids of chrysanthemums. Similarly, Mr. Jones, a retired salesman for the past several years, has been actively involved in breeding, training, and selling quarter horses. He seems to find as much satisfaction in his avocation as he did his vocation. It is a mistake to assume that money is the only thing that pushes people to work hard at a given task. While every individual must have enough income to guarantee a secure existence, once assured of a secure income there are a wide range of activities and interests that can totally engulf the person. Regardless of whether they are paid for the activity, if it brings a sense of accomplishment, a degree of status, self-respect, and some recognition from others with a similar interest, it can be fulfilling.

Most older Americans who feel good about their retirement will freely attest to the fact that the most enjoyable aspect of their retirement lives is the freedom of choice now available to them. They can now choose what activities they do or don't want to get involved in, the amount of time they want to invest, and at what point they want to withdraw. Freedom from the responsibilities of the job and childrearing can be seen as one of the major advances of later life. At no other time throughout the entire life cycle is one granted so many choices in which there are no expectations or normative pressures placed on the individual to conform or behave in a particular manner. Each age in life has its particular advantages and disadvantages. The freedom to choose in the later years would appear to be a major advantage of this age.

MALADJUSTMENT

The point has been made in previous chapters of this text that older persons are confronted with a series of losses. Older persons often find themselves in the position of trying to hang on to a lifestyle that they found comfortable during their adult years but now find difficult to maintain.

The position taken by most gerontologists is that maladjustment in later life is the result of psychological and social stresses placed on individuals as they attempt to adjust to the various problems with which they find themselves confronted.

The greatest stress seems to be placed on the disadvantaged. A review of 34 different studies of these problems found that 29 of them concluded that the lowest status groups had the highest rates of psychosis and hospitalization.[18] Most researchers have found a negative relationship between socioeconomic status and severe mental illness. A study done by Locke and others found that the rates of hospital admissions for mental disorders in old age were several times higher among those with elementary school education or less compared to those with high school educations, when controlled for sex and race.

Gerontologists and social scientists generally believe that mental illness among the disadvantaged is greater because they are placed under greater stress than other social groups. They are often living on inadequate diets, in poor housing, and in deteriorating communities. Leighton has done research indicating that community disintegration is a major factor contributing to mental illness.

Erdman Palmore points out what he considers to be the social stresses of old age which are experienced by the advantaged as well as the disadvantaged. These include

1. Loss of income
2. Loss of role and status
3. Loss of a spouse (bereavement)
4. Isolation through disability
5. Loss of cognitive functioning

This list indicates some of the variety of social, psychological, and physical stresses with which older Americans are often confronted. Retirement usually reduces the income of older persons by about 50 percent. Without raising the question of the adequacy of retirement incomes, no one questions that a 50 percent reduction in income is an adjustment that may produce stress. With retirement, the loss of role and status associated with being an employed and responsible member of the community often brings a sense of meaninglessness and uselessness for older Americans. The loss of a lifelong spouse is perhaps most devastating to the individual. This represents a deterioration of the personal, private, and most intimate aspects of his or her life. Isolation through disability and a loss of cognitive function, while having social and psychological consequences, are primarily a result of physiological decline.

Older persons, then, are confronted with different kinds of stress. One source of stress is social and begins at the time of retirement, often retirement forced on the individual by mandatory retirement rules; it has the effect of removing the individual from his or her career and the mainstream of life and simultaneously reduces his or her income. The loss of a spouse creates stress which seems to have the strongest personal and psychological implication for the individual. Finally, stress can be the result of physiological decline which simultaneously has the social effect of isolating the individual.

Older persons, because of the losses they experience in later life, often feel threatened by their environment and unable to cope with their problems.

Incidence of Maladjustment

Robert Butler and Myrna Lewis believe that the best evidence available indicates that about 85 percent of the elderly, or approximately 19 million, will adjust to the problems of aging without any serious emotional problems and difficulties, even though some of these live in conditions known to be conducive to emotional problems. The remaining 15 percent are believed to suffer from some type of emotional problem. Considerably more than 15 percent of the older population live under conditions known to be related to mental illness even though they may have experienced no problems. Twenty-five percent, approximately five million persons, live in poverty or near poverty conditions which are known to produce emotional strain. An additional million are estimated to have a serious physical illness, and still another million are social isolates. Thus it has been estimated that seven million older persons live in conditions known to be conducive to maladjustment and mental illness.[19] Fortunately, the coping mechanisms adopted by many of the persons living under these conditions prevents them from having serious emotional and adjustment problems.

Carole Allen and Herman Brotman report:

> Older people use mental health services at about half the rate of the general population. Five percent of patients admitted to psychiatric facilities (both inpatient and outpatient) are 65 and older. Among the elderly, admission rates are generally higher for women, for younger elderly aged 65 to 74 and those with no spouse.[20]

The remaining 10 percent of the older population believed to be suffering from emotional problems are admitted to local hospitals and mental health clinics, receive outpatient psychiatric care, or go untreated.

The classification of the most common disorders, which was developed by Butler and Lewis and coded in the Charles Harris book, includes:

1. Late-life schizophrenia (also called *paraphrence* or *senile schizophrenia*)—generally, a newly developed schizophrenic disorder is rare in older persons.
2. Affective psychoses—may include involutional melancholia and manic-depressive psychoses.
3. Psychotic depressive reaction—refers to severe depressions related to some definable life experience.
4. Paranoid states—psychotic disorders presenting a delusion usually persecutory or grandiose as the main abnormality.
5. Neuroses—may include anxiety neurosis, hysterical neurosis, depressive neurosis, and hypochondriacal neurosis.
6. Personality disorders—defects in personality development of a lifelong nature.[21]

As a result of the fact that these disorders can have physiological as well as psychosocial causes, it is often difficult for the psychiatrist to determine the precise cause of the problem.

Other effects of stress experienced by some in the aging process include suicide, drug abuse, and alcoholism. One in five suicides in the United States is committed by a person over 65, though this age group represents approximately 1 in every 10 persons in the United States. Suicides are disproportionately higher among older persons. The pattern of suicide for men tends to increase with age. The suicide rate for women, on the other hand, peaks in the middle years (45–54) and declines thereafter. (See Table 5–2.) The reasons for the different ages at which the suicide rates peak for men and women remain unexplained at the current time. One wonders why women would experience the greater stress and hence the higher suicide rates in the middle years while men experience the greater stress and higher suicide rates in the later years.

Another and almost totally uninvestigated area of stress in the older population is the relationship between their physical health and their mental health. For some older persons who are dying and who know that they are dying, suicide may represent a form of euthanasia. Those who are dying and in pain and are aware of the fact that the longer they live the worse the pain will be may find suicide the solution to their problems. The following case illustrates the circumstances leading to the suicides of some older persons. Dr. Bryan was a psychology teacher at a well-known university. After a number of trips, x-rays, and medical diagnoses they located the cause of his recurring headaches. Professor Bryan was told that he had inoperable brain cancer. Moreover, he was told

Table 5–2 Suicides per 100,000
Population by Age and Sex in 1974*

AGE	MALE	FEMALE
5 to 14	1.4	0.4
15 to 19	11.0	3.2
20 to 24	24.1	6.2
25 to 29	23.8	8.1
30 to 34	22.6	8.7
35 to 39	23.1	9.8
40 to 44	22.5	12.4
45 to 49	25.8	13.2
50 to 54	27.3	12.8
55 to 59	30.7	11.2
60 to 64	29.7	9.3
65 to 69	30.5	8.3
70 to 74	36.4	7.6
75 to 79	42.5	7.7
80 to 84	45.2	5.7
85 and over	45.2	3.8
All ages	18.1	6.5

*Based on U.S. Public Health Service data.

he would die sometime in the next six months and between now and the time of his death the headaches would come more regularly and be more painful. Professor Bryan finished out the spring semester of his classes, made out his final grades, cleaned off his desk, and went out behind his office and shot himself. Who can say, given the circumstances in which he found himself, whether this was a rational or irrational decision?

Currently very few studies have been done on drug abuse by the elderly. Lawrence Krupka and Arthur Veneer did study drug use among the elderly and they found 67 percent of their sample used at least one over-the-counter drug and 98 percent consumed a social drug daily. They considered alcohol, caffeine, and nicotine to be social drugs. The older drug users in this study averaged 2.0 prescriptions, 1.8 over-the-counter, and 1.8 social drugs daily. This meant that 5.6 drugs were consumed per individual with males averaging 7.5 and females 4.7.[22] One is led to suspect that it is a different kind of abuse than that which we read about among younger persons. One might guess that the refilling and overuse of prescriptions, the saving of unused medicines for a later date, and the willingness of medical doctors to be liberal in granting prescriptions to older persons is more likely to be their source of drugs rather than the black market. One suspects that older persons are more likely to justify the misuse of drugs as good for their health rather than a kind of counterculture movement which we find among the young.

Overall, one might expect older persons to be the least likely group to be classified as alcoholic. Phyllis Snyder and Ann Way point out that older Americans are less likely to drink than younger Americans and if they do drink they are more likely to be moderate rather than heavy drinkers. Leslie Drew observed that alcoholism is a self-limiting disease which burns out as the alcoholic ages. Either it burns out, or in some cases the alcoholic dies before reaching old age. While this is the overall pattern, Janet Glassock estimated that there are more than 3 million alcoholics over the age of sixty in the United States.

Sheldon Zimberg identified two types of older alcoholics: one type for whom alcoholism has been a lifelong pattern and another type for whom alcoholism appears to be a reaction to the stresses of growing old. Undoubtedly the latter form of alcoholism is the one that responds most readily to treatment.

Snyder and Way outlined some of the major causes of alcoholism among the elderly:

1. *Loneliness*—nearly 60 percent of admissions to a Chicago treatment facility were widowed, separated, or divorced.
2. *Retirement*—sometimes due to a loss of self worth.
3. *Leisure*—increased leisure time leading to an involvement of the older person in a variety of recreational activities which encourage one to drink.[23]

Margaret Bailey and her associates found the peak periods in the prevalence of alcoholism to be in the ages from 45 to 54 and from 65 to 75. Elderly widows showed the highest rate of alcoholism.[24] The period of 45 to 54 would appear to be one of shifting roles from the young to the middle years. Often the children have left home and the individual is beginning to recognize the first signs of some of the inevitable physiological losses. No one has yet investigated whether role changes and altered lifestyle of the middle years create stress which some attempt to resolve by the use of alcohol. Similarly, one wonders if the 65- to 74-year-olds are adjusting to the role changes that accompany retirement and the onset of old age and if this does not create stress which some will attempt to assuage through the use of alcohol. These are unanswered questions which should prove fruitful topics for researchers interested in the problems of alcoholism and aging.

Neither suicide, drug abuse, nor alcoholism in later life have been studied extensively by gerontologists or social scientists. Therefore, there is simply not enough evidence available at the present time to connect the social ills of later life to alcoholism, drug abuse, and suicide.

CONCLUSION

We view personality development as a lifelong process in this chapter. The three principal components of personality discussed have been the physiological, the psychological, and the social. The individual at birth is considered to have a genetic composition which may predispose him or her to be nervous, relaxed, energetic, lethargic, etc. In addition, the individual has a variety of biological drives and urges which demand attention and ultimately must be satisfied in some fashion. Psychologically the individual receives, processes, and incorporates new information into a view of his or her environment and a strategy of coping with it. Over time the individual develops personal traits and habits as he or she learns to cope with a variety of social situations. These traits and habits become a fairly stable part of personality and guide the individual through a variety of diverse social situations. Over the life cycle one acquires new roles and responsibilities. While the personal traits predispose an individual to behave in a well-established manner when confronted with a new role, the norms of society demand a certain kind of behavior, which is independent of personality, for all who occupy that role. Thus the social structure and normative role expectations force changes in personality throughout the entire life cycle.

Later life and personality were further discussed in terms of adjusting to a series of losses. As a result of aging, physiological decline, the loss of previous roles and status, and changing societal expectations, the individual often finds later life to be of increasing insecurity and develops a growing inability to cope with his or her environment. While the majority of older Americans develop coping mechanisms with which they compensate for the inevitable losses of old age, some do not; and personal emotional problems, as well as alcoholism, drug abuse, and suicide, have been seen to be a result of these older Americans' inability to cope with the stresses of later life.

KEY TERMS

personality types:	personality
reorganizer	field-dependent personality
focused	field-independent personality
disengaged	internally oriented persons
holding on	externally oriented persons
constricted	social structuring
succorance-seeker	self
apathetic	"I" and "me" concepts
disorganized	

SUGGESTED READINGS

ALLEN, CAROLE, AND HERMAN BROTMAN, *Chartbook on Aging in America.* White House Conference on Aging, 1981.

BAILEY, MARGARET, PAUL W. HABERMAN, AND HAROLD ALKNE, "The Epidemiology of Alcoholism in An Urban Residential Area," *Quarterly Journal Studies of Alcohol,* 26 (1965).

BENGTSON, VERN L., *The Social Psychology of Aging*, pp. 9–10. Indianapolis: Bobbs-Merrill, 1973.

BIRREN, J. E., AND OTHERS, "Interrelations of Mental and Perceptual Tests Given to Healthy Elderly Men," in *Human Aging*, ed. J. E. Birren and others. Washington, D.C.: Public Health Service Pub. No. 986, 1963.

BIRREN, J. F., *The Psychology of Aging*. Englewood Cliffs, N.J.: Prentice-Hall, 1964.

BOTWINICK, J., "Geropsychology," in *Annual Review of Psychology*, eds. P. H. Mussen and M. R. Rosensweig. Palo Alto, CA: Annual Reviews, 1970.

BOTWINICK, J., AND L. W. THOMPSON, "Individual Differences in Reaction Time in Relation to Age," *Journal of Genetic Psychology*, 112 (1968), 73–75.

BROADHURST, P. L., AND H. J. ERPENCK, "Emotionality in the Rat: A Problem of Response Specificity," in *Studies in Psychology*, eds. C. Banks and P. L. Broadhurst. Aylesbury Bucks, Eng.: Hazell, Watson & Viney, Ltd, 1965.

BROMLEY, D. B., *The Psychology of Human Aging*. Baltimore, Md.: Penguin, 1966.

BUHLER, C., "Old Age and Fulfillment of Life with Considerations of the Use of Time in Old Age," *Cocta Psychologica*, 19 (1961), 126–48.

BUTLER, ROBERT AND MYRNA LEWIS, *Aging and Mental Health: Positive Psychosocial Approaches*. St. Louis: C. V. Mosby, 1977.

CANESTRARI, R. F., "Research in Learning," *The Gerontologist*, 7, no. 2, pt. 2 (1967), 61–66.

CARSON, ROBERT, C., *Interaction Concepts of Personality*. Chicago: Aldine, 1969.

CASE, H. W., S. HULBERT AND J. BEERS, *Driving Ability as Affected by Age*. University of California at Los Angeles: Institute of Transportation and Traffic Engineering (Report 70-18), 1970.

CLARK, M., AND B. C. ANDERSON, *Culture and Aging*. Springfield, Ill.: Chas. C Thomas, 1967.

DENNIS, W., "Creative Productivity between the Ages of 20 and 80 Years," *Journal of Gerontology*, 21 (1966), 1–8.

DREW, LESLIE, "Alcoholism as a Self Limiting Disease," *Quarterly Journal of Studies on Alcohol* (Dec. 1968), pp. 963–68.

FRIED, M., *Social Differences in Mental Health in Poverty and Health*, eds. J. Rosa, A. Antonovska, and K. Zola. Cambridge, MA: Harvard University Press, 1969.

FREEDMAN, DANIEL G., "Constitutional and Environmental Interactions in Rearing Four Breeds of Dogs," *Science*, 127, no. 3298 (1958), 585–86.

FRENKEL-BRUNSWIK, ELSE, "Adjustments and Reorientation in the Course of the Life Span," in *Psychological Studies of Human Development*, ed. Raymond Kuhlen. New York: Appleton-Century-Crofts, 1963.

FREUD, SIGMUND, *An Outline of Psychoanalysis*, trans. James Strachey. New York: W. W. Norton & Co., Inc., 1963.

FURRY, C. A., AND P. B. BALTES, "The Effect of Age Differences in Ability: Extraneous Performance Variables in Assessment of Intelligence in Children, Adults and the Elderly," *Journal of Gerontology*, 28 (1973), 73–80.

HARRIS, CHARLES, *Fact Book on Aging: A Profile of America's Older Population*. Washington, D.C.: National Council on the Aging, Inc., 1978.

HEINE, PATRICKE JOHNS, *Personality in Social Theory*, Chicago: Aldine, 1971.

JUNG, CARL G., "The Stages of Life," trans. R. F. C. Hull, in *The Portable Jung*, ed. Joseph Campbell. New York: Viking, 1971.

KALISH, RICHARD A., *Late Adulthood: Perspectives on Human Development*, p. 47. Monterey, CA: Brooks/Cole, 1975.

KIMMEL, DOUGLAS C., *Adulthood and Aging*. New York: John Wiley, 1974.

KRUPKA, LAWRENCE, AND ARTHUR VENEER, "Hazards of Drug Use Among the Elderly," *The Gerontologist*, 19, no. 1 (1979), 90–95.

LEHMAN, H. C., *Age and Achievement*. Princeton, N.J.: Princeton University Press, 1953.

LEVINSON, DANIEL J., AND OTHERS, "Stages in Adulthood," in *Socialization and the Life Cycle*, ed. Arnold Rose, pp. 279–93. New York: St. Martin's Press, 1979.

LEIGHTON, A., "Is Social Environment a Cause of Psychiatric Disorder?" *Psychiatric Epidemiology and Mental Health Planning*, eds. R. E. Monroe, J. D. Klee, E. B. Brody, pp. 337–45. Washington, D.C.: American Psychiatric Association, 1967.

LOCKE, B. Z., M. KERAMER, AND B. PASAMANICK, "Mental Diseases of the Senaim at Mid-Century," *American Journal of Public Health*, 50 (1960), 998–1012.

LOWENTHAL, MARJORIE, AND OTHERS, *Four Stages of Life*. San Francisco: Jossey-Bass, 1975.

MAUGHAM, W. SOMERSET, *The Summing Up*. New York: Doubleday, 1938.

MISCHEL, WALTER, "Continuity and Change in Personality," *American Psychologist*, 44, no. 11 (1969), 1012–18.

MISCHEL, WALTER, *Personality and Assessment*. New York: John Wiley, 1968.

NEUGARTEN, BERNICE, *Middle Age and Aging*, p. 137. Chicago: University of Chicago Press, 1968.

NEUGARTEN, BERNICE L., AND DAVID L. GUTMAN, "Age-Sex Roles and Personality in Middle Age; A Thematic Apperception Study," *Psychological Monographs*, 72, no. 17, Whole No. 470 (1958).

NEUGARTEN, BERNICE, ROBERT HAVIGHURST, AND SHELDON TOBIN, "Personality and Patterns of Aging," in *Middle Age and Aging*, ed. Bernice Neugarten. Chicago: University of Chicago Press, 1968.

NEUGARTEN, BERNICE L., "Summary and Implications," in *Personality in Middle and Later Life*, ed. Bernice Neugarten. New York: Atherton Press, 1964.

NEUGARTEN, BERNICE L., ROBERT J. HAVIGHURST, AND SHELDON S. TOBIN, "The Measurement of Life Satisfaction," *Journal of Gerontology*, 16 (1961), 168–74.

PALMORE, ERDMAN, "The Effects of Aging on Activities and Attitudes," in *Normal Aging*, ed. Erdman Palmore. Durham, N.C.: Duke University Press, 1970.

REICHARD, SUZANNE, FLORINE LIVSON, AND PAUL PETERSON, *Aging and Personality*. New York: John Wiley, 1962.

RILEY, M. W., A. FONER, AND ASSOCIATES, *Aging and Society, Volume 1. An Inventory of Research Findings*. New York: Russell Sage, 1968.

SCHONFIELD, D., "Learning and Retention," in *Contemporary Gerontology: Concepts and Issues*, ed. J. E. Birren. Los Angeles: Andeurs Gerontology Center, 1969.

SNYDER, PHYLLIS K., AND ANN WAY, "Alcoholism and the Elderly," *Aging* (January-February 1979), pp. 8–11.

ZIMBERG, SHELDON, "The Elderly Alcoholic," *The Gerontologist* (June 1974), pp. 222–25.

6

AGE NORMS, AGE CONSTRAINTS, AND ADULT SOCIALIZATION

To know how to grow old is the masterwork of wisdom, and one of the most difficult chapters in the great art of living.

Amiel
Journal, September 21, 1874

In the previous chapter we discussed the physiological, psychological, and social changes that a person must adjust to in his or her later life. While the last chapter focused heavily on the psychological adjustment to these events, this chapter will look more closely at the social aspects of aging.

Observing ten-year periods throughout the life cycle, Kalish notes:

> To grasp what has happened during the past decade, you must examine more than one dimension of your past existence. It is immediately obvious that you have had ten years of experiences—pleasant and unpleasant, exciting and boring, warming and embittering, ego building and ego destroying.[1]

Older persons often find their lives considerably changed during the later years. Their children have most often left home and gone to establish their own families. They are retired and find themselves spending considerably more time around their homes with their husband or wife. They usually have considerably less income on which to attempt to maintain their preferred lifestyle. Most have experienced some chronic health problem to which they must adjust. They have probably lost former friends due to death and frequently have lost touch with their younger counterparts in the community. Thus, the lives of older persons may be considerably altered during the later years.

Goslin defines socialization as

> The process by which individuals acquire the knowledge, skills and dispositions that enable them to participate as more or less effective members of groups and society.[2]

Socialization is a process of learning how one is expected to behave in a given role or social situation. Socialization is a lifelong process since change is a constant part of one's life. We are always assuming new roles and positions in the social system. Some of the difficulties inherent in the changes of life are mitigated by the fact that they are often anticipated, desired, and prepared for. A young man or woman may spend considerable time anticipating and planning for their forthcoming marriage. Hope chests, bachelor parties, wedding plans, showers, and so on, may all be part of the process. Sociologists have coined the phrase "anticipatory socialization" to refer to this phenomenon. Thus the person imagines what it is going to be like to assume the new, and in this case, desired role. While the actual performance of the role may not be exactly what the person had expected, he or she will probably feel more comfortable in the new role as a result of his or her previous preparations.

One problem that older Americans are confronted with as they plan for the next phase of their lives is that some of the roles they will be assuming are positive and desirable and others are not. Retirement after forty years of striving to succeed in a career may be desirable. Being a widow or widower, or being sick, are usually roles that are not desired. Thus, older Americans must for the first time in their lives look forward to a variety of factors in their future that have undesirable consequences for them. If one looks back over one's entire life, this is the first time that future events are not viewed positively and anticipated with high expectations. The child looks forward to adulthood and can't wait to reach the age of 21. The junior executive looks forward to becoming the president of the company. Older persons, for the first time in their lives, look forward to their future with some degree of antipathy. Everything in their future is not necessarily going to be good.

Still, however, the evidence indicates that there is considerable planning and preparation for the future on the part of middle-aged and older persons. Considerable anticipatory socialization does take place. A study by Cox and Bhak indicated that as early as age 55, some Americans sell their large homes in which they raised their families and move to smaller houses or apartments that are located nearer to desired services.[3] Thus well in advance, many Americans prepare for the later years.

There are societal norms and expectations about how one is to act at any age in life. A mother may scold her seven-year-old son "to grow up and act his age," and the 70-year-old man may be referred to as a "dirty old man" because he shows an interest in the opposite sex when he is at an age when society believes he should no longer be interested in sex. At any age in life there will be discrepancies between how one is expected to act and how one would individually like to act.

In a youth-oriented culture such as the United States, one often does not like to think of himself or herself as getting old. By thinking of oneself as old, the individual loses the privileges of the adult and middle years. Phillips reports a study done at Elmira and Kips Bay, New York, in which respondents were asked if they identified themselves as being old, middle-aged, or young. A measure of psychological adjustment and maladjustment was then given to the respondents. Psychological adjustment was defined as "the efforts of an individual to satisfy his personal needs as well as to live up to the expectations of others."[4] Maladjustment was defined as "behavior which does not completely satisfy the individual and social needs of the person, even though it may reduce his drive tension."[5] The evidence indicated that a significantly higher proportion of the maladjusted respondents are found among those who identify themselves as being old. (See Table 6-1.) This relationship held when controlled for employment status, marital status, and age.[6] Apparently, identifying oneself as old in a youth-oriented society is not a healthy thing to do.

LIFE SPACE

One factor which clearly illustrates the changing social environment of older Americans is the concept of "life space." One thinks of a newborn child's world in terms of life space with limited but expanding horizons. The child's life space may be a single room in a house or apartment. Much of the child's first years are spent in a single room where he or she sleeps, eats, and plays. The child of one to three begins to walk and move around, and his or her life space becomes the

Table 6-1 Percent Maladjusted Respondents by Age Identification

AGE IDENTIFICATION	ELMIRA		KIPS BAY	
	%	N*	%	N*
Middle-age	31	(343)	28	(287)
Old	58	(118)	49	(199)

In this table and in the following one, N refers to the total number in each category. The sum of those in the employed and retired categories, as well as those who are married or widowed, is somewhat less than the total number of respondents in each sample. In the former case housekeepers are omitted from the samples, while in the latter instance respondents who never married are excluded.
*Total number in each category

Source: Bernard S. Phillips, "A Role Theory Approach to Adjustment in Old Age," *American Sociological Review*, 22 (1957), 216.

entire apartment or house. The child from three to six years of age begins to travel in his or her yard and perhaps one block of the neighborhood. Thus, his or her life space is increasing. Upon entering school he or she is now allowed to move about in a school district or neighborhood of several blocks.

The mature adult's life space has become the whole world. He or she is confronted with both national and international issues, is expected to be an active participant in the community, to regularly take part in local and national elections, and occasionally to go to war.

Older persons find their life space beginning to shrink. Upon retirement they find themselves not going to the office, not being involved in major business decisions, and tending to travel more frequently in their neighborhood rather than throughout the city. Eventually, declining health, poor vision, or related problems may force them to quit driving, and thus they are even more likely to stay in their own neighborhood. Ultimately they may find themselves staying in their own house or apartment most of the time. Health reasons may limit their leaving the house. Thus both the physical and social environments of older Americans are usually ones that gradually shrink. Socially one no longer sees his or her cronies at the office, lifelong friends die, and the opportunity to make new friends may be limited. Upon the death of a spouse, one no longer fits comfortably in a group of married couples.

ROLE

Roles are defined as socially acceptable and expected ways of behaving, associated with a particular job, function, or task. In simple terms, a role is a pattern of expected behavior associated with a position in society. The norms of expected behavior are very strong, and there is much pressure to conform placed on people who occupy a certain role. Sociologists have maintained that one can better predict a person's behavior based on knowledge of the position he or she holds, than one could based on knowledge of the idiosyncratic aspects of an individual's personality. For example, all ministers behave somewhat alike regardless of their personalities.

In Chapter 6 we observed that one's role in a social setting is usually accompanied by another, reciprocal role. Thus if there is a mother, there is a child. If a teacher is expected to lead interesting lectures and discussions, there is a student who is expected to be responsive, attentive, and ask pertinent questions about the topic.

Since change is an integral part of life, the individual is often in the process of discarding old roles and learning new ones. Thus a girl may no longer be a teenager, but a bride; and then in a few years, she may no longer be solely a wife, but a wife and mother.

Some of the roles the individual assumes throughout the life cycle are desired and sought by the individual, while others are expected and forced on him or her by others. A young man may want to become a husband but not be anxious to be a father. Regardless of his latent reservations, if children are born in the marriage he will be expected to assume the role of father.

Each role carries with it a given status. Status refers to the position of dominance or subordination associated with the role. The role of father in a family carries high status, privilege, and power. The role of son carries low status, privilege, and power. The father makes decisions and directs the son's early life. The son is expected to comply.

There are both advantages and disadvantages attached to the roles that one assumes in later life. The major advantage that many older Americans express at the time of retirement is that for the first time in their lives they are free to choose what roles and activities they want to become a part of. Up until retirement, many of the roles that adults assume are expected and carry heavy demands for the individual's time, energy, and effort in order to successfully fill them. For example, one goes through the endless work of rearing and nurturing children that involves constant attention, changing diapers, feeding, during the early years of the child's life, followed by close and careful concern for the next several years. Most parents breathe a sigh of relief once the children are reared and successfully launched on their own lives and careers. Parenthood, while it may be a desired role, carries heavy demands on the individual's time, energy, and effort. Moreover, the norms surrounding parenthood are so strong that no self-respecting individual seriously considers abandoning this role once it is assumed.

The retired couple usually have their children reared, no longer must go to work every morning, and can now choose what they want to do and not do. There is probably greater freedom of choice for older Americans than for any other age group. One is free to choose whether to become a volunteer working at the local hospital or to go to the golf course every day. One can choose whether to remain in Chicago throughout the year or to move to Florida during the winter months. On the other hand, the older couple may decide to pick up their belongings and move permanently to Florida. There is probably a wider range of choices of roles to assume for older Americans than for any other age group in our society. Even the roles that are forced on the elderly by the social system allow considerable freedom and discretion on the part of the old person. For example, one becomes a grandmother and grandfather through no choice of his or her own. The grandparent role, however, allows one to spoil the grandchildren, if he or she so chooses, without being responsible for their discipline.

On the other hand, while there is greater freedom of choice in old age, the roles that are available for the individual to choose among are not highly valued in the society and do not bring one a high status. Most of these roles, whether leisure, recreational, volunteer, or family, are less valued than the roles assumed by the adult and middle-age groups in the population.

Phillips, in examining a number of role changes among the elderly and

Table 6–2   Percent Maladjusted Respondents by Role

	ELMIRA		KIPS BAY	
ROLE	%	N*	%	N*
Employed	22	(171)**	27	(161)**
Retired	42	(98)**	40	(200)**
Married	27	(173)**	30	(221)**
Widow or widower	40	(217)**	47	(180)**
Age 60–69	29	(277)**	31	(254)*
70 or over	52	(187)**	40	(233)*
Not treated differently	34	(366)**	32	(355)**
Treated differently	53	(87)**	48	(118)**

*Difference is significant at the .05 level.
**Difference is significant at the .01 level.

Source: Bernard S. Phillips, "A Role Theory Approach to Adjustment in Old Age," *American Sociological Review,* 22 (1957), 216.

correlating these with adjustment, found that the retired were more likely to be maladjusted than the employed; the widowed were more likely to be maladjusted than the married; and those over 70 were more likely to be maladjusted than those under that age.[7] (Table 6–2.) It would appear that role changes in later life, just as those at an earlier age, involve some adjustment on the part of the individual. This study does not indicate how long those individuals had been retired or widowed, and therefore there is no way to determine if they ultimately adjusted to the new role.

The information on the desirability of the retirement role is confusing at this time, however. Richard, Livson, and Peterson found that those respondents who were both older and retired had greater ego strength, indicated less projection of hostility, had fewer obsessional defenses, were more open, freer from anxiety, and were less depressed. They concluded that the period of greatest difficulty was the 64–69 age range when the transition to new roles and circumstances is still in process. Once the transition has taken place, the strength cited above appeared.[8]

Bell found, in a study of retirement adjustment, that 12 percent of his sample had increased their community contact after retirement and experienced an increase in life satisfaction. This suggests that the more time the individual invests in community contact after retirement, the more positive is the change in life satisfaction. Bell concluded that community involvement gave the individual rewards similar to those that he or she had received from employment. Families of retired individuals were apparently not able to provide these precise satisfactions.[9]

Old people find themselves at a time when, as we have just discussed, there is less social pressure placed on them for role performance, and they are freer to choose from among a variety of roles that they may enter. Simultaneously, older persons are in a better position to resist social pressure when it is experienced by them. They no longer have to worry about pleasing the boss or establishing business and political ties in the community. They are therefore freer to ignore social pressure and follow their individual inclinations. Kimmel observes:

> Women, as they age, seem to become more tolerant of their own aggressive egocentric impulses; while men, as they age, seem to become more tolerant of their own nurturant and affiliative impulses.[10]

The lack of concern for social pressure can be seen in the following letter thanking a friend who sent a radio as a gift. Her final response to her roommate seems to illustrate total honesty and the total lack of social constraint which older persons experience:

Dear Mr. Gary:

Just a short note of thanks to you and your associates in the Adult Education Association for the more than generous donation which you gave to the Senior Citizen's Fun Fund (SCFF) recently. Your kind contribution meant a new clock radio for me. Thank you so much for the lovely gift. It is just wonderful that an absolute stranger like yourself would take time off from his own business to remember people like us. I am 82 years old and I have been here at the home for 16 long years. They treat us well, but the loneliness is sometimes hard to bear.

My roommate, Mrs. Eisenblatt, is a very nice person but is very stingy. She has a radio but she never would let me use it and she turns it off when I come into the room. Now, because of your thoughtfulness, I have my very own radio.

My son and daughter-in-law are very nice and they come to visit me once a month. I appreciate it, but also understand their sense of obligation. This makes your gift all the more wonderful because it was given not as a sense of duty, but from a feeling of compassion from a fellow human being.

Today Mrs. Eisenblatt's radio went out of order and when she asked me if she could use mine, I told her to go f_____ herself.

Yours truly,

Kimmel, in reviewing past studies of personality changes in later life, argues that the life cycle of an individual involves moving from an early period of expansion, in which one is rapidly learning and acquiring new roles and is very careful to note the observations of others about their behavior in young adulthood, to a period of balance between external and internal pressures in the middle years, to an increasing focus on internal processes in old age and much less concern for external pressures.

AGE SYNCHRONIZATION

Most people have an idea of what age in life is most appropriate for the accomplishment of the major life tasks. They consider age a factor in the judgment of their peers' successes and failures as well as their own. One often hears people refer to themselves as marrying early or late which implies that they have an idea of what the right age is to marry. There appear to be three major areas of accomplishment which require some coordination in a person's life. These are family, career, and age group. Gubrium speaks of these as spheres in which both within the sphere and between spheres persons can be seen as being late, early, or on time. One may enter a career early but marry late. On the other hand, one may marry in the early twenties at about the right time, enter a career simultaneously, which is also about the expected time, but not achieve the career success he or she expected by the middle forties. The lack of synchronization of the major events in one's life creates anxiety for the individual. Gubrium states:

> For the most part, an individual in our society marries in his early twenties, completes the childbearing period in his late twenties, reaches a career and income peak in his late forties or early fifties, is widowed sometime thereafter and begins to consider himself old in his mid seventies.[11]

An individual who is divorced in the thirties, reaches a career peak in the early forties, and remarries in the late forties would, according to Gubrium, experience considerable tension and conflict due to the lack of synchronization between the different spheres of his or her life.

Table 6–3 indicates the results of an earlier study done by Neugarten and others regarding what people felt was the best age to achieve given critical life tasks. While these represent a cross section of ages and opinions, there are sometimes differences in attitude based on the age of the respondent. Neugarten reports that a 20-year-old felt it would be perfectly all right for a 17-year-old to marry as long as the boy had a job. A 45-year-old man, on the other hand, felt that it would be foolish to marry at that young an age, and that the couple would both suffer later.

It still remains true, however, that there is a desirable age in most people's minds to marry, raise one's children, achieve career success, and retire. Upon meeting someone for the first time, Americans quickly observe the age and sex of the individual and then draw some conclusions about his or her behavior. Age is a critical social category carrying with it certain societal norms and expectations.

Merton developed a typology to categorize deviant behavior based on the individual's conformity to culturally prescribed goals and the normative expectations regarding how one was to achieve these goals. Gubrium modified the table somewhat to explain the conformity or deviance of individuals from the timing of major life events. Gubrium identifies the sources of time-disoriented relationships: inconsistencies within social spheres such as marrying early and

Table 6–3 Consensus in a Middle-Class, Middle-Aged Sample Regarding Various Age-Related Characteristics. Fifty Middle-Aged Men and 43 Middle-Aged Women Were Asked to Indicate the Age for Which Each of These Statements Is Most Descriptive.

	AGE RANGE DESIGNATED AS APPROPRIATE OR EXPECTED	PERCENT WHO CONCUR	
		Men	*Women*
Best age for a man to marry	20–25	80	90
Best age for a woman to marry	19–24	85	90
When most people should become grandparents	45–50	84	79
Best age for most people to finish school and go to work	20–22	86	82
When most men should be settled on a career	24–26	74	64
When most men hold their "top" jobs	45–50	71	58
When most people should be ready to retire	60–65	83	86
A young man	18–22	84	83
A middle-aged man	40–50	86	75
An old man	65–75	75	57
A young woman	18–24	89	88
A middle-aged woman	40–50	87	77
An old woman	60–75	83	87
When a man has the most responsibilities	35–50	79	75
When a man accomplishes most	40–50	82	71
The prime of life for a man	35–50	86	80
When a woman has the most responsibilities	25–40	93	91
When a woman accomplishes most	30–45	94	92
A good-looking woman	20–35	92	82

Source: Reprinted from "Age Norms, Age Constraints, and Age Socialization," *American Journal of Sociology,* 70 (1965), 710–17, by B. L. Neugarten, J. W. Moore, and J. C. Lowe, by permission of The University of Chicago Press. © 1965 by The University of Chicago Press.

having one's children late; inconsistencies between social spheres, for example having children late at about the time one's career is peaking; or inconsistencies both within and between spheres, such as being divorced and starting a second family in the late forties while not achieving a career peak until the late fifties. Gubrium borrows the Merton typology to show all the possible arrangements of time-ordered events in one's work career (see Table 6–4).

Conformity in this typology, according to Gubrium, would be having socially acceptable career goals and arriving at these goals at expected times.

Innovation would be the case when the individual accepts and internalizes the major societally prescribed career goals but is not able to follow the culturally prescribed timing of these events. For instance, one individual may fully plan to be a medical doctor but finances force him or her to drop out of medical school and take a job. Five years later he or she reenters the program and ultimately completes the training, but is several years behind his or her cohorts. Professional women who drop out of school to have children and reenter the program after their children enter the first grade would be another example.

Table 6-4 Responses to Time-Disoriented Relationships Based on the Merton Typology

	CAREER GOALS	GOAL TIMING
1. Conformity	+	+
2. Innovation	+	−
3. Ritualism	−	+
4. Retreatism	−	−
5. Rebellion	+	+

Source: Jaber F. Gubrium, *Time, Role and Self in Old Age* (New York: Human Sciences Press, 1976), p. 120. © 1976 by Human Sciences Press.

In the pattern called *ritualism,* the people have given up on achieving the culturally prescribed goals, but they conquer any lingering guilt feelings by acting as though they still plan to achieve the goal. They may work very hard at a job from which they know they will never be promoted. Their behavior becomes ritualistic.

In *retreatism* the persons have given up on the prescribed goals and the time for achieving these goals. They are not the least bit concerned about goals or the timing of events in their life. Gubrium describes their behavior as nonnormative. He believes they are most often lifelong isolates.

In *rebellion* you find persons who believe that the culturally prescribed goals and the timing of these events are wrong. They want to revamp and restructure the current social order, creating a new system which they believe will be better. They may keep or reject some of the prescribed goals, and similarly keep or reject some of the expected timetables, depending on their view of what the social system ought to be. The Gray Panthers, led by Maggie Kuhn, who want to bring greater privileges and status to older Americans, would be typical of the rebellion pattern by which individuals hope to reform society.

Gubrium believes that middle-aged and older people who view the schedule of events as under their control perceive themselves as younger and more internally in control of their lives than do those who view the scheduling as externally imposed.

NORMATIVE CONSTRAINTS

At every age in life, society feels that it has a significant investment in the individuals—their footsteps must be guided carefully so as to make them responsible, productive members of society. Socialization is a process of training persons to assume the roles they are expected to occupy during the next years of their lives. Both formally and informally, most socialization and training are directed at children and young adults in order to teach them to fill the roles they must assume as adults if the system is to run well. Informally, parents provide a role model which the children may emulate in order to learn the expected pattern of behavior. Formally, individuals are lectured to by parents, sent to public schools and colleges, and frequently sent to specialized training programs by the company that employs them.

While great expense, time, energy, and effort go into socializing the individuals to assume adult roles, practically no training goes on forty years later to prepare them to leave the world of work and retire in a meaningful fashion. Neither the government, higher education, nor private business has been willing to invest in socializing the individuals for the roles they will be assuming in later life.

In terms of age constraints, the older one becomes the more likely he or she is to believe that there is a proper way for the individual of a given age to behave, or a proper age to marry, etc. On the other hand, the older a person becomes the less likely he or she is to perceive constraints being placed on his or her behavior by society or the generalized other.[12]

Thus, in later life most of the constraints placed on the individual's behavior are by his or her own constraints, that he or she has acquired and internalized through a lifetime of experiences. (Society has generally been little concerned about what older Americans do or don't do.) The French sociologist Emile Durkheim coined the term *anomie* to refer to states of normlessness in which the rules of life change so rapidly that one does not know how to conduct himself or herself. Anomie, or states of normlessness, were thought by Durkheim to be extremely confusing, disconcerting, and frightening to the individual. Durkheim believed that anomie was one of the causes of suicide. The fact that society places very few normative constraints on older persons, and in fact is not too concerned about how they behave, along with the knowledge that the incidence of suicide rises dramatically for men after the age of 65, tends to lead one to believe that Durkheim was correct in asserting that anomie was a cause of suicide. The suicide rate for women, however, is highest between 45–55 and declines in the later years. Therefore, it does not follow the typical pattern of the male. Research on this subject has neither explained the reason for the sex difference nor explored whether the concept of anomie is a useful concept to explain the patterns of suicide for older persons.

Only the future will determine if society will be concerned enough about older individuals to be anxious about the appropriateness of their behavior. At the present time there appear to be relatively few constraints placed on older Americans and a general lack of concern for their lives taken by the larger system.

ATTITUDES TOWARD OLD AGE

The most negative attitudes about older Americans are often expressed by children. Serock and others, in a study of children's attitudes toward older persons, found many of the stereotypes about old people being expressed by children. They quote:

"They are wrinkled and short," "They have gray hair," "They don't go out much," "They chew funny," "Old people sit all day and watch T.V. in their rocking chairs," "They have heart attacks and die."[13]

The children in this study also saw themselves as taking care of older people, getting them their slippers, taking them to the doctor, and occasionally even referred to the fact that they would have to bury them. In a similar study conducted by Judith Burke the children identified older adults as sad, lonely, and not busy; older adults were bypassed on items like "knows a lot" and "I prefer to have this person as a teacher." In a study of knowledge of aging in an elderly population, Helen West and Walter Levy found old people shared many of the same stereotypes of old people that were held by younger age groups. Males were found to be more biased against the old than females and the very old were most biased of all.

While the children in this study expressed all the traditional stereotypes of aging, the Harris study conducted for the National Council on Aging of the adult population was a little more optimistic. Harris found that 74 percent of the public now see the old as friendly and warm, 64 percent as wise from experience, 41 percent as physically active, 35 percent as effectual and proficient, 29 percent as adaptive, and only 5 percent as sexually active.[14]

SOCIAL CLASS DIFFERENCE

The adjustment to old age has only superficially been viewed from the position of one's social class background. Somewhat like the treatment of minority groups, old people are often viewed by the general public as all being alike when in fact they come from different social class backgrounds, have spent much of their lives in different occupations, and have had quite disparate life experiences. Tissue studied the retirement adjustment of middle- and lower-class Americans and found some unexpected differences in the two groups.

Blue-collar workers have generally lived on smaller incomes and been less affluent throughout their lives. The low incomes accorded them by Social Security and other retirement programs often represent only a slight decrease from what they were previously used to. The middle class, on the other hand, is used to secure income and a desirable style of life throughout their adult years. The income loss, if they are forced to rely almost solely on Social Security, is heavy. Moreover, the lower status and near poverty which some older Americans are forced to accept is a considerably greater loss in status for the middle class than it is for the lower class.

It is specifically these issues that Thomas Tissue addressed when comparing middle- and lower-class Americans during the retirement years. Tissue compares the plight of the middle-class retiree to that of "social skidders" in adult life. "Social skidders" are defined by sociologists as people who started in a higher social class or social status position and find themselves going downward to a less desirable position. This skidding can be intergenerational, such as a son who must accept a lower position than the father, and intragenerational, such as a person who is unsuccessful in his or her career and finds himself or herself being demoted. Wilensky and Edwards found "social skidders" to be more rigidly conservative than nonskidders and to hold onto a more rigid middle-class value structure.[15] Tissue states:

> Like a man falling from a skyscraper, our skidder reaches not in the direction of his fall, but back up the structure.[16]

The working class, by comparison, more frequently maintains an intact family unit, is more likely to be living with a spouse, and regularly see children and other family members (Tables 6–5 and 6–6). Middle-class respondents, according to Tissue, are more likely to read, attend movies, participate in hobbies, and watch television. Many of these activities illustrate their capacity for solitary enjoyment. Twenty-nine percent of the middle-class respondents report themselves as not too happy with their current life compared to 17 percent of the working class who report themselves as not too happy. Tissue reports:

> In other words, feeling that retirement was working out worse than anticipated and that freedom from responsibility and additional free time were not the major benefits of old age and missing at least some part of one's previous job was a response pattern more common to those with higher socioeconomic origins.[17]

Table 6–5 Life Space and Perceived Life Space

	MIDDLE CLASS	WORKING CLASS
Life space		
Low (0–49 contacts)	47%	32%
High (50 plus contacts)	53	68
	100%	100%
	(127)	(129)
Perceived life space*		
Severe loss (in at least 4 of 5 roles)	55%	40%
Moderate to no loss (in 3 or fewer roles)	45	60
	100%	100%
	(127)	(129)

*Significant at .02 level.

Source: Thomas Tissue, "Downward Mobility in Old Age," in Socialization and the Life Cycle, ed. Peter J. Rose (New York: St. Martin's Press, 1979), p. 356. Reprinted with permission of the Society for the Study of Social Problems.

Table 6–6 Family

	MIDDLE CLASS	WORKING CLASS
Currently lives with spouse*	23% (127)	36% (129)
Lives in own home*	17% (127)	28% (129)
Children living in California* (For those with living children)		
Has none	11%	26%
Has one	28	30
Has two	29	20
Has three or more	32	24
	100% (104)	100% (105)
Sees at least one child daily (For those with living children)	26% (103)	38% (105)

*Significant at .05 level.

Source: Thomas Tissue, "Downward Mobility in Old Age," in *Socialization and the Life Cycle,* ed. Peter J. Rose (New York: St. Martin's Press, 1979), p. 356. Reprinted with permission of the Society for the Study of Social Problems.

Being dissatisfied with their retirement life, the middle class gives strong verbal support to the ethic of hard work for its own sake and a belief that one's fate is the result of one's abilities rather than luck or chance. They appear to be more committed and more conservative in clinging to middle-class values than the general population. Is this the result of their status loss and their reaching back to a more preferred time in their life and the values that they believed in then? Only future research will be able to determine if this is the case. Wilensky and Edwards would suggest that "social skidders" respond by exaggerated allegiance to the values of the system in which they perceive that they have failed.

CONCLUSION

No individual is ever entirely free to do exactly what he or she would like to do but rather is conditioned by a socialization process that teaches one how one is to behave and respond in social situations. Sociologists refer to roles as being expected patterns of behavior associated with certain jobs, functions, or tasks in society. Since life involves a gradual, but constant process of change, one is often learning to assume new roles and relinquishing old roles. Moreover, there are social expectations about the desirable age to assume certain roles. Ideally one marries and enters a career in one's early twenties, has children in the middle twenties, achieves a career peak in the middle forties, has the children launched by the late forties, and retires in the early to middle sixties.

The problem for many adults is that they cannot always assume the roles at precisely the expected age, and sometimes family and career goals are not reached at the prescribed time. Time-disoriented life patterns cause the individual some degree of frustration and strain, according to Gubrium.

There are both advantages and disadvantages to the assumption of retirement roles. The advantage is that society does not feel that it has a large stake in what the person does during the retirement years. Older persons are freer to choose among a variety of different roles than perhaps any other age group. Simultaneously, while there are normative constraints placed on persons to make their behavior conform at any age in life, there seems to be less pressure on older persons to perform the roles in a prescribed manner than there is on any other age group. Old age involves considerable freedom from external social pressure. It should be said, however, that by this age in life most persons have internalized society's norms into a well-developed conscience which directs most of their behavior and does not require external controls. The major problem with the roles assumed by older persons is that they are perceived by others to be generally low in status, privilege, and power.

Thus while one has greater freedom to choose among a variety of roles in later life, most of these are not highly valued roles in the society. They often involve a loss of status for older persons. This loss of status is perhaps greatest for middle-class Americans who have, prior to retirement, most often maintained responsible positions in the community, and who, at the time of retirement, experience the greatest loss in income, privilege, and power.

KEY TERMS

anticipatory socialization	conformity
life space	innovation
role	ritualism
status	retreatism
socialization	rebellion
anomie	

SUGGESTED READINGS

BELL, BILL D., "Role Set Orientations and Life Satisfaction: A New Look at an Old Theory," in *Time, Roles and Self in Old Age,* ed. Jaber F. Gubrium, pp. 148–64. New York: Human Sciences Press, 1976.

BURKE, JUDITH LEE, "Young Children's Attitudes and Perceptions of Older Adults," *International Journal of Aging and Human Development,* 14, no. 3 (1981–82), 205–22.

COX, HAROLD, AND ALBERT BHAK, "Determinants of Age Based on Residential Segregation," *Sociological Symposium,* no. 29 (Winter 1980), pp. 27–41.

CUMMING, E., AND W. HENRY, *Growing Old: The Process of Disengagement.* New York: Basic Books, 1961.

DURKHEIM, EMILE, *Suicide.* New York. Free Press, 1951.

GOSLIN, DAVID H., *Handbook of Socialization Theory and Research.* Skokie, Ill.: Rand McNally, 1969.

GUBRIUM, JABER F., *Time, Roles and Self in Old Age,* p. 113. New York: Human Sciences Press, 1976.

HARRIS, LOUIS, AND ASSOCIATES, *The Myth and Reality of Aging in America.* Washington, D.C.: The National Council on the Aging, Inc., 1975.

KALISH, RICHARD A., *Late Adulthood: Perspectives on Human Development,* p. 47. Monterey, CA: Brooks/Cole, 1975.

KIMMEL, DOUGLAS C., *Adulthood and Aging,* p. 313. New York: John Wiley, 1974.

MERTON, ROBERT, *Social Theory and Social Structure,* p. 140. New York: Free Press, 1957.

NEUGARTEN, B. L., J. W. MOORE, AND J. C. LOWE, "Age Norms, Age Constraints and Age Socialization," *American Journal of Sociology,* 70 (1965), 710–17.

PHILLIPS, BERNARD S., "A Role Theory Approach to Adjustment in Old Age," *American Sociological Review,* 22 (1957), 212–17.

REICHARD, S., F. LIVSON, AND P. C. PETERSON, *Aging and Personality: A Study of 87 Older Men.* New York: John Wiley, 1962.

SEROCK, KATHY, AND OTHERS, "As Children See Old Folks," in *Focus Aging,* ed. Harold Cox, pp. 102–103. Guilford, CT: Dushkin, 1978.

TISSUE, THOMAS, "Downward Mobility in Old Age," in *Socialization and the Life Cycle,* ed. Peter J. Rose, pp. 356–67. New York: St. Martin's Press, 1979.

WEST, HELEN L., AND WALTER J. LEVY, "Knowledge of Aging in An Elderly Population," *Research on Aging,* 3, no. 2 (June 1981), 202–210.

7
AGING MINORITY
GROUP MEMBERS

After all there is but one race—humanity.

George Moore
The Bending of the Bough, Act III

Many social scientists believe that relations between dominant and minority groups can be identified and defined on the basis of the power variable. Eitzen argues that from this perspective the first and most crucial aspect of a minority group is that it is dominated by a more powerful group. A second characteristic of a minority group is that it is comprised of people whose characteristics differ significantly from the dominant group. These characteristics must be easily visible to the casual observer; they must make a difference. A third characteristic of minority group members is that they are stereotyped and often condemned by the dominant group. Stereotypes (often negative generalizations) about the minority group are held in the minds of the dominant group. These stereotypes provide the dominant group a rationale for keeping the minority group down and are sometimes accepted by the minority group itself. Common stereotypes that one often hears are that blacks are lazy, and that women are overly emotional. The final characteristic of minority groups is that they are all singled out for different and unfair treatment. Whether the discrimination is subtle or blatant, the effect is always detrimental to the best interests of the minority group and frequently detrimental to the dominant group.

One can see, therefore, that the descriptive criteria of a minority group from this perspective include relative powerlessness, visible differentiation from the majority, negative stereotyping, and discrimination.

Eitzen delineates some of the bases of minority group status:

1. Race, which is based on genetic differences among individuals and often results in differential treatment.
2. Ethnicity, which identifies one as a member of a distinct subculture, which is in one way or another different from the dominant culture.

3. Religion, which also is used as the basis for placing people in inferior positions. Jews have been persecuted because of their religious identity. The Amish are merely looked down upon by the dominant groups.

4. The impoverished comprise a minority group in most societies.

5. Sex, which singles women out for different treatment than men. Women are often considered incapable of leadership and relegated to less important roles in the social system.

6. Homosexuals and other subgroups are often identified as deviant by the dominant group in the society and therefore treated in a discriminatory manner.

7. The aged are often relatively powerless and discriminated against by the dominant group.

8. The deformed, handicapped, and obese frequently experience discrimination because they are different.[1]

Jackson, in her work on minority aging, defines Anglo-American men as the dominant group. She then specifies what she believes to be the minority groups in the United States:

1. Black American women
2. Black American men
3. American Indian women
4. American Indian men
5. Asian American women
6. Asian American men
7. Hispanic American women
8. Hispanic American men
9. Anglo American women[2]

Whether the aged are or are not a minority group was discussed in Chapter 2. There are those such as Rose and Peterson who believe that the aged share negatively defined physiological characteristics of being old which are easily observable and can therefore be used as the basis for different treatment. Moreover, they are generally negatively defined by others in the social system and receive less income and share a lower status than other age groups. Recognizing their unequal treatment, Rose and Peterson believe they band together and identify themselves as being discriminated against and thereby form a subculture. Gordon Streib has argued against older persons being considered a minority group. He doubts the exclusiveness of the group since all persons who live long enough will eventually become a member. Simultaneously, Streib believes old people are much too heterogeneous, coming from different social class, racial, and ethnic groups to form a common identity at age 65.[3]

It is probably true that the aged in American society do not think of themselves as a minority group, do not share a group identity, and do not form a subculture. On the other hand, many people are required to retire at age 70, do lose occupational roles and status at that time, are forced to live on approximately half the income they received during their earlier years, and have limited resources to maneuver as they attempt to find solutions to their current problems. In these ways older persons, whether recognizing themselves as a minority group or not, are discriminated against and do receive differential treatment.

If one accepts the fact that older persons in American society face unique problems not experienced by other age groups, then it becomes relevant to ask what the consequences are of being a member of a minority group and also of being old. One often encounters the concept of being placed in double jeopardy—being old and black; or of triple jeopardy—being old, black, and female. In this chapter an attempt will be made to look at some of the unique problems confronting aging members of minority groups.

DEMOGRAPHIC CHARACTERISTICS
OF THE MINORITY ELDERLY

There has been a tendency to lump all different groups into two categories for statistical analysis and presentation of the data. Thus, we often see tables headed by columns: nonwhite and white. The lumping of all minorities into the nonwhite category blurs many of the distinctions among the aging minorities.

American Indians, for example, generally have a shorter life expectancy than blacks, but one would not be aware of this when these two groups are placed in the nonwhite category. Blacks have more households headed by females than the Japanese but this also could not be discerned if both groups are placed in the nonwhite category.

In terms of the numbers of the various minority groups in the United States that live beyond age 55, we find whites to be the largest group, followed by blacks, Hispanics, Pacific Asians, and American Indians. The 55+ group of whites who are noninstitutionalized numbers 41,204,000; the comparable black group numbers 3,872,000; the Hispanic, 1,113,000; the Pacific Asian 275,000; and the American Indian 89,000 (Table 7–1).

There have been quite disparate growth patterns of the various minority groups in the United States in the last seventy years. Ultimately this affects the number of old minority group members we find for these groups. Jacquelyne Jackson reports that between 1900 and 1970 the total Japanese population increased by 683 percent, while the blacks were increasing by 255 percent. Both in terms of numbers and percentage increases, the growth rates of the aged were greatest for Asian Americans and least for the American Indians.

The black population has been moving out of rural areas and into the large cities. In 1978 the Bureau of the Census found that 55 percent of all black aged lived in the central cities.[4]

In 1978, 84 percent of the Hispanic elderly population lived in metro-

Table 7–1 Population of Elderly Minority
Group Members

RACE	AGE	NUMBER
White	55+	41,204,000
Black	55+	3,872,000
Hispanic	55+	1,113,000
Pacific Asian	55+	275,000
American Indian	55+	89,000

Source: "Policy Issues Concerning the Elderly Minorities," DHHS Publication No. (OHDS) 80–20670
(Washington, D.C.: Federal Council on the Aging,
1979), p. 20.

Table 7–2 Minority Populations in Urban Areas

	WHITE	BLACK	HISPANIC
Number Living in Urban Areas	10,700,000	2,080,000	924,000
Percent of Total Group	27	55	84

Source: "Policy Issues Concerning the Elderly Minorities," DHHS Publication No. (OHDS)
80–20670 (Washington, D.C.: Federal Council on the Aging, 1979), p. 27.

politan areas (Table 7–2).[5] The older Pacific Asians tend to be concentrated in
Los Angeles, Honolulu, San Francisco, San Diego, Boston, New York, and
Washington. The census information does not specify the exact numbers of Pacific Asians at the present time. The data of the Census Bureau is even less complete regarding the American Indians. The percentage of American Indians
who lived on identified reservations ranged from 3 percent among the Catawla
to 77 percent among the Pueblo. According to the final report on the first National Indian Conference on Aging, there is a growing shift of the elderly Indian
population to the urban areas.[6]

  The life expectancy pattern for all aging minorities follows a general
trend of lagging far behind the white life expectancy at birth but of almost being
equal by age 65 and exceeding the white life expectancy thereafter. The life expectancy in 1977 of whites at birth was about five years greater than nonwhites,
but this gap is considerably reduced by age 65. Since 1900 the gains in life expectancy have been greater for blacks than for whites. The U.S. Department of
Health, Education, and Welfare reports that from 1900–1976, the average
length of life for blacks and other nonwhite groups increased by 35.3 years compared to 25.9 years for whites. For women, life expectancy is almost identical at
age 70 (14.4 for white females and 14.3 for black females and others) and is re-
versed at age 75 with the blacks living longer.[7] (See Table 7–3.)

  Elderly Hispanics comprise only about 4 percent of the total Hispanic
population. Even though it is generally accepted that the life span of Hispanics is
much shorter than that of their white counterparts, concrete data are
nonexistent.

In a report prepared for the National Advisory and Resource Committee, Dr. Fujii reported that even though the proportion of the Pacific Asian elderly to the population of Pacific Asians is very small, those who reach 65 years of age live longer in comparison to their white counterparts.[8]

In 1978 the National Clearinghouse of Aging reported on life expectancy of the American Indian. At birth the life expectancy for the Indian was reported to be lower than for whites. By age 45 the gap had diminished. In 1970, American Indians 45 years old had a life expectancy of 29.1 years compared to 30.6 years for whites. At age 55, the American Indians had a life expectancy of 22.0 years compared to 22.3 for whites. At 65, the American Indians had a life expectancy of 15.4 years compared to 15.2 for whites.

It is often assumed that the black family is more extended (including brother, sisters, aunts, uncles, and cousins) than the white and includes an informal support network of relatives providing daycare services, parental surrogates, and related services more commonly handled by other organized groups for the white family. The Federal Council on the Aging found that most older blacks own their own homes and in most cases are the heads of households. In 1978 elderly black women headed 32 percent of black families where the head of the household was 65 and over. Approximately 41 percent of these elderly households headed by black women had children under 18 living with them, in comparison to 9 percent of families headed by elderly white women.[9]

According to the Asociacion Nacional Pro Personas Majores's final report on the Second National Hispanic Conference on Aging, the widely held belief that the Hispanic elders live in extended family situations simply is not true. In 1975, only 9.7 percent of the elderly of Spanish origin, the majority of whom were women, lived in extended-family situations. Sixty percent lived in husband-wife arrangements, and the other 40 percent (most of whom were women) lived alone.[10] Census data indicates that only 18 percent of the Hispanic elderly age 55 and over live alone or with nonrelatives in comparison to 24 percent of the total United States population 55 and older.[11] The Federal Council on the Aging data indicates that within the Hispanic communities, neighbors, friends, and churches provide the elderly with some support services.

The family structure of some of the Pacific Asian groups was affected by past U.S. immigration laws, which prevented Asian males from bringing their families with them to the United States. The Federal Council on the Aging reports that proportions of Pacific Asian households headed by men living alone were twice as high in 1970 as the comparable proportion for the total U.S. population. Thus, many Asian men are deprived of family support during their later years. For Asians who do live in a family setting, the information is at the present confusing. Studies at San Diego State University indicate that families and neighbors serve both as a coping mechanism for older persons and as traditional support networks.[12] Other studies of Asian families have reported a slow disintegration of family structure.[13]

Past studies have indicated that older American Indians still play an important role in the extended family, particularly those living on the Indian reservations.[14] The increasing movement of the Indians off the reservations to urban areas has often resulted in the acculturation of the young American Indians. Thus, the extended Indian family appears to be rapidly eroding in the United States.

As one might expect, the education levels attained by the minority groups are often considerably lower than those attained by the whites. The Federal Council on the Aging reports:

> The median levels of educational attainment in the U.S. in 1978 for whites 60–64 (12.2), 65–69 (11.6), 70–74 (10.1) and 75 and over (8.8), while for elderly blacks 60–64 (8.5), 65–69 (7.9), 70–74 (6.6) and 75 and over (5.9).[15]

The Federal Council on the Aging report further indicated that 38 percent of the 60+ Hispanic females and 43 percent of their male counterparts had been to school for less than five years. The median number of years of education for the entire Hispanic population was 6.6 for males and 5.9 for females.[16]

Like the elders of other minority groups, three-fifths of older American Indians have completed less than eight years of schooling and only 2 percent had completed four or more years of college.[17]

INCOME AND EMPLOYMENT

The general pattern that we find in the elderly minorities beyond age 55 is one of higher rates of unemployment and lower incomes than the general population. The Federal Council on the Aging reports that older black men (55+) had an unemployment rate of 5.3 percent compared to 2.6 percent for the white group. Older black women had an unemployment rate of 4.5 percent compared to 3.0 percent for their white counterparts. Two-person black families with the head aged 65+ in 1977 had a median income of $5201 compared to the same group of white families with a median income of $8700.[18] Approximately one in three blacks aged 55+ lived in poverty in 1978. Thirty percent of all blacks aged 55+ lived in poverty in contrast to 10 percent of the whites.[19]

In 1977 the median income for Hispanics was $7538, which falls in between the median incomes for blacks and whites. The rate of unemployment for Hispanics 55 and older was 5.8 percent, which is higher than both the black and white groups.[20]

There were no current figures on the median incomes and unemployment rates of older Asian Americans. The Pacific Asian Research Project noted that in 1969 the median annual income for Japanese males was $266 less than that for white males; the figure for Japanese females was $128 less than that for white females.[21]

In terms of employment and income, American Indians seem the most deprived. Because of limited education and lack of opportunity to develop their abilities, American Indians are usually employed in low-paying, unskilled roles in mining, forestry, and manual labor. The income of older American Indians was well below that of all other groups. The median income for males 65+ was $1654; for females, $1162. Moreover, fear of losing their government support in the form of social security, supplemental security income, and food stamps prevents many of the Indians from selling their arts and crafts in order to supplement their income.[22]

While social security is the primary source of retirement income for both the dominant and minority elderly, there are significant differences in the social security benefits received by the various groups. Since social security benefits are based on past earnings as a general rule, all the minority groups receive smaller benefits than white males. Past discrimination in employment has kept most of the minority group earnings low throughout their working years thus resulting in lower social security benefits during retirement. In 1970 black workers, both men and women, received social security pensions averaging $250 per year less than those for whites.

Home Ownership

We find disparate patterns of home ownership among the various minority elderly. The Bureau of the Census estimates that 71 percent of all black families headed by elderly (60+) persons owned their homes in comparison to 84 percent of all white families. Since home ownership is relatively high among blacks, they are least likely of all the minorities to live in public housing or government-subsidized rental units.[23]

Fifty-four percent of elderly Hispanics own their own home and 46 percent are renters. In terms of home ownerships, the Hispanic group seems to be in poorer circumstances than the whites and the other minority groups.

A study done by the San Diego Center on Aging found that 83 percent of older Japanese owned (or were buying) their own homes. Only 3 percent of this group were living with their adult children.[24] The Japanese Americans appear to be as well off as whites in terms of home ownership. The studies made no attempt to assess the quality or value of the homes owned by the different groups.

There were no available data on home ownership by American Indians. The Federal Council on the Aging reports that elderly Indians were more likely to live in two- (or more) person households and in rural areas than elderly persons of all races.

Sex Composition

Sex composition varies considerably among the elderly ethnic minority groups. Jacquelyne Jackson reports that there were more females than males among Koreans, whites, blacks, Japanese, Hispanics, and Indians (in descending order). There were more males than females among the Filipino and Chinese. Thus, there were 64 males per 100 females among the Koreans, but there were 431.4 males per 100 females among the Filipinos.[25]

Living Arrangements

Jackson identifies differences between the living arrangements of the blacks, Hispanics, and whites (Table 7–4). The greater proportion of black and Hispanic female-headed families in comparison to whites can in part be explained by the difference in the longevity of the males in these three groups. Black and Hispanic men, who are more likely to have a shorter life expectancy than whites, leave more widows who become the female heads of family.

Moving in with relatives is more common among women because they are more likely to be widowed and poor. The 1977 data indicate, however, that among blacks a slightly larger proportion of males than females 65–74 years of age were living with other relatives (Table 7–4).

The proportion of aged persons living with family members has been decreasing for both males and females of all ethnic and racial groups. The trend for all aged persons is to maintain their independence as long as possible and not to move in with other relatives. The availability of age-segregated and government-subsidized housing has made it less necessary for older persons to move in with other family members. Most older persons apparently prefer to live near their children but not with them as long as they can maintain independent living arrangements. The more economic conditions improve for older Americans, the less likely they will be to live in multigeneration families.

SOCIAL ASPECTS OF AGING
FOR MINORITY GROUP MEMBERS

Sociologists, in viewing the effect of aging on minority group members, are concerned about the changing role and status of these persons, the conditions that bring about these changes, and societal reactions to these changes.

Anyone's life course involves a series of role changes that accompany significant social events in one's life. One common pattern: The child begins school, graduates from elementary school and enters high school, graduates from high

Table 7–3 Life Expectancy by Sex, Race, and Age, 1976

AGE	WHITE		BLACK	
	Male	*Female*	*Male*	*Female*
0	69.7	77.3	64.1	72.6
65	13.7	18.1	13.8	17.6
70	10.9	14.4	11.3	14.3
75	8.5	11.2	9.7	12.2
85	5.1	6.4	7.2	9.1

Source: National Center for Health Statistics, *Vital Statistics of the U.S., 1976*, Vol. II, Sec. 5 (Washington, D.C.: U.S. Department of H.E.W., 1976).

Table 7–4 Living Arrangements of Blacks, Hispanics, and Whites, by Sex, 65–74 and 75+ Years of Age, 1970 and 1977

RACE/ETHNICITY AND SEX	YEAR AND AGE			
	1970		1977	
	65–74	75+	65–74	75+
Black females				
% primary individuals	31.8	33.1	32.0**	41.0**
% family heads	17.8	17.1	19.0**	22.3**
% wives of family heads	31.9	15.2	35.7**	12.4
% with other relatives*	15.7	31.3	10.7	22.7
% secondary individuals	2.8	3.3	2.6	1.6
Black males				
% primary individuals	21.6	24.5	16.8	32.8**
% of family heads	66.5	56.0	65.9	50.6
% with other relatives*	7.0	14.2	12.6**	14.0
% secondary individuals	4.9	5.3	4.7	2.6
Hispanic females				
% primary individuals	21.4	25.0	27.1**	29.6**
% family heads	12.6	12.2	10.8	17.8**
% wives of family heads	38.8	18.4	37.8	15.1
% with other relatives*	25.6	42.8	23.1	35.2
% secondary individuals	1.6	1.6	1.2	2.3**
Hispanic males				
% primary individuals	13.9	16.2	14.8**	—
% family heads	74.4	59.1	71.3	—
% with other relatives*	10.1	22.4	13.4	—
% secondary individuals	1.6	2.3	0.5	—
White females				
% primary individuals	33.2	41.1	36.5**	49.3**
% family heads	7.8	9.8	7.4	8.5
% wives of family heads	45.4	21.0	47.9**	20.8
% with other relatives*	12.2	26.3	7.0	19.8
% secondary individuals	1.4	1.8	1.2	1.6
White males				
% primary individuals	13.0	20.3	12.1	20.1
% family heads	81.1	66.0	81.2**	71.9**
% with other relatives*	4.6	13.6	5.1**	6.8
% secondary individuals	1.3	0.1	1.6**	1.2**

*In 1977, "with other relatives" includes individuals in primary or secondary families or others not in subfamilies.
**Indicates percentage increase between 1970 and 1977.

Source: Jacquelyne J. Jackson, *Minorities and Aging* (Belmont, CA: Wadsworth, 1980), p. 134. © 1980 by Wadsworth, Inc. Reprinted by permission of Wadsworth Publishing Company.

school and enters college, graduates from college and enters an occupation, marries, has children, watches the children leave home, becomes a grandparent, retires, experiences the death of a spouse and ultimately, dies himself. At each of life's junctures there are new roles and statuses that are assumed by the individual and that bring new responsibilities requiring new skills. From the sociological perspective, one's life can be viewed as a series of adjustments to rather predictable and periodic changes in one's social position.

In discussing the adjustments of later life, Irving Rosow defines *roles* as the expected behavior considered appropriate for any set of rights and duties. He defines *status* as representing a formal office or social position that can be clearly identified by name, for example, president of the Chamber of Commerce. The person occupying this position can be classified and located within the social structure.[26]

Some of the major institutionalized roles which Rosow identifies are occupation, social class, family, and age. He is not sure, however, that there is a consensus in society about what the age norms (expected patterns of behavior for persons of a given age) are.

He argues that the greatest role and status changes among the elderly occur when the individual has lost the central institutionalized roles and statuses in family, occupation, and community. The major status losses, from this perspective, would be retirement, widowhood, and inability to perform public roles as the result of failing health. The more important institutional roles grow steadily during adulthood, peaking in late middle age.[27]

Role emptying is a term used by Rosow to indicate the shrinking responsibilities and duties within a role which often occurs during the later years of life. One is a parent but no longer has many parental responsibilities since the children have left home. As a result of their loss of responsibility and function, the aged are often seen as socially expendable. A major problem of the later years is that individuals are not socialized for old age and that roles of the elderly are not specific or structured.[28]

Formal institutionalized roles that center around occupation and community functions are most often performed by middle-aged adults. Rosow identifies the informal roles as more prevalent among the very young and very old and center on family, social groups, and neighborhoods. He believes the quality of life of older persons could be considerably improved by strengthening their informal roles.

Families, social groups, and neighborhoods tend to be comprised of individuals from the same race and social class background. They are, therefore, most often homogeneous groups. As a result, Jackson argues that if Rosow's suggestions for strengthening the informal roles and social networks of older persons became public policy, they would perpetuate the segregation of society.[29] Rosow appears to have advocated these changes as a means of improving the status and position of older persons in society. It is doubtful that he intended to perpetuate the continued segregation of social groups and neighborhoods although this could be one of the results.

SERVICE NEEDS OF THE ELDERLY MINORITIES

Throughout history, the family has been the group responsible for its older members. The treatment of the elderly, whether favorable or unfavorable, was considered primarily a family matter. Modern industrial nations, with their ability to produce surpluses of goods and services, made retirement possible. Since the advent of social security and other federally funded programs, there has been a tendency to shift the responsibility for aged family members from the family and to the government and other institutions. Of the actual government funded social services provided for older persons, many have felt that most of the services went principally to the white group and that considerably fewer services were provided for aged minority group members.

The myth used to justify the fact that elderly members of minority groups did not receive the quantity and quality of services they would seem to deserve is that the typical minority group family is considered to be more extended than the white family and that it looks after its older members, thus rendering government services unnecessary. It is often observed that the family support systems for American Indians, Asian Americans, blacks, and Hispanics are very strong. By way of comparison, the extended family of aged whites is reputedly weaker than that of other ethnic groups, making government services to them more necessary.

In fact, the lack of services to older minority group members has meant that their families have had either to provide for them or to abandon them. Minority families might well have liked to shift the responsibility for their older members from themselves to the government, but they have not had the opportunity of doing so. The myth of the stronger family support system for minority elderly is believed by some to have been invented by public planners as a rationalization for not providing more services for the minority elderly.

The findings of the Federal Council on the Aging study indicate the following special problems of the minority-group elderly that should be considered by government planners:

1. Language and cultural barriers to services;
2. Fewer median school years completed than those completed by the total elderly population;
3. Low-paying, blue-collar jobs (many without social security or retirement benefits);
4. Inadequate benefits from federal income supplement programs;
5. Fewer opportunities for training and employment for those on income maintenance programs;
6. A struggle against skyrocketing inflation, high taxes, and increasing energy costs;
7. Poor housing conditions, reflective of a federal housing policy unresponsive to minority needs;

8. A fear of the increasing incidence of crime committed against their age group;

9. Insufficient social and health care services, both mental and physical;

10. An underrepresentation of members of their ethnic groups on federal, state, and local policymaking bodies;

11. An emotional and mental attachment to their ethnic communities (i.e., natural support networks);

12. A fear of being removed from their cultural surroundings and placed into institutions such as nursing homes and other long-term care facilities; and

13. An underrepresentation of the number and socioeconomic characteristics of each of their ethnic groups by the census.[30]

The Federal Council on the Aging, after conducting a symposium, hearings, and meetings to discuss the problems of services to the minority elderly, identified the following problems, charging that current programs

1. Are designed without taking into account cultural diversities within the aging population;

2. Overlook the traditional role of many older minorities in their extended families;

3. Do not adequately involve the minority aging communities and their advocates in planning and implementation procedures;

4. Suffer from a shortage of bilingual and bicultural staff on the federal, state, regional, and local levels;

5. Underestimate the need of older minority subgroups for mental health services;

6. Do not provide sufficient funds to minority colleges for the training of minority personnel, and for research in the field of minority aging;

7. Use reporting and coding systems that do not accurately represent, and differentiate between the number of older minorities who are in need and those who are recipients of services;

8. Lack coordination between federal policies and policies of state and local levels of government.[31]

SUBCULTURAL AND VALUE DISPARITIES BETWEEN THE DOMINANT GROUP AND MINORITY GROUPS

Assimilation is used by sociologists to mean the fusion of different and often disparate groups of individuals into one homogeneous unit. America, at the outset, was made up of a variety of different ethnic groups coming primarily from northwestern Europe, and had a reputation for being a melting pot in which these groups were gradually assimilated into one national culture. Later immigrants frequently came from southeastern Europe, Asia, and other parts of the world. While the early immigrants were Caucasians, the later immigrants were frequently comprised of different racial groups. While assimilation was in the early history of the country the most common pattern, it has not been the only pattern, and it has been selective. Assimilation has generally occurred more rapidly for Caucasians and more slowly for members of other racial groups. Americans whose racial features set them apart from Caucasians have not found assimilation so easy. The prevailing pattern in America has been the integration of Caucasian ethnic groups and the segregation of other groups.

While assimilation refers to a blending of two cultures, *amalgamation* means a biological interbreeding of two peoples of distinct physical appearance until they become one stock. As with assimilation, amalgamation has more commonly taken place between different ethnic groups comprised of Caucasians than between Caucasians and other racial groups. The fact that the study of aging minority group members is considered a problem area in social gerontology indicates that members of several different ethnic and racial groups have not been fully assimilated into American society and in fact are part of a subculture sufficiently different to be identifiable. Moreover, members of these subcultures are seen as having unique problems in later life that have in the past resulted from their minority group status.

The history of blacks from the slave period to the present is one of (1) assimilation from a variety of national and cultural backgrounds to American society and (2) indoctrination with the prevailing values. If slavery did not destroy most of the previous cultural heritage of the slaves, it certainly limited blacks' communication with the previous culture as well as the opportunity of maintaining previous cultural traditions, rituals, and practices. Blacks often adopted the values of the white plantation community, somewhat modified by their slave status. Names, religious beliefs, and a variety of other values were frequently transmitted to the slaves through the white plantation owners and their families. While blacks were thus indoctrinated with certain white attitudes, the rigid system of segregation and discrimination prevented them from being totally assimilated into the white community. While amalgamation between blacks and whites during the slave period was usually the result of a relationship between white slave owners (or their sons) and black women, formal marriage was quite uncommon. Since the Civil War, amalgamation has been the exception rather than the rule in black/white relations.

Given the fact that American blacks have generally been in the country for several generations and that in public schools and the society at large they have been indoctrinated with the prevailing values of the culture, one critical question is to what degree can we consider the problems of elderly blacks to be unique from whites or other ethnic groups?

Generally, black social gerontologists have argued that the problems of older blacks should be seen as unique. Gossie Harold Hudson, chairman of the Division of Social Services at Lincoln University, asserts:

Regrettably most whites and many blacks do not label the problems of older blacks as Special, avoiding thereby careful or even superficial examination of their own prejudice.[32]

Duran Bell and others argue that black problems are primarily a result of economic deprivation and that any difference found between older blacks and older whites as a group would disappear altogether if social class differences were removed. They argue that if you compared lower-class blacks and lower-class whites, few racial differences in health or income are found. Gail Zellman and Duran Bell further assert that future research on minority elderly should pose implicit interracial comparisons with a recognition of the importance of social class comparisons. André Hammonds believes, however, that even if the strength of the relationship in which elderly blacks and whites are compared is diminished, by social-class comparisons the relationship will have merely been interpreted and not explained away. In actuality both blackness and socioeconomic status must be understood in attacking the problems of black elderly. Hammonds concludes that the problems of the black aged are unique and to some extent shared by all elderly blacks. The black elderly have experienced relative deprivation throughout their lives, being lower than whites in income, in opportunities of mobility, health, and housing, and in other ways. Being poor in old age is not a novel experience for blacks, since many of them have been poor most of their lives. Many elderly whites, on the other hand, become poor for the first time in their lives when they retire. The problem of elderly blacks is unique according to Jacquelyne Jackson because these people have suffered from institutionalized racism throughout their entire lives and therefore confront the problems of aging from a social position different from others.

Richard Seiden examined white and nonwhite suicide rates throughout the life cycle. He found that both white and nonwhite suicide rates increase throughout the teen years and into early adulthood (about age 30); then the black suicide rate begins to drop while the white suicide rate continues to rise (Figure 7–1). Seiden, like Hammonds and Jackson, argues that blacks experience economic and social deprivation early in life and develop coping mechanisms very early to deal with unfair situations. These coping mechanisms are carried into later life and help explain the lower suicide rate for blacks after age 30, according to Seiden. He asserts that because of racism the nonwhite elderly have been shut out of most positions of occupational power and authority. Therefore, retirement does not lead to the same loss of status for blacks that it does for whites.

THE ASIAN AMERICAN

Most of the aged Chinese Americans today represent the first-generation Chinese Americans. F. L. K. Hsu argues that the values which they brought with them to America were quite different from the prevailing values of American

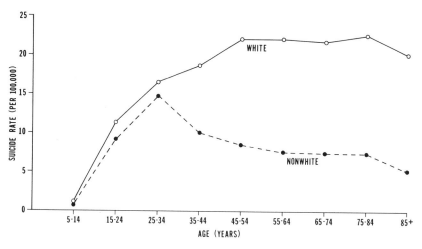

Figure 7–1 Suicide by Age and Race, U.S., 1975
Source: National Center for Health Statistics

society. Hsu believes that Chinese society discourages financial independence from parents and the extended family, instead encouraging interdependence. American values of individual achievement, upward mobility, and competitiveness were alien to Chinese beliefs. Hsu asserts that for Chinese Americans reared to believe that children should not become financially independent of their parents, contemporary American values are most disconcerting. While in the homeland, the elderly maintain control over income, property, and jobs; no such control can be exercised in the United States. The only absolute claim the elderly Chinese can attempt to place on their children for respect is community pressure. In China the upward mobility of an entire generation would have been impossible according to Hsu, whereas in the United States it was possible. Thus the first-generation Chinese Americans have great difficulty maintaining the family form, lifestyle, and senior status that they had been taught to cherish in their homeland.[33]

Richard Kalish and Sharon Moriwaki point out that by law the first-generation Japanese American could not own property. Property was often purchased in the name of a son or daughter, the natural child of the alien Japanese. What this meant was that the first-generation Japanese could neither own property nor obtain citizenship until so late in their lives that financial security was difficult to achieve. In the homeland, ownership of property and the accumulation of financial resources would have allowed the older Japanese to maintain a position of leadership and respect in the eyes of younger family members and thereby assure themselves that their children would look after them during their later years. Many of today's aged Japanese were even less likely to accumulate property because of their initial expectations of returning to their homeland after making their fortune. When unable to do so, it was most often too late in life to establish the rule of primogeniture, by which the eldest son would care for parents in their later years. Even the property bought in the name of the children was confiscated during World War II. Ultimately most of the property was restored after the war.

Richard Kalish and Sharon Moriwaki state:

> The Issei, the fruits of his most productive years often destroyed by the lengthy incarceration, and his dominant role having been effectively undermined, was forced to return to what he had been doing—often required to work with his sons or sons-in-law not as a respected patriarch but an equal or even subordinate.[35]

Kalish and Moriwaki observe that Americans who value autonomy and independence often become quite concerned when adult children turn from their elderly parents and fail to grant them a respected senior status. How much more upsetting this must be in a culture in which independence and autonomy are negatively valued in the first place!

Hsu observes that competition was not alien to traditional Chinese culture but that the purpose of the competition was to enhance the family rather than the individual. Elderly Chinese who are part of an extended family have a feeling of belonging, meaning, and pride through group identification that older Chinese Americans are often denied.

Some of Japanese values are congruous with American values. Hard work, achievement, self-control, dependability, manners, and thrift seem to be values shared by both cultures. Elderly Chinese would appear, for a variety of reasons, to have more value conflicts as immigrant Americans. Elderly Chinese in traditional China were part of a network of primary relations stemming from the family. Usually all sons inherit the family wealth or land equally.[36]

Many of the early Chinese and Japanese immigrants to the United States intended to make their fortune and then return to a superior status in their homeland. For this reason, these early immigrants most often tried to indoctrinate their children with the traditional attitudes and values of their native land, according to Kalish and Moriwaki. As with other ethnic groups the second generations were more likely to adopt the standards of conduct of the country in which they were born rather than those of their parents' homeland. This contributed to considerable generational strain between the older family members and their children.

Kalish and Moriwaki observe that the older Chinese and Japanese were often caught in an ideological dilemma:

> On the one hand, they recognized and at least to some extent accepted the values of their adopted homeland that being a burden to children is bad, that having the privacy and independence of one's own home is good, that the education of grandchildren should not be sacrificed for

the care of grandparents. On the other hand, they recall their earlier learning that the older person is entitled not only to financial support, but to personal care and virtual devotion.[37]

The pattern of adjustment of American Indians to the dominant American culture is different from that of any other minority group. While others came to this country expecting to have to make adjustments and changes, the Indians in contrast have been cultural islands resistant to the spread of the white population and culture. The tribes that settled in the Southwest have, to a considerable degree, been able to isolate themselves and maintain a separate culture. The intense settlement of the eastern half of the United States led to the rapid disintegration of many of the eastern tribes.

The percentage of the Indian population that is aged 65+ is also smaller. High birth and death rates have kept the Indian population young; half are less than 20 years of age. The percentage distribution by age resembles that of the total U. S. population in 1880.[38]

As a rule, the early Indian tribes treated their older members fairly well and provided them with valued roles for their later years.

Many of the American Indian tribes had developed a variety of ways to provide food for their older members. These methods ranged from the sharing of food among the hunting and gathering tribes such as the Shoshone and Plains Indians to the assumption of family responsibility for older members such as prevailed among the Pueblo.[39] The role of the bearer of tribal traditions and a role as healer of the sick were often reserved to older tribal members. Ceremonial knowledge was paid for by younger Indians, who sought this information from their elders. Similarly, payment was made for the treatment of illness, for dispelling demons, and for divining the whereabouts of lost articles. The old occasionally took on a religious aura in the eyes of the young Indians, who felt that the older members of the tribe had extraordinary supernatural powers.[40]

The Hopi were one of the exceptions to the above "rule" and accorded respect to their elders only as long as they performed a useful function. After senility set in, old age was considered a burden, and the old were often neglected.[41]

The murder of older tribal members was relatively rare among American Indians. John Ewers points out the exception.

> The Iroquois, however, did allow an older man to give a large feast, during which a favorite son would administer the coup de grace from behind.[42]

Among the nomadic tribes the feeble were often abandoned.

Jerrod Levy maintains, however, that Indian tribes generally treated older members with deference and respect. Older Indians most often assumed the roles of leading, educating, and advising, roles usually associated with middle age in the American culture. Perhaps one other factor that contributed to the high status given older Indians is their paucity relative to the numbers of the younger generation, who therefore saw them as no threat.

The movement and restriction of the Indians to reservations and the destruction of wildlife brought an end to the Indian cultures, according to Levy. The development of new economic activities has further destroyed the social organization and culture of American Indians.

The nomadic tribes have had finally to settle in one location and have been forced to do wagework often provided by the federal government. The federal government's stock reduction program forced the older stockowners to give their grazing rights to their heirs and thus stripped them of managerial roles and the prestige that accompanies those roles.[43] Similarly, free medical services are competing with the healing rituals practiced by older tribal workers. Levy states:

> The domestic skills of the traditional aged are less important in a small household. Now almost all the children are either in government boarding school or public school. Much of the domestic economy for the younger wage workers involves knowledge of English and arithmetic to cope with the cash stores that are springing up all over the reservations. Social change has resulted in the destruction of education and the advisory functions of the experienced older person.[44]

Thus, with American Indians, as with most other cultures, rapid social changes tend to undermine the traditional roles and statuses assumed by older persons while creating new roles and opportunities for the young.

The Indian cultures are distinct from other minority groups in that they never wanted to be assimilated into the white American culture. While the ideal of a melting pot of persons of different cultures and ethnic groups tends to permeate the values of most Americans, the Indians would appear to prefer cultural pluralism. They fail to see the superiority of the American culture and often are not desirous of being a part of it.

CONCLUSION

America—with its historic emphasis on the assimilation of a variety of different national, religious, and ethnic groups into a common culture—still contains a variety of minority groups that have not totally become a part of the American way of life. America has much more rapidly assimilated Caucasians of a variety of national, ethnic, and religious backgrounds than it has assimilated other racial groups. The American Indians did not want to be assimilated and thus tried to isolate themselves from the dominant culture. The Pacific Asians had the disadvantages of generally being late immigrants to the country, of being a different racial group, and of arriving in the country after it was relatively settled. As a result of all these factors, they have not been entirely assimilated into the American culture. The different Asian ethnic groups often share values and beliefs that are not consistent with the ideology of the American culture. This becomes a particular problem for the elderly members of these groups who find themselves unable to establish the kind of relationship with the younger generation they had come to expect as part of their cultural traditions. Their children have often begun to adopt at least some of the American values and considerable generational strain is the result.

There are a number of themes running through all the research on minority groups. Members of minority groups generally receive lower incomes and have fewer job opportunities than do members of the dominant group. First-generation immigrants in particular are required to take the least preferred jobs at the lowest salaries. Members of minority groups generally have a shorter life expectancy up to age 65 than does the dominant group but at some point beyond that age a longer life expectancy. Because of past discrimination, members of minority groups usually receive smaller retirement incomes, are more likely to live with extended relatives, are less likely to be able to maintain independent living in the later years, and are generally less well educated than the dominant group. They often receive fewer government services than the dominant group. The argument often heard as a rationalization is that the families of minority groups are very tightly integrated and that they consider it important to look after their older members. This rationalization provides something of a vicious circle, since, if the government provided needed services to older members of minority groups, it would probably not be necessary for their families to assume this responsibility.

Research on the unique and unusual problems of the minority elderly has so far been limited. One would expect second- and third-generation members of ethnic minorities to become assimilated into the dominant culture. Assimilation, however, probably creates intergenerational strain between first-generation immigrants and their children and solves none of the problems of the first generation, who are now in their later years. To what degree the American Indian will be able to remain in isolated enclaves where the original culture can be maintained is debatable. The data tend to suggest a movement of the younger Indians off the reservations and into urban areas.

Whatever the future trends may be, minority groups currently find themselves confronted with a variety of often unique and difficult problems that have most often been ignored by the federal planners of social services for older Americans.

KEY TERMS

role	stereotypes
status	assimilation
role emptying	amalgamation

SUGGESTED READINGS

ATCHLEY, ROBERT C., *The Social Forces in Later Life.* Belmont, CA: Wadsworth, 1977.

BELL, DURAN, PATRICIA KASSCHAU, AND GAIL ZELLMAN, *Delivering Services to Elderly Members of Minority Groups: A Critical Review of the Literature.* Santa Monica, CA: Rand McNally, 1976.

EITZEN, D. STANLEY, *Social Problems.* Boston, MA: Allyn & Bacon, 1980.

EWERS, JOHN C., "The Hore in Blackfoot Indian Culture," *Bureau of American Ethnology Bulletin,* 159 (1955).

FEDERAL COUNCIL ON THE AGING, *Policy Issues Concerning the Elderly Minorities.* Washington, D.C.: DHHS Publication, no. 80-20670, 1979.

HAMMONDS, ANDRÉ, "Poverty and Older Black Americans: A Demographic Portrait" (unpublished paper).

HSU, F. L. K., *The Challenge of the American Dream: The Chinese in the United States.* Belmont, CA: Wadsworth, 1971.

HUDSON, GOSSIE HAROLD, "Some Special Problems of Older Americans," *Crisis Magazine,* March 1976.

ISHIZUKE, C. KAREN, AND OTHERS, *The Older Japanese, Latino, Black, Chinese, Quamanian.* San Diego: Center on Aging, San Diego State University, 1978.

JACKSON, JACQUELYNE J., *Minorities and Aging.* Belmont, CA: Wadsworth, 1980.

KALISH, RICHARD A., AND SHARON MORIWAKI "The World of the Elderly Asian American," *Journal of Social Issues,* 29, no. 2 (1973), 187–202.

KENNARD, E. A., "Hopi Reactions to Death," *American Anthropologist,* 39 (1937).

LEVY, JERROD, "The Older American Indian," in *The Older Rural Americans,* ed. E. Grant Youmans, pp. 221–37. Louisville: University of Kentucky Press, 1967.

NATIONAL ADVISORY AND RESOURCE COMMITTEE, *Pacific/Asian Elderly Research Project.* Special Services for Group, Inc., May 1978.

ROSE, A., AND WARREN PETERSON, *Older People and Their Social Worlds,* pp. 3–16. Philadelphia: F. A. Davis, 1965.

ROSOW, IRVING, "Status and Role Change through the Life Span," in *Handbook on Aging and the Social Sciences,* eds. Robert H. Binstock and Ethel Shanas, p. 462. New York: Van Nostrand Reinhold, 1976.

SEIDEN, RICHARD, "Mellowing with Age: Factors Influencing the Nonwhite Suicide Rate," *International Journal of Aging and Human Development,* 13 (1981), 265–83.

STREIB, GORDON F., "Are the Aged a Minority Group," in *Middle Age and Aging,* ed. Bernice Neugarten. Chicago: University of Chicago Press, 1968.

U.S. BUREAU OF THE CENSUS, "Household and Family Characteristics," *Current Population Reports,* no. 340, Table 3 (March 1978), p. 20.

U.S. BUREAU OF THE CENSUS, *Current Population Survey* (unpublished data, March 1978).

U.S. DEPARTMENT OF HEALTH, EDUCATION AND WELFARE, ADMINISTRATION ON AGING, "The Older Black Population," *Statistical Reports on Older Americans,* no. 5 (1976).

U.S. Department of Health, Education and Welfare, Public Health Service, Office of the Surgeon General, Division of Public Health Methods, "Health Services for the American Indians," *Public Health Service Publication,* no. 531 (1957).

U.S. Department of Health, Education and Welfare, Public Health Service, *Vital Statistics of the U.S.,* Vol. II, Section 5 (1976).

Yee, Dona, "The Older Chinese" (statement presented at the San Francisco Meeting of the Minority Elderly, June 1979).

8

FAMILY PATTERNS
IN LATER LIFE

*Marriage is the relation between man and woman in which the
independence is equal, the dependence mutual, and the
obligation reciprocal.*

Louis Kaufman Anspacher
Address, Boston (December 30, 1934)

The typical couple of two generations ago had a life expectancy which enabled
them to live together for approximately 31 years after the marriage, two years
short of the time when their fifth child was expected to marry. As a result of
declining family size and the improved survival prospects of the American population since 1900, the typical husband and wife of today are likely to see all their
children marry and in all probability have one-fourth of their married life to live
when the last child leaves home. Thus, by the time most married couples are
approaching the age of retirement, their children have already matured, married, and established independent households. Consequently, the typical older
family today is comprised of simply the husband and wife. Approximately two-
thirds of all aged persons are husband-wife couples living alone, most of whom
maintain their own households.

While the previous work of family sociologists was heavily concentrated
on the initial adjustment to marriage and the inevitable consequences of the first
child on the husband-wife relationship, sociologists today are now becoming interested in the opposite end of the family life cycle. Paradoxically, as the earlier
research had indicated that the birth of the first child was the biggest single adjustment problem faced by the young married couple, current family research
indicates that the nature and quality of the husband-wife relationship may be
just as much affected 25 years later when the last child leaves home. For many
couples, after a quarter of a century of assuming the roles and responsibilities of
mother and father to growing children, it may be quite a change in lifestyle to
return exclusively to the roles of husband, wife, companion, and lover. Nadine
Brozan points out that while many middle-age couples are adjusting to the

"empty nest" and the transition from parent to companion, they may be simultaneously confronted with the responsibility of caring for aging parents. At any age in life, changes in previous roles, expectations and patterns of behavior result both in individual and social adjustments which must be successfully negotiated. The adjustments and family patterns which emerge following such events as the last child leaving home, the growing dependence of aging parents, retirement of the husband, and the withdrawal of the family from previous levels of involvement in the social system will be the principal foci of this chapter. From the perspective of the symbolic interactionist, the critical factors in the successful adjustment of older couples is their ability to assume and successfully perform in new roles and the value placed on these roles by significant others in their social milieu.

CHANGING ROLES AND THE AGING FAMILY

Early in the retirement years older couples must make a number of important decisions about their lives which include such things as whether to

1. Remain in their current home with its past history and memories, or move to a new home or apartment.
2. Remain in the same community or move to a different one, perhaps a retirement community.
3. Remain active in current organizations, join new ones or simply not be bothered with affiliations of this nature.
4. Try to locate geographically near children and close friends or move to a different section of the country.
5. Seek activities mutually satisfying to both husband and wife or participate independently.

All of these choices are in one way or another related to the style of life one desires. This preferred style of life ultimately will dictate the roles one becomes actively involved in and the roles one will give up during the later years.

These choices also assume the older person is in good health and able to live independently. In the event of financial dependence, poor health, or related problems, there may be role reversals in the family by which the children make these decisions for aging parents. Past research has often examined the question of the conflict between striving to get ahead by children and the responsibility of caring for their aged parents. Since it is the middle-class group which has the strongest mobility striving, one might expect the upper-class group (those who no longer strive for mobility) and the lower-class (those who have given up) to be more concerned about their aged parents. The findings of a study by Paul and Lois Glasser did not show this to be the case.[1] They found no significant relationship between social class mobility and supporting parents. However, it was found that the more mobile the children, the more likely they were to give help to their parents.

Evidence from the Glassers' work and other studies indicates that caring for aging parents is often a concern of families in the middle years. The problems require a decision by the aged or their children. Should the children take the parent(s) into their home? Should the aged be given financial support by their children? Should the adult children contribute time and energy to help care for their sick parent(s)?

Many of these critical decisions, whether made by the older person or their children, are accompanied by role loss, and result in decreased interaction between the aging persons and others in the social system to which they belong. These are seen as both qualitative and quantitative changes in social interaction that the aging family experiences. This would be the pattern expected by the disengagement theorists.

Most middle-class Americans adhere to the values centered around the importance of leading active lives and thus believe that for those activities and roles which the individual was forced to give up at the time of retirement, new substitutes should be found. The aging person is not expected to alter either the pace or style of life during the retirement years.

From a symbolic interaction perspective, the retired family, rather than trying to disengage from previous roles or vigorously seek new ones, are most likely to maintain those roles they enjoy and choose others from a variety of new ones which are available to them because of their increased leisure time.

Bert Adams speaks of the categories of retirement roles assumed by older families.[2] These are

1. The positively-oriented disengaged who were glad to give up work roles. They are frequently working-class in background.
2. The negatively-oriented disengaged who hate to give up work roles. They are more frequently middle-class in background and likely to believe that they have given up a highly valued part of their lives.
3. The self-employed who have never given up the major life roles and probably never intend to.

What needs to be added to Adams's typology is a fourth category, the actively reengaged who are finding new and useful roles and activities that previous work-related responsibilities would not have allowed time for.

The symbolic interactionists maintain that what is defined as useful and meaningful activity at any age in life is in part determined by significant others in one's social milieu and their definition of the situation. When one's friends and close associates of the same age are retiring and when numerous new roles and opportunities are available to the aging individual, then disengagement need not follow, or if it does occur, it need not be negatively labeled. Life can have newfound meaning and excitement can be created by the very fact that one is free to choose among a variety of available roles, that one's lifelong friends and associates are making similar choices, and that new activities may prove to be just as satisfying as previous work-related activities. Participation in such programs as the Retired Senior Volunteer Program, which involves retired Americans in a variety of charitable and humanitarian causes, may be just as important to the self-confidence of older Americans as their previous work roles. Self-esteem can easily be maintained when one sees that one's activities are useful, needed, and defined as important by significant others, even if they are done voluntarily for little or no economic remuneration.

Thus it would seem that the aging family need not be a disengaged or totally active family but rather selectively engaged.

CONJUGAL: HUSBAND-WIFE RELATIONS IN OLD AGE

Studies by Blood and Wolfe, Pineo, as well as Rollins and Feldman, have examined family patterns over the life cycle. Blood and Wolfe, and Pineo both reported a decrease in shared activity of husbands and wives from the beginning of marriage to the end.

Pineo speaks of marital "disenchantment," which is defined as a decline in marital satisfaction and decrease in intimacy. While disenchantment occurs for both husbands and wives in a marriage, it apparently occurs earlier for husbands than for wives. The reason for this seems to be related to the fact that men tend to romanticize their wives more than wives do their husbands, with the result that the wives may fall faster and further from their husbands' idealization. Pineo has concluded that marriage over time is a process of gradual disenchantment with the marriage in general and the partner in particular.[3]

A careful examination of the husbands' and wives' marital satisfaction by Rollins and Feldman indicates different patterns over the family life cycle in the subjective-affective state of each individual. These include:

1. Husbands seem to be much less affected by the state of the family life cycle in their subjective evaluation of marital satisfaction, with husbands' satisfaction varying only slightly from the beginning through the childrearing phase.
2. Wives experience a general decrease in marital satisfaction during the childbearing and childrearing phase of the marriage until the children leave home. After the last child leaves home both the husband and wife are similar in marital satisfaction.
3. For men there is an apparent setback in marital satisfaction just before the husband retires.

The implications of these patterns would seem to be that childbearing and childrearing have a rather profound and negative effect on the marital satisfaction for wives. The most difficult time for the husbands seems to be when they are anticipating retirement. Thus, marital satisfaction for husbands appears to be more influenced by their occupational experiences in comparison to wives who are more often influenced by the advent and developmental years of children in their families.

While the family adjustment patterns over the life cycle indicate variations in family satisfaction related to the wife's childrearing responsibility and the husband's stage of career development, there has been very little research related to the exclusive adjustment patterns experienced by older Americans. Felix Berardo observed that researchers have for a long time generally concentrated their efforts on the early phases of the life cycle to the neglect of the later stages.

In terms of the opportunity for husband and wife to have time together, to share common interests, and to have the opportunity to develop greater mutual respect and understanding, the pattern over the family life cycle would seem to be curvilinear. The early phase of marriage, prior to the advent of the first child, seems to offer the husband and wife maximum opportunity for this kind of personal involvement and marital cohesion. The birth of the first child and the increasing time demands of the husband's career substantially reduce the time the husband and wife have to spend together in the middle years. The last child leaving home, and the approaching retirement of the husband once again return the opportunity for greater involvement, shared activity, and marital cohesion on the part of the husband and wife.

This is consistent with the findings of both the Rollins and Feldman, and Rollins and Cannon studies which report a curvilinear trend with a decline in marital satisfaction following the initial years, a leveling off, followed by an increase during the postretirement years. Streib and Schneider observed that the loss of work role for husbands often resulted in expanded activity in other ongoing roles (i.e., husband, grandfather, etc.) which had remained latent. It would appear then that a part of the retirement process for men is the shifting of emphasis from occupational to family activity. Richard Kalish suggests that retirement and a general disengagement from previous career and social responsibilities for the husband in particular serves the function of allowing older men to maintain family activities as long as possible. This does not mean that men during the working years necessarily ignored family roles and responsibilities. It does mean that they will now have more time to dedicate to exclusive family roles. Morris Medley found that family life and standard of living were significant determinants of life satisfaction for both sexes at each stage of adulthood.

Family sociologists have not at the present time resolved the inconsistency of the earlier studies of the family life cycle reporting a decline over time in marital satisfaction and the later studies indicating a curvilinear relationship. Future research will undoubtedly clarify this issue.

For many reasons, in the postretirement years, conjugal relationships and adjustment patterns are probably a continuation of adjustments made earlier in the life cycle. Fried and Stern, for example, found that nearly all of the older couples whom they interviewed and who rated their marriage as satisfactory, had a previous history of good marital relations. Moreover, almost half of these marriages had become even more satisfactory as the partners aged. On the other hand, most of the older couples who rated their marriage as unsatisfactory stated it "had been unsatisfactory more or less from the beginning," and approximately half the marriages deteriorated further as the partners advanced in years. For many older couples, then, marital adjustment in the later years is simply a reflection of the adjustment worked out earlier in life.

"Ideal types" are used by sociologists to describe those cases taken to a logical extreme in order to illustrate a particular type of relationship or pattern of behavior. Perhaps no person or group may perfectly equate the "ideal type" but they are very similar to it in their pattern of behavior.

Medley identified what he believed to be three ideal types of marital relationships found among older couples:

1. Husband-wife
2. The parent-child
3. The associates

Medley describes the "husband-wife" relationship as one in which the couple stresses the intimate and shared nature of their relationship. These persons focus their marriage around husband and wife roles, although not necessarily to the exclusion of other roles. Couples characterized by the husband-wife relationship are likely to feel that the interpersonal interaction with one's spouse is the most rewarding aspect of marital life.

In the "parent-child" marriage one partner assumes the role of parent and the other the role of child. The spouse assuming the parent role behaves in a nurturing, protective, and dominant fashion toward the other partner. Concomitantly, the spouse assuming the child role behaves in a submissive and dependent manner. Failing health of one of the marital partners may quickly lead to this type of relationship.

The "associates" are couples who most often act as friends and although they appreciate one another's company, they find their most rewarding moments outside of the intimacy of the husband-wife relationships. The associates are apt to be efficient in the business of managing marital and family life. The friendship experienced by the pair, coupled with satisfaction derived from their parental and extrafamily roles, is likely to enhance the perpetuation of the relationship.

Thus, there is no single pattern of husband-wife relationship which leads necessarily to a good marital adjustment in later life. What we find are a variety of different marital relationships which some couples find satisfying depending on their individual needs and preferences.

SEXUAL ADJUSTMENT

One problem Americans confront in achieving an adequate sexual adjustment in the later years is the generally negative view held by society on this subject. Society considers a young man's interest in the opposite sex as normal and expected, even to the point of worrying a little when there appears to be a lack of interest. At a later age, however, this same interest is negatively labeled and we hear the jokes about "dirty old men." The result is that a young man not interested in the opposite sex is a cause for concern but an older man continuing to show an interest in sex is also cause for concern. It is difficult to understand why society would come to expect all other biological systems to function throughout life except the sexual one.

Lobsenz observes that many Americans apparently feel that sexual interest declines with age, that sexual exertion may be dangerous to one's health in old age and therefore, most older people tend to give up sex more or less completely. Research findings from Kinsey, Masters and Johnson, and Pfeiffer of the Duke University Center for Study of the Aging find the above beliefs to be in error. The findings of all these studies indicate that men and women in a state of general good health are physiologically able to have a satisfying sex life well into their seventies, eighties, and beyond. Kinsey found that four out of five men over the age of 60 were capable of intercourse and that there was no evidence of sexual decline in women beyond the age of 60. A research project at Duke University followed a sample of respondents for 20 years and interestingly enough, Pfeiffer reports that 15 percent of the men and women studied showed a steadily rising rate of sexual interest and activity as they got older. Duke University's findings indicated that two out of three men are sexually active past 65, and one of five is still active in his eighties.

The Masters and Johnson data indicated a slowdown in sexual activity with aging but not total cessation. They found that the male's capacity for erection and climax and a woman's capacity for orgasm were slowed but not terminated by the aging process.

The slowing of sexual activity during the later years was most carefully explored by the researchers during the Duke longitudinal study. The pattern was found to be quite different for men than it was for women.

Approximately 80 percent of the healthy and socially active males reported continued sexual interest at the beginning of the study. Ten years later no significant drop in this proportion was found. While expressing continued interest in sexual activity, the proportion who were still sexually active dropped from 70 percent at the beginning of the study to 25 percent ten years later. While interest remained high in the males, the actual sexual activity decreased considerably in the later years.

Of the healthy and socially active females only about one-third reported continued sexual interest at the beginning of the study. This proportion did not change significantly over the next ten years. Approximately one-fifth of these women were still having sexual intercourse regularly over the next ten years. Fewer women than men, therefore, were still sexually interested and active, but of those who were active, aging did not seem to diminish the activity.

Busse and Pfeiffer believe the lower level of sexual interest and activity among the aging females may be in part explained by a lower level of sexual interest expressed by women as compared to men throughout the life cycle. Kinsey and others reported a lower frequency of sexual outlets for women than for men at all ages. Furthermore, Busse and Pfeiffer assert that declining sexual interest and activity for women may have occurred before their entry into the study (before age 60). Their data indicated that the median age of cessation of intercourse occurred nearly ten years earlier in women than in men.

The principal explanation for the cessation in sexual activity in women, however, still appears to be a decline in interest on the husband's part. Nearly all of the women attributed responsibility for the cessation of sexual intercourse to their husbands, and the men in general agreed.

The Kinsey studies indicated that married and nonmarried men did not appreciatively differ in the degree of sexual interest and activity. Married women by comparison differed substantially from nonmarried women, with very few of the nonmarried women reporting any sexual activity, and less than 20 percent reported any sexual interest.

Like other areas of the older person's life, sexual adjustment tends to follow patterns set in the middle years and these are likely to continue well into the seventies and eighties. Couples who have not remained sexually active during the middle years are likely to find that the older years bring decreased interest and responsiveness to sexual stimulation. Masters and Johnson report:

> The most important factor in the maintenance of effective sexuality for the aging male is consistency of active sexual expression. When the male is stimulated to high sexual output during his formative years and a similar tenor of activity is established for the 31 to 40 year age range, his middle-aged and involutional years are marked by constantly recurring physiologic evidence of maintained sexuality. Certainly it is true for the male geriatric sample that those men currently interested in relatively high levels of sexual expression report similar activity levels from their formative years.[4]

The report indicates a similar continuity from the middle years among women. Masters and Johnson state:

> In brief, significant sexual capacity and effective sexual performance are not confined to the human female's premenopausal years. Generally, the intensity of physiologic reaction and duration of anatomic response to effective stimulation are reduced . . . with the advancing years. Regardless of involutional changes in the reproductive organs, the aging human female is fully capable of sexual performance at orgasmic re-

sponse levels, particularly if she is exposed to regularity of effective stimulation.[5]

When the opportunity for sexual fulfillment in old age is present, Masters and Johnson's evidence indicates that sexual ability does appear to deteriorate in old age, particularly among men. Masters and Johnson believe the problem of sexual adjustment in later life is psychological rather than physical. Factors which they believe can contribute to sexual impotence at any age are (1) boredom with one's partner, (2) preoccupation with career and economic pursuits, (3) mental and physical fatigue, (4) overindulgence in food and drink, (5) physical and mental infirmities, and (6) poor performance.[6] It is apparent that with the aging male the most critical factor is fear of failure and the emotional threat to identity and masculinity which this brings. Older wives are likely to lack insight into the fear of failure problem and take their husbands' lack of interest as a personal rejection and most often respond in such a way as to further compound the problem. Counseling the female, in this case, could probably readily eliminate the problem.

For older females, the Masters and Johnson data indicate that there are several major factors which serve to limit sexual responsiveness, which include (1) steroid starvation which makes coitus painful, (2) lack of opportunity for regular sexual outlet, (3) the Victorian concept that women should not have an interest in sexual activity, (4) physical infirmities, and (5) the fact that some women never learn to respond to sexual desire and use menopause as an excuse for total abstinence.[7]

Hormone therapy was found to eliminate the pain associated with coitus experienced by some older women, resulting in the conclusion that there is no time limit to female sexuality.

Butler and Lewis feel that medical doctors have been shirking their responsibility of informing their older patients about medical problems and sexual performance. A man or woman with a heart condition, for instance, ought to know that a coronary attack during sex occurs much less often than the patient may fear is the case and can be avoided by taking nitroglycerine pills prior to the sexual experience. Similarly, a women who experiences vaginal discomfort should be encouraged to have hormonal replacement therapy. Furthermore, if a doctor has a choice among the varying techniques of surgery, he or she should consider the sexual effects in making his or her decision.

Thus, the older couple potentially has some problems of sexual adjustment not confronted by the younger couple. Evidence strongly indicates, however, that any difficulties can be overcome, and that human sexuality is not terminated with advancing years. The most crucial factor for sexual adjustment in the later years seems to be the opportunity for regular sexual stimulation and involvement. Thus, according to Douglas Kimmel, the principal factor involved in limiting sexual activity for the aging person is male attrition which leaves the female without a sexual partner and with little opportunity to find another.

RETIREMENT YEARS
AND MARITAL ADJUSTMENT

While physical, economic, and emotional factors may contribute to the retirement adjustment of older Americans, the accommodation of the husband to the retirement role appears to be crucial. Aaron Lipman observed that the husband's concept of self was acquired from his occupational role, as a worker, and from the familial role as a husband and father. Their two roles are clearly demarcated both geographically and temporally. Life on the job involves a different location with different actors, goals, and status. There is obviously some interpenetration of the roles due to the fact that the male's success in family roles is in part determined by his success in the occupational role. Thus, through the occupational role the husband manages to develop and sustain a satisfactory self-image and status in the home.

The wife's self-concept has, in the past, been tied to her management of the internal and domestic affairs of the household. The homemaker role has the most continuity in the life of the wife. The homemaker role, Ruth Cavan observes, seems the most basic, transcending all others. The mother role rises to a crest, declines, and disappears. Paid employment comes and goes. Homemaking as a role continues from the day after the wedding to the end of the marriage. Thus by virtue of her significance in the household and the attendant social roles of wife, homemaker, and companion, the woman manages to develop and sustain an acceptable self-image and status throughout her adult life.

Retirement, in the past, has altered the husband's role situation while leaving the wife's relatively unchanged. While many wives in retired families are able to continue satisfactorily their traditional role as homemakers, a similar pattern of role continuity is denied the husband. The role of wage earner, which he had conceived as his primary role, is suddenly withdrawn. Structurally he is isolated from the occupational system, which can lead to adjustment problems. If the married male is to adjust to retirement, he must necessarily redefine his social function and his familial roles.

Some insights into this problem are provided by Lipman's study of a group of primarily upper socioeconomic class retired couples residing in metropolitan Miami. He found, among other things, that successful marital adjustment following retirement depends on the extent to which the husband replaces a self-conception functionally related to employment and the associated instrumental role of provider by developing a substitute expressive role in the home. As Lipman states:

> In retirement since man can no longer attain the work and achievement goals, striving for them and adherence to them is associated with poor adjustment. A feeling of usefulness and purposefulness is achieved by the male increasingly through the assistance with household activities, and emphasizing expressive qualities such as giving love, affection, and companionship to his wife. A new and meaningful functional role is thus created that aids in individual adjustment.[8]

Other of the Lipman data led him to question the rather widespread assumption that women experience little or no role discontinuity, following their husband's retirement, but simply retain their traditional role of housewife. He found that the husband's increased involvement in household activities and his emergent expressive orientation necessitates a reciprocal shift in the wife's domestic role and her self-image. The wife can no longer view her major role primarily as a good housekeeper and homemaker. But the wife and husband must move from the previously defined sex-differentiated instrumental roles toward a common area of identity and role activities, which includes sharing and cooperation; where similar expressive qualities such as love, understanding, companionship, and compatibility become the most important things they can both give in marriage.

The next generation of retirees may find the division of labor between husband and wife at the time of retirement much easier to negotiate. Families today are much more likely to have both the husband and wife working outside of the home. Thus, throughout their careers, housework, in all probability, has been shared. This being the case, retirement may be less problematic. A new problem may emerge for the next generation, however. If both husband and wife are not the same age then one may be under pressure to retire earlier in order that the couple may initiate their retirement plans. One partner retiring considerably earlier than the other may feel somewhat deprived by the fact that travel and other activities must be postponed until his or her spouse's retirement.

Finally, it should be emphasized that retirement need not necessarily have a deleterious effect upon conjugal relations in old age. Streib found when he asked a sample of adult children to assess their family situation and their relationship with the father following retirement, these responses were obtained: (1) Over 70 percent said the father's retirement had not created any serious difficulties; (2) 30 percent felt retirement had brought the father closer to his immediate family, and 68 percent reported no change at all in this respect; (3) 93 percent felt the father had as much to say about family matters as he had had in the years preceding retirement. These responses indicate that there is considerable stability and harmony in family roles and relationships in retirement.

INTERGENERATIONAL FAMILY RELATIONS

Marvin Koller, in discussing multigenerational families, defines a generation as

> cohorts or thousands of persons who will share similar, but not identical experiences because they are born, live, and die within a common historical period.[9]

The thread that links multiple generations together with a system of shared belief, norms, values, and cultural traditions is the family. Family units often transcend more than one generation and inculcate their members with a system of shared beliefs. The longevity of the current population means that families may periodically interact with other family members spanning three and four generations.

Ethel Shanas refers to four-generation families as "the New Pioneers." She observes that four-generation families are becoming more common and are creating a complex system of family interrelationships. What to call each family member of each generation—the generation differences between the first and last generations—and who is the head of the four-generation family—are just a few of the problems identified by Shanas.

The most often heard argument regarding multigenerational family interaction is one of the demise and deterioration of multigenerational families with regard to any meaningful and reciprocal relations between generations.

Many family sociologists have argued that modern urban mass society had the effect of creating the isolated nuclear family in which extended family ties were either minimized or nonexistent. At the time of completing the educational training, the young man or young woman was expected to establish himself or herself in a career, marry and move to a household away from the influence of either sets of parents. Industrial organizations prefer and often demand a mobile labor force which can be periodically moved as production and employee development demand. This system of values often resulted in younger family members being geographically separated from either set of in-laws and his or her extended relatives. Thus it was felt that the isolated nuclear family was likely to be the most common one in modern industrial nations. Multigenerational or extended family ties were expected to be a thing of the past.

Research evidence into changing family forms and functions in the last twenty-five years simply have not found this to be the case. Eugene Litwak in a study of extended family ties tested two hypotheses:

1. That occupational mobility is antithetical to extended family relations;
2. That extended family relations are impossible as a result of geographic mobility.

Litwak's research found that the extended family form exists in modern urban society among middle-class families, that extended family relations are possible in an urban society, that geographical propinquity is an unnecessary condition of these relationships, and that occupational mobility is unhindered by the activities of the extended family. Some of the extended family activities include advice, financial assistance, temporary housing, and similar assistance given during such movement.[10]

Troll, Miller, and Atchley discuss the stereotypes of the modern family. They believe the most common stereotype is that the young couple are expected to establish a home independent of both sets of parents (neolocal), raise their children with the advice of child psychologists rather than the wisdom of the grandparents, and be economically independent by virtue of the young husband's own efforts and successes. They concluded:

> In actual fact, most young couples seem to live reasonably close to both sets of parents, receive either help in the form of services (such as babysitting) or money (more in the middle class) and visit frequently.[11]

The evidence indicates, then, that the isolated nuclear family expected to emerge in modern industrial nations simply has not come to pass. Three- and four-generation family units who interact with and assist each other frequently in a variety of different circumstances seem the most common pattern.

Sussman and Burchinal found that a variety of help patterns exist between family members including the exchange of services, gifts, advice, and financial assistance. Moreover, the exchange of aid among family members flows in a variety of different directions including from parents to children and vice versa, among siblings and less frequently from more distant relatives. Financial assistance, apparently, more often flows from parents to children.

Social activities of family units are also a source of emotional support for family members. Many family sociologists believe that the difficulty of developing satisfactory primary relationships outside of the family in urban areas makes the extended family even more important to the individual.

The extended family interaction and assistance pattern found in this country carries with it a system of satisfaction and support for older family members. Shanas and Streib found that married children were willing to assume responsibility for aged parents including financial aid, providing a home for them, and locating close to the residences of their aged parents.[13]

What research findings indicate then is that there is a two-direction flow of assistance in multigenerational family units. Adult members of the family during their working years contribute both financially and socially to the children during the early years of their marriage. Simultaneously, adult members of the family contribute financial aid, social support, and sometimes a home for older members of the family. The protective function of the family, as it looks after all its members, is still one of its more useful and integrating activities. While some of the support functions for older members of the society have been shifted off of the family and onto the government (such as retirement income) the family still provides many and often the most crucial services for its older members. Sussman and Stroud in a series of studies found that illness of an older member of a family group resulted in an almost instantaneous response from all other family members. The ill person is most often the recipient of large amounts of aid, service, and social attention during hospitalization or after his or her return to the community.[14]

The family still provides a very personal, primary, and immediate response to the needs of its elder members. While government services are important to America's elders, it is doubtful that it could ever replace vital family support functions.

GRANDPARENTHOOD

A cross-national study of older persons in 1962 found that 40 percent of the persons over 65 in the United States had great-grandchildren; 23 percent in Denmark and 22 percent in Britain were also at the top of four-generation families.

Peter Townsend found that in Britain, the average woman becomes a grandmother at 54 and a great-grandmother at 72; men averaged three years later.[15] In Britain and the United States, 75 percent of old people with children live no longer than thirty minutes away from them.

Increased life expectancy coupled with the earlier age at marriage, a shorter child-rearing period, and fewer children, have exposed more middle-aged and older couples to the role of grandparenthood than at any other period in history. While this is true, interestingly enough the phenomenon of grandparenthood has been relatively ignored by researchers in both psychology and sociology.

An anthropological study of Dorian Apple provides us one of the best clues to the critical determinants of the quality of the relationship between grandparents and grandchildren. Using ethnographic data from seventy-five cultures, she concludes that in societies where grandparents retain considerable household authority either because of economic power or the traditionally high status granted them, the relationship between grandparents and grandchildren is most often formal and unfriendly. On the other hand, in societies in which the grandparents' generation retains little control or authority over the grandchildren, grandparents and grandchildren typically have egalitarian and warm relationships. Thus, Apple concludes that friendly relationships between grandparents and grandchildren will occur where the family structure does not allow grandparents to exercise family authority.

Similarly, Sue Updegraff found that most often American grandparents engage in companionable and indulgent relationships with their grandchildren, and they usually do not assume any direct responsibility or control over their behavior. It seems apparent that only in the case of their being orphaned do grandparents give direct aid or take full responsibility for the grandchildren. The majority of grandparents do exhibit considerable pride and pleasure from involvement with their grandchildren.

A study by Neugarten and Weinstein identified five major styles of grandparenthood:

1. The *Formal* are those who follow what they regard as the proper and prescribed role of grandparents. Although they may give presents and

babysit with grandchildren they maintain clearly drawn lines between parenting and grandparenting and leave the parenting exclusively to the parents.

2. The *Fun Seeker* is a relationship to the grandchild characterized by informality and playfulness. They join the child in a variety of activities specifically for the purpose of having fun, almost as a playmate. The emphasis is on mutual gratification.

3. The *Distant Figure* is the grandparent who emerges from the shadows on holidays and special occasions. Contact with the grandchildren is fleeting, but benevolent.

4. The *Surrogate Parent* is most often practiced by grandmothers who are caring for the children while the mother works.

5. The *Reservoir of Family Wisdom* is a pattern centering around the grandfather and is distinctly authoritarian. The grandfather is the dispenser of special skills and resources.

The most frequent pattern was the formal style which comprises 33 percent of all grandparents, followed by 26 percent who were fun seeking, 24 percent the distant figure style, 7 percent the parental-surrogate, and 4 percent the reservoir of family wisdom. Neugarten and Weinstein found the fun seeking was more often followed by younger grandparents and the formal style more often by older grandparents.

Nye and Berardo in their book point out that women are much more likely than men to look forward to assuming the grandparent role and to undergo considerable anticipatory socialization. They often visualize themselves as grandmothers well ahead of the birth of the first grandchild.

The image of grandmother in most women's minds is a positive one that they are most likely to desire. The role presents some anxiety, however, for young grandmothers who still view themselves as attractive since it is a threat to a youthful self-image.[16]

Nye and Berardo further observed that most men become grandfathers at the time when they are reaching the apex of their occupational careers. Their primary identity is still attached to the work role and consequently they postpone much involvement in the grandparent role until the years following retirement.

The grandparent role can be somewhat onesided and selfish if not carefully guarded by the individual's assuming the role. To be able to play with, pamper, and spoil the child while not being responsible for the child's behavior or discipline seems a bit unfair. In this situation the parents become responsible for all negative sanctions on behavior while the grandparents become the distributors of rewards. The other extreme would be for the adult offspring to expect the grandparents to always be available for babysitting duty on a minute's notice, to leave the children for extended periods of time while they vacation, or sometimes to totally turn the responsibility for rearing the children to the grandparents.

Richard Kalish observes that the closeness between grandparents and grandchildren might be due in part to the circumstances in life that they share. They are both groups that do not have much power to influence the decision makers, both are constantly reminded of their nonproductive roles, both are seen as leading a life of leisure, both are living with their time unstructured, both are thought to be inadequately educated, and both are seen as being poor and weak. One wonders, however, if they are this aware of the similarity of their circumstances or if they perceive of their positions in this manner since their ages place them at such diverse points in the life cycle.

Most grandparents, whether initially enamored with the grandparent role or not, come to enjoy the role due to the fact that it involves a minimum of obligations and responsibilities while allowing for much personal fulfillment and need gratification.

WIDOWHOOD

Sooner or later all older married persons must face the possibility of their partner's death, or conversely the fact that they will die and their spouse will be removed from intimate family relationship during the later years. Since the husbands generally die at a younger age than their wives, the widowed status is more common to women than to men, but it does happen to both.

The last half-century has seen the widowed female consistently outnumbering her male counterpart and the margin is ever-widening. In 1940 there were twice as many widows as widowers. During the next decade widows increased by 25 percent while the number of widowers rose by only 3 percent. In 1960 widows outnumbered widowers by 3.5 to 1 and by 1980 this discrepancy had increased to the current ratio of more than 4 to 1.

The individual making the transition from the married to the widowed status is confronted with a variety of personal and familial problems. That the transition is not always successfully accomplished is reflected in the statistics which indicate that widowed persons rather consistently show higher rates of mortality, mental disorders, and suicide. The death of a spouse is particularly devastating to older persons because they have become so accustomed to a style of life that is heavily involved with, and dependent upon, their marital partners.

Lopata is concerned with role transitions in widowhood, and how these transitions may be affected by a particular society's structure, composition, and culture. In Lopata's view, when changes occur in an individual's social relations and role involvements, one usually goes through a series of stages, including:

1. Official recognition of the event.
2. Temporary "disengagement" or withdrawal from established lines of communication.

3. Limbo—this may involve ritualized action of unusual or emergency nature not considered part of the normal pattern.
4. Reengagement.

Lopata points out the role changes and altered lifestyles of women in four different societies. The chosen lifestyle often depends upon the woman's involvement in her former role of wife and the way in which this role is connected to her other sets of social relations. In some groups, for instance, a wife may have obligations to her in-laws which extend until long after the husband's death.

Levirate is practiced among the Kgatlo in Africa for caring for widows. Levirate is when a brother of the deceased husband takes his place in providing for the widow and her children, and sometimes fathers more children with her. In this tribe, all the males in the family will cooperate to obtain a "bogadi" or bride price. The man who marries the woman has exclusive rights to her while he is living, but after death, other males in the family may also claim rights to her. Any children who are born of the widow and "substitute" husbands are called "children of the rafters" and are considered as belonging to the original husband, becoming his rightful heirs.

In traditional India around A.D. 200, legal rules were developed which greatly restricted the social life space of women. The ideal age for marriage was about 9–10 years, and remarriage of the widow became outlawed. The wife was expected to "revere her husband as a god," and when the husband died, his death was usually viewed as the result of some sin his wife had committed. The ideal act for the widow became "suttee," or burning death of the widow on the funeral pyre of her husband. Although the British outlawed this custom in 1829, it was still practiced in some areas of the country for some time.

In traditional China, the husband's family usually acquired extensive rights over the wife, as the result of a very high bride price. On the other hand, remarriage among the working class was often discouraged because a woman's labor was highly valued and she was the only adult who could support her aged in-laws and her young children.

American widows, according to Lopata, seemingly have more possible alternatives than widows in most other societies. In theory, the widow may stay single or remarry at any time she chooses; she can choose a mate from any but a small incestly defined group; she can continue relations with her own family, or her husband's family, or both, and she can fill her time with a career or voluntary associations.

There seems to be much confusion among family sociologists regarding who experiences greater difficulty at the death of a spouse, the husband or the wife. Felix Berardo's evidence indicates that for a variety of reasons survivorship adaption may be more difficult for the older husband, since the role of the wife remains relatively unchanged upon the death of her spouse. She continues to perform her household tasks such as cleaning and cooking, in much the same manner as when her husband was alive. Indeed the ability to maintain certain standards of good housekeeping often represents a challenge and a test of the degree to which the older women is avoiding "getting old."

Consequently, a large proportion of aged widows can maintain separate quarters and are capable of taking care of themselves. Moreover, the older widow is more likely than the widower to be welcomed into the home of her married children and to find a useful place there.

In the case of the aged widower, however, the loss of the wife produces marked changes in his pattern of living. If the wife was the homemaker and housekeeper, all these responsibilities for maintenance and upkeep of the household now fall on him. The husband who loses his wife is now faced with the problems of preparing his meals, doing the cleaning, maintaining the budget, and providing himself with other types of general care. In addition to the necessity of becoming proficient in domestic roles, the widower must find an adequate substitute for the intimacy of that primary relationship once provided by his wife.

The widower's problems of adjustment may be further compounded by the loss of his occupational role. For most of a man's adult life, his work has been a principal source of identity and self-conception. Retirement severs that identity and often removes the husband from contact with friends and coworkers. The combined retiree-widower status often places the widower in a position of social isolation leading to reduced communication and interaction with significant others.

Berardo has noted that widowers were least likely to

1. Be living with children;
2. Have a high degree of kin interaction or to be satisfied with extended family relationships;
3. Receive from or give to children various forms of assistance;
4. Have friends either inside or outside the community or to be satisfied with their opportunities to be with close friends.

Bell, on the other hand, has argued that the role of widow may be socially and psychologically more difficult than that of the widower for a variety of reasons. He argues that in American society

1. Marriage is generally more important for the woman than the man and that the loss of the role of wife is more basic to the woman;
2. The widow is more apt to be forced to "go it alone" because in comparison to the widower she receives less encouragement from family and friends to remarry;
3. The widow faces much more difficulty in providing and caring for herself and her children because her financial resources usually are considerably less than those of the widower;

4. There are far greater numbers of widows than widowers, and the majority of them are widowed at advanced ages; therefore, it is much more difficult for the surviving wife than for the surviving husband to change her status through remarriage.

This latter point may be the crucial one with regard to the contrasting adjustment patterns of widows and widowers. The surplus of women over the age of 65 is such that there is no doubt that the widower who wants to remarry can do so, while the widow may want to remarry but simply not have the option to do so. In every decade since the turn of the century, the remarriage rate for widowers has been more than double that of widows, and with each successive increment in age the disparity widens, so that for persons 55 years or older, the remarriage rate for widowers is approximately five times as great. A woman who has been widowed at age 25 may find some small comfort in the knowledge that she has more than a ninety percent chance for remarriage. At age 45, however, this probability is reduced to one in three and at age 65 it drops to one in 32.

The conclusion would seem to be that widows and widowers both face adjustment problems at the death of a spouse. The widower may have a more readily available solution to his problem since a second marriage is most often possible. The fact that women so outnumber men during the later years makes a second marriage much more likely for a man than for a woman. Moreover, it is not unusual for an older man, especially one who has a substantial income, to find a woman approximately his own age or several years younger who will be willing to marry him. The aged woman, on the other hand, has much less opportunity for a second marriage.

One critical aspect of the successful adjustment on the part of widows or widowers is their degree of dependence on the marital partner. In the parent-child relationship in which one partner assumes a maternalistic or paternalistic concern in the care and supervision of the other partner, the death of a spouse may prove devastating. The overly dependent spouse may have over long years of dependence lost the necessary inclination, capability, and skill to be self-sufficient.

ALTERNATIVE LIFESTYLES

An alternative family pattern that has emerged among a segment of older Americans is that of living together without the formal marital contract. There are a variety of social, legal, and financial pressures placed upon older people that encourage this kind of family arrangement. First, many retirement programs pay the surviving spouse a monthly income, but are void if a remarriage occurs. Thus, many widows in particular feel that remarriage will bring an economic penalty in the form of lost financial security. In this instance, living with a partner without a formal marriage is a way of maintaining economic independence while meeting personal, emotional, and psychological needs which the sharing of one's life with another person brings.

A second factor is the property that a couple may have accumulated throughout life and now is under the control of the surviving spouse. Children may discourage the marriage of an aging mother or father for fear that upon the death of this person, his or her assets will be in the hands of the second marital partner who is related to them only by marriage. Thus an older couple who chooses to live together will reduce pressures from their children not to marry for fear of losing the parent's inheritance. The major danger for an aging couple who decides on this course of action is the feeling of guilt which may accompany such arrangements. Mores and norms regarding acceptable and unacceptable behavior in heterosexual relations which have been acquired over long years of living are not easily changed. These residual feelings of guilt and anxiety may be a cost that older couples who choose this kind of family arrangement may have to bear.

Due to the greater longevity of women, and differences in the age of the partners at the time of marriage, the average wife outlives her husband from five to fifteen years. The net result is an imbalanced sex ratio and a surplus of women during the later years. Awareness of this situation and the problem that it creates led Kassel to suggest that polygyny after 60 ought to become an established American family pattern. Kassel believes that allowing one man to have several wives after 60 would offer the following advantages to older Americans:

1. Older women would have the opportunity to reestablish a meaningful family group.
2. Mealtime would regain a social atmosphere and the elderly would eat a more balanced diet.
3. The opportunity to pool funds would insure a more adequate income for older families.
4. In case of illness there would be others around to care for the sick person and less of a need for a nursing home.
5. Household duties could be shared and would, therefore, be lighter.
6. This would solve the problem of insufficient numbers of sex partners for older women.
7. Loneliness and social isolation would be curbed.
8. Group insurance would become less expensive and more feasible for older persons.

While Kassel's suggestion of polygynous marriage is intriguing, it seems not to be readily occurring in the United States. He first suggested this pattern in an article in *Geriatrics* in 1966. Since then neither medical doctors, psychiatrists, nor social gerontologists have seen fit to recommend this family style to older Americans. While feasible, this pattern of living would seem to clash with attitudes and values acquired over a lifetime. Older Americans as a group seem less prone to experiment with alternative styles of life than other age groups. One wonders, therefore, if Kassel seriously expected polygyny after 60 to become an established family pattern or was merely putting the reader on.

Remarriage of older persons who have lost a spouse through death does seem to be a more common and accepted pattern among older persons. Jessie Bernard in discussing this phenomena states:

> That the high proportion of successful remarriages, especially among the widowed, suggests that the loneliness of the later years might well be assuaged if older men and women were encouraged to remarry. Popular attitudes cannot be changed at will, of course; but if it is at all possible to create an attitude sympathetic to love and romance in the later years such an attitude might help.[17]

Remarriage seems to be the most realistic solution for single older persons who hope to maintain the approval of relatives and friends of their lifestyle. As previously stated, the biggest single deterrent to this pattern is the shortage of available men in the later years.

SECOND MARRIAGES IN LATER LIFE

A century ago the extended family was considerably more common in the United States than it is today. The result was that older widowed persons often moved in with their children, were given a place in the family, and found many family roles which they were capable of performing.

Modern industry requires a mobile labor force which can be moved from place to place. Hence, one does not always live in the same community with extended family members. While Litwak's work indicated that families do provide support for their members even if they are geographically widely separated this does not usually include providing them a permanent place of residence. Aging parents prefer to maintain their independence and are not anxious to move in with their children. Their children often have their own children to raise and are not anxious to have their aging parents move in with them. Figure 8–1 indicates that both men and women living with children and other relatives became less common between 1960 and 1979. Currently less than 5 percent of the men and less than 15 percent of the women are living with children and other relatives. Older persons who find themselves without an immediate family due to the death of a spouse now have only a few choices available to them. They may live alone, move into a home or apartment with another widowed person, or remarry if a suitable partner is available.

The story of Amy indicates the reluctance of older persons to give up their independence and move in with their children. Amy was just one year younger than her husband Bill, who was 67 when he died in 1978. She remained living in the house that she and her husband had built a number of years before. She had known that her husband was dying for two years so she had more time than many widows to decide about remaining in her home. Amy had no intention of selling her home at all until two years later when the upkeep became too much for her and she felt compelled to do so. After selling her house she moved

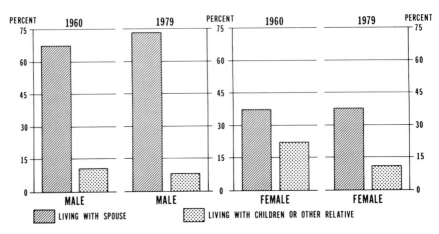

Figure 8-1 Living Arrangements, Persons Aged 65 and Older, by Sex, 1960 and 1979

Source: Bureau of the Census

into a small apartment complex located not too far from the home of her son. Amy has always been independent. The only circumstance that slowed her down at all was the continuing problem with her eyes, suffering from glaucoma, then cataracts, and then a detached retina. The following year Amy, because she was going blind, was forced to give up her apartment and move in with her son. She proclaims this was the most difficult decision of her life since she did not want to give up her independence and did not at all like the idea of imposing on her children. Her failing eyesight, however, left her no other choice.

A second marriage in later life has been most carefully examined by McKain, who has written a book entitled *Retirement Marriage*. McKain argues that disengagement from employment and other social activities related to the work role makes the family the single most important factor in the life satisfaction of older Americans. McKain further believes that marriage is a positive force in health maintenance and that older men and women who remarry are probably adding years to their lives.[18]

While children may not prefer to have their aging parents live with them, their support in the case of a second marriage was found to be most helpful. McKain states:

> One of the most important ingredients in a successful retirement marriage is a wholesome relation between the old couple and their children. Especially fortunate were those parents whose children lived nearby, visited their parents occasionally and stood ready to help the elderly couple in an emergency.[19]

It seems highly likely that second marriages in later life will become more common in the future than they have been in the past. Moreover, McKain's work indicates that marriage in later life contributes much to the

health and well-being of older Americans. Only the unavailability of an acceptable partner would seem to prevent this from becoming an even more common
phenomenon.

CONCLUSION

Individuals and families over the course of a lifetime find themselves adjusting
to and being shaped by a variety of changing circumstances and forces. Koller in
his work on the multigenerational family used the power variable to illustrate the
change in one's position in society over a lifetime. (Figure 8–2.) The young in
Koller's view are low in power and generally dependent on the parent generation for their support and survival. The parent generation in their middle years
are at the peak of their power and occupy the positions of greatest trust and
responsibility in the system. The old in Koller's diagram are in a period of
declining power. Intertwined with the power variable are such factors as
changing role, status, and privilege, which shift simultaneously over the life
cycle.

Older families, because they are in a position of declining power and
privilege, must adjust to new roles, statuses, and altered styles of life. Over time,
older couples see their children marry and leave home, the husband or wife or
both retire from full-time employment, and the family may move to a smaller
home or apartment.

Many changes in family life during the later years are seen as desirable.
The husband and wife, free of occupational and childrearing demands, are now
able to spend time in other desired ways. Often neglected family roles can now
be assumed. The husband and wife find that they have more time for each other
as well as time to dedicate to grandchildren and other family matters. They are
now free to choose among a variety of social activities, volunteer chores, recreational and social pursuits. Older persons frequently point out that the advantage

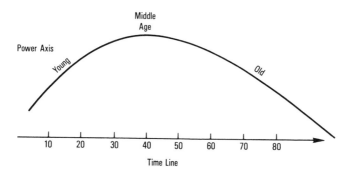

Figure 8–2

Source: Adapted from Marvin R. Koller, *Families: A Multigenerational
Approach* (New York: McGraw-Hill, 1974), p. 216.

of retirement is that it allows one the freedom to choose what one would like to do with their time. During most of the adult years, they found themselves doing what was expected of them.

On the other hand, the older couple often must adjust to some undesirable changes in their lifestyle. The retirement of one or both married partners means a reduced income, and often a loss in status in the eyes of their former associates and friends. The later years may be accompanied by the development of chronic health problems, declining energy, and the death of a spouse. One ultimately may have to give up one's independence, and move in with children, to government housing or a nursing home. Dependence on one's children involves a role reversal in the relationship. While formerly being the advisor and counselor of their children's problems, older persons now find themselves being advised and counseled.

In the study by Cox, Bhak, and Kline on the life satisfaction and marital adjustment of older Americans, two distinct personality types were identified and found to be quite different in their adjustment to the problem of older families. The internally oriented individuals were those who believed the rewards they received followed from or were contingent upon their own behavior. The externally oriented were those who felt that the rewards they received were controlled by forces outside of themselves and over which they had no control. The internally oriented believed that there was a direct causal chain between their behavior and the resultant reward or punishment. The externally oriented believed that reinforcement was not contingent upon actions of their own, but was the result of luck, fate, or chance, and was, therefore, unpredictable. The internally oriented tend to be self-directed; the externally oriented are inclined to be fatalistic. Older married couples who were internally oriented were found to experience greater marital cohesion, to have a better marital adjustment in the later years, were more satisfied with their life, and perceived the greater difficulties for themselves following the death of a spouse.

KEY TERMS

life cycle	internal orientation
ideal type	external orientation
generation	

SUGGESTED READINGS

ADAMS, BERT N., *The Family: A Sociological Interpretation.* Skokie, Ill.: Rand McNally, 1975.

APPLE, DORIAN, "The Social Structure of Grandparenthood," *American Anthropologist,* 58 (August 1956), 656–63.

BALLWEG, JOHN A., "Resolution of Conjugal Role Adjustment After Retirement," *Journal of Marriage and the Family,* 29 (May 1967), 277–81.

BELL, ROBERT R., *Marriage and Family Interaction,* pp. 412–16. Homewood, IL: Dorsey, 1963.

BENGTSON, VERN L., AND JOSEPH A. KUYPERS, "Generational Difference and the Developmental Stake," *Aging and Human Development,* 2 (1971), 249–60.

BERARDO, FELIX M., "Social Adaptation to Widowhood Among a Rural-Urban Aged Population," *Washington Agricultural Experiment Station Bulletin,* 689 (December 1969), 28–29.

BERARDO, FELIX M., "Widowhood Status in the United States: Perspectives on a Neglected Aspect of the Family Life Cycle," *The Family Coordinator,* 17 (July 1968), 191–203.

BERNARD, JESSIE, *Remarriage.* New York: Dryden, 1956.

BLOOD, R. J., AND D. M. WOLFE, *Husbands and Wives: The Dynamics of Married Living.* New York, Free Press, 1960.

BROZAN, NADINE, "The Sandwich Generation," *Aging,* ed. Eleanor Goldstein, Social Issues Series (1980), Article 52.

BURGESS, ERNEST W., "Family Living in the Later Decades," *The Annuals of the American Academy of Political and Social Science,* 279 (January 1952), 111–12.

BUSSE, E. W., AND F. PFEIFFER, *Behavior and Adaptation in Later Life.* Boston, MA: Little, Brown, 1969.

BUTLER, R. N., AND M. I. LEWIS, *Sex After Sixty.* New York: Harper & Row, 1976.

CAVAN, RUTH S., "Self and Role Adjustment in Old Age," *Human Behavior and Social Pressures,* ed. Arnold M. Rose, pp. 526–35. Boston, MA: Houghton Mifflin, 1962.

COX, HAROLD, ALBERT BHAK, AND ARTHUR KLINE, "The Motivation and Marital Adjustment Patterns of Older Americans," *Family Perspective,* 12, no. 1 (Winter 1978), 41–51.

COX, HAROLD, GURMEET SEKHON, AND CHARLES NORMAN, "Social Characteristics of the Elderly in Indiana," *Proceedings Indiana Academy of Social Sciences* (1978), pp. 186–98.

CUMMING, ELAINE, "Further Thoughts on the Theory of Disengagement," *International Social Science Journal,* 15 (1963), 377–93.

CUMMING, ELAINE, AND WILLIAM HENRY, *Growing Old: The Process of Disengagement.* New York: Basic Books, 1961.

DAVIDSON, MARIA, "Social and Economic Characteristics of Aged Persons (65 Years Old and Older) in the United States in 1960," *Eugenics Quarterly,* 14 (1967), 27–44.

DUETSCHER, IRWIN, "Socialization for Postparental Life," *Human Behavior and Social Processes,* ed. Arnold Rose, p. 507. Boston, MA: Houghton Mifflin, 1962.

FARBER, BERNARD, *Family Organization and Interaction,* pp. 29–30. San Francisco: Chandler, 1964.

FRIED, EDRITA G., AND KARL STERN, "The Situation of the Aged Within the Family," *American Journal of Orthopsychiatry,* 18 (January 1948), 31–54.

GLASSER, PAUL H., AND LOIS N. GLASSER, "Role Reversal and Conflict Between Aged Parents and Their Children," *Marriage and Family Living,* 24 (1962), 46–51.

JACOBSON, PAUL H., "The Changing Role of Mortality in American Family Life," *Lex et Scientia*, 3 (April-June 1966), 117–24.

KALISH, RICHARD A., *Late Adulthood: Perspectives on Human Development*. Monterey, CA: Brooks/Cole, 1975.

KASSEL, V., "Polygamy After 60," *Geriatrics*, 21 (1966), 214–18.

KERCKHOFF, ALAN C., "Husband-Wife Expectations and Reactions in Retirement," *Journal of Gerontology*, 19 (January 1964), 510–16.

KIMMEL, DOUGLAS C., *Adulthood and Aging*. New York: John Wiley, 1974.

KINSEY, ALFRED C., AND ASSOCIATES, *Sexual Behavior in the Human Female*. Philadelphia: Founders, 1953.

KOLLER, MARVIN R., *Families: A Multigenerational Approach*. New York: McGraw-Hill, 1974.

LIPMAN, AARON, "Role Conceptions of Couples in Retirement," *Social and Psychological Aspects of Aging*, ed. Clark Tibbitts and Wilma Donahue, pp. 475–85. New York: Columbia University Press, 1962.

LITWAK, EUGENE, "The Use of Extended Family Groups in the Achievement of Social Goals: Some Policy Implications," *Social Problems*, 6 (Winter 1959-60), 177–87.

LOBSENZ, N. M., "Sex and the Senior Citizen," *The New York Times Magazine*, January 20, 1974.

LOPATA, HELENA Z., "Role Changes in Widowhood: A World Perspective," in *Aging and Modernization*, ed. Donald O. Cowgill, L. D. Holmes, and D. Lowell, pp. 299–308. New York: Meredith, 1972.

MARIAS, JULIAN, *Generations: A Historical Method*, trans. Harold C. Raley. University: The University of Alabama Press, 1970.

MASTERS, WILLIAM H., AND VIRGINIA E. JOHNSON, *Human Sexual Response*. Boston, MA: Little, Brown, 1970.

MASTERS, WILLIAM H., AND VIRGINIA E. JOHNSON, *Human Sexual Inadequacy*. Boston, MA: Little, Brown, 1970.

McKAIN, WALTER C., *Retirement Marriage*. Storrs: University of Connecticut, 1969.

MEDLEY, MORRIS, "Marital Adjustment in the Post Retirement Years," *The Family Coordinator*, (January 1976), pp. 5–11.

MEDLEY, MORRIS, "Life Satisfaction Across Four Stages of Adult Life," *International Journal of Aging and Human Development*, 11 (1980), 193–209.

METROPOLITAN LIFE INSURANCE COMPANY, "Widows and Widowhood," *Statistical Bulletin*, 47 (May 1966), 3–6.

NEUGARTEN, BERNICE L., AND KAROL K. WIENSTEIN, "The Changing American Grandparents," *Journal of Marriage and the Family*, 26 (May 1964), 199–204.

NIMKOFF, M. F., "Changing Family Relationships of Older People in the United States During the Last Fifty Years," *The Gerontologist*, 1 (1961), p. 96.

NYE, F. IVAN, AND FELIX M. BERARDO, *The Family: Its Structure and Interaction*. New York: Macmillan, 1973.

PFEIFBER, ERIC, "Sexuality in the Aging Individual," in *Sexuality and Aging*, ed. Robert L. Solnick, pp. 26–32. Los Angeles: Ethel Percy Andrus Gerontology Center, The University of Southern California Press, 1978.

PINEO, PETER C., "Disenchantment in the Later Years of Marriage," *Marriage and Family Living*, 23 (1961), 9–10.

ROLLINS, B. C., AND K. L. CANNON, "Marital Satisfaction Over the Family Life Cycle: A Reevaluation," *Journal of Marriage and the Family,* 36 (1974), 271–83.

ROLLINS, B. C., AND H. FELDMAN, "Marital Satisfaction Over the Family Life Cycle," *Journal of Marriage and the Family,* 33, no. 1 (1970), 20–27.

ROSE, ARNOLD M., AND WARREN A. PETERSON, *Older People and Their Social World,* p. 26. Philadelphia, PA: David, 1965.

SHANAS, ETHEL, "Older People and Their Families: The New Pioneers," *Journal of Marriage and the Family,* 42, no. 1 (February 1980), 9–15.

SHANAS, ETHEL, AND OTHERS, *Older People in Three Industrial Societies,* p. 285. New York: Atherton, 1968.

SHANAS, ETHEL, AND GORDON STREIB, *Social Structure and the Family: Generational Relations.* Englewood Cliffs, NJ: Prentice-Hall, 1965.

STREIB, GORDON F., "Family Patterns in Retirement," *Journal of Social Issues,* 14 (1958), 60.

STREIB, GORDON F., "Integenerational Relations: Perspectives of the Two Generations of the Older Person," *Journal of Marriage and the Family,* 27 (November 1965), 469–74.

SUSSMAN, MARVIN B., AND LEE BURCHINAL, "Kin Family Network: Unheralded Structure in Current Conceptualizations of Family Functioning," *Middle Age and Aging,* ed. Bernice Neugarten, pp. 247–54. Chicago: University of Chicago Press, 1968.

SUSSMAN, MARVIN B., AND W. STROUD MORRIS, "Studies in Chronic Illness and the Family." Unpublished paper, Western Reserve University and Highland View Hospital, 1959-1964.

THOMPSON, WAYNE E., AND GORDON F. STREIB, "Meaningful Activity in a Family Context," in *Aging and Leisure: A Research Perspective into the Meaningful Use of Leisure Time,* ed. Robert W. Kleemeier, pp. 177–211. New York: Oxford University Press, 1967.

TIBBITTS, CLARK, "Origins, Scope and Fields of Social Gerontology," *Handbook of Social Gerontology,* ed. C. Tibbitts, pp. 3–26. Chicago: University of Chicago Press, 1960.

TOWNSEND, PETER, "The Emergence of the Four-Generation Family in Industrial Society," *Proceedings of the 7th International Congress of Gerontology, Vienna,* 8 (1966), 555–58.

TROLL, LILLIAN F., SHEILA J. MILLER, AND ROBERT C. ATCHLEY, *Families in Later Life.* New York: Wadsworth, 1979.

UPDEGEROFF, SUE G., "Changing Role of the Grandmother," *Journal of Home Economics* (March 1968), pp. 177–86.

9

WORK, LEISURE, AND RETIREMENT PATTERNS

The only true retirement is that of the heart, the only true leisure is the repose of the passions. To such persons it makes little difference whether they are young or old; and they die as they had lived with graceful resignation.

William Hazlitt
The Feeling of Immortality in Youth

INTRODUCTION

Work, free time, and leisure are differentially distributed to individuals over the life cycle. During the formative stages of life—during childhood, adolescence, and early adulthood—ample amounts of free time and leisure are available to the individual. Furthermore, during these stages free time and leisure carry none of the negative connotations of frivolity, idleness, or sinfulness that they often connote during the adult years. Children and young adults are presumed to need considerable free time to grow, develop, and mature.

During the adult years (early twenties to 65), however, American values dictate that commitment to work is to be the central life interest of the individual, and too much indulgence in free time and leisure pursuits is considered to be an indication of laziness and self-indulgence. One's identity, self-respect, and status are generally tied to involvement in the occupational career world and success therein.

Upon retirement the amount of free time and leisure expands dramatically, but this is often difficult for the individual to accept. The difficulty of this adjustment is in part related to habit and inertia and in part related to the long years of commitment to the work world and the values surrounding that world. The lifestyle one develops during a long work history of 40 to 50 years (in which

)ne's life is entirely structured around the nine-to-five workday, and much of remaining social life is directly or indirectly connected with colleagues and work-related acquaintances) is not easily altered upon retirement. Similarly, the commitment to productivity, goal attainment, upward mobility, and other basic work-related attitudes and values is not easily forgotten upon retirement. Thus, it is easy to understand the difficulty older Americans face in embracing free time and leisure during the retirement years. Melching and Broberg have gone so far as to suggest a national sabbatical system which would give the individual one year off for every seven years of employment during his or her life as a means of adequately preparing the individual for the retirement years.

The adjustment problem Americans are often confronted with as they pass through different phases of the life cycle is that the transition from one phase to another is often not gradual and smooth but rather abrupt and disjointed.

The term *role continuity* has been used by sociologists to describe that the activities one is involved in and the roles he or she is assuming at one stage of life are an adequate preparation for what will be expected of him or her at the next phase of life. What we find in American society is often a pattern of role discontinuity rather than continuity. Thus it is not clear that the large block of free time and leisure granted to youth is in any way an adequate preparation for the family responsibilities and work demands of early adulthood. Similarly, the work demands and numerous incentives for the individual to be productive during adult life seem not to be an adequate preparation for the free time and leisure activities of the retirement years. Thus, passing from one phase of the life cycle to the next in American society is often a somewhat difficult transition.

In this chapter we will discuss the meaning, relevance, and effect of changing opportunities and demands for work, free time, and leisure that the individual is confronted with during the adult and later phases of the life cycle.

WORK

The meanings of such diverse activities as work, leisure, and retirement to the individual member of a social system are often quite complex and difficult to discern in any kind of understandable fashion. The relevance of work and leisure activities for an individual is often paradoxically intertwined in his or her thinking. Consequently, the concept of work has been difficult for sociologists to precisely define.

Robert Dubin, for example, defined work as continuous employment in the production of goods and services for remuneration.[1] This definition ignores the fact that there are necessary tasks in society carried out by persons who receive no immediate pay. Mothers, fathers, housewives, and students do not receive pay for their valued activities.

Everett Hughes sees the meaning of an occupation in broad terms. He states:

> that an occupation, in essence, is not some particular set of activities; it is
> the part an individual plays in an ongoing set of activities.[2]

Hughes's definition involves less concern with the economic or remunerative aspects of work and greater concern for the social and relational aspects of work life.

Richard Hall attempts to incorporate both the economic and social aspects of the meaning of work and states:

> an occupation is the social role performed by adult members of society
> that directly and/or indirectly yields social and financial consequences
> and that constitutes a major focus in the life of an adult.[3]

Clifton Bryant similarly tries to include both the economic and social aspects of work life in his definition of labor: "Labor is any socially integrating activity which is connected with human subsistence."[4] By "integrating activity" Bryant refers to sanctioned activity which presupposes, creates, and recreates social relationships. The latter two definitions seem to take a broader and more complete view of work in the individual's total life.

One of the limitations of these definitions, which Hall observes, is the fact that they ignore school and occupational experiences prior to the period of full employment which are essential preparations for any occupational roles that one may assume.[5] Miller and Form have delineated four parts of the work life which include: initial, trial, stable, and retirement periods. The initial phase includes part-time jobs that a person may have as he or she passes through adolescence. While these jobs may be important in developing work habits and attitudes, they are not truly occupations since they are recognized as temporary. At the other end of one's life cycle, the retirement period, the individual is not involved in an occupation, but the individual's personality and behavior patterns have been strongly imprinted by the occupational identity acquired over the long work career. Viewing the individual's work life as progressing through these stages has the effect of minimizing the financial reward and maximizing the social and psychological meaning attached to work by the individual worker and others who comprise his or her social world.

The advantage of definitions that attach strong importance to the meaning and social aspects of an occupational role is the fact that they recognize the importance of work roles for which there is no, or very little, economic reward. The homemaker, while not receiving pay, may contribute considerably to a spouse's career and success. The college student in the period of anticipatory socialization and preparation for an occupation role may not be receiving any economic benefits. The retired salesperson living on a social security check is receiving no money as an immediate result of involvement in an occupation.

The most appropriate definitions of work, therefore, seem to be those that emphasize the social and role aspects of an occupation which an individual reacts to and is shaped by, whether he or she is financially rewarded for assuming these roles or not. From the perspective of the symbolic interactionists, one's work life and the roles one assumes during the workday will come, in time, to shape the individual's self-concept, identity, and feelings about oneself, and therefore strongly affect one's organization of personality and behavior. Moreover, from this perspective, the individual's choice of occupation is probably strongly affected by the desire to establish, maintain, and display a desired identity.

Of critical concern to gerontologists is the link between work and retirement. If the individual uses his or her occupation to establish, maintain, and display a desired identity during the working years, how can this identity be supported during his or her retirement years? This question will be addressed later in this chapter when the concept of leisure is discussed.

Historical Perspectives on the Meaning of Work

One of the most distinguishing features of contemporary urban society is the conscious expectation that one should derive meaning from one's work. Historically, there has often been the view that work was the province of the slave or the deprived classes and that the elites had more important things to do with their time.

The single best analysis of the meaning of work in different historical periods is that done by Adriano Tilgher.[6] In the Greek era a clear distinction was made between manual and intellectual labor, and manual labor was looked upon as a curse and nothing else. Generally, Greeks grudgingly accepted agriculture as not unworthy of a citizen because it brings a livelihood and independence. Greek landowners, however, delegated all manual work to slaves. Gentlemen were expected to develop the arts. Because of this value structure regarding work, the Greeks made significant contributions to art and literature but very few technological discoveries. Greeks felt that the mechanical arts were brutalizing to the mind and if pursued would result in one becoming unfit for thinking and truth. Free artisans were scorned as hardly better than slaves.

The Roman view was very similar to that of the Greeks. Cicero accepted agriculture and business as honorable if they were to lead to early retirement and the life of a country gentleman. The Romans also delegated most of the physical labor to slaves.

Current beliefs about the relevance of work in one's life seem to have emerged from the early Hebrew-Christian traditions. The early Hebrew tribes believed that men work because it is their duty to expiate the original sin committed by their forefathers in the early paradise. If man does not find his food like animals and birds, but must earn it, this is because of his sinful nature. Early Christian belief followed the Jewish tradition, regarding work as punishment placed on man by God because of man's original sin. It is the duty of every Christian to give work to the unemployed. Idleness is akin to original sin. Thus, work is never exalted as anything of value in itself, but only as an instrument of purification. Note that the concept of work was mostly negative, emphasizing its penal nature. The first hint of any positive meaning attached to work emerged from the early Christian belief that the fruits of one's labor could legitimately be shared with the less fortunate. With this view, work could be seen to serve useful social and humanistic functions. The result was that work was seen as having positive consequences, rather than only existing as punishment for one's sins. This view of work was apparently maintained through the Middle Ages; work was appropriate for all people as a means of spiritual purification; very gradually it began to assume other positive connotations as well. Consistent with this view, early Catholic leaders insisted that every member of the clergy should earn his own living by the work of his own hands. The effect of the Church requiring the clergy to work was to raise the value of labor in men's minds. If the priests, the religious leaders of the community, worked, then work was not merely the providence of the less fortunate.

St. Thomas Aquinas drew a hierarchy of professions and trades according to their value to society. The hierarchy placed agriculture first, handicrafts second, and commerce last. He kept money lending and usury as outcasts since interest is not earned by work, and since the only righteous sources of property and profit are work and inheritance.

Martin Luther added further dimensions to the Christian beliefs about work. Accepting the premise that work is the redeemer of fallen man, he added the idea that work has both penal and educational characteristics, and that everyone should work. Work, he thought, is the universal base of society, the real cause of differentiation of social classes. He was unsympathetic toward commerce and asserted that the purpose of work should be maintenance and not profit. He discouraged any idea of upward mobility, arguing that to seek by means of work to pass from one class to another goes against God's laws. Thus, according to Luther, God assigns to everyone his place, and one best serves God who stays in one's place.

Luther may be credited then with attaching positive value to all forms of work, since he believed that work is a form of serving God and there is just one best way to serve God: to do most perfectly the work of one's occupation. Thus Luther swept away all distinctions regarding the superiority of one kind of work to another. Every variety of work has equal spiritual dignity. All occupations are useful and equal in the common life of mankind.

John Calvin and the early Protestant thinkers added further dimensions to man's view of work, which Weber so ably pointed out were to lead to the justification of commerce and banking and lay the groundwork of modern capitalism.[7]

Calvin followed the earlier Christian concept that work is the will of God, but added the belief that profits and the accumulation of wealth are an indication of God's favor. The results of work (profit) should be used to finance other ventures which bring greater profits, further indications of God's pleasure. This represents a dramatic shift in earlier religious values regarding work, since man now has an obligation to God to attempt to achieve the greatest and most rewarding occupation. Thus, striving for upward mobility is morally justified, if not mandated. Luther's concept that upward mobility is bad and that all callings are equal in the sight of God was swept away.

Tilgher and others have observed that the "religion of work," so fundamental in modern industrial society, is beginning to falter in the twentieth century as a new orientation toward recreation and leisure develops. The evidence, to date, does not support this position. Morse and Weiss, in a study of American workers, found that the vast majority would continue working even if they were given the opportunity to maintain their lifestyle without working.[8] Weber's observations of the positive consequences of the "Protestant Ethic" on the attitudes and behavior of the workers in Western industrial nations apparently still carry considerable relevance.[9]

Some would argue that the cohorts currently entering the work force, being socialized in a different historical period, may be less commited to the work ethic than their parents and grandparents. While this is possible, it does not seem likely. More realistically it would seem that young people, just entering the economic marketplace, hold different attitudes than their parents toward work, but it is likely that these attitudes will change as they are socialized into an occupation and the work world. Vanlue asked a sample of social workers whether they derived more pleasure from their work life or their nonwork life.[10] The data indicated that prior to age 40 the respondents most often indicated that their greatest satisfaction came from their nonwork life. From age 40 on, however, respondents rather consistently indicated that their greatest satisfaction came from their work life. One wonders, then, if the purported discrepancy between younger and older workers' commitment to work is not more a function of age and their location in the life cycle than any fundamental change in attitudes toward work held by the generation currently entering the labor market. One might speculate that deriving greater satisfaction from work after the age of 40 might be a result of the fact that workers after this age are likely to be assuming the most powerful and prestigious positions in the organizations in which they work. Further, the high status which accrues to the individuals who occupy these valued positions contributes to a positive self-concept and results in the individuals holding much more positive attitudes toward work and work-related roles. If this were the case, it might contribute to our understanding of why some older workers are reluctant to retire.

Individual Motivation to Work

The subject of what has motivated people to work has been often investigated, but relatively few conclusions have been reached. The source of the difficulty seems to be the broad and diverse range of satisfactions which individuals can derive from their work lives.

The increasing complexity of modern society has led to the belief that many people work merely as a means toward the end of earning a living. Indeed,

Dubin's study of the "central life interests" of industrial workers concludes that work and the workplace do not generally constitute important foci of concern for this group. Orzack in a study of professional nurses found that 79 percent listed work as their central life interest while Dubin in a study of industrial workers found that only 24 percent listed work as a central life interest. This seems consistent with the oft-repeated phrase that white-collar workers live to work, and blue-collar workers work to live.

The danger, however, lies in overgeneralizing and reaching an oversimplistic conclusion which would imply that work is only a means to an end for most American workers.

Morse and Weiss found in their national sample of employed men that work gives them a feeling of being tied into the larger society, of having something to do, of having a purpose in life—functions which would not likely be found in nonwork situations. The conclusions drawn from this study seemed to be (1) that working is more than a means to an end; (2) that a man does not have to be at the age of retirement to be threatened by unemployment; and (3) that working serves other functions than an economic one for men in both middle- and working-class occupations.

Morse and Weiss asked industrial workers why they would continue to work even if they had enough money to live. The workers listed the following positive reasons: (1) they enjoy the kind of work; (2) they want to be associated with people; (3) they want to keep occupied; (4) the work justifies my existence; (5) the work gives me a feeling of self-respect; and (6) it keeps me healthy and is therefore good for a person. A number of negative responses, however, resulted from the same question. These included: (1) I would feel lost or go crazy; (2) I would feel useless; (3) I would feel bored; (4) I would not know what to do with my time; (5) I would work out of habit; and (6) I would work in order to keep out of trouble.

Weiss and Morse believe that not working would require considerable readjustment. The employed person does not often have alternative ways of directing his or her energy or of gaining a sense of identity and relationship to his or her society which are sufficiently important to take the place of work.

Victor Vroom attempts to delineate components of work motivation.[11] The first component is wages and all the economic rewards associated with the fringe benefits of the job, which people desire and which, therefore, serve as a strong incentive to work.

A second motivational inducement to work is the expenditure of physical and mental energy. Man seems to need opportunity for activity and the expenditure of energy in some meaningful way, and work provides this opportunity. Vroom notes that often animals will engage in activity as a consequence of activity deprivation.

A third motivation, according to Vroom, is the production of goods and services and is directly related to the intrinsic satisfaction the individual derives from successful manipulation of the environment.

A fourth motivation is social interaction. Most work roles involve inter-action with customers, clients, or members of identifiable work groups, as part of the expected behavior.

The final motivation is social status, since the individual's occupation is perhaps the best single determinant of one's status in the community.

The conclusion would seem to be that the various motivations for work undoubtedly assume different configurations for different people and occupa-tional groups. Social interaction may be most important for some while eco-nomic considerations may be most important for others. For still others the in-trinsic satisfaction derived from the production of goods and services may be all important. Thus the research in industrial sociology related to the worker's mo-tivation has not as yet produced a single adequate explanatory theory of work motivation. Future researchers will undoubtedly have to grapple with this problem.

The critical question for gerontologists is whether the same psychologi-cal and social motivational factors that thrust the individual into the occupation, career, and work patterns for the major part of their adult life can be channeled in a similar manner into their involvement with leisure activities during the re-tirement years. Can the individual find the same satisfaction, feeling of worth, and identity in leisure activities that he or she did in work-related activities? Streib and Schneider assert that this is possible and argue that the husband, wife, grandmother, grandfather roles may expand and become more salient in the retirement years; while simultaneously, the assumption of public service and community roles are now possible because of the flexibility of their time. The changing activities and roles, in their opinion, need not lead to a loss of self-respect or active involvement in the mainstream of American life.

FREE TIME

If we can think of nonwork time as free time or leisure, it is apparent that the technological revolution in industry which has occurred during the last one hun-dred years is making possible an ever-increasing amount of free time. Kaplan estimates that free time increased from about 2.18 hours per day in 1850 to about 7.48 hours per day in 1960. Similarly the amount of vacation time has been ever increasing. In 1970, 40 percent of both men and women in the labor force had accumulated vacation time of four weeks or more. If one thinks of retirement as free time, Juanita Kreps estimated that men born in 1960 will have nine more years of nonworking time than men born in 1900.

Harold Wilensky observes, however, that most of the gains in free time have occurred in the manufacturing and mining industries and since the 1940s, in agriculture. Professionals, executives, officials, civil servants, and self-employed persons have apparently not gained much of an increase in leisure time. The distribution of free time across the total population is not one of universal increase in free time, but rather a selective increase in certain occupations. While the pattern of increasing amounts of free time is not universally true for all occupations, Don Mankin believes that eventually this trend will extend to all of them. As hours of work decrease, vacation periods become longer and more numerous, and retirement is allowed at younger ages, the free time available to the individual steadily grows, according to Mankin.

Sebastian De Grazia's book *Of Time, Work and Leisure* points out, however, that even if we concede greater amounts of time away from the job it does not necessarily imply greater amounts of free time or leisure. De Grazia maintains that the amount of free time and leisure available to Americans has not increased appreciably since 1850.

His argument is that American society, and indeed each community, weaves its work and nonwork time together. Greater amounts of nonwork time are usually quickly absorbed by family, social, and community obligations placed on the individual, so that he or she actually gains nothing in the amount of available free time and leisure. In De Grazia's own words:

> Since 1850 free time has not appreciably increased. It is greater when compared with the days of Manchesterism or of the sweatshops of New York. Put alongside modern rural Greece or ancient Greece, though, or Medieval Europe and Ancient Rome, free time today suffers by comparison, and leisure even more.[12]

LEISURE

Work, Free Time, and Leisure

While never totally resolving the problem of what the distinction is between work and leisure, a number of social thinkers have attempted to clearly define the dimension of each. The layman has the general view that work is something we do in order to get paid and leisure is time spent away from work. While considerably more sophisticated, Ronald Pavalko's definition follows similar lines when he states:

> Clearly work and leisure are interrelated. While no universally agreed-upon definition of leisure exists, the most satisfactory way of thinking about leisure is as "free time." In this sense leisure is the reciprocal of work.[13]

Haworth and Smith assert that this distinction is not entirely accurate, however, since they believe that one can have free time but not necessarily have leisure. De Grazia follows this line of reasoning when he states:

> Work is the antonym of free time but not of leisure. Leisure and free time live in two different worlds ... anybody can have free time. Free

time is a realizable idea of a democracy. Leisure is not fully realizable, and hence an ideal not alone an idea. Free time refers to a special way of calculating a special kind of time. Leisure refers to a state of being, a condition of man, which few desire and fewer achieve.[14]

Stanley Parker has also rejected the notion of free and nonfree time. Parker attempts to graph out various aspects of both work and leisure using a line continuum (see Table 9–1).

Work is defined as the activity involved in earning a living, plus necessary subsidiary activities such as traveling to and from work. Work obligations involve doing things outside of normal working hours associated with the job, such as voluntary overtime, grading papers, working on one's expense account, and so on. The physiological needs follow the traditional definitions of these needs: sleeping, eating, and related activities. Nonwork obligations might include parental responsibilities, redecorating the house, and other routine responsibilities almost everyone is forced to meet. These are what some authors define as semileisure. Leisure in Parker's scheme is time free from obligations either to self or to others—time in which to do as one chooses.

Parker is attempting to refute the tendency to continuously refer to work in terms of time, and to leisure in terms of activity. (He argues that the two worlds of time and activity are not the domains of work nor leisure respectively, but are both dimensions of work and leisure.) Table 9–2 indicates that there is no reason to conceive either of work or leisure as being unidimensional, as has often been done in the past. Leisure does take up time, and we do engage in activity in work.

Table 9–1

WORK TIME		NONWORK TIME		
Work	Work Obligations	Physiological Needs	Nonwork Obligations	Leisure

Source: Stanley Parker, *The Future of Work and Leisure* (St. Albans, Eng.: Granada Publishing Ltd., 1971.)

Table 9–2

	ACTIVITY		
	CONSTRAINT -- FREEDOM		
Work Time	Work Employment	Work Obligations (connected with employment)	Leisure in Work
Non-Work Time	Physiological Needs	Nonwork Obligations	Leisure

Source: Stanley Parker, *The Future of Work and Leisure* (St. Albans, Eng.: Granada Publishing Ltd., 1971.)

Table 9–3

		DISCRETION	
		CHOSEN	DETERMINED
Work Relation	Independent	1. Unconditional Leisure	3. Complementary Leisure
	Dependent	2. Coordinated Leisure	4. Preparation and Recuperation

Source: John Kelly, "Work and Leisure: A Simplified Paradigm," *Journal of Leisure Research,* 4, no. 1 (1972), 50–62.

Kelly proposed a model for conceptualizing leisure along two dimensions: (1) the amount of choice the individual has in undertaking the activity and (2) the relation of the activity to work.

Unconditional leisure, as Table 9–3 indicates, is chosen freely and is unrelated to one's work. Examples might be hunting, fishing, or traveling, if they were totally unrelated to one's work. Coordinated leisure is freely chosen but related to the occupation in some way. The machinist working in a home workshop or the professor reading a work-related journal would be examples. Complementary leisure reflects the role expectations associated with one's occupation. Voluntary organizations, such as unions and professional associations in which persons in given occupations are expected to participate, would be an example of complementary leisure. Preparation and recuperation in the model are activities that are related to the occupation and are not freely chosen. The person who is too exhausted by working to do anything except watch TV, or the teacher who is preparing for tomorrow's class, would be examples of this use of nonleisure.

Atchley seems to follow this trend and defines leisure as activities pursued as ends in themselves. They are unplanned and unrequired. Leisure is primarily action directed generally toward self-satisfaction.

One problem confronted by Americans as they face the reality of increasing free time, and hence the potential for leisure, is an appropriate belief system and value structure with which to incorporate free time. As previously observed, Luther, Calvin, and later religious leaders of the Protestant Reformation extolled the virtues of hard work, self-denial, and thrift as the means of salvation. Thus, work had spiritual value while leisure consequently became identified with "idleness," "frivolity," "sinfulness," and "unproductive" activities. Consequently, increased leisure often represents a crisis of values for many Americans as a result of its incompatibility with the prevailing Protestant work ethic.

Bennett Berger has pointed out that the use of leisure by youth and the unemployed is often a concern of public officials, social workers, and clergymen who are convinced that leisure activities ought to be wholesome and morally acceptable.

Related to the concern regarding the ethical and moral considerations of leisure is concern for the overemphasis on the passive and consumptive leisure activities of many persons who do not appear to desire challenge in their leisure activities. Mankin is concerned that as leisure time increases, our society will develop more expensive versions of amusement parks, nightclubs, recreational vehicles, adult games, and travel clubs. Mankin believes that these activities emphasize passive consumption in leisure on the part of a consumer-oriented public and are not conducive to the individual's growth and development.

Pavalko in his text points out the patterns of leisure activities by different occupational groups, which Clark delineated in his study of 574 men in Columbus, Ohio. Respondents at the highest occupational prestige level were most likely to attend theatrical plays, concerts, special lectures, conventions, meetings of fraternal organizations, play bridge, visit an art gallery, study, and entertain at home. The second group of respondents, in terms of occupational status, mentioned such things as out-of-town weekend visiting, attending football games, and attending parties. Level 3 respondents mentioned playing golf more often than anyone else, and men at Level 4 were more likely than others to mention working on automobiles. Respondents at the lowest prestige level were most likely to mention fishing, or hunting, raising a garden, playing poker, spending time in a tavern, and pleasure driving.

While these are diverse recreational and leisure activities in which no single pattern is apparent, perhaps a more careful examination might reveal some trends. If we were to analyze the leisure pursuits of the different occupational groups in terms of whether the activity is physical or intellectual, it would seem that the upper status occupational groups, who primarily are involved in jobs taxing one's mental capacities (often involving the manipulation of symbols or ideas), pursue primarily intellectual activities such as listening to a lecture, visiting an art gallery, or similar activities during their free time. Respondents at the two lower levels were most likely to engage in activities that were physical in nature such as hunting, fishing, or working on the car. Since their work activities are also for the most part physical, there seems to be some continuity between the work and nonwork life. Workers employing mental skills on the job pursue intellectual activities in their leisure, and workers with physical jobs pursue physical activities in their spare time. Thus we see considerable similarity between the kinds of activities pursued in the work and leisure lives of American workers.

Both Wilensky[15] and Dumazediers[16] suggest that future researchers direct their attention to thinking of leisure in terms of a three-fold typology which views leisure as (1) an extension of work and continuation of one's personal development; (2) neutral and entertainment; and (3) opposition and recuperation. What seems to need to be added to the typology is a fourth category of leisure that is not an extension of work life but independent of work life and strongly related to the individual's identity and self-concept. From a symbolic-interaction perspective, leisure, in the true sense of the word, will be meaningful as an independent phenomenon which is different from work only when the individual attaches his or her identity, his or her opinion of himself or herself, to some of the activities that he or she pursues in his or her leisure time. Thus some of his or her collective self-concepts would be determined by the roles he or she assumes in leisure activities as well as the roles he or she assumes in work activities. Only in this way can leisure be truly meaningful to the individual, and only in this way can a self-concept begin to emerge which is not totally dependent on work and career. This would involve changing attitudes and values regarding work and leisure, and the legitimization of leisure activities, which postindustrial society would seem to demand.

From the symbolic-interaction perspective it would be argued that a person's choice of leisure activities is fundamentally related to his or her concept of self. Glasser, in a study of shopping habits and human motivation, concluded that the purpose of a shopping expedition was to reaffirm the person's perception of his or her identity and to compare this with an ideal identity. Making purchases was a secondary goal. Numerous studies have concluded that the overwhelming compulsion governing all of an individual's actions and attitudes is the pursuit of a desired identity. This desired identity is a composite of ideas that one holds about behavior, ethical standards, physical appearance, and lifestyle.

Haworth and Smith comment:

> Each person is engaged, unconsciously, in a continued quest, firstly to perceive clearly what this desirable identity is, secondly to achieve it within himself, and thirdly to display it.[17]

Undoubtedly, either consciously or unconsciously, the leisure activities which one pursues are related to this ideal self and are a reflection of the identity the individual would most like to establish.

RETIREMENT

Demographic and economic trends in American society have resulted in an ever-increasing number of retired Americans. Streib and Schneider observed that for retirement to become an institutionalized social pattern in any society, certain conditions must be met, among which are: that there must be a large group of people who live long enough to retire; the economy must be sufficiently productive to support segments of the population which are not included in the work force, and there must be some well-established forms of pension or insurance programs to support these people during their retirement years.

The rapid growth in both the number and percentage of the American population 65 and above since 1900 was observed in Chapter 1. Currently, approximately 25 million Americans are in this age category. While the number and proportion of the population over 65 years of age have been increasing steadily, the proportion of those who remain in the work force has decreased steadily. Labor force participation rates in 1900 indicated that nearly two-thirds of those over 65 worked. Frank Sammartino reports that by 1947 approximately 47.8 percent of men 65 and over were still in the work force. By 1975 only 21.7 percent of the men 65 and older were still in the work force. There appears to be a somewhat greater convergence in the work and retirement patterns of men and women when comparing the 1900 period with the 1970 period. The earlier pattern of work histories for men and women seemed to be for men to enter the work force earlier and retire later. Women tended to enter the work force later and retire earlier. Douglas Kimmel concluded that the current trends indicate that women are entering the work force earlier and working longer. Men, on the other hand, enter the work force later and retire earlier. Thus, the work histories of men and women are becoming very similar although the men, as a group, still have longer work histories than women. Not only are more women remaining in the labor force throughout their entire adult lives but more women are entering the labor force. Carole Allen and Herman Brotman point out that in 1950 three out of ten U.S. workers were women. In 1980, four out of ten U.S. workers were women. During this same time period 25 to 40 percent of the work force over 45 years of age were women.

The trend for both men and women for the past 30 years has been for larger numbers of them to choose to retire early. Allen and Brotman point out that in 1968 forty-eight percent of all new Social Security payment awards to men were claimants under 65. By 1978, this had increased to sixty-one percent. In 1968, sixty-five percent of all new Social Security awards to women were to claimants under 65. In 1978, the figure had increased to seventy-two percent. Allen and Brotman state:

> The early retirement rate for male and female workers was 66 percent in 1978. The most recent figures available from the Social Security administration indicate that since 1977, the number of people retiring early has declined slightly (to 64 percent in 1980). It is too early to tell whether or not this is a reversal of the early retirement trend.[18]

Simultaneously, fewer persons are choosing to remain in the labor force beyond the age of 65. Herbert Parnes points out that after age 65, the participation of men in the labor force drops sharply with fewer than three of ten men over 65 remaining in the labor force. Of those that remain, Allen and Brotman observe that less than one-third of all 65 and older workers were employed on a full-time basis.

In an earlier chapter the multiplicity of problems that the individual is confronted with at the time of retirement was observed. Some of these were the lowering of income; the loss of status, privilege, and power that were associated with one's position in the occupational hierarchy; a major reorganization of life's activities since the nine-to-five work day becomes meaningless; a changing definition of self due to the fact that most individuals over time come to shape their identity and personality in line with the demands of their major occupational roles; a considerable degree of social isolation if new activities are not found to replace previous work-related activities; and a search for new identity, meaning, and value for one's life. Obviously, the major reorganization of one's life that must take place at the time of retirement is potentially a source of adjustment problems for those individuals who must negotiate the change. Critical to the adjustment is the degree to which one's identity and personality structure were attached to the work role. For those individuals in which the work identity is most central to their self-concept, the one from which they have derived the greatest personal satisfaction, retirement will represent somewhat of a crisis. For others, in which the work identity was not central to their self-concept, nor their major source of personal satisfaction, retirement should not represent much of a problem.

Institutionalization of Retirement

There are often paradoxically different views on the meaning of retirement in the individual's mind. On the one hand, the individual is likely to view retirement as a well-deserved right earned by long years of hard work in a particular occupation. On the other hand, there is the tacit feeling that one is being forced out of a chosen career and the opportunity for gainful employment.

The emergence of retirement as an institutionalized pattern seems in part a result of the declining crude birth rate. With fewer young dependents to support, it is now possible to support older dependents. Simultaneously, the rapid increase in mass production means that not as large a labor force is needed to produce the nation's goods and services; older workers are freed of the need to work until the time of their death. Atchley asserts that the growth of the federal bureaucracy further facilitated the retirement of the older workers. A large government bureaucracy, in his opinion, became the political counterpart of an economic corporation which facilitated the pooling of the nation's resources, thus allowing a segment of society to be supported in retirement.

Robert Kleemeier has listed six key factors which he believes explain the decline of the elderly in the labor force:

1. The tendency for certain types of expanding job openings to be filled by women, rather than by elderly men because of the better training of the women.
2. The decline in self-employment which has always been a leading type of gainful activity for elderly men.
3. The rising general-income level which has made it possible for an increasing proportion of older persons to live in retirement.

4. The growth of old age assistance payments, old age insurance benefits, and private pension plans in the last forty years.

5. Increasing mechanization of agriculture and consolidation of farms, explaining the increase in retirement in rural areas.

6. The rise in the relative importance of large firms since there is clear evidence that both age discrimination in hiring and compulsory retirement policies are more likely to be found in the larger firms.

Undoubtedly, all of the factors have resulted in the institutionalization of retirement as a universal social pattern in American society. Whether inflation and the strain on Social Security funds resulting from the increased number of persons arriving at retirement age will cause a reversal of the trend toward early retirement or not remains to be seen. If the current trend toward early retirement continues, it becomes crucial that Americans begin to alter some of their basic attitudes and values regarding the importance of work and leisure in one's life. Retirement would seem inevitably to involve some alterations in one's priorities regarding work and leisure. A successful retirement adjustment seems to demand that the individual be able to establish and maintain a desired identity while in the pursuit of leisure activities.

Retirement Adjustment:
Social Factors

Using a variety of indicators of retirement adjustment, most of the past studies have often focused on two variables as the critical ones: namely, the kind of work the individual was involved in prior to retirement with its concomitant style of life, or the individual's preretirement attitude.

Simpson, Back, and McKinney view the former variable as the critical one, and speak of the disjunctive effects of retirement, asserting that work is one of the most important avenues for integrating the individual into the social system by giving him or her his or her identity, style of life, and social-participation patterns. Beginning with the assumption that work places the individual and his or her family in the hierarchy of the social structure, they argue that retirement undercuts the individual's major social support by removing him or her from the work world in which these supports are rooted. They conclude it is not retirement per se which is responsible for the individual's lack of self-anchorage and adjustment in retirement, but rather their work histories which do not allow them to develop other social ties in the larger system.

Their findings indicate that orientation toward work is the main influence shaping preretirement attitudes and consequently postretirement adjustment among upper white collar workers, that income deprivation in retirement is the main influence on retirement adjustment for the semiskilled workers, and that none of the explanations accounted for much variability within the middle stratum.

Streib and Schneider focused on the attitudinal orientation of being willing or reluctant to retire as the critical factor in retirement adjustment. Their findings indicated that those persons who are favorably disposed toward retirement are much more likely to retire than those who are reluctant to do so, and the former are simultaneously more likely to make a favorable retirement adjustment. This was true regardless of whether they voluntarily chose to retire or they were administratively retired by the company they worked for.

Streib and Schneider, though they viewed retirement as a major role disjuncture due to the loss of the work role, were led to some conclusions differing from previous research regarding the effects of the loss. Viewing role sets and role change as a dynamic process, they found that the loss of the work role does not inevitably lead to either adjustment problems or disengagement. Many retirees, after losing the work role, expanded activity in other ongoing roles (that is, as husband, wife, grandmother, grandfather, friend, and so on) which had often remained latent, and simultaneously assumed new roles such as citizenship and service roles. Their findings suggest that many retirees are able to successfully cope with the role realignment precipitated by retirement.

Streib and Schneider, utilizing a role approach to study the problems of retirement adjustment, suggest that an alternate approach would be to view the problem in terms of reference groups which are significant for work and retirement, namely: families, friends, cliques at work, and so on.

Following the Streib and Schneider suggestion that the use of reference groups and the symbolic-interaction perspective would be a useful way to study retirement adjustment, Cox and Bhak made a study of the effect of reference groups on both preretirement attitudes and postretirement adjustment. Their work indicated that family, close friends, and work group cliques were critical determinants of how the individual viewed retirement both prior to and after the event. They concluded that it was these critical reference groups that were shaping the individual's preretirement attitudes and hence his or her postretirement adjustment.

Psychological Factors
and Retirement Adjustment

Atchley perceives a number of phases the individual will go through in his or her attempt to make an adequate retirement adjustment:

1. Preretirement phase in which the individual's concerns are whether he or she will have an adequate income and what leisure interests should be pursued.
2. Honeymoon phase in which the individual wallows in his or her newfound freedom of time.
3. Disenchantment phase in which there is a letdown as he or she adjusts to the slower pace of life.

4. Reorientation phase in which the depressed person attempts to pull himself or herself together.

Reichard, Livson, and Peterson conducted a study of personality types associated with good and bad retirement adjustment. The personalities they identified as making good adjustments to retirement were the "mature," the "rocking-chair men," and the "activity oriented."

The "mature" were described as relatively free of neurotic conflict; they were able to accept themselves realistically and to find genuine satisfaction in activities and personal relationships. Feeling their lives had been rewarding, they were able to grow old without regret.

The "rocking-chair," because of their general passivity, welcomed the opportunity to be free of responsibility and to indulge in their passive needs in old age.

The "activity oriented" were unable to face passivity or helplessness in old age; they warded off their dread of physical decline by keeping active.

The poorly adjusted men included two types—the "angry men" and the "self haters." The "angry men" were unable to reconcile themselves to growing old and therefore became very bitter in the process. The "self haters" looked back on their past lives with a sense of disappointment and failure, but unlike the "angry men," they turned their resentment inward, blaming themselves for their misfortunes.

More recently Atchley, in his book on the sociology of retirement, argues that the individual's ability to adjust to retirement is directly related to the priority of goals in his or her life. Maintaining that everyone has personal goals, Atchley believes that achievement of these personal goals is the fundamental means by which one develops a strong sense of personal worth. The individual's goals might include such personal qualities as honesty, ambition, cheerfulness, and kindness. Material goals held by the individual might include such things as achieving ownership of land, house, farm, and so on. Still other goals, according to Atchley, might involve successful role performance such as being a good parent, lawyer, or artist. The individual's priority of goals, Atchley feels, will directly affect the ease or difficulty with which he or she adjusts to retirement. Thus, people who are committed to a hierarchy of personal goals with their career at the top, might find retirement more difficult than for people who place a lower priority on their career. People who stress the importance of personal qualities might place their job far down the list, and thus retirement would not be much of a problem. Still others, with a strong emphasis on achieving materialistic goals, would find retirement difficult to adjust to in direct proportion to the degree that it interferes with the chance to achieve materialistic goals. Atchley states:

> The crucial question, however, is whether retirement is a consequential change, a change that is important enough to necessitate a reorganiza-

tion in the upper level of the individual's hierarchy of personal goals. If not, then retirement produces no actual change in the criteria the individual uses to select from among the behavioral alternatives available to him.[19]

Critical Aspects of Retirement

The principal focus of many of the past studies of retirement adjustment has been whether the individual can find meaningful activities in retirement by which he or she can maintain a positive self-concept. Back and Guptil found:

> The overriding point of interest has been that retirement leads to a feeling of loss of involvement for males in this study. Without the job around which their lives had been built for some forty or fifty years, these retired men were unable to avoid feeling less useful, less effective and less busy than the men who were still employed. Different conditions of life in retirement did little to alter these findings.[20]

Other than the void left by the loss of the job and the value and meaning it has in the individual's feelings of usefulness and involvement, most of the remaining consequences of retirement are positive ones. The data indicate the negative orientation toward the self tends to decrease with age as the personality approaches closure.

Contrary to the popular belief that at retirement people get sick and die, the data indicate that the health of retired persons is as good or better than when they were working, and that there is no significant difference in preretirement and postretirement mortality rates if age is controlled.

Cottrell and Atchley found that retirement as such had little influence on such variables as depression, anxiety, anomie, or self-stability.[21] Cottrell and Atchley argue that there is little or no evidence that retirement is in any way related to the common problems of older Americans. They believe that the most common problem of retirement is the limitation that it places on income.

One further effect of retirement is to reduce the set of individuals one interacts with. In retirement, family and close friends come to comprise the social world of older Americans.

In discussing the concept of "significant others," Stryker states:

> This concept represents the recognition that, in a fragmented and differentiated world, not all persons with whom one interacts have identical or even compatible perspectives and that, therefore, in order for action to proceed, the individual must give greater weight or priority to the perspectives of certain others. To speak then of significant others is to say that given others occupy a high rank in importance for a given individual.[22]

While not referring specifically to the concept of significant others, numerous studies have observed the importance of maintaining close friendship ties for the successful adjustment of older Americans. Erik Erickson postulates that the capacity for intimacy is one of the major developmental tasks of life. Zena Blau's study of the structural constraints of friendship of the aged documents the importance of the prevailing age–sex–marital status patterns in the establishment of friendships. Arth, in his study of friendship in an aging population, is concerned with the importance of close friends in the social world of older Americans but does not define closeness. Rosow's study of friendship patterns under varying age density conditions imputes the importance of close friends to the successful adjustment of older Americans.

Lowenthal and Haven were the first to carefully consider the quality of the social relationships of older Americans. Using the concept of a "confidant" they observed that the healthiest and happiest of older Americans often seem to be those who were involved in one or more close personal friendships. They concluded that the maintenance of a stable intimate relationship is more closely associated with good mental health and high morale than is high social interaction or role status or stability of interaction and role.

All of these studies suggest that signficant others are of major importance to the successful adjustment of older Americans.

The composition of any individual's social world can be seen in terms of concentric circles or spheres of social involvement as illustrated in Figure 9–1. The first circle is the primary group of husband, wife, children, and a few very close friends. The second circle would indicate a wider range of associates such as well-known friends in the individual's work, social clubs, fraternal and religious organizations. The second circle constitutes the individual's "proximate others." In the third circle would be a much larger group of casual acquaintances in the work and social world of the individual. These are usually considered by sociologists as secondary group associations.

It is the secondary associations that tend to be reduced after retirement.

Figure 9–1

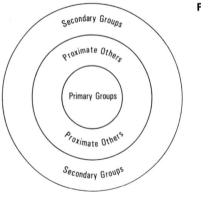

Therefore the importance of family and close friends (the two inner circles on the diagram) is magnified, and these people can appropriately be labeled the significant others of older Americans. The significant others will have the greatest impact on the individual's successful or unsuccessful retirement adjustment.

The Case of Compulsory Retirement

Over the long course of civilization's development, work demands have been constant and persistent for those who hoped to survive. Providing the necessary food and shelter in preindustrial society required the constant effort of as many hands as possible. Children started doing the simpler tasks early in their lives and old people, while reducing their work loads gradually, still worked, for the most part, until the day they died. The level of productivity of most preindustrial societies was such that free time and leisure were scarce commodities and work was most highly valued.

Industrialization initially brought little change in the demand for and value placed on labor, but did begin to produce surpluses and gradually led to a point where physical survival as such was no longer problematic. The ever-increasing productivity of the industrially developing nations ultimately led to both the reduction of work time in terms of hours per week and work life in terms of years on the job. Early in the twentieth century child labor laws were passed reducing considerably the involvement of children in factory and other kinds of work. These laws were seen as desirable by labor groups who felt that their workers would be paid better if they did not have to compete with child labor. The 1930s brought Social Security and the mandatory retirement policies of companies which attempted to force the older workers out in order to make room for younger employees. Although Congress passed a law in 1978 making mandatory retirement prior to age 70 illegal, most companies still do everything possible to encourage their employees to retire prior to age 65.

The United States, as well as other industrially developed nations, now seems to be approaching the postindustrial period in which jobs have become a scarce commodity. Women and blacks in the past, were frequently discriminated against in employment and found themselves being the last hired and first fired during fluctuations of the business cycle. The civil rights and women's liberation movements have resulted in federal regulations which prevent any kind of blatant discrimination against these groups. Women, in particular, were often not regularly employed in the past but are demanding full employment today. This, coupled with modern technology and increasing productivity, has resulted in the inability of the economic system to provide enough jobs for all eligible citizens desiring work.

The result of these trends is increasing pressure to force the older worker to retire earlier in order to make room for younger workers and those members of minority groups demanding equal opportunity for employment. As previously observed, all the evidence points to the fact that as one grows older, jobs become increasingly hard to find and the ones the older workers are able to find often pay poorly. In periods when there is high unemployment the older worker who is not protected by having worked long years with a company (thus accumulating considerable seniority) is most likely to be unemployed. Similarly, older workers employed by a company that moves to a new location are least likely to move because of the multiplicity of family and social ties that they have in a particular community.

Work commitments of older workers, while generally being highly valued, are also inflationary to some degree. From the perspective of business and management, older workers must be paid higher salaries, receive greater fringe benefits, and be granted greater vacation time. Thus older workers cost the company more. One can easily see why mandatory retirement policies are often considered to be good for business. From the individual's point of view, forced retirement is often perceived negatively due to the fact that income is reduced, the opportunity to work removed, and there seems to be little or no cash value for a lifetime of commitment to a particular organization.

Alton Johnson and his associates have listed the arguments in favor of mandatory retirement:

1. Employment and promotion opportunities for younger workers are thereby created.
2. Older workers are less desirable than younger workers, since they generally have declining mental and physical capacities, are more difficult to retrain, are less educated, and are more inflexible with regard to work rules and scheduling.
3. All workers are treated alike and thus less productive older workers are not humiliated by being singled out for dismissal.
4. Social Security and pension benefits provide income opportunities for older workers that younger workers do not have.
5. A mandatory age of retirement makes planning easier for both employers and employees.[23]
6. An older work force is more costly for employers due to related fringe benefits such as health and insurance plans.
7. Mandatory retirement may be the only practical way of dismissing older workers who are insulated by existing seniority systems.

Johnson and his associates offer equally persuasive arguments against mandatory retirement:

1. Such policies discriminate against older workers.
2. Chronological age is a poor indicator of ability to perform work.
3. Mandatory retirement results in the loss of income, health, and identity of older workers.

4. Mandatory retirement reduces Social Security benefits for some workers who are at the highest earning years. This is especially true for late entrants in the labor force such as married women.

5. Older workers have skills and experience that younger workers do not, thus mandatory retirement reduces the total output of the economy.

6. Mandatory retirement increases the number of retirees, raising Social Security expenses and burdening the remaining members of the work force.[24]

Historically, most people have retired voluntarily because of poor health. While this has been true in the past, the emergence of less physically demanding jobs and improved medical technology may result in other factors leading to the retirement decision. William Pollman, in a study of Chrysler Corporation employees who retired early, concluded that adequate retirement income was the most common reason given for retirement. If adequate retirement income were assured, the decision to retire apparently would be voluntarily arrived at by a majority of workers.

Preretirement programs undoubtedly would do much to ease the fears of many older workers and to facilitate for them a smooth transition to the retired state. Unfortunately, most of the large companies that currently have any preretirement programs offer their workers, at most, only discussions of what the workers can expect to make in retirement.

The business community and educational institutions have been willing to invest large amounts of money, time, and effort socializing the individual for a particular occupation or career. This socialization includes both the training of practical skills as well as proper attitudes and values. During the later phase of the career and the life cycle, however, there seems to be little interest in, or effort invested in, preparing the individual to withdraw from an occupation. Thus business and education seem to be following the general societal pattern of being greatly concerned in preparing the individual to assume the role but little concerned about his or her ability to disembark from a previously occupied role.

Recognizing the inadequacies of current retirement counseling programs, and looking toward the future in terms of what the priorities of retirement decisions and planning should include, the following would seem to be the most desirable suggestions:

1. The development of adequate preretirement programs to prepare the worker for retirement.

2. A more flexible retirement policy in which the age of retirement is not mandatory.

3. Maximum freedom for the individual to choose and plan for the point at which he or she will retire.

Whether these goals will be achieved in the future remains to be seen.

CONCLUSION

Work, leisure, and retirement are different dimensions of human life, all of which must, in one way or another, be incorporated into the individual's style of life and defined in such a way as to give meaning to the individual's existence.

The "Protestant Ethic," so aptly described by Weber, maintained that work was the redeemer of fallen man and leisure an indication of frivolity and man's sinful nature, a belief that has made it somewhat difficult for Americans to easily embrace leisure activities.

The industrial and technological revolutions, on the other hand, have resulted in a shorter work day and a shorter career history for all Americans. The result is that a growing number of the citizenry experiences increasing free time in their daily lives and more years in retirement without the appropriate value structure to make the additional opportunity for leisure activities a meaningful part of their lives.

Ultimately one's identity, and self-concept, will be shaped as much by leisure pursuits as by work roles. This shift in emphasis away from the all inclusiveness of the relevance and importance of work roles to one's sense of worth has not been entirely negotiated by most Americans. The work of Morse and Weiss indicates the pervasiveness of the "work ethic." The effect of changing values and the increasing acceptance of leisure activities in industry and other institutions in American society is difficult to gauge. One can only surmise that social change will occur, at whatever pace, and that future shifts in the American way of life are inevitable as the balance between work and leisure activities swings further in the direction of leisure.

KEY TERMS

leisure   work
role continuity   free time
role discontinuity

SUGGESTED READINGS

ALLEN, CAROLE, AND HERMAN BROTMAN, *Chartbook on Aging in America.* Washington, D.C.: Administration on Aging, 1981.

ARTH, M., "American Culture and the Phenomenon of Friendship in the Aged," in *Social and Psychological Aspects of Aging,* eds. C. Tibbitts and W. Donahue, pp. 522–34. New York: Columbia University Press, 1962.

ATCHLEY, ROBERT, *The Sociology of Retirement.* Cambridge, MA: Schenkman, 1976.

BACK, KURT W., AND CARLETON S. GUPTILL, "Retirement and Self Rating," in *Social Aspects of Aging,* eds. Ida H. Simpson and John C. McKinney. Durham, NC: Duke University Press, 1966.

BERGER, BENNETT, "The Sociology of Leisure: Some Suggestions," in *Work and Leisure,* ed. O. Erwin Smigel, pp. 21–40. New Haven, CT: College and University Press, 1963.

BIER, WILLIAM C., ed., *Aging: Its Challenge to the Individual and to Society.* Bronx, NY: Fordham University Press, 1974.

BLAU, ZENA SMITH, "Structural Constraints on Friendship in Old Age," *American Sociological Review,* 26 (1961), 429–40.

BRYANT, CLIFTON, *The Social Dimensions of Work.* Englewood Cliffs, NJ: Prentice-Hall, 1972.

CAPLOW, THEODORE, *The Sociology of Work.* Minneapolis: University of Minnesota Press, 1954.

CLARK, ALFRED C., "The Use of Leisure and Its Relation to Levels of Occupational Prestige," *American Sociological Review,* 21 (June 1956), 301–307.

COTTRELL, FRED, AND ROBERT ATCHLEY, *Women in Retirement: A Preliminary Report.* Oxford, Ohio: Scripps Foundation, 1969.

COX, HAROLD, AND ALBERT BHAK, "Symbolic Interaction and Retirement Adjustment: An Empirical Assessment," *International Journal of Aging and Human Development,* 9, no. 3 (1978–1979), 279–86.

DE GRAZIA, S., *Of Time, Work and Leisure.* New York: Twentieth Century Fund, 1962.

DRAKE, JOSEPH T., *The Aged in American Society.* New York: The Ronald Press, 1958.

DUBIN, ROBERT, "Industrial Workers World: A Study of the Central Life Interest of Industrial Workers," *Social Problems,* 30 (January 1956), 131–42.

DUMAZEDIERS, J., *Lo Spettacalo.* London: Collier-Macmillan 1972.

DUMAZEDIERS, J., *Towards a Society of Leisure.* London: Collier-Macmillan, 1967.

DURKHEIM, EMILE, *The Division of Labor in Society,* trans. George Simpson. New York: Free Press, 1947.

ERICKSON, ERIK H., "Identity and the Life Cycle, " *Psychological Issues,* monograph. New York: International University Press, 1959.

FOX, ALAN, *A Sociology of Work in Industry.* New York: Macmillan, 1971.

GLASSER, R., *The New High Priesthood: The Social and Political Implications of a Marketing Oriented Society.* London: Macmillan, 1967.

GREENE, MARK R., *Preretirement Counseling, Retirement Adjustment, and the Older Employee.* Eugene, OR: Graduate School of Management and Business, 1969.

HALL, RICHARD, *Occupations and the Social Structure.* Englewood Cliffs, NJ: Prentice-Hall, 1975.

HAVIGHURST, R.J., AND OTHERS, eds., *Adjustment to Retirement.* The Netherlands: Koninklijke Van Gorcum and Corp. N.V., 1969.

HAWORTH, J. T., AND M. A. SMITH, *Work and Leisure.* Princeton, NJ: Princeton Book Company, 1975.

HOFFMAN, ADELINE M., *The Daily Needs and Interests of Older People.* Springfield, IL: Chas. C Thomas, 1970.

HUGHES, EVERETT C., *Men and Their Work.* New York: Free Press, 1958.

JOHNSON, ALTON, CHRISTOPHER FORREST, AND FRANK SAMMARTINO, "Mandatory Retirement," in *Monographs on Aging,* no. 1, pp. 18–19. Madison, Wisc.: Faye McBeath Institute on Aging and Adult Life, University of Wisconsin, 1979.

Kaplan, M., *Leisure: Lifestyle and Lifespan*. Philadelphia: Saunders, 1979.

Kimmel, Douglas, *Adulthood and Aging*. New York: John Wiley, 1974.

Kleemeier, Robert W., ed., *Aging and Leisure*. Fair Lawn, NJ: Oxford University Press, 1961.

Krause, Elliot A., *The Sociology of Occupations*. Boston, MA: Little, Brown, 1971.

Kreps, Juanita M., ed., *Employment, Income and Retirement Problems of the Aged*. Durham, NC: Duke University Press, 1963.

Lowenthal, Marjorie Fiske, and Clayton Haven, "Interaction and Adoption: Intimacy as a Critical Variable," *American Sociological Review*, 33 (1968), 20–30.

Manis, Jerome and Bernard Meltzer, *Symbolic Interaction: A Reader in Social Psychology*. Boston, MA: Allyn and Bacon, 1972.

Mankin, Don, *Toward A Post-Industrial Psychology*. New York: John Wiley, 1978.

Melching, Dolores, and Merle Broberg, "A National Sabbatical System: Implications for the Aged," *Gerontologist*, 14 (April 1974) 175–81.

Merton, R. K., L. Broom, and L. S. Cottrell, "The Study of Occupation," in *Sociology Today*. New York: Harper and Row, Pub., 1965.

Miller, Delbert, and William Form, *Industrial Sociology*. New York: Harper and Row, Pub., 1969.

Morse, Nancy, and R. S. Weiss, "The Function and Meaning of Work and the Job," *American Sociological Review*, 20, no. 2 (April 1955), 191–198.

Nosow, Sigmund, and William Form, *Man, Work and Society*. New York: Basic Books, 1962.

Owen, John D., *The Price of Leisure*. Montreal, Canada: McGill-Queen's University Press, 1970.

Parker, Stanley, *The Future of Work and Leisure*. New York: Holt, Rinehart & Winston, 1971.

Parnes, Herbert S., *Work and Retirement: A Longitudinal Study of Men*. Cambridge: The Massachusetts Institute of Technology, 1981.

Pavalko, Ronald W., *Sociology of Occupations and Professions*. Itasca, IL: F. E. Peacock Publishers, 1971.

Pollack, Otto, *The Social Aspects of Retirement*. Homewood, IL: Richard D. Irwin, 1956.

Pollman, A. William, "Early Retirement: Relationship to Variation in Life Satisfaction," *Gerontologist*, 11, no. 1, part 1 (1971), 43–49.

Reichard, S., R. Livson, and P. C. Peterson, *Aging and Personalities*. New York: John Wiley, 1962.

Rhee, H. A., *Human Aging and Retirement*. Geneva: General Secretariat, International Social Security Association, 1974.

Riley, Matilda, Marilyn Johnson, and Anne Foner, *Aging and Society*. New York: Russell Sage, 1972.

Roberts, Kenneth, *Leisure*. London: Longman Group Limited, 1970.

Rosenburg, George S., *The Worker Grows Old*. San Francisco: Jossey-Bass, 1970.

Rosow, Irving, *Social Integration of the Aged*. New York: Free Press, 1967.

Sammartino, Frank, "Early Retirement," in *Monographs on Aging*, no. 1. Madison: University of Wisconsin, Faye McBeath Institute on Aging and Adult Life, 1979.

SIMPSON, I. H., K. W. BACK, AND J. MCKINNEY, "Work and Retirement," in *Social Aspects of Aging*, p. 45. Durham, NC: Duke University Press, 1966.

SIMPSON, IDA HARPER, *Social Aspects of Aging*. Durham, NC: Duke University Press, 1966.

STREIB, GORDON F., AND CLEMENT J. SCHNEIDER, *Retirement in American Society*. New York: Cornell University Press, 1971.

STRYKER, SHELDON, "Symbolic Interaction as an Approach to Family Research," *Marriage and Family Living*, 21 (1959), 111–119.

TIBBITTS, CLARK, AND WILMA DONAHUE, eds., *Social and Psychological Aspects of Aging*, pp. 529–34. New York: Columbia University Press, 1962.

TILGHER, ADRIANO, *Work: What It Has Meant to Men Throughout the Ages*, trans. Dorothy Fisher. New York: Harcourt Brace Jovanovich, Inc., 1930.

VANLUE, NANCY, "The Sex Differential As It Relates to Public Welfare Personnel's Job Satisfaction." Unpublished master's thesis, Indiana State University, 1974.

VOLLMER, HOWARD M., AND DONALD L. MILLS, eds., *Professionalization*. Englewood Cliffs, NJ: Prentice-Hall, 1966.

VROOM, VICTOR, *Work and Motivation*. New York: John Wiley, 1964.

WEBER, MAX, *The Protestant Ethic and the Spirit of Capitalism*, trans. Talcott Parsons. London: George Allen and Unwin, 1935.

WILENSKY, HAROLD L., "Professionalization of Everyone," *American Sociological Review*, 70 (April 1964) 137–138.

WILENSKY, HAROLD L., "The Uneven Distribution of Leisure: The Impact of Economic Growth on Free Time," in *Work and Leisure*, ed. Erwin O. Smigel, pp. 21–40. New Haven, CT: College and University Press, 1963.

WILLIAMS, RICHARD H., CLARK TIBBITTS, AND WILMA DONAHUE, eds., *Processes of Aging*. New York: Lieber-Atherton, 1963.

10

LIVING ENVIRONMENTS IN LATER LIFE

Old Parents

For reasons we could not control
This Home has now become our home,
We may not live amongst our own
We who are blind and aged grown.

Our children must their own lives lead,
Their own tasks do; their own times need.
Here we live in calm and rest—
Indeed, for us, this is the best.

To God nor man bemoan our fate
But join in friendship; cast out hate.
Let peaceful living be our goal
As befits a human soul.

Yiddish verse written by an 83-year-old
resident of a home for aged people,
translated by Shura Saul

Old age, as described earlier, is often a period of shrinking life space. This concept is crucial to our understanding of the housing problems and choices of older Americans. As older persons lose strength, experience health losses, and begin generally to feel less in control of their environment, they are likely to restrict their mobility to the areas where they feel most secure. For most older persons this means that they spend much of their time in their immediate neighborhood and increasing amounts of time inside their own house or apartment. The older one becomes the more likely he or she is to spend every moment at home. Hansen has estimated that persons over 65 spend 80 to 90 percent of their lives in the domestic (home) environment.[1] In comparing older persons with other groups, only small children and those living in institutions are so house and neighborhood bound.

The house, neighborhood, and community environment is, therefore, more crucial to older persons than it is to other age groups. The contact that older persons have with the home and outside neighborhood can be very stimulating or can be very foreboding, dangerous, and threatening. Across the country older Americans find themselves living in a variety of circumstances ranging from some of the most desirable to some of the most undesirable neighborhoods. Similarly they are found living in some of the most exclusive homes as well as some of the most modest. Fifty percent of the elderly are housed in structures that were built in 1939 or earlier.[2]

Older persons are often in the position of trying to hold onto a house and a neighborhood in which they lived most of their lives. Their current location often has for them a long history and much sentimental value attached to it. Harris found that although almost 75 percent of the respondents can find some undesirable conditions existing in their neighborhoods, over 95 percent of them do not wish to move as a result of those conditions. Harris found that the elderly were less likely to move than the general population; those that do move tend to stay in the same county to about the same degree as the general population.[3]

Montgomery made a study of older persons who lived in a small community in Pennsylvania and found that 76 percent of those interviewed were born in or near the community and 81 percent had lived in their current dwelling for ten or more years. Seventy-eight percent of this sample liked their neighborhood very well and 76 percent liked their house very well.[4]

Erich Fromm has argued that people need a sense of place, a feeling that they belong in their environment. Perhaps a house and neighborhood for the older persons provides this sense of place that Fromm described.[5]

The fact that a high proportion of older Americans own their own homes and the fact the majority of them do not want to move does not mean that they have no problems with their current housing, however. Kalish states:

> Neither should this figure be interpreted to mean that older people have no housing problems. First, a high proportion of their homes are extremely old and often rundown, second, many are located in high-crime areas, where older people are especially likely to be victims, third, rising property taxes often take a substantial portion of the older person's income, leaving no money for repairs, and finally, the elderly often remain in their homes because they have no adequate alternative.[6]

Older couples who give serious thought to their housing problems may come to the conclusion that with the children raised and grown the large house is becoming a drain on their physical energy and economic resources. They may rationally decide then to move to a smaller house or apartment. It is quite possible that the proceeds of the sale of the old house may be inadequate for the purchase of a newer smaller dwelling.

In this chapter, an attempt will be made to discuss the housing needs of older Americans and to relate these to the choices that are available to them.

RESIDENTIAL SEGREGATION OF THE AGED

Residential segregation refers to the fact that a high proportion of identifiably different kinds of people may be located in distinct zones and neighborhoods of a community. Thus, young people may be disproportionately found in given neighborhoods while older people may be found in other neighborhoods. Similarly certain areas of a city are known for their high concentrations of given ethnic groups.

Where a person lives in the community is not an accidental or unstructured event but rather indicates a great deal about the person's social status. McKenzie, Park, and Laumann have all argued that there is a direct link between territorial organization and culture and that a city's spatial order is a reflection of its social order.[7]

Many of the past studies in sociology used income, occupation, and education as indicators of one's social status and made predictions regarding one's residential location. They expected and found that persons of similar social class lived in similar sections of the city. Duncan and Duncan used occupations as an indicator of residential segregation and found that persons whose occupations approach the extremes of the occupational status scale were more residentially segregated than those persons whose occupational status was nearer the center of the scale. Sociologists would expect the most unique status group to be the most segregated since their status position is most distinct.[8]

Feldman and Tilly, in a later study of social status and residential segregation, concluded that education, used as a measure of style of life, accounts for a substantially larger part of the variation in the association than does income used as a measure of resources.[9]

Still more recently, Coleman and Neugarten, in their study of Kansas City, found that their respondents invariably referred to the resident's geographic location as an example of a complex stratification system. The subjects ranked neighborhood not only in terms of the individual's present social or financial status, but also in terms of the person's status goals.[10]

Later studies began to use age as a critical variable for determining one's location in the urban community. Eisenstadt observed that age differences are among the most basic and crucial aspects of human life and destiny. All societies are confronted with age-related role changes and the progression of power and capacities connected with age changes. Thus the transition from youth to old age is subject to social and cultural definitions.[11]

To the degree that age groups are differentially located along family, career, and status positions in society, we should expect to find them differentially located in the urban community. While not much work has been done on identifying age concentrations of young and middle-age persons in the urban community, Cowgill's work was instrumental in identifying concentrations of older people in the 56 large cities studied. Cowgill, using the Spencerian principle that increasing mass results in increasing differentiation of parts including spatial segregation of heterogeneous elements, suggests that the size of the community may be a critical determinant of age segregation. Miller later found that this trend had increased in the 1960s. In the seven cities which she studied there was a marked increase in the degree of segregation of the aged.

Some would argue that the residential segregation of older persons in the urban community is a result of social class and status position of this particular group. Others would argue that this is a result of changing family needs. Foote and his associates had earlier traced in some detail the changing housing needs resulting from the changing size of the family and stage of the life cycle, including the shrinking stage in later life.

Golant notes, however, that changing needs do not lead to an automatic adjustment and that, particularly in old age, there is much inertia that retards such adjustments. He contends that concentrations of the elderly are more likely to result from immobility than mobility. Goldscheider's work on the mobility patterns of the older population does not seem to totally support Golant's inertia and immobility explanations of concentrations of older people in the urban community. He found that 30 percent of the fifty years and older population move at least once over a five year period and that 10 percent of this group move annually. It seems unlikely that inertia alone would account for the age concentrations of the older population. What must be remembered is that most but not all older persons are residentially stable, nor, for that matter, are all younger persons mobile.

Cox and Bhak conducted a study of age segregation in an average-size Midwestern city to determine if the age segregation patterns which Cowgill and Miller found in the large urban community were equally true for smaller cities. They predicted that the young (20–24) and the old (65+) could be considered distinct status groups, sharing some very similar and other very dissimilar problems in relation to the general population. They argued that these two age categories are comprised of people who are generally not totally involved in occupation and career, who are dependent on others for their income and security, and who are often excluded from the mainstream of American life. The young are not totally involved in the occupational status hierarchy because they are either in the education years, for those who seek a college degree, or the apprentice years, for those who do not. Neither of these groups is well established in their career pattern. The college students have not entered an occupation. The noncollege students in the apprentice programs often experience frequent job changes as they attempt to acquire the necessary occupational skills. The old, because they have arrived at the age of retirement, are similarly not actively involved in occupational and career activities. The age groups in between 25 and 65, on the other hand, are likely to be involved in occupations and careers, greatly concerned with status and upward mobility, and inextricably enmeshed in the political, economic, and social structure of the culture. Cox and Bhak's predictions were:

1. The "dependent groups" (20–24 and 65+) would be more residentially segregated than the "active groups" (25–64).
2. Within the "dependent groups" the young (20–24) and the old (65 and older) will be located in distinctly different zones of the city.

Table 10–1 indicates that the general pattern of these findings conformed to the direction predicted by Cox and Bhak. The residential-segregation scores form a distinct U-shaped curve in which the young and old age groups were found to be more residentially segregated than the group in between. The 20–24 age group received a residential segregation score of 26.5 which was the highest score of all the groups. The 75 and older age group received a residential segregation score of 21 which was the second highest score. The 65–74 age group received a residential segregation score of 13.5 which was the third highest score.

Cox and Bhak's prediction that the young and old would live in distinctly different zones of the city was also borne out by the data. Their argument was that these two groups, while being defined as dependent, would represent distinctly different status groups, one being in the preoccupational category and the other in the postoccupational category. In order to test the validity of this hypothesis, the city's Standard Metropolitan Statistical Area was divided into

Table 10–1 Differences in Residential-Segregation Scores of the Area by Age Groups*

AGE GROUP	RESIDENTIAL SEGREGATION SCORE**
20–24	26.5
25–34	10.5
35–44	12.0
45–54	8.0
55–64	10.0
65–74	13.5
75+	21.0

*High scores indicate greater residential segregation.
**Determination of the residential segregation scores for these age groups was done in the same manner as Duncan and Duncan's 1955 study of occupational rank and residential segregation. This involves the tabulations of two distributions. The first distribution consists of the proportion of each age group residing in each census tract. The second distribution is obtained by computing the proportion of all other age groups combined, except the group being measured in each tract. The index of residential segregation is then one-half the absolute value differences of the two distributions for each age group, taken tract by tract.

Source: Harold Cox and Albert Bhak, "Determinants of Age-Based Residential Segregation," *Sociological Symposium*, no. 29 (January 1980), 35. Reprinted by permission of the authors and *Sociological Symposium.*

Table 10–2 Differences in Mean Residential-Segregation Scores for Selected Age Groups by Ecological Zones*

AGE GROUP	ECOLOGICAL ZONE						
	1	2	3	4	5	6	7
20–24	26.00	13.00	8.25	16.25	10.50	15.00	10.50
65–74	16.50	22.25	24.50	14.75	15.00	9.25	4.25
75+	16.25	24.75	21.50	14.25	8.25	11.00	5.50

*Ecological zones, comprised of configurations of census tracts concentric with the center of the city, move outward from Zone 1 to Zone 7.

Source: Harold Cox and Albert Bhak, "Determinants of Age-Based Residential Segregation," *Sociological Symposium,* no. 29 (January 1980), 36. Reprinted by permission of the authors and *Sociological Symposium.*

concentric zones in much the same manner suggested by Park and Burgess. Zone 1 represented the central city and Zone 7 represented the regions farthest from the central city; the intermediate Zones 2–6 fell in between. As Table 10–2 indicates, locating the zone with the largest proportion of various age groups resulted in a clear pattern. The 20–24 age group was most heavily concentrated in Zone 1. The 65–74 age group was most heavily concentrated in Zone 3. The 75-and-above age group was most heavily concentrated in Zone 2. From the perspective of where they are located, the dependent groups are least likely to live in Zone 7, which represents the suburban neighborhood and outskirts of the city. This pattern is considerably stronger for the two older age groups. Cox and Bhak argued that the zones of low population density are too isolated and devoid of the minimum social interaction which seems to be desired by members of the older age groups. This study further found that as early as age 55, changes in housing are being seriously considered by older persons as they begin to anticipate retirement and the alterations in their lifestyle that are to be forthcoming.

Older persons are found in disproportionate numbers in large urban communities and in small towns throughout the country. Their location in zones surrounding the downtown districts in the urban community provides maximum access to the concentration of local services essential to the regular needs of the elderly, such as grocery stores, drug stores, hospitals, banks, and bus services. The scattered and widely spread suburbs make services needed by the elderly more widely scattered and less accessible.[12]

The urban community also carries some undesirable aspects for its elder residents.

The more aged and infirm elders will find innumerable barriers to their use of the services. The urban communities are designed for the average thirty-year-old male who is healthy, strong, mobile, and thereby capable of negotiating the environment with ease.

There are many barriers for older persons in the urban community which may include irregular surfaces, long flights of stairs, crowded buses with high steps, and the high crime rates.[13] The cultural diversity in urban communities which young people find attractive may be a further source of insecurity and fear for the elderly. In addition one finds low quality housing, deteriorating neighborhoods, crowding, congestion, and noise in the urban community.

The small town is heavily inhabited by farm families who find their farms too isolated in later life and move into the more heavily inhabited rural village and small town, as well as by some urban residents who move back to their childhood hometowns after retiring because it is cheaper to live there. These communities are likely to provide easy access to grocery stores, drug stores, and restaurants. They are, moreover, relatively free of crime. They are primarily homogenous in make-up; most of the residents are white, of northern European descent, and largely Protestant. They provide for older persons a quiet, secluded enclave from which they can feel free and secure from many of the stresses and strains that accompany the diversity and speed of social change in the large urban community. Unfortunately, often the small size and geographic isolation of these small towns has meant that government service programs for older Americans are not available.

DESIGN AND ENVIRONMENTAL FACTORS
IN SENIOR HOUSING

Architects, in designing houses and apartments for senior citizens, have planned housing which has year-round adequate systems of temperature and climate control, an adequate source of sun and artificial light, and an adequate control of noise. They have simultaneously kept the living space small and easy to maintain. Within the living quarters they have tried to minimize the need to lift, bend, pull, or climb. Bathrooms and showers have had safety features added to minimize falls and the risk of bodily injury. While these design features are helpful and a decided improvement, what must be remembered is that the house, apartment, or living space of an older person is one part of an entire environment which includes neighborhoods and communities.

Kalish argues that what the older person needs is a sense of place, a feeling of relatedness, a sense of environmental mastery, privacy, and psychological stimulation.[14] Following Fromm's work, Kalish maintains that the homes of the elderly should satisfy their need to identify with a place, a dwelling, a neighborhood, village, city, or landscape. People of all ages need to be able to interact frequently with other human beings but older persons need this opportunity in particular, in order to keep from becoming lonely, depressed, isolated, and preoccupied with themselves. Carp in one study found that older residents of the enriched environment seemed to respond to their housing by reengaging in social life.[15] Failure to master and control one or more aspects of one's environment can lead to a growing sense of inadequacy, incompetency, and self-doubt on the part of older persons. A supportive environment, on the other hand, can lead to an enhanced sense of competency which tends to assist older persons in their efforts to remain independent for as long as possible. People at any age in life need psychological stimulation. Older persons, because of declining health, widowhood, or a variety of other losses that they have experienced, may not be able to look forward to a better tomorrow. Psychological stimulation and diversion, therefore, may prove to be a significant booster of the morale and outlook of these persons. Lack of enough to do and lack of new stimulating experiences result in the older persons having too much time to become preoccupied with themselves and their personal problems. Finally, persons of all ages need periods in which they can withdraw from others, as well as from the stimulation and stress of their environment, in order to regroup their energy and efforts and restructure their thoughts before meeting any new challenges. They need privacy and a time to be with themselves. Privacy can be an expression of territoriality for human beings.

The designers of homes for the elderly must be aware of both physiological and psychological needs of older persons. They must take into account the total environment of the homes they are constructing. Unfortunately, architects and behavioral scientists do not always speak the same language, nor even attempt to communicate. Therefore, from the point of view of the behavioral scientists, the homes constructed for older persons often leave much to be desired.

Since the health, energy, competence, and life space of the older person is often declining, the environments created for older persons should be as supportive of competence and self-confidence as possible. Unfortunately gerontologists have not always been able to agree on which environmental factors are most crucial and desirable. The question of age homogeneity versus age heterogeneity in the neighborhoods of older people is a case in point. Rosow in a study of older persons living in apartments in Cleveland concluded that friendship patterns varied in direct proportion to the number of aged peers living nearby. Age homogeneity yielded the larger number of friendships and increased the amount of visiting. His work strongly supports the notion that age segregation is good for the older person.[16] The concept of segregation of any kind does not fit well, however, with American ideals and values concerning democracy, equality, and social justice. Segregation of any kind is assumed to be bad. There have been others who have argued that being in contact with only other old people is depressing. One cannot help but be aware that one's friends are aging and dying. A social group made up of just older persons carries the constant reminder of one's own declining health and ultimate death. Gerontologists frequently argue that age-integrated neighborhoods should produce higher morale and greater stimulation for the older person. Studies which systematically attempt to determine the solution to this question seem always to conclude that the age-segregated environment is best for the older person. However, Powell Lawton, in discussing this movement of older persons to senior housing, states:

Several impact studies by Carp, Lipman and our own center show that to varying degrees a favorable change is experienced by elderly people during the year following such a move, particularly in the areas of organization activity, social interaction and perceived changes in life satisfaction. Finer detailed examination of some of the processes involved in such an increase in well-being seems to indicate that the physical proximity of age peers and the establishment of a normative system appropriate to the level of competence of the average elderly tenant are major factors in beneficial effect.[17]

Similarly, Bultena and Wood made a study comparing men who lived in four age-segregated communities in Arizona and compared them with men of the same age who have remained in integrated communities. The results indicated that the morale of those living in the retirement communities was significantly higher.[18] It is the general belief of gerontologists that the older one becomes the more crucial are the environmental factors in determining one's degree of life satisfaction. In discussing this matter, Lawton proposes an environmental docility hypothesis which in its simplest form states:

> The less competent the individual in terms of personal disability or deprived status, the more susceptible is his behavior to the influence of immediate environmental situations.[19]

Even competent older persons are influenced by environmental factors, and Steven Gambert studied what happened to competent nursing home patients when they were placed in a room with a confused and mentally incompetent roommate. They found many undesirable effects on the competent subjects from these placements, including loss of recent memory, passive aggressiveness, and increased anxiety. Most of their subjects became less friendly, more remote, and depressed.

The attempts to change and improve the lives of older persons through environmental manipulation can be seen, and is being instituted, in four different ways, according to Lawton. In the first of these the individual initiates and the point of application is the individual. These older persons actively seek stimulations, strive toward self-determined goals, and are alert to the need for change in themselves, Lawton believes. In the second, the individual initiates the change; the point of application is the environment. Activity of this nature on the part of older persons involves attempts to redesign one's own environment in such a way as to maximize the congruity between one's own needs and the offering of the environment. Migration to a pleasanter climate or to a neighborhood or community where health care is more readily available would be an example of this kind of environmental improvement. In the third technique the individual responds to a treatment that is applied individually by a therapist. This involves the person's being a good cotherapist. The factor that distinguishes this type of change from growth is the activity of a professional in the change system. In the final pattern the individual responds to a change applied to the environment. Social designers and architects have attempted with varying degrees of success to construct need-fulfilling environments. Past studies have indicated that a change in environment will be most effective in changing behavior when the individual is at a threshold level of competence. One example might be the individual who is about to lose his or her physical or financial ability to maintain his or her lifelong home and therefore must move to a smaller and more easily kept apartment. Since they are at a threshold of losing the ability to maintain a home, a change to a more manageable apartment might increase their sense of competence and independence.

Regnier has developed a table to indicate the age-related losses that older persons are likely to experience and the changes which may be required in one's environment in order to adjust to these expected losses (Table 10–3).[20]

A word of caution might be appropriate at this point. The solution to all older persons' personal losses is not necessarily a move to a different and more manageable and supportive environment. Briggs has pointed out that movement from a familiar to a strange environment induces numerous stresses. There is most often a strong attachment by the person to the familiar living arrangements. Present arrangements, while leaving something to be desired, are most often predictable and have been a part of the older person's life for a long time. Moving requires adjustments and causes some amount of emotional trauma in persons of all ages. Elders may simply not be able to withstand another adjustment if they have recently experienced a series of personal losses in their lives.

Table 10–3 Age-Related Environmental Changes and Personal Losses

50–65	65–75	75–87	80+
Loss of relationship to younger friends and acquaintances of children. Loss of neighborhood role to schools and youth. Home is too large, but mortgage payments are low and equity high.	Loss in relation to work environment, loss of mobility due to lessened income. Dissolving of professional work associations and friendships. Move to apartment, smaller home, or struggle with increased maintenance costs of larger home.	Loss of ability to drive independently. Must rely on bus or relatives and friends. Connections with community, church associations slowly severed. Move to more supportive housing, such as apartments with meals and maid service. Maintenance costs for single-family house unmanageable.	Losses of ability to navigate in the environment. Loss of strong connection with outside neighborhood. Dependence on supportive services. Move to supportive environment necessary, such as nursing home, home for the aged, or siblings' home.

Source: Victor Regnier, "Neighborhood Planning for the Urban Elderly," in *Aging,* eds. Diana S. Woodruff and James E. Birren (Belmont, CA: Wadsworth, 1975), p. 299.

HOUSING AND COMMUNITY CHOICES
OF OLDER AMERICANS

Many older persons have no choice regarding where they will live. They are so poor that they must try desperately to hold onto whatever meager quarters they have at the present time. For middle- and upper-income elderly, however, there are probably more choices of housing and neighborhoods available to them than they have ever had before in their lives.

Many elderly, who can well afford to move, ultimately decide to remain in their current homes because of what the home represents to them in terms of their adult life. It is here that they raised their children, entertained, visited with neighbors, loved, fought, and struggled with life's many problems. Their current homes are filled with family traditions and sentiments which they may not want to break. The choice to remain where one has lived most of his or her life allows the person to continue living in a familiar environment, to continue in a well-known neighborhood interacting with familiar neighbors and lifelong friends. Moreover, the individual is in an area with familiar stores and accessible service centers. To move entails a variety of adjustments required in the new neighborhood. It is easy to see why the choice of many older persons is to remain where they are currently living.

If the decision is made to move out of the old house and neighborhood, however, a variety of choices are available to the older person. It is probably good advice for the older person not to make a decision to move until thinking it over carefully for several weeks or longer and never to make a decision to move during a time of stress such as following the death of a spouse. No decision should be made for six months after the death of one's husband or wife in order to avoid a wrong decision, made under traumatic conditions, and not possible to reverse at a later point in time.

One choice often made by middle-class Americans is to move to a retirement community. This usually involves a move to a different state since many of the retirement villages are located in such Sun Belt states as Florida, Texas, Arizona, and California.

Many of the retirement communities are almost self-contained. They include shopping centers, churches, restaurants, recreation centers, golf courses, swimming pools, and sometimes medical centers. The advantages of the retirement communities include accessibility to needed services, limitless possibilities for social contacts and friends while allowing for independence and privacy. The major drawback of retirement communities is the cost, which often puts them out of reach of any other than the most affluent older Americans. Peterson and Larson, in a study of Sagina Hills in Southern California, found that 55.4 percent of the residents had been engaged in professional or managerial occupations before retirement, compared to the 25.3 percent of these occupations within the population at large.[21]

Bultena and Woods found that although residents of retirement communities do admit to having less contact with family members than do elderly residents of the general community, they seem to have more friends available, have generally higher morale, and perceive their own health as better.[22]

Mobile home parks are often available to persons who can't afford retirement communities but want to move to the Sun Belt. Residents usually pay a monthly rate which includes trailer space, utilities, laundry, and recreational facilities. Most of the trailer parks have swimming pools, recreation rooms, and organized social activities.

Many of the residents of mobile home parks originally intended to live there only during the winter months but later decided to remain the year round. Hoyt found in a study of mobile home residents that 12 percent of the residents remained for 10 months or more each year. Fifty-eight percent of them owned the same homes they owned during their working years and returned to them during the summer months. An additional 10.3 percent had purchased a different home but also returned to it during the summer months. Thus the majority of the residents of mobile home parks live there during the winter months and return to their original homes during the summer months.[23]

Hoyt, whose study took place at a trailer park in Bradentown, Florida, found that the trailer park residents were not integrated into the larger community but were integrated into the social structure of the trailer park. Eighty-two percent of the residents reported that they obtained all or most of their recreation within the park. Many reported that they originally moved there because of climate but that they stayed for social reasons.

When asked why they preferred living in the trailer park, a variety of reasons were given. The two most common responses were sociability (46.4%) and same status and interests (42.6%). Other reasons included "more and better activities" (28.4%), "not so lonesome" (14.8%), "everyone's the same age" (7.7%), "mutual aid" (42.6%), and "less disturbance" (18.7%). Thus a variety of factors make the trailer parks attractive to retired persons.

A number of church groups sponsor retirement houses for the aged. The accommodations range from modest living to very elaborate arrangements. These homes generally offer a life care arrangement in which the tenant pays a founders fee upon moving in and monthly rent thereafter. Most of these, like the retirement communities, are so expensive as to be out of the reach of the majority of older Americans.

The federal government, through the office of Housing and Urban Development, has made funds available to build high-rise apartments for senior citizens across the country. The relatively small amount of land required makes it possible to build these in large urban areas and near shopping centers and needed services. These are mainly inhabited by the less-affluent older Americans.

Another choice available to the less-affluent older person is the retirement hotel. This is usually an old hotel or apartment house located near the downtown area of the city. It may provide maid service and have a common dining room. It offers the older person ample amounts of social contact and simultaneously the opportunity for privacy. Unfortunately, these hotels are often located in poor neighborhoods in which the elderly are much more likely to be the victims of crime.

HOUSING COSTS

Rosow found that the older persons who were most dissatisfied with their housing were those in the low-income brackets. Economic problems were at the core of the housing problems of older Americans, he concluded.

Since the average older family's income is about half as large as that of younger families, it is easy to understand why the older family spends a larger percentage of its total income on housing. In actual dollars, however, the older family spends less on housing than young families do. Most often this means that older families live in less desirable homes than their younger counterparts.

While many older families simply do not have enough income to maintain their current housing, they most often have too much income to gain entry into public housing that requires income must be less than a designated figure for residency. Thus the income barriers often found in public housing put pressure on middle-income older persons who do not have enough money to maintain their own homes, but who cannot qualify for public housing.

Harris found that in 1973, 65 percent of the housing units in the U.S. were owner occupied. For the over-65 population 70 percent of the houses were owner occupied. The older one becomes, however, the less likely one is to live in one's own home. The 1970 census indicated that of the dwellings occupied by 60- to 64-year olds, 71 percent were owner occupied; of 65- to 74-year-olds, 68 percent of these were owner occupied and the 75-and-above group, 66 percent were owner occupied. Older persons are often ultimately forced to give up on maintaining their own homes and move into some other housing arrangement, whether in government housing or with other family members. Harris further found that 82 percent of the owner-occupied housing was free and clear of any mortgage.[24]

Harris, in comparing black and white home ownership, states:

> The black aged are only slightly more likely to own (57%) their homes as to rent (43%), compared to white elderly households, of whom, 71% lived in their own homes.[25]

For older persons who rent their homes, they are much more likely than the general population to be paying 25 percent or more of their income in rent. (See Figure 10–1.)

In terms of the quality of the homes that they live in, the elderly are slightly more likely than the total population to live in housing units lacking

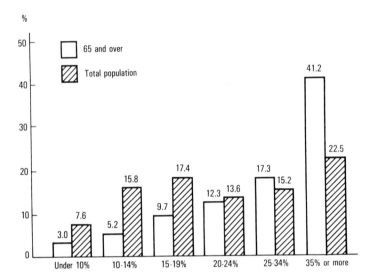

Figure 10–1   Gross Rent as Percent of Income by Age, 1973

Source: Charles Harris, *Fact Book on Aging* (Washington, D.C.: The National Council on the Aging, Inc., 1978), p. 179.

some or all plumbing features. This is more often the case for blacks than whites and more frequently true in rural areas. Montgomery, Stubbs, and Day found in their study of housing in rural America that federal programs designed to assist the rural elderly in home improvements simply were not being effectively implemented. They concluded that the rural elderly were not inclined to seek assistance from the government and that federal programs like the Cooperative Extension Service, the Farmers Home Administration, and the Federal Housing Administration were not actively offering them any assistance.

Housing costs take a substantially larger share of the incomes of older persons and therefore become more of a burden for several reasons, according to Harris:

1. The inflation of real estate prices means that the elderly are unlikely to be able to sell their homes and find new houses which they can afford to buy.
2. The average homeowner pays 3.4 percent of his income in property taxes while the older homeowner pays 8.1 percent.
3. Higher utility costs, the current energy shortages and problems, have hit the hardest on those with fixed incomes.
4. Maintenance costs for all homeowners have risen dramatically but this has most affected the older person who is frequently living in older housing.
5. There is age discrimination in mortgage regulations which work against the old.

6. The elderly are required in some states to sign over their homes to state welfare departments in order to obtain old age assistance.[26]

It is an error to assume that the housing needs of the individual are likely to remain constant over the entire life cycle, or that the homes the elderly live in are ideally suited to them. While younger families may have a problem of overcrowding, older families may have a problem of undercrowding when they attempt to live in housing too large for them to maintain and afford.

The Federal Housing Program has addressed some of the housing problems of older Americans. As of 1975 about one-fourth of federally sponsored housing units were specifically designed for the elderly.

Section 8 of the Federal Housing Program provides for low-income housing assistance. Families assisted under this program may pay no more than 25 percent and might pay as little as 15 percent of their gross incomes for rent.

Section 8 is also the first housing program that permits the construction of congregate housing units which are most needed by certain groups of older Americans whose health or finances no longer permit them to live independently.

SOCIABILITY

It is apparent that housing and neighborhood choices affect the opportunity for the social interaction of older Americans. Rosow, in discussing the social integration of neighborhoods, believes that the critical factors for integration are long-term residence, neighborhood stability, social homogeneity, and intact primary groups. Moreover, the number of old people's friends will vary with the proportion of their older neighbors. Regardless of the number, these friends will consist disproportionately of older rather than younger neighbors.

While Rosow's arguments regarding neighborhood friendship patterns have been found to be true, they are, apparently, more true for lower-class persons than they are for middle-class persons.[27] Rosow found that the middle-class older person is significantly more likely to have more than one friend than is the working-class older person. In the working class there is greater local dependency for friendship than in the middle class. While the middle-class older person has more friends both generally and specifically in his or her section of town than the working class, the working class was found to be far more dependent on neighbors as a source of friendship and social life.[28]

Rosow's work indicates that the older person's local friends vary with the proportion of old neighbors, and these friends are drawn basically from older neighbors. Regardless of the number of friends, the aged select their friends most often from older rather than younger neighbors, and this tendency increases with the residential density of old people.[29]

Friendship patterns of older persons are very similar then to that of all age groups. Friendships are most often formed between persons of similar status, notably of age, but also of sex, marital status, social class, beliefs, and lifestyle. Proximity to persons of similar status is a facilitator of social involvement for older Americans.

While social involvement may be more or less desired by persons at any age in life, Rosow described different social participation types in his sample:

1. Cosmopolitans (32%). This group, which was largely middle class in background, had the least contact with neighbors, and no desire for more friends.
2. Phlegmatic (4%). This group had low contact with neighbors, no good friends, and wanted no friends.
3. Isolated (19%). This group had high contact with neighbors and strongly wanted more friends.
4. Sociable (25%). This group had high contacts with neighbors and wanted no more friends.
5. Insatiable (20%). This group had high contacts with neighbors but still wanted more friends.[30]

The neighborhood environment, and opportunity for social interaction and involvement, is evidently much more important for lower-class persons than it is for middle-class persons. The lower class, throughout their lives, seem to be less integrated into the total community and therefore have fewer resources on which they can draw, other than from the neighborhood, in order to establish friends. This problem becomes more pronounced in later life.

INSTITUTIONALIZATION

While approximately 5 percent of the older population reside in a nursing home at any one time, eventually 25 percent of all older persons will spend some time in a nursing home setting. Gottesman reports that of all older persons currently institutionalized, one in seven are in a psychiatric facility; all the rest are in nursing homes.[31]

It is a mistake to assume that the only persons who enter nursing homes are those that are very sick or dying. Often the person enters the nursing home when his or her support system in the community breaks down. This may be at a time when one's spouse dies, and one realizes that it is no longer possible to maintain one's home or to live independently. If no family members live in the immediate area, the individual often comes to realize that he or she has no other choice except a move to a nursing home. Studies have shown that many of of these persons who ultimately enter a nursing home have been marginal throughout most of the later years. They frequently have been unable to cope adequately with the outside world and have been unable to utilize either family or community support systems in order to maintain their independence.

Nursing homes, like prisons and mental hospitals, are total institutions. Total institutions have control over the entire life of the individual. These are places where a large number of like-situated individuals together lead an enclosed, supervised, and carefully administered life. Upon entering the institution, individuals lose control of so much of their lives and environment that Goffman labels them "inmates."[32] The individual most often loses control of his or her personal property and sometimes even the loss of his or her full name. The insult to one's self-concept and self-confidence is extensive. The individual may react by a disidentifying process. The new resident often states that he or she doesn't belong there. He or she is often treated as equal, however, with those that he or she believes to be considerably less competent.

The impersonalization of persons in nursing homes often includes feeding and bathing in an assembly-line fashion, treating all the patients alike with no regard for individual differences, inability to call patients by their first names, complete disregard of the patient's sentiments or complaints, only speaking to the patients in order to give orders, and tying to their beds patients who cause trouble.

There is a kind of circular process by which one who is already disoriented is inculcated into the total institution and as a result further loses his or her identity. Dress, manners, and conversations are under constant scrutiny. The result is almost total visibility and a complete lack of privacy. Most total institutions tend to be operated under the caste system model. The staff is in total control and constantly disciplines the residents.

Psychologists and psychiatrists have developed a description of the neurotic syndrome that tends to develop in persons who reside in total institutions. The person is characterized as apathetic, expressionless, disinterested. This is often accompanied by the deterioration of personal habits regarding dress, cleanliness, and personal appearance.[33]

It is well recognized by psychiatrists today that behavior manifestations previously believed to be senility are often instead neuroticism, anxiety, and lack of ego strength, which frequently result from a decline of participation in the environment and induced sensory deprivation.[34]

Barnes, Sack, and Shore describe in detail the downward spiral of senility, indicating the progressive loss of self-esteem which may occur among older persons. The spiral ends in their ultimate death (Figure 10–2). The deterioration begins at Point 2, when society may demand that the older person relinquish his or her accustomed roles which leads to a loss of self-esteem (3). This may be accompanied by failing health and pressure placed on the older person to become dependent (4 and 5). Institutionalization (6) may then lead to a further loss of self-esteem and personal confusion (6–7–8). The older person retreats into the more pleasant memories of their past (9), is now considered beyond hope by others (10), and this may eventually terminate with death (11–12).

The morale and self-concepts of personnel working in nursing homes may in part be determined by the negative attitudes toward nursing homes on

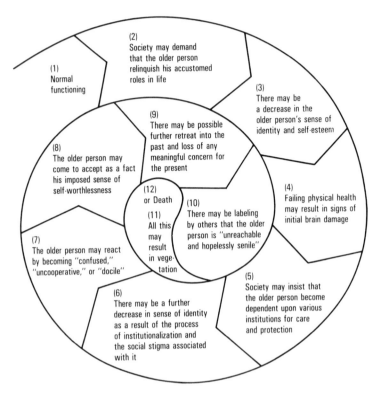

Figure 10–2 The Spiral of Senility
The patient may not go through all the stages shown nor in the order
shown; however, all stages have been observed clinically in different
patients at different times. Note that a consistently observed pattern in the
spiral is the progressive decrease in self-esteem, ending in death.

Source: E. K. Barnes, A. Sack, and H. Shore, "Guidelines to Treatment
Approaches," *Gerontologist,* 13 (1973), 513–27. Reprinted by permission
of *The Gerontologist.*

the part of the population. Most often thought of as the place where people go to
die, the staff of the nursing home are frequently seen as caretakers. Kalish observes the expressions of some nursing home staffs such as "time to water the
vegetables" or of one nursing home administrator who referred to himself and
his colleagues as the "human garbage collectors." All such comments seem to be
a reflection of the fact that society does not place a high value on caring for its
older and sometimes dying persons. Thus nursing home personnel have difficulty maintaining a sense of pride in the important tasks that they are required
to perform.[35]

Because nursing homes are expensive to operate and many families simply do not have the funds to pay for the care of their elderly members, many
facilities have not attempted to provide intellectual or sensory stimulation for

their patients. This would have meant adding more staff which would for most be prohibitively expensive. The advent of the federal Medicare/Medicaid program has helped many older persons and their families bear some of the expenses of nursing home treatment. This has lead to the upgrading of the nursing home programs.

Physical therapists and recreational directors are now found in most of the large nursing homes.

Industrial sociologists have dichotomized organizational structures into two ideal types. The "bureaucratic" model and the "professional" model are often characterized as models which represent the opposite ends of the continuum of organizational structure.

The "bureaucratic" model is described as (1) a hierarchy of offices and authority with increasing centralization of power; (2) increasing specialization; (3) specifications, standardization, and formalization of the rules; (4) authority residing in the office; (5) impersonalization of operation; (6) merit appointment; and (7) essentially a "closed system."[36]

The "professional" model by comparison includes the following characteristics: (1) horizontal patterns of authority with a minimum of centralized authority; (2) a division of labor based on professionalization of authority; (3) authority resting on professional expertise and competence rather than the sacredness of the office; (4) considerable autonomy given the subunits of the organization; (5) stress placed on employee commitment to organizational goals; (6) stress on informal rules and primary relations; (7) responsibility delegated to the lower levels of the organization, and (8) essentially an "open system."[37]

Corwin has pointed out that employee roles in bureaucratic organizations are likely to stress uniformity of the clients' problems, uniform rules and work procedures, little responsibility of the employee for decision making, and primary responsibility to the organization and administration. On the other hand, professional roles depend on the opposite conditions, which include stress on informal rules and regulations, horizontal patterns of authority, the uniqueness of clients and of the skills of the personnel, and primary loyalty to the clients and colleagues rather than to the organization.[38]

The current organization of nursing homes seems to approximate the bureaucratic model in both organizational structure and employee attitudes toward their roles. The client in the nursing home would be much better served if both the organizational structure and employee beliefs about their legitimate occupational role could be moved in a more professional direction.

Kalish reports:

> Most nursing home staff members have had no training in the field before coming to their home, receive little or no in-service training and are very poorly paid. Relatively few of them enjoy the task they are required to perform and many are not particularly attracted to working with people.[39]

RELOCATION

Relocation from a familiar to a strange environment involves some stress and numerous adjustments at any age in life. For the very old who may be already confused and experiencing several other problems simultaneously, a move can be overwhelming. The older person who moves leaves behind the current living arrangements which are comfortable and predictable and enters a new environment which is different and initially somewhat unpredictable.[40]

Earlier research had tended to indicate that mortality rates for the elderly moving to and between nursing homes were substantially higher than actuarial expectations for those of their age group and higher than the death rate for those on the waiting list.[41] The more recent work of Borup, Gallego, and Hefferman indicates that this is not the case. They state:

> Programs developed for the purpose of reducing mortality of relocated patients should focus on those factors which extend life of the elderly rather than focus on the stress of relocation since relocation does not cause an increase in mortality. This is not to minimize the need for programs which attempt to reduce stress since relocation is a stress experience for most patients. However, it should be remembered that the stress of relocation does not bring about an increase in mortality.[42]

Thus, the evidence on the negative effects of relocation of older Americans is controversial at the present time. There seems little doubt that stress is involved and that adjustments have to be made. Whether this stress is serious enough to cause death is not certain. The work of Borup and others suggests that it is not.[43]

CONCLUSION

The data indicates that one's location in the urban community is not an accidental phenomenon but rather that there is a direct link between physical space and social distance. Past work of social ecologists has indicated that where a person lives in the urban community indicates a great deal about the personal status and position in society (McKenzie, 1927; Park, 1952; and Lauman, 1966). Coleman and Neugarten found that respondents referred to the resident's geographic location in the urban community as a complex stratification system. Those older residents in the urban community are most likely to be located in the zones immediately around but not in the downtown district. These locations seem to offer the older person the maximum access to needed services and transportation with the minimum of effort on their parts. Unfortunately, these urban areas are often zones of high crime, congestion, and a physical environment structured primarily for a healthy 30-year-old. There are aspects of the urban environment and its location that carry with them undesirable side effects for older Americans. The elderly seem to shy away from the more sparsely settled and spacious suburban zones.

For the elderly living in rural areas the small towns seem to be the preferred location. This tends to keep farm families in closer proximity to friends, family members, and the community without being as isolated as remaining on the farm. The small towns provide easy access to grocery stores, drug stores, restaurants. Moreover, one is near a group of persons of similar age, status, and life history. Sociability is maximized. Some urban residents have found that moving to a small town reduces the cost of living considerably.

Beyond the urban and rural choices of older Americans are a whole range of other choices. The person planning for retirement may decide to remain in his or her current house and neighborhood with its long history and personal value, move to a smaller house or apartment, or perhaps move to a retirement community in the Sun Belt. Inevitably there are advantages and disadvantages of any decision that is made. Hoyt found in his study of trailer park residents that most of them returned to their original homes during the summer months.

One problem for the elderly in choosing the house and community where they will live is the cost. Residents of retirement communities were found to have most often been professional or managerial workers during their employment years and to have had considerably higher incomes than the average old person. For the very poor, government housing through the HUD programs has often been the solution to their problems. Middle-income older persons often find themselves in a situation in which they have too high an income to gain admission to government-sponsored housing, and they are too poor to move to the more exclusive retirement communities. The financial strain to keep up their current homes may be the greatest on this group.

The relative desirability of age-segregated versus age-integrated housing and communities at this time seems to be in favor of age-segregated housing. Generally speaking older persons in age-segregated communities have more friends, more informal visiting, and higher morale. This is more true for blue-collar workers who have fewer resources, financial or social, to maintain contacts outside of their immediate neighborhood.

Nursing homes are generally viewed negatively by older persons because they represent a loss of independence and ultimately death. Less than 5 percent of persons over 65 actually reside in nursing homes. These persons were often marginal in terms of their ability to maintain community or family support for their independent living. The death of a spouse, the tearing down of the apartment or hotel that they lived in, and similar events are often the precipitating events that lead to their institutionalization. Thus, most residents of nursing homes entered at the time that their support system broke down. The desirability or undesirability of the nursing home environment is a topic that is under debate at the present time, and gerontologists do not have enough information to give definitive answers.

KEY TERMS

Spencerian principle
environmental docility hypothesis
total institutions
bureaucratic organizational model
professional organizational model
social ecologist

social participation types:
  cosmopolitans
  phlegmatic
  isolated
  sociable
  insatiable

SUGGESTED READINGS

BARNES, E. K., A. SACK, AND H. SHORE, "Guidelines to Treatment Approaches," *Gerontologist*, 13 (1973), 513–27.

BORUP, JERRY H., DANIEL T. GALLEGO, AND PAMELA G. HEFFERMAN, "Relocation and Its Effect on Mortality," *The Gerontologist*, 19, no. 2 (1979), 135–40.

BRIGGS, JOHN C., "Ecology as Gerontology," *The Gerontologist*, 8, no. 2 (1968), 78–79.

BROTMAN, H. B., *Facts and Figures on Older Americans: An Overview, 1971.* Washington, D.C.: Department of Health, Education and Welfare, 1972.

BULTENA, G. L., AND V. WOOD, "The American Retirement Community: Bane or Blessing?" *Journal of Gerontology*, 24 (1969), 209–17.

CARP, F. M., *A Future For the Aged: Residents of Victoria Plaza, Austin.* Austin: University of Texas Press, 1966.

CARP, FRANCES, "Life Style and Location Within the City," *The Gerontologist*, 15 (February 1975), 27–34.

COLEMAN, RICHARD P., AND BERNICE L. NEUGARTEN, *Social Status in the City.* San Francisco: Jossey-Bass, 1971.

CORWIN, RONALD G., *Militant Professionalism*, p. 63. New York: Appleton-Century-Crofts, 1970.

COWGILL, DONALD J., "Segregation Scores for Metropolitan Areas," *American Sociological Review*, 27 (June 1962), 400–402.

COX, HAROLD, AND ALBERT BHAK, "Determinants of Age-Based Residential Segregation," *Sociological Symposium* (January 1980), 27–41.

DUNCAN, OTIS D., AND BEVERLY DUNCAN, "Residential Distribution and Occupational Stratification," *American Journal of Sociology*, 60 (March 1955), 493–503.

EISENSTADT, S. N., *From Generation to Generation: Age Groups and Social Structure.* New York: Free Press, 1956.

FELDMAN, A. S., AND C. TILLY, "The Interaction of Social and Physical Space," *American Sociological Review*, 25 (December 1960), 877–84.

FOOTE, NELSON, AND OTHERS, *Housing Choices and Constraints.* New York: McGraw-Hill, 1960.

FROMM, E., *The Art of Loving.* New York: Bantam, 1963.

GOFFMAN, E., *Asylums*, p. 1. New York: Anchor, 1961.

GOLANT, STEPHEN M., "The Residential Location and Spatial Behavior of the Elderly," *Research Paper No. 143.* Chicago: University of Chicago, Dept. of Geography, 1972.

GOLDSCHEIDER, CALVIN, *Population, Modernization, and Social Structure.* Boston: Little, Brown, 1971.

GOTTESMAN, L. E., C. E. QUARTERMAN, AND G. M. COHN, "Psycho-social Treatment of the Aged," in *The Psychology of Adult Development and Aging,* eds. C. Eisdorfer and M. Lawton, p. 56. Washington, D.C.: American Psychological Association, 1973.

HANSEN, G. D., "Meeting Housing Challenges, Involvement: the Elderly," in *Housing Issues: Proceedings of the Fifth Annual Meeting, American Association of Housing Educators.* Lincoln, NE: University of Nebraska Press, 1971.

HARRIS, CHARLES, *Fact Book on Aging: A Profile of America's Older Population,* p. 185. Washington, D.C.: The National Council on the Aging, Inc., 1978.

HOYT, G. C., "The Life of the Retired in a Trailer Park," *American Journal of Sociology,* 59 (1954), 361–70.

KALISH, RICHARD A., *Late Adulthood: Perspectives on Human Development,* p. 97. Belmont, CA: Brooks/Cole, 1975.

LAUMANN, E. O., *Prestige and Association in an Urban Community.* Indianapolis, IN: Bobbs-Merrill, 1966.

LAWTON, POWELL, "Social Ecology and the Health of Older People," in *Aging in America: Readings in Social Gerontology,* eds. Cary S. Kart and Barbara B. Manard, p. 320. Sherman Oaks, CA: Alfred, 1976.

LIEBERMAN, M. A., "The Relationship of Mortality Rates to Entrance to a Home for the Aged," *Geriatrics,* 16 (1961), 515–19.

McKENZIE, R. D., "Spatial Distance and Community Organization Patterns," *Social Forces,* 5 (June 1927), 623–38.

MILLER, SHEILA J., "Segregation of the Aged in American Cities." Unpublished paper, Wichita State University, 1967.

MONTGOMERY, JAMES E., ALICE C. STUBBS, AND SAVANNAH S. DAY, "The Housing Environments of the Rural Elderly," *The Gerontologist,* 20, no. 4 (1980), 444–51.

MONTGOMERY, J. E., "Social Characteristics of the Aged in a Small Pennsylvania Community," *College of Home Economics Research Publication,* no. 233. State College, PA: The Pennsylvania State University, 1965.

PARK, R. E., AND E. W. BURGESS, *The City.* Chicago, IL: The University of Chicago Press, 1925.

PARK, ROBERT E., *Human Communities.* New York: Free Press, 1952.

PETERSON, JAMES A., AND CUBI E. LARSON, "Social-Psychological Factors in Selecting Retirement Housing." Revised version of a paper read at the Research Conference on Patterns of Living and Housing of Middle Age and Older People, Washington, D.C., 1972.

REGNIER, VICTOR, "Neighborhood Planning for the Urban Elderly," in *Aging,* eds. Diana S. Woodruff and James E. Birren, p. 303. New York: Van Nostrand Reinhold, 1975.

ROSOW, IRVING, *The Social Integration of the Aged.* New York: Free Press, 1967.

SPENCER, HERBERT, *First Principles.* New York: D. Appleton and Company, 1896.

STEINFELD, EDWARD, JAMES DUNCAN, AND PAUL CARDELL, "Toward a Responsive Environment: The Psychosocial Effects of Inaccessibility," in *Barrier Free Environments,* ed. Michael Bednar. Stroudsburg, PA: Dowden, Hutchinson, and Ross, 1977.

TAUMANN, E. O., *Prestige and Association in an Urban Community.* Indianapolis, IN: Bobbs-Merrill, 1966.

THOMPSON, JAMES D., *Organization in Action,* pp. 4–7. New York: McGraw-Hill, 1967.

WEINER, MARCELLA B., ALBERT J. BROK, AND ALVIN M. SANDOWSKY, *Working with the Aged,* p. 38. Englewood Cliffs, NJ: Prentice-Hall, 1978.

WEBER, MAX, *The Theory of Social and Economic Organization,* trans. A. M. Henderson and Talcott Parsons, ed. Talcott Parsons, p. 38. New York: Free Press, 1947.

WILTZIUS, FRANCES, AND STEVEN GAMBERT, "Importance of Resident Placement within a Skilled Nursing Facility," *Journal of American Geriatric Society,* 29 (September 1981), 418–21.

ZUSMAN, J., "Some Explanations of the Changing Appearance of Psychiatric Patients," *International Journal of Psychiatry,* 4 (1967), 216–37.

11
DEATH AND DYING

For you the to-come, but for me the gone-by; you are panting to live, I am waiting to die.

Richard Le Gallienne
An Old Man's Song

Epicurus is quoted as saying:

Thus that which is the most awful of evils, death, is nothing to us, since when we exist there is no death, and when there is death we do not exist.[1]

While Epicurus appears to have philosophically accepted death as something that need not concern the living, many people experience some anxiety over the thought of dying and most must at some time in life find adequate means of coping with the anxieties and fears about their own death.

Throughout history, death has been a distinct possibility for all age groups and has commonly occurred at any point in the life cycle.

Up until the last century the highest percentage of deaths occurred within the first ten years of age. This mortality is still found in many of the primitive cultures throughout the world. Robert Blauner points out:

Among the Sakai of the Malay Peninsula, approximately 50 percent of the babies born die before the age of three; among the Kwinai tribe of Australia, 40–50 percent die before the age of 10.

Fifty-nine percent of the male deaths in Nigeria among the "indigenous" blacks were children who had not reached their fifth birthday. Thirty-five percent of an Indian male cohort born in the 1940s died before the age of 10.[2]

The Industrial Revolution, accompanied by an ever-advancing medical technology, has reduced death among children, teenagers, and young adults. Death in industrial societies is most common among those who have retired from work, who have completed their parental responsibilities, and who are beyond the age of 60.

Since death most often occurs among the old in industrial nations, the majority of the adult population have been able to reduce their anxieties and latent fears. While the individual recognizes the fact that someday he or she will die, any lingering concerns about death can be controlled by removing them from the realm of the immediately probable. Thus death is most often thought of as happening to someone who is very old. It is not going to happen to me today, tomorrow, or even next year. Sometime—forty, fifty, or sixty years from now—I may die, but that's so far off, why worry about it? Thus fear of death in modern society is more easily managed than in the past.

IMPACT OF DEATH ON SOCIETY

The death of those who comprise a social group can cause considerable strain and tension as the group attempts to reorganize itself in the absence of the deceased. Methods of coping with the crisis of death can be seen in the smaller groupings such as families, as well as the larger groups such as work forces and even societies. Robert Blauner observes that there are complex interrelationships between how society is organized, how the death crisis is managed, what its death practices are, and how they are linked to the social structure.[3]

Blauner further observes that death is most disruptive in primitive and preindustrial society primarily because of the age at which the population is most likely to die. Death that strikes the young and those in their adult years seems more devastating to the social order. In these societies death frequently strikes those who are involved in functional activities which are critical for the society. Thus, replacements must be quickly found and much effort made to reorganize without the deceased, or disruption of an entire way of life is likely to follow.

By way of contrast, in the West and most of the industrial societies, death, we have already noted, is more likely to be among the very old.

The United States and other Western nations find death highly concentrated among the elderly. These deaths are much less disruptive to the business and productive forces of the system. Some have argued that mandatory retirement is a convenient way of removing older persons from the labor force so that their death will create no disruption in the flow of goods and services.

The general devaluing of the old in American society is often seen as a means of segregating them and thus reducing the significance of their death. Herty observes a similar pattern in primitive societies:

> Primitive societies hard hit by infant and child mortality characteristically do not recognize infants and children as people; until a certain age they are considered as still belonging to the spirit world from which they came, and therefore their death is often not accorded ritual recognition—no funeral is held.[4]

From a societal perspective it could be argued that the ideal time to die would be when one's family was raised and lifework completed. This would cause the minimum disruption in both family life and the economic system.

If one accepts the argument that disengagement is good for older persons since they supposedly no longer have the energy to compete with younger persons it could also be seen to be desirable for society as well. The disengagement and segregation of older Americans results in the decreasing likelihood of someone dying on the job or in public places. Furthermore, since World War II there has been a growing tendency to remove death from the home and place it in hospitals and nursing homes. The bureaucratization of all institutions and activities of modern society that Max Weber so aptly described has now reached as far as dying. Bureaucratization, as Weber saw it, is a process of ordering and routinizing both everyday and unusual events in order to make all aspects of life as predictable as possible.

Removing death from the home, replacing the church with the funeral parlor, and secularization of beliefs about death, seem to be a part of segregating the dying and bureaucratizing the dying process. Death is a traumatic event that tends to arouse strong emotions among the friends and loved ones of the deceased. Bureaucracies usually attempt to maintain as smooth a functioning organization of persons and activities as possible. All disruptive problems and contingencies are to have a routine method of handling, according to the bureaucratic model. Thus in modern societies that tend to be bureaucratically structured, there is a desire to make the management of death as routine and systematic as possible, with a minimum disruption to the current social order. Placing the dying in hospitals and nursing homes under the supervision of a professional medical staff, rather than keeping them in the home where many would prefer to die, is just one example of the bureaucratization of death. Removing the deceased from homes and churches and placing them in funeral parlors is another example of the same process. William K. Kephart, in a study of death in Philadelphia, found that 90 percent of funerals occurred in funeral parlors rather than in homes and churches.

Doctors and nurses also have a tendency to avoid and isolate the terminally ill. In a study done by L. Le Shan, observing how quickly nurses responded to the service lights of the sick, it was found that the nurses were much slower in responding to a summons from a patient defined as terminally ill than to calls from patients not so classified.

Fergenberg and Fulton observed that many hospitals will go to great lengths to hide the fact that a patient has died. David N. Sudnow observes that the hospital morgue is usually on the ground floor with a private loading platform so that the public need not see the departure of the deceased. Similarly, hospitals protect other patients and the public by moving the dying to another room when the end is foreseen, and by not removing the body during visiting hours.

David Haber and others found that most of the nursing homes in their study attempted to minimize information and discussions of the death of other residents. While this was true, most of the residents of the nursing home said they would prefer to know about the death of other patients.

It seems apparent that American society has gone far in its effort to bureaucratize the process of dying. From families to medical staffs, the sentiment seems to be to isolate the dying and make death as painless as possible and at the same time minimally disruptive of the system. Even the modern funeral has tended to become less emotional and eulogistic and more a reading of scriptures that give a philosophic view of death. For those who would argue that the bereaved individual must experience a certain amount of grief before he or she can adjust to the death of associates and loved ones, the current routines surrounding death seem to deny any opportunity for the expression of this human emotion. On the other hand, too much emotionalism can be negative, supporting the notion that an irreparable tragedy has taken place. Scripture reading can have the virtue of focusing the attention of the bereaved on acceptance, reconciliation, and understanding—all of which can help them adjust ultimately to their own encounter with the experience. One of the most unfortunate aspects of the bureaucratization of death in American society is that the dying must spend much of their last few days in isolation.

ATTITUDES TOWARD DEATH

Perhaps the most widespread attitude toward death is fear. All people, however, at some point in time, must see their own death as a part of life and develop some coping mechanisms to deal with this most undesirable reality. Anthropologists often dichotomize the aspects of the cultures they are studying into their sacred and secular aspects. The sacred elements of the culture are usually embodied in the religion of a group of people and are used by them to explain aspects of reality that they do not fully understand or control. On the other hand, the secular (often defined as those things relating to the material world) is used to refer to all those aspects of our environment which we can control. While modern science has dramatically increased the secular aspects of our culture and reduced the sacred, life and death seem to be aspects of reality that defy scientific explanation. Bronislaw Malinowski believes that hope for a life after death is the only thing that makes the fear of death manageable. Religion reduces the fear of death, for most people, by offering the hope of eternal life. In speaking of the fear of death, Malinowski states:

> Religion steps in selecting the positive creed, the comforting view, the culturally valuable belief in immortality in the spirit of the body and in the continuance of life after death.[5]

Throughout much of a person's life, death seems remote and in the indefinite future. Thus, our anxieties, fears, and apprehensions are kept at the subconscious level of our mind. C. W. Wahl's view is that death is the cessation of being:

> We also see that death as a cessation of being involves aspects of reality inadmissible to the omnipotent and narcissistic self and for that reason strong defenses are developed against its recognition.[6]

Humans seem to continually develop defense mechanisms by which we psychologically insulate ourselves from the reality of death. We regularly emphasize the accidental cause of death such as disease, mishaps, or advancing age, and demote death from a necessary reality to a mere accident. More realistically, death, as is birth, is a part of life that each individual must experience.

One event that arouses all the latent fears of death is the loss of a close friend or relative. Here we not only feel the loss of a loved one, but also come face-to-face with the fact that all lives must come to an end. All of our fears are brought to the conscious level.

Another event that breaks down our defenses regarding death is assassination of a well-known public figure, such as was John F. Kennedy. When the president—the most powerful national figure, with whom we have all in some way identified—is cut down in his prime, one cannot help but be aware how thin the thread is that ties each of us to mortal life. The public reaction to the Kennedy assassination was a reflection of trauma that death produces among the living. Mourning for a well-known public figure or a loved one may in part be motivated by the recognition that someday we too must die.[7]

While the fear of death is universal, the acceptance of death is considered a mark of true maturity. Frances C. Jeffers and Adrian Verwoerdt, in a study of how the old face death, categorized the different ways that people view death. Some, in their study, viewed it as the cessation of this life but felt that death is merely a stepping-stone to another life. Others viewed death as an enemy that was interfering with and disrupting one's life pattern. Another group saw death as an opportunity for reunion with departed friends and relatives. Some saw death in terms of reward or punishment—as a transition to a better state of being if life has been lived well, or a worse state of being if life has been lived poorly. Others were sincerely curious about death. The anticipation or unknown, uncertain nature of death seemed to intrigue them. The final group saw death with a sort of resignation. They believed that death was the end and that there was nothing else to follow.

Jeffers and Verwoerdt found six different coping mechanisms people use to deal with their fear of death:

1. Strong religious beliefs, enabling people to accept death.

2. Acceptance derived from positive social relationships with one's children and grandchildren, which connect one's family to the next generation, thus giving meaning to one's life.

3. Inheritance planning, which shows the acceptance of death (whereas not planning might indicate superstition—e.g., making out a will brings about an early death).

4. Denial of the impending death by rationalization, suppression, and extenuation (to treat death as of small importance).

5. Retreat from the source of the anxiety; this may take the form of avoiding other people and declining social roles and responsibilities, thus protecting oneself from the painful loss of significant others. Drugs or alcohol may be used to insulate oneself from the pain.

6. Mastery of death through attempted resolution of the crisis. This may take the form of counterphobic mechanisms; attempting to appear young; hyperactivity (in which one becomes so involved in life and engaged in so many social roles that there is no time to think about death); introspection and review of one's life in order to develop a sense of self-meaning so that both successes and failures can be realistically accepted.

In terms of their realistic acceptance of death, Wendell M. Swenson found that persons with more fundamental religious convictions looked forward to death more than those who have less fundamental religious beliefs. Persons residing in nursing homes have more positive, forward-looking attitudes than do those who live alone. Nursing-home residents regularly see their friends die. They can also see some of those around them linger on when death would be less painful. Therefore, they are more inclined to accept death as a desirable end for many older persons. Less educated persons in the Swenson study were more likely to be evasive about death, which probably indicated an inability to resolve the anxieties surrounding death. Widowed persons were more likely to evade the issue of death than were single, separated, or married persons. Why widows would be more fearful of death is difficult to explain. Those persons who indicated they had a large number of outside interests tended to be actively evasive about death. It would appear that older persons who feel that they have much to live for would like to evade the reality of their own death. Similarly those persons who reported good health are most often actively evasive about death, while those who report poor health look forward to death in a more positive manner.

Scientific studies of the effect of a person's religious beliefs on his or her attitude toward death are inconclusive. While most studies report that religious convictions tend to reduce one's fear of death, I. E. Alexander and M. M. Adlerstein, in their studies on the psychology of death, report that manifest anxiety about death is found to be significantly higher in the religious group. Frances C. Jeffers, Claude Nichols, and Carl Eisdorfer, on the other hand, report that fear of death seemed to be a factor more pronounced in those people who consider themselves nonreligious. It may be wrong to jump to the conclusion that belief in an afterlife will alter one's fear of death. This later study revealed that 77 percent of the respondents stated that they were sure of an afterlife, 21 percent stated that they were not sure, and 2 percent said that there was no afterlife. Apparently, many of those self-described as nonreligious still believe in an afterlife.

Assuming that the acceptance of one's death is a sign of emotional maturity, is the choice that one might make about when one will die also a sign of maturity? The following is an illustration of the choice that one couple made about their own death:

> One Canadian couple in their 80's is an example. The woman was dying of cancer. Her husband did not want to live without her. They borrowed a car from their neighbor, parked it behind their house and ran a hose from the exhaust pipe into one of the windows. With rags they sealed themselves inside, airtight, and started the engine. In the note they left behind they promised not to leave the motor running. They didn't. As soon as the car was filled with carbon monoxide, they turned off the engine.[8]

The prevailing ethical and religious values in American culture tend to encourage one to view suicide as an irrational and unpardonable act committed by persons who are emotionally distraught. One is not inclined to think of a suicide being committed by a person who has carefully analyzed the circumstances of his or her life and concluded that death is the most reasonable choice available. In the above illustration the husband apparently felt that to continue living without his wife would be meaningless. Therefore, to him death was the more reasonable choice.

THE MEANING OF DEATH

Our forebears had an unwavering belief in a kind of personal afterlife, a concept of eternity as sacred time. Death to them was always accompanied by the possibility of atonement and salvation.

Modern society with the growth of secularism has seen the waning of the traditional belief in personal immortality and a lack of transcendent significance associated with death. For many people death is not seen as a transition to an afterlife but rather the end of the line. For these persons death has become a "wall" rather than a "door." It is often seen as a loss of identity, an extinction.

In a society that emphasizes the importance of the future, the prospect of no future to some people is an abomination. Hence, death and dying invites their hostility, recrimination, and denial.

American culture has attempted to cope with death by disguising it and pretending that it does not exist. Those with strong religious convictions speak of the deceased as passing on or joining their forefathers. To those without religious conviction this represents euphemistic language; they believe we should speak merely of the deceased as dead.

Robert J. Kastenbaum in attempting to explain all the possible meanings of death discusses four different views of death. The first of these sees death as the great leveler. While all societies are stratified and structured with differential reward systems for those considered to be of greater or lesser importance, death terminates all such distinctions. The rich and the poor, the powerful and the weak, the lord and the servant, all eventually die. Thus death is the great leveler of all mankind. In Kastenbaum's view, death warns those who set themselves above others to keep their pride and ambition within limits.

In opposition to this view of death as the great leveler is that of death as the great validator. Death from this view is seen to support the life status or distinction of the individual. Thus, the rich have elaborate and ornate funerals with much pomp and ceremony and many of the expensive trappings that such events require, whereas the poor have much more humble funerals. Burial plots themselves are often more or less expensive to purchase. The fact that many cities have cemeteries segregated on the basis of where blacks and whites can be buried is a reflection of a belief in death as a validator of one's existence.

The third view of death, Kastenbaum believes, is that of a radical alteration of one's relationships. One part of this change consists in a reunion with previously deceased relatives and friends. This reflects the desire to be rejoined with people from one's life who have gone before. The other part of the change consists in one's separation from living friends and loved ones. Knowledge of one's impending death may prove painful for the individual or loved ones because of the implicit separation.

In the fourth view, death is seen as the ultimate solution or the ultimate problem, according to Kastenbaum. Both at the individual and the group level during periods of prolonged stress or conflict the annihilation of the perceived opponent is one solution to the problem. Thus one individual may take another's life as well as his own, and nations go to war against other nations. On the other hand, death as the ultimate problem can be seen in the feeling that the death of individuals can threaten society as a whole. Death is an end of one's opportunity to experience, to achieve, and to exist.

The fact that death has such paradoxical and diverse meanings is a reflection of its defiance of intellectual understanding and explanation. Many individuals at different points in time embrace different meanings without realizing the inconsistency of their own thoughts on the matter.

Regardless of the meaning attached to death by the individual, whether religious or nonreligious, or whether there is or is not a belief in life after death, older Americans must over time come to accept the reality of their own impending death. At any age in life there may be adjustments made to death. Sometimes the individual must face the death of significant others in the form of friends and loved ones; sometimes a person must face the reality of his or her own death and its effect on loved ones.

Victor W. Marshall, in studying residents of Glen Brae, a retirement community, found that most had come to accept and even legitimize their impending death. In discussing the legitimation of death, Marshall states:

> All legitimation of death must carry out the same essential task—they must enable the individual to go on living in society after the death of significant others and to anticipate his own death with, at the very least, terror sufficiently mitigated so as not to paralyze the continued performance of the routines of everyday life.[9]

Of 79 residents at Glen Brae who were asked if they would like to live to be 100 years old, none answered unconditionally "yes." Nineteen residents gave conditional "yes" answers, the conditions most often being good health and not constituting a burden on others. Sixty of the residents answered with an unconditional "no."

Marshall gives examples of the manner in which Glen Brae's residents have come to legitimize their own death. An 81-year-old widow, when asked how old she would like to live to be, answered:

> Heavens! I've lived my life. I'd be delighted to have it end. The sooner the better. I nearly went with a heart attack. It would have been more convenient to go when my daughter was in _____ rather than in _____. I feel I've lived my life and I don't want to be a care to anybody. That's why I'm glad to be here (Glen Brae). No, I don't want to mourn when I go. I've had a good life. It's time.[10]

Another resident responds to the question of whether it would be desirable to live to be 100 by saying:

> No point, I have no one to depend on me. And I've looked after my few descendants I have. And I haven't any great problem to resolve.[11]

Arlie Hochschild believes that the acceptance of death by older persons is often a process of role modeling by which they see their friends and acquaintances die and come to realize how it will be for them. The legitimation of death for older persons often involves the acceptance of a shared system of meanings regarding the importance and relevance of life and death. Peter Berger and Thomas Luckmann maintain that the legitimation of death, like any other process, is best accomplished socially as part of a conversational process by which attitudes, values, and beliefs can be expressed and shared by members of the group. Having significant others to discuss death with seems critical to the acceptance and legitimation of one's own death. In order for values and meaning about significant life events to become accepted, they must be shared.

CRITICAL QUESTIONS ABOUT DEATH

Human anxiety about death has made it difficult to discuss in a rational manner when, where, why, and how people die. The prevailing attitude of the general public seems to be that one should cling to life as long and as desperately as it is possible to do so. Suicide by a friend or loved one is most often met with shock and disbelief by the living.

Arnold Toynbee and others, in discussing the various ways people have come to reconcile themselves to death, see basically two different methods of resolving their fears. Hedonism is the first of these and involves making sure that we enjoy life as much as possible before death snatches it from us. "Let us eat, drink, and be merry for tomorrow we may die," best expresses the philosophy of those who accept hedonism as a means of relating to their ultimate death. The problem that Toynbee sees with this philosophy is that instead of leading to a good life it often leads to anxieties, fatigues, and maladies that if severe and drawn out long enough may actually make the person look forward to death.

Pessimism is the second philosophical resolution of the death issue that may be embraced; basically, it concludes that life is so wretched that death is the lesser evil. The Greek poet Sophocles is known to have stated that "it is best to have never been born, but second best to go back again as quickly as possible to whence one has come."[12]

One indicator of pessimism might be suicide. If life is of such little value, then suicide might be a more acceptable means of ending life. In some instances one might expect that suicide could be considered meritorious. While no stigma was attached to suicide in the Greco-Roman world, the practice was not nearly as common as it has been in East Asian countries.

Hindu society practiced a form of suicide called *suttee*, by which it was deemed meritorious for a widow to immolate herself on her husband's funeral pyre. During the Vietnam war, Buddhist monks and nuns committed suicide by burning themselves to death, as a form of political protest.

Christianity, of Jewish origin and firmly planted in the Greco-Roman world, has always been strongly opposed to suicide. Christians have generally deprived suicides of burial in consecrated ground. For Christians death is exclusively God's prerogative, and hence human intervention is wrong. The Christian prohibition against committing suicide discourages the terminally ill from considering taking their own lives in order to avoid further pain. Toynbee and others state:

> The Christian inhibition against suicide applies, a fortiori, to giving incurably and painfully ailing human beings the merciful release that humane Christians give, as a matter of course, to animals when they are in the same plight.[13]

Modern American society, heavily imprinted with Judeo-Christian traditions, has approached the subject of euthanasia (mercy killing) with considerable anguish and trepidation. David Johnson and Roy Neubecker, in a study of attitudes toward euthanasia, found that persons with strong religious convictions were more likely to believe that life should be maintained regardless of its condition. The termination of life by any means or for any reason is still considered to be God's province. There is some inconsistency in this logic in that few argue against medical technology saving or prologing life, which would seem to be equally an invasion of God's province. Current thought seems to consider the prolongation of life, in whatever state, the province of man (aided by medical technology); but the ending of life is God's province. Law in the United States prohibits killing, for any reason, whether merciful or malicious.

The ability to prolong physical life long after the individual is unconscious and has no hope of improvement by medical technology has forced the subject of euthanasia into the world's consciousness. Modern proponents of euthanasia have raised the following questions:

1. Should those whose brains, as a result of stroke, function only at an autonomic nonvoluntary level, and who have no hope of improving, have their lives terminated in the most merciful way available?
2. Should a severely defective fetus be aborted through medical means if the abortion does not occur spontaneously?
3. Should profoundly retarded persons who are totally dependent on others for all their needs have their lives terminated mercifully?
4. Should persons suffering from advanced senility and who have no hope of recovery, have their lives terminated in the most merciful way available?[14]

While the questions of euthanasia apply to persons at every age in life, they are likely to apply most frequently to older Americans, who find themselves in various states of declining health.

The proponents of euthanasia are increasing. Wayne Sage in one study found that 77 percent of the members of the American Association of Professors of Medicine were found to be in favor of the practice. Fifty-four percent of college students accepted the idea. The only ones against euthanasia were the patients themselves; most of a sample of nursing-home patients wanted to be allowed to die normally.

There are basically two kinds of euthanasia. In voluntary euthanasia, life-sustaining medicines or machines are withdrawn at the patient's request. In passive euthanasia, the doctor does nothing to prolong the patient's life, who then is allowed to die in his or her own time.

In order to safeguard against the abuses of voluntary euthanasia the proponents have suggested that any forthcoming legislation require the consent of the patient, who must be over 21 years old; the agent of euthanasia must be a physician who shall have consulted with another physician or some specified authority. Some would argue for a period of time between the request for euthanasia and the act itself, during which the patient is allowed the opportunity of changing his or her mind. Given these safeguards, the proponents of new legislation argue that it is cruel to prolong intense suffering in someone who is mortally ill and desires to die.

The proponents of euthanasia further argue that a person has the right to decide whether he or she should continue to live or not and that such a decision can be reached after rationally weighing the benefits of continued living against the suffering involved.

The opponents of euthanasia argue against any change in the current law, first, because they doubt that acts of killing would always truly be merciful for patients requesting them. Second, they argue that even when death would seem more merciful and the patient might not want to continue living, these rationales may justify suicide and the withholding of life-prolonging treatment, but they do not justify an act of killing. They further argue that a very small number would actually be helped by new legislation since those not competent even over age 21 would not fit the requirements. Finally, they warn against the possible abuses and errors that might result from a relaxation of the present strong prohibition against killing.

O. Ruth Russel in *Freedom to Die* proposed the following possible solutions to the difficulties of euthanasia:

1. Ratification of a constitutional amendment that would recognize the right to death in addition to the rights to life, liberty, and the pursuit of happiness.
2. Amendment of the suicide laws so as to allow a doctor to provide the patient with the means to end life (this, of course, would not help the unconscious, paralyzed, or mentally deficient).
3. Amendment of the criminal code so that euthanasia would not be defined as murder. Euthanasia could then be considered a compassionate rather than a criminal act.
4. Contest, through litigation, the right of the state to deny a person the right to euthanasia.
5. Inclusion in the definition of death the state of brain death. This would allow euthanasia to be administered to persons who could never recover from an illness or deformity that had reduced them to a passive physical state.
6. Enactment of a euthanasia law that would protect from prosecution for murder those doctors who performed passive euthanasia by not prescribing life-sustaining medicine for a patient who is not of "testamentary capacity."
7. Legalization of active euthanasia for a patient who has made a written declaration for euthanasia.

The critical point of the euthanasia debate for older Americans is related to the question of when a person should be allowed to die. Most older

Americans prefer a quick death to a long, lingering illness. Similarly, most of them do not want to be a burden to their families. Lingering illnesses tend to drain the family both financially and emotionally.

Victor W. Marshall quotes how some residents of Glen Brae indicated they preferred to die:

1. "I hope . . . when the end comes, it'll be snappy. You know, I know one person here who carries a cyanide pill with him . . . I think he dreads a terrible siege."
2. "I hope when the time comes it will come fast. I've given the doctors instructions that way."
3. "I'd just like to go to sleep and never wake up. Kind of cowardly but I haven't anyone to say goodbye to."[15]

Aware of the nearness of their death, they want their dying to be of no trouble to themselves or anyone else.

The physician is often left with an impossible dilemma in serving older patients. In most states, to remove an intravenous tube from a dying patient is currently defined as murder. The act of not inserting it in the first place is not defined as murder.

Critical Questions for Older Patients

Richard A. Kalish discussed the inevitable questions that older persons, their families, and their doctors must ultimately decide. The first of these for the older patient is, "Where to die?" While most would prefer to die in their homes amid familiar surroundings, as observed earlier in this chapter, the trend has been for old people to more and more frequently die in hospitals and nursing homes. This undoubtedly has come about partly because the hospitals and nursing homes are better equipped to deal with the dying person. Simultaneously, however, it does remove considerable family tension and strain that can surround the care for a dying family member in the home. Therefore, most families probably prefer that their older members who are terminally ill not remain in the home. Kalish quotes one highly emotional housewife exclaiming that she would never be able to live in their home again if her aged father died there.

Thus while the elderly most often prefer to die at home with their possessions surrounding them and in the presence of loved ones, they are not likely to be allowed to do so. A variety of medical, family, and financial pressures often result in the decision to allow them to die in hospitals and nursing homes.

A second critical question is whether the older patient has the right to know when he or she is dying. Some argue that the patient should be informed of his or her condition. This, it is felt, will lead to a more natural and relaxed relationship between the patient and his or her friends and loved ones since no one will have to pretend that everything is all right and the patient is going to recover. Simultaneously, it allows the patients some time to make any final preparations for their death in the form of dispensing of property, financial arrangements, and plans for other family members. Others believe, however, that the patients should be protected against such knowledge which is seen as possibly closing out hope and perhaps hastening death. They feel that many patients simply would not be able to adjust to the knowledge of their impending death and that instead of giving them time to make any final arrangements it would merely put them in a state of depression during their final days.

The final question for the older patient, according to Kalish, is "At what point do you cease to be yours?" When are you no longer responsible for what is happening to you? At some point many dying patients become either semiconscious or unconscious. Inevitably, decisions have to be made by family members or medical personnel regarding how great an effort should be made to keep the patient alive. The physician's ability to reduce discomfort through sedation sometimes results in the patients leading a vegetablelike but comfortable existence.

Human knowledge of how to prolong life has resulted in the ultimate question of when it is unwise to prolong it further. Earl MacQuarrie's story is an example of the decision that must sometimes be made regarding this question. Earl was admitted to the hospital to undergo open-heart surgery. Prior to his surgery, Earl had a stroke and was in such a poor condition that the doctors could not operate with any reasonable hope of success. After carefully examining Earl for the next 48 hours, the doctors advised Earl's wife that they could probably keep him alive for 6 months to a year by the use of respirators and other machines that would assist his body in all its vital functions. If they did nothing other than give him sedation, he would die within a week. Earl's wife bravely recommended that Earl be allowed to die naturally with no special efforts made by the doctors to prolong his life.

ADJUSTMENTS TO DYING

Each individual at various times in life and in various ways comes to develop means of coping with and adjusting to the inevitability of his or her own death. Most people, while recognizing the finiteness of mortal life, still consciously or subconsciously resist information that suggests that their death is imminent. What happens to one who is told that "the time has come" and that he or she is dying?

Elisabeth Kübler-Ross, in working very closely with dying patients, came to conclude that there are five stages of adjustment that the person goes through in the attempts to adjust to his or her death. The first of these is denial, in which the individual refuses to believe that he or she is dying and attempts to insulate himself or herself from anyone or anything that indicates that he or she is dying. The second stage involves the gradual recognition that he or she is dying: He or she can no longer deny the evidence, and he or she becomes angry and resentful. All kinds of questions arise at this time, most of which center on the theme, "Why is this happening to me?" The third stage of adjustment is one of bargaining and an attempt to postpone the inevitable. The person figuratively bargains with his or her maker, stating (consciously or subconsciously), "If I do such-and-such, God, will you let me live?" In the fourth stage, a sense of depression and loss sets in. The person has now come to realize that he or she is dying and that there is nothing that he or she can do to bypass the inevitable. The fifth stage, according to Kübler-Ross, is one of acceptance, in which one attempts to utilize the remaining time to set one's affairs in order prior to death.

While Kübler-Ross is to be credited with pioneering work in dealing with the adjustments of the dying, certain questions are currently being raised about her work. Some gerontologists wonder whether each patient must necessarily go through these five stages of adjustment in exactly the manner that Kübler-Ross predicted or whether each patient must go through all of them. Others wonder whether gerontologists have not been so quick to accept the reality of these five stages of adjustment that they have not been adequately examined and empirically tested for their accuracy. Regardless of the accuracy of these stages, it would be a mistake to expect every single dying person to progress through them in a timely, predictable manner.

The problem of adjustment to dying is first of all a problem for the dying persons, but it is secondly a problem for others who must interact with them in any therapeutic or social manner. Medical doctors and nursing personnel have been trained primarily to save and prolong life. To them, the dying person may seem a failure of their science. Moreover, professional persons who have not resolved their own anxiety about death may avoid the dying patient because of their anxiety.

When informed of the results of the Le Shan study, nurses were surprised to learn how much longer it took them to respond to the calls of the terminal patients. Wilber H. Watson, in a study of nursing homes, found that 90 percent of dying patients were placed in the rooms farthest from service, office, or assistance centers. Similarly Kübler-Ross, in a study of senior medical students, found that the students complained that the physicians avoided the terminally ill on rounds. Avoidance of the dying is one way of insulating oneself from both a sense of powerlessness to help and the inevitability of death as a part of life.

Family members go through similar stages of adjustment to the knowledge of the death of a loved one as does the person himself or herself. An early reaction is often one of shock and disbelief. How can this be true? Often they deny the facts of the diagnosis and shop around for another doctor who might give a different diagnosis. Some turn to fortune tellers and faith healers. They may take the patient to expensive clinics. Ultimately, if the second opinion is the same as the first one, they must accept the reality with which they are faced.

Ideally the physician, the family, and the patient should be able to discuss the patient's dying in a meaningful, sympathetic, and supportive manner.

This, however, depends on the acceptance by all three of the dying person's condition. If the family and the dying person, or the doctor and the dying person, try to keep this a secret from each other, they will keep a barrier between them that makes it more difficult for both. Kübler-Ross believes that the patient and the family will both be able to adjust to, and deal more realistically with, a problem that they can openly discuss.

Avery Weisman, in an article on the common fallacies of the dying patient, believes that the doctor is crucial to the patient's acceptance of his or her death. He further argues that the doctor's misconception of death may distort the dying patient's image of it. Weisman lists seven widespread fallacies about death that he has found:

1. Only suicidal and psychotic people are willing to die. Even when death is inevitable, no one wants to die.

2. Fear of death is the most natural and basic fear of man. The closer one comes to death, the more intense the fear becomes.

3. Reconciliation with death and preparation for death are impossible; therefore one should say as little as possible about it to dying people, turn their questions aside, and use means to deny, to dissimulate, and to avoid open confrontation.

4. Dying people do not really want to know what the future holds, otherwise they would ask more questions. To force a discussion or to insist on unwelcome information is risky. The patient might lose all hope. He might commit suicide, become depressed, or even die more quickly.

5. After speaking with family members, the doctor should treat the patient as long as possible. Then, when further benefit seems unlikely, the patient should be left alone, except for relieving pain. He will then withdraw, die in peace, without further disturbance and anguish.

6. It is reckless, if not downright cruel, to inflict unnecessary suffering on the patient or his family. The patient is doomed; nothing can really make any difference. Survivors should accept the futility but realize that they will get over the loss.

7. Physicians can deal with all phases of the dying process because of their scientific training and clinical experience. The emotional and psychological sides of dying are vastly overemphasized. Consultation with psychologists and social workers is unnecessary. The clergy might be called upon but only because death is near. The doctor has no further obligation after the patient's death.[16]

These fallacies, according to Weisman, become reasons for not getting involved with the dying. Weisman believes that the first three are used to justify withdrawal and the establishment of more distance between the doctor and patient. The fourth implies that the patient doesn't want to talk about death. The fifth and sixth presume that the patient is not responsible; the patient's silence suggests ignorance and complacency. The final fallacy assumes that the physician is all-knowing about both his or her own feelings and those of his or her patient. Weisman argues that the professional must deal with fallacies such as these and treat each dying patient as an individual person, not as a stereotyped group.

The "hospice" movement in Western Europe and the United States advocates a philosophy of caring for the terminally ill in a humane manner. Lynette Jordon advocates that hospices be special places for treating the terminally ill which would be an alternative to allowing them to die in their homes or in hospitals. A specially trained staff assists the terminally ill person in psychological, spiritual, and personal ways. St. Christopher's Hospice, London, is considered a model of its kind. The staff attempts to care for not only the patient's physical, psychological, and spiritual needs but also the needs of family members. Each patient at St. Christopher's controls his or her own intake of drugs so as to remain an integrated and functioning individual as long as possible. The length of stay at St. Christopher's is two to three weeks on the average; 16 percent die about 26 hours after admission.

Hospices aim at (1) lightening the burden for both the dying patient and his or her family; (2) helping the patient maintain dignity; and (3) minimizing the trauma for remaining family members.

The hospice movement is currently a rapidly expanding one in both Western Europe and the United States.

BEREAVEMENT

The death of a friend, loved one, or lifelong spouse is often difficult for the individual to accept. One's sense of powerlessness can be heightened since obviously one was unable to prevent the death. The feeling of powerlessness is simultaneously accompanied by a sense of loneliness, loss, and social isolation. These are the beginnings of the human emotion called grief.

Grief is best described as a physiological, psychological, and sociological reaction to loss. Physiologically, the individual may suffer from crying spells, upset stomachs, headaches, fainting, diarrhea, and profuse sweating. Psychologically, the individual goes through various stages of adjustment to the loss, ranging from disbelief to despair. Sociologically, family and friends may simultaneously grieve for the deceased and thus the experience is shared. The social significance of the event may be most far reaching. A wife is now a widow, a husband a widower, the company is without an employee, and the city council without a member. In one or another way the entire world is changed by each and every death.

The fact that the grief period is a difficult time for those who experience it can be seen in the results of a study of Bernard Benjamin and Chris Wallis on the mortality of widows and widowers. The immediate six months following the death of a wife was followed by a 40 percent increase in the death rate of a sample of adult men. This was followed then by a return to the same death rate as married men. Apparently the shock of widowhood weakens the resistance to other causes of death. Howard Becker, discussing bereavement, says

> The sorrow of love is ever attached to the beloved object, and in diverse ways, strives to maintain all that remains of the former union.[17]

Persons experiencing grief tend to go through somewhat predictable and patterned responses as they attempt to adjust. These include protest, despair, detachment, and reorganization. The protest reaction immediately follows the death and includes the emotions of denial, disbelief, and anger. The first stage is one of numbness and disbelief. This is often accompanied by weeping and bodily complaints.

The next stage is one of despair, characterized by considerable restlessness, disorganization, and searching behavior. The restless behavior during this period is characterized by pacing and searching, or walking in a disorganized and restless manner. During this stage the individual searches for the lost person for a variety of reasons: First, there is need to confirm that the person is gone; second, a need to use the lost person as the basis for one's grief.

Detachment is the stage in which the bereaved begins to pull back from the lost person. The bereaved has now begun to recognize the reality of his or her loss. Some of the former ties are now beginning to be broken; energies are beginning to be directed to other areas of concern as they become diverted from the lost person. Often the bereaved will withdraw from others and from everyday duties. This period of being alone is a time for doing one's final grieving. It is often a time of forgetfulness; the bereaved may go to the drug store and forget why he or she went. However, these are the grieving person's attempts to return to normal tasks, and should not be viewed negatively.

The final stage of adjustment to the loss of a loved one is that of reorganization. A sign that the reorganization has occurred is the ability of the grieving person to talk about the lost person without severe emotional upheaval. The ability to remember the deceased in favorable terms without continuous crying is another sign of final adjustment. The individual will at this time begin to return to former roles including job, social groups, and community activities. W. M. Lamers and others have observed the therapeutic value that funerals have for helping the bereaved person resolve grief.[18]

The time necessary for grieving is difficult to determine and obviously subject to individual differences. The grieving is complete when the person returns to a normal living pattern with no lingering feeling of guilt. Many people in the United States today feel that one year is an appropriate time, and that "heavy" decisions—selling one's house and moving, remarrying, taking a job (or changing jobs)—should wait for at least a year after the death of a spouse. Decisions hurried during the grieving period are often wrong decisions.

For most people today, dying takes place over a longer period of time than in the past. This causes numerous problems for family members and the patient. During a long illness a family member grieves as a mother is taken from the home to the hospital; the husband and children grieve because they have lost a wife and mother. Anticipatory grief refers to the fact that a person may grieve when anticipating the death of a loved one. K. C. Aldrich, in comparing anticipatory and conventional grief, says:

> Conventional grief can be prolonged indefinitely. Anticipatory grief, on the other hand, has a finite endpoint dependent on external circumstances of the physical occurrences of the anticipated loss. Also, conventional grief decelerates or diminishes in degree as time passes, while anticipatory grief theoretically should accelerate.[19]

A period of anticipatory grief may provide some opportunity to grieve in advance but may produce feelings of guilt and thereby complicate the working-through process. The individual who anticipates ahead of time the death of a loved one may experience considerable emotional strain. Prolonged illness in which the death is anticipated and considerable grieving occurs prior to the actual event may result in the family being "all grieved out" by the time of the death. While social custom demands further grieving, the family may only feel relieved.

The grieving person can be considerably aided by friends and family. David Maddison and Wendy L. Walker found that widows who made the best adjustments to the death of a spouse were those that perceived their social environment as an active and helpful one. Widows without a supportive social network experienced greater difficulty with their grief.

Some societies have developed formal customs to assist the grieving person in recovering from his or her loss. The "Irish Wake" involved much ceremony surrounding the burial of the deceased, followed by a period of drinking and brawling. This was one of considerable social support for the grieving individual. More recently the United States has seen the emergence of widow-to-widow programs by which someone who has experienced considerable grief in the past attempts to help another person who is currently grieving adjust to his or her loss.

CONCLUSION

In all probability, from prehistoric times to the present, human beings have been awed by the gift of life and dismayed by the presence of death. Although through the skills of modern science people have developed some control over the conception of children and the ability to prolong life through the use of scientific technology, life itself and death are subjects that defy scientific explanation and reason.

Both people's fear of death and the ability of the sciences to prolong life (even if only in a sedated and vegetablelike state) have created some difficult questions for modern society concerning when, where, how, and why people die. There has been a tendency to institutionalize and bureaucratize death. The old are more likely to die in hospitals and nursing homes and less likely to die at home. Similarly, funerals are more likely to take place in a funeral parlor and less likely to be held in a home or church. We have chosen to let modern society turn the dying and the dead over to specialists for their care and attention. For the generation of young Americans currently growing up, this means that they are less likely to have to confront the issue of death directly in their own lives.

The fear of death seems almost universal and is something everyone must ultimately deal with. Vern L. Bengtson and others found age to be a critical factor in explaining one's fear of death. The young perceive death as so far in the future that it evokes little concern. The middle-aged are likely to be increasingly aware of the slowing of certain biological functions and the finiteness of their lives but often have not had time to resolve their fear of death. The old have most frequently come to accept death as inevitable and evidence fewer anxieties about it.

The death of acquaintances, friends, and loved ones arouses many latent fears of death in humans. During times of mourning, we grieve not only for the dead but for ourselves and the fact that someday we must die. The period of grieving is necessary as part of the adjustment of an individual to the loss of a significant other, an adjustment that is helped if the situation surrounding a death allows for, encourages, and supports the necessary grieving. Much of the formal ritual surrounding the funeral ceremony is designed to assist the grieving individual. The ability to resolve one's own grief is best accomplished in a supportive environment in which the assistance of the living to the grieving person is readily available. Family, friends, and religious convictions often assist the individual in adjusting to the loss of a loved one.

KEY TERMS

bureaucratization
introspection
secularism
significant others

hedonism
euthanasia
anticipatory grief
bereavement

SUGGESTED READINGS

ALDRICH, K.C., "Some Dynamics of Anticipatory Grief," in *Anticipatory Grief*, ed. B. Schoenberg and others, pp. 3–9. New York: Columbia University Press, 1974.

ALEXANDER, I.E., AND M. M. ADLERSTEIN, "Studies in the Psychology of Death," in *Perspectives in Personality Research*, pp. 65–92. New York: Springer, 1960.

BECKER, HOWARD, "The Sorrow of Bereavement," *Journal of Abnormal and Social Psychology*, 27 (1933), 391–410.

BENGTSON, VERN L., JOSE B. CUELLAR, AND PAULINE K. RAGAN, "Stratum Contrasts and Similarities in Attitudes Toward Death," *Journal of Gerontology*, 32, no. 1 (January 1977), 76–89.

BENJAMIN, BERNARD, AND CHRIS WALLIS, "The Mortality of Widowers," *The Lancet*, 2 (August 1963), 454–56.

BERGER, PETER, AND THOMAS LUCKMANN, *The Social Construction of Reality: A Treatise in the Sociology of Knowledge*, p. 102. Garden City, NY: Doubleday Anchor, 1967.

BLAUNER, ROBERT, "Death and Social Structure," *Psychiatry*, 29 (1966), 378–94.

BLUESTEIN, VENUS W., "Death-Related Experiences, Attitudes, and Feelings: Reported by Thanatology Students in a National Sample," *Omega*, 6, no. 3 (1975), pp. 207–18.

BOWERS, M., AND OTHERS, *Counseling the Dying*. New York: Thomas Nelson, 1964.

COX, HAROLD, "Mourning Populations: Some Considerations of Historically Comparable Assassinations," *Death Education*, 4, no. 2 (Summer 1980), 125–38.

ELLIOT, T.O., "Bereavement: Inevitable, but not Unsurmountable," in *Family Marriage and Parenthood* (2nd ed.), eds. H. Becker and R. Hill. Cambridge, MA: Heath, 1971.

EPSTEIN, CAROLE, ESTER BALHIN, AND DAVID BUSH, "Attitudes Toward Classroom Discussions of Death and Dying Among Urban and Suburban Children," *Omega*, 7, no. 27 (1976).

FEIFEL, H., AND A.B. BRAUNSCOMB, "Who's Afraid of Death?" *Journal of Abnormal Psychology*, 81 (1973), 282–88.

GLASER, BARNEY G., AND ANSELM L. STRAUSS, *Awareness of Dying*. Chicago: Aldine, 1965.

HOCHSCHILD, ARLIE, *The Unexpected Community*, p. 88. Englewood Cliffs, NJ: Prentice-Hall, 1972.

JACKSON, N. EDGAR, *When Someone Dies*. Philadelphia: Fortress Press, 1973.

JEFFERS, FRANCES C., AND ADRIAN VERWOERDT, in *Behavior and Adaption in Later Life*, eds. Ewald Busse and Eric Pfeiffer, pp. 163–81. Boston, MA: Little, Brown, 1969.

JEFFERS, FRANCES C., CLAUDE NICHOLS, AND CARL EISDORFER, "Attitudes of Older Persons Toward Death: A Preliminary Study," *Journal of Gerontology*, 16, no. 1 (January 1961), 53–56.

JORDAN, LYNETTE, "Hospice in America," *The CoEvolution Quarterly* (Summer 1977).

JORGENSON, DAVID E., AND RON C. NEUBECKER, "Euthanasia: A National Study Survey of Attitudes Toward Voluntary Termination of Life," *Omega*, 11, no. 4 (1980), 281–91.

KALISH, RICHARD A., "The Aged and the Dying Process: The Inevitable Decisions," *Journal of Social Issues*, 21 (1965), 87–96.

KANE, JOHN J., "The Irish Wake: A Sociological Appraisal, " *Sociological Symposium,* 1 (Fall 1968), 11–16.

KASTENBAUM, ROBERT J., *Death, Society, and Human Experience.* Saint Louis: C.V. Mosby, 1977.

KEPHART, WILLIAM K., "Status After Death," *The American Sociological Review,* 15 (1950), 635–43.

KÜBLER-ROSS, ELISABETH, *On Death and Dying.* New York: Macmillan, 1969.

LAMERS, W.M., "Funerals are Good For People—M.D.'s Included," *Medical Economics,* 46 (June 23, 1969), 104–7.

LESHAN, L., "The World of the Patient in Severe Pain of Long Duration," *Journal of Chronic Diseases,* 17 (1964), 119–26.

LEVITON, DANIEL, "Death Education," in *New Meanings of Death,* ed. Herman Feifel, pp. 253–72. New York: McGraw-Hill, 1977.

MADDISON, DAVID, AND WENDY L. WALKER, "Factors Affecting the Outcome of Conjugal Bereavement," *British Journal of Psychiatry,* 113 (1967), 1057–67.

MALINOWSKI, BRONISLAW, *Magic, Science, and Religion and Other Essays.* New York: Free Press, 1948.

MARSHALL, VICTOR W., "Socialization for Impending Death in a Retirement Village," *American Journal of Sociology,* 80 (1975), 1124–44.

OBERSHAW, RICHARD J., *Death, Dying, and Funerals.* Burnsville, MN: Grief Center, 1976.

PENNISTON, D.H., "The Importance of Death Education in Family Life," *The Family Coordinator* (1963), pp. 15–21.

RUSSEL, O. RUTH, *Freedom to Die: Moral and Legal Aspects of Euthanasia.* New York: Human Science Press, 1975.

SAGE, WAYNE, *Choosing the Good Death.* Guilford, CT: Dushkin, 1978. Also in *Focus Aging,* ed. Harold Cox.

SCHNEIDMAN, EDWIN S., *Death: Current Perspectives.* Palo Alto, CA: Mayfield, 1976.

SELDES, GEORGE, ed., *The Great Quotations.* New York: Simon & Schuster, 1967.

SHEATSLEY, PAUL B., AND JACOB FELDMAN, "The Assassination of President Kennedy: A Preliminary Report on Public Reactions and Behavior," *Public Opinion Quarterly,* 28 (Summer 1964).

SILVERMAN, PHYLLIS ROLFE, "The Widow to Widow Program: An Experiment in Preventive Intervention," in *Death: Current Perspectives,* ed. Edwin S. Schneidman, pp. 356–66. Palo Alto, CA: Mayfield, 1976.

SMITH, T.E.,"Cocos Keeling Islands: A Demographic Laboratory," *Population Studies,* 14 (1960), 94–130.

SUDNOW, DAVID N., *Passing On: The Social Organization of Dying.* Englewood Cliffs, NJ: Prentice-Hall, 1967.

SWENSON, WENDELL M., "Attitudes Toward Death in an Aged Population," *Journal of Gerontology,* 16, no. 1 (January 1961), 49–52.

WAHL, C.W., "The Fear of Death," in *The Meaning of Death,* ed. H. Heifel. New York: McGraw-Hill, 1959.

WATSON, WILBER H., "The Aging, Sick and the Near Dead: A Study Distinguishing Characteristics and Social Effects," *Omega,* 7, no. 2 (1976), 115–24.

WEBER, MAX, *Essays in Sociology,* trans. and ed., H.H. Gerth and C. Wright Mills, pp. 196–98. New York: Oxford University Press, 1953.

WEISMAN, AVERY, "Common Fallacies about Dying Patients," in *Death: Current Perspectives,* ed. Edwin Schneidman, pp. 443–52. Palo Alto, CA: Mayfield, 1976.

ZEIGENBERG, LOMA, AND ROBERT FULTON, "Care of the Dying: A Swedish Perspective," *Omega,* 8, no. 3 (1977), 215–29.

12
ECONOMICS OF AGING

The harvest of old age is the recollection and
abundance of blessings previously secured.

Marcus Tullius Cicero
De Senectute, XI

ECONOMIC NEEDS OF OLDER AMERICANS*

In order to discuss the adequacy of the income and economic resources of the elderly we must first determine the specific characteristics and needs of this particular group of people. Using 65 and above as our definition for old, one finds a group of persons who generally have no children remaining at home, who are retired, who own their own home, and whose expenses are likely to be lower than they were during the middle years, except for medical expenses, which are likely to be higher and to climb steadily as one ages. Schulz observed that when one gets very old, one is likely to experience exceptionally higher expenditures for chronic illness, hospitalization, and sometimes institutionalization. Declining health and increasing medical expense can destroy savings and raise the economic needs of older Americans dramatically. Further, the newly retired, sometimes referred to as the young-old, are likely to have more adequate incomes than the old-old (those who are 75 and above).

Today's retirees, many of whom experience economic deprivation, have been a relatively quiet, noncomplaining group. They are fairly hardened to their deprivation by their experiences of living in a historical/cultural environment that included two world wars and a major depression. Many of the current retirees have lived on limited resources throughout much of their lives. Moreover, they are generally more conservative in their attitudes toward government services than is the adult population today. They often consider government services to be welfare and are opposed to being the recipients of welfare programs.

Previously we observed that less than 5 percent of elderly Americans are living in nursing homes. A Midwestern survey of older Americans found that 44.3 percent of the noninstitutionalized sample were living alone, 41.3 percent

*I would like to express my appreciation to Philip Bibo, an Associate Professor of Economics at Indiana State University, for his assistance as the coauthor of this chapter.

were living with a spouse, 4.4 percent were living with children, 0.8 percent were living with a spouse and children, and 1.2 percent had some other living arrangement.[1] The great majority of this sample of older Americans were either living with a spouse or living alone. Those living independently have the same need for housing, clothing, transportation, and utilities as younger persons in the population.

Although they have fewer expenses than during the childrearing years, the elderly have the same individual needs as any other person during his or her adult years. In terms of medical costs, their needs are greater than others in the adult population. The basic problem for the elderly then becomes to maintain an adequate standard of living during the later years on a relatively fixed and unchanging retirement income. This problem is compounded by the fact that older persons:

1. Generally receive considerably less income than those in the working years.
2. Are living in a country in which inflation is a relatively constant phenomenon, so that each year their income will buy less.
3. Have no means of increasing their income at this stage of life.

It is easy to understand why some older Americans become depressed during later life. They often have inadequate incomes, they can see that with inflation their money will buy less, and they have no visible means for increasing their incomes. They may feel that all they have to look forward to in the future is the same income and reduced purchasing power.

INCOME

The income of older Americans consistently falls below that of other age groups in the adult population. Most older Americans have incomes below $6000 a year. Family heads tend to earn more than unrelated individuals (Table 12–1). Brotman reported a median income of $8057 for heads of families who were 65 and above. This compared with $14,698 for heads of families between the ages of 14 and 64. For unrelated individuals the median income in 1975 was $3311 for the 65+ group and $6460 for the 14–64 age group (Table 12–1).

In 1978 these figures had increased somewhat but the pattern was the same. The median income for men 65 and over was $5526; for women 65 and over, $3088; for families whose head was 65 and over, $9110; for families of all other age groups, $16,009; for unrelated individuals 65 and above, $3829; and for unrelated individuals below the age of 65, $5907 (Table 12–2). When considering individuals or families, income of blacks will be approximately one-third less than the incomes of whites during old age.[2]

Table 12–1 Trends in Median Money Income of Families and Unrelated Individuals by Age, 1960–1975

YEAR	FAMILIES			UNRELATED INDIVIDUALS		
	Heads 14–64	Heads 65+		Heads 14–64	Heads 65+	
	Amount	Amount	% of 14–64	Amount	Amount	% of 14–64
1960	$ 5,905	$2,897	49.1	$2,571	$1,053	41.0
1961	6,099	3,026	49.6	2,589	1,106	42.7
1962	6,336	3,204	50.6	2,644	1,248	47.2
1963	6,644	3,352	50.5	2,881	1,277	44.3
1964	6,981	3,376	48.4	3,094	1,297	41.9
1965	7,413	3,514	47.4	3,344	1,378	41.2
1966	7,922	3,645	46.0	3,443	1,443	41.9
1967	8,504	3,928	46.2	3,655	1,480	40.5
1968	9,198	4,592	49.9	4,073	1,734	42.6
1969	10,085	4,803	47.6	4,314	1,855	43.0
1970	10,541	5,053	47.9	4,616	1,951	42.3
1971	10,976	5,453	49.7	4,783	2,199	46.0
1972	11,870	5,968	50.3	5,018	2,397	47.8
1973	12,935	6,426	49.7	5,547	2,725	49.1
1974	13,823	7,505	54.3	6,080	2,984	49.1
1975	14,698	8,057	54.8	6,460	3,311	51.3

Source: Herman B. Brotman, "Income and Poverty in the Older Population in 1975," *The Gerontologist,* 27, no. 1 (1977), 23. Quoting U.S. Bureau of the Census data. Reprinted by permission of *The Gerontologist.*

Table 12–2 1977 Median Total Money Income and Percent with Incomes Below $6000

	MEDIAN	PERCENT WITH INCOME BELOW $6000
Men Age 65 and Over	$ 5,526	55
Women Age 65 and Over	3,088	83
Families Age 65 and Over	9,110	26
Families (All Ages)	16,009	13
Unrelated Aged Individuals	3,829	75
Unrelated Individuals (All Ages)	5,907	51

Source: U.S. Bureau of the Census, "Consumer Income," *Current Population Reports,* Series P-60, no. 116 (Washington, D.C.: U.S. Government Printing Office, 1978).

Table 12–3 1977 Total Money Income* of Persons 65 and Over, by Sex

TOTAL MONEY INCOME	MEN	WOMEN
Less than $2,000	6%	29%
$ 2,000–3,999	27	40
4,000–5,999	22	14
6,000–7,999	15	7
8,000–9,999	9	4
10,000–14,999	10	4
15,000–19,999	5	1
20,000–24,999	2	**
25,000 and Over	4	1
Total	100%	100%

*Money income includes salaries and wages; self-employment income; social insurance benefits; welfare payments; dividends, interest, and rents; pensions, alimony, and contributions from others; and unemployment, veterans', and workmen's compensation payments.
**Less than 1 percent.

Source: U.S. Bureau of the Census, "Consumer Income," *Current Population Reports*, no. 116 (Washington, D.C.: U.S. Government Printing Office, 1978).

Comparison between the incomes of men and women reveals that the men consistently receive more during the retirement years. Table 12–3 indicates that the lower earning levels include a higher percentage of women than men. The 65+ age group who earned less than $2000 was comprised of 29 percent of the women but only 6 percent of the men. The category of earnings from $2000 to $3999 was comprised of 40 percent of the women but only 27 percent of the men. Looking at the other end of the table, we find 21 percent of the older men earning $10,000 or more while only 6 percent of the women earn $10,000 or more.

As these figures indicate, older persons living alone tend to have less income than older persons living in families or younger persons. Brotman observed that four-fifths of those living alone had annual incomes under $6000, or no greater than $114 per week, in comparison to younger persons living alone or with nonrelated persons, in which less than one-half had incomes below $6000. At the other end of the economic scale Brotman notes that one-fifth of older families had incomes of $5000 or above in comparison to one-half the younger families that had above $5000. One-twentieth of the unrelated individuals and one-fifth of younger persons had incomes of $12,000 or more.[3]

While it is generally true that the older population is disadvantaged when compared to other age groups in the general population, their gains in income have been more rapid than any other age group for the last two decades. Carole Allen and Herman Brotman observe:

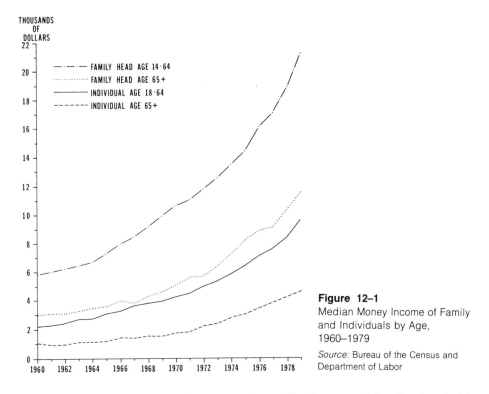

Figure 12–1
Median Money Income of Family and Individuals by Age, 1960–1979

Source: Bureau of the Census and Department of Labor

Between 1960 and 1979 alone, the median income of families headed by a person 65 or older increased nearly fourfold (3.9 times), a rate somewhat greater than that of younger families, whose income increased 3.6 times. As a result, the median incomes of old families rose from 49 percent to 53 percent of the younger families during this time period. The rate of increase for individuals 65 and older was even greater—their median income rose from 41 percent to 48 percent of the younger persons.[4]

While this is a distinct improvement in the median incomes of older persons, it is still true that in 1979 the median incomes of older families and individuals alike remained roughly one-half of their younger counterparts' (see Figure 12–1).

POVERTY

The poverty index figure for a nonfarm two-person family with a head age 65 or more was $4200 in 1979. The one-person level was established at $3500 that same year. The unit of poverty index is calculated by determining the minimum amount of adequate food for the family unit, and then the cost of that food at prevailing prices is determined by pricing foods in retail stores. Schulz observed that this food allotment was originally devised for emergency periods only and that no one is expected to have to live for a long period of time on these very minimal amounts. He believes that these food diets would be detrimental to health over an extended period of time.[5]

It is apparent from Figure 12–2 that the older persons are much more likely to have incomes which place them below the poverty line than younger persons. While this is true, the overall proportion of elderly with incomes below the poverty line has been decreasing. There were 28 percent of the 65+ group who fell below the poverty line in 1966 and there were only 16 percent who fell below the poverty line in 1979. Both increases in the median incomes of older persons and the decreases in the percentage of those falling below the poverty level have occurred primarily because of increases in Social Security benefits mandated by Congress and increases in the number of persons receiving private pensions.

The Department of Health, Education, and Welfare has established the "near-poor" threshold as 25 percent above the poverty line. Harris observes that in 1975 the near-poverty level for older persons was $4040 for a family and $3015 for a single person. Twenty-five percent of the elderly fell below the near-poverty level of income at that time (Table 12–4).

Blacks in comparison to whites are significantly more likely to fall below the near-poverty level, and women are much more likely than men to fall below it. The black female in old age is most likely to find herself in a state of poverty or near poverty. Harris points out that the proportion of elderly blacks who are poor is almost two-and-one-half times the proportion of elderly whites who are poor. In 1975 over half the elderly blacks fell below the near-poverty line. In 1974, more than 40 percent of the elderly widows were classified as poor and of those living alone 70 percent were poor.

Schulz points out that another method of measuring poverty is the Bureau of Labor Statistics Retired Couples Budget. The retired couple has been

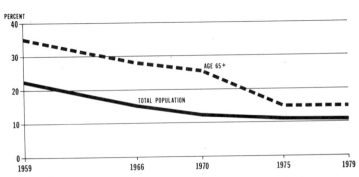

Figure 12–2   Poverty Rate of Total Population and Persons 65 and Over, 1959–1979

Source: Bureau of the Census

Table 12–4 Number and Proportion of Persons in Households with Incomes Below the Near-Poverty Level, All Ages and 65+, by Race and Family Status, 1975

RACE AND FAMILY STATUS	ALL AGES		65+	
	*Number**	*%*	*Number**	*%*
Total, all races	37,182	17.6	5,495	25.4
In families	30,127	15.8	1,290	15.8
Unrelated Individuals	7,055	34.9	3,304	48.2
White	26,595	14.5	4,516	23.0
In families	20,898	12.6	979	13.2
Unrelated Individuals	5,697	32.5	2,823	45.5
Black	9,788	40.6	926	51.6
In families	8,560	39.5	306	45.5
Unrelated Individuals	1,227	51.1	448	74.8

*Numbers in thousands

Source: U.S. Bureau of the Census, "Money Income and Poverty Status of Families and Persons in the U.S." (advanced report), *Current Population Reports*, Series P-60, No. 103, September 1976.

defined by the bureau as a husband 65 and over and his wife. They are living in their own home without any assistance and are in reasonably good health. The budget is not designed to indicate poverty levels but rather a moderate style of life. Schulz states:

> In general, the representative list of goods and services comprising the standard of budget reflects the collective judgment of families as to what is necessary and desirable to meet conventional and social as well as physical needs of families in the present decade.[6]

In 1978 the Bureau of Labor Statistics set three levels of retirement budget:

1. Lower level: $5031
2. Intermediate level: $7198
3. Higher level: $10,711

The majority of older Americans could not reach the intermediate budget, since most of them make less than $6000 a year. Data from the Indiana survey indicated that those individuals who made $8000 or more tended to score high on the life satisfaction measure. Those making less than $8000 tended to score lower. Those having incomes of less than $8000 usually report low levels of life satisfactions, and those earning from $8000 to $10,000 reported higher levels of life satisfaction. Those making above $10,000 scored high on life satisfaction but not significantly higher than the group from $8000 to $10,000. Eight thousand dollars would appear in the eyes of older persons to be the current figure necessary to maintain an adequate standard of living.

SOURCE OF INCOME

The major sources of income for the elderly are very difficult to determine precisely. Figure 12–3 is an update of an earlier survey done by the Social Security Administration. This is broken down by families and for unrelated individuals. As this table indicates, Social Security and Railroad Retirement combined is the biggest source of income for most older Americans, with over 90 percent of them receiving some benefits. This is followed by income from property, which 64.4 percent receive; wage and salary incomes, 41.7 percent; and retirement income in the form of private pension plans and annuities, 35.7 percent.

While Figure 12–3 represents the percent of families and individuals receiving income from various sources, Grad and Foster in a report for the Social Security Administration indicate the percentage breakdown of the total income of older persons as contributed by the various sources. While 90 percent of older persons receive some Social Security benefits, these benefits account for

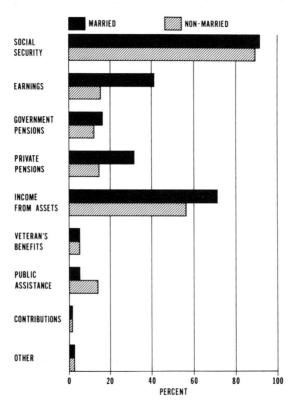

Figure 12–3
Percent of Older Persons Receiving Money Income from Each Source, 1978

Source: Bureau of the Census

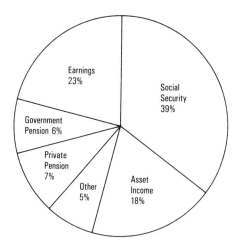

Figure 12–4

Source: Income of the Population 55 and Older,
(Washington, D.C.: Social Security Administration
1979), 1980

only 39 percent of the total earnings of older Americans. In addition, earnings account for 23 percent, asset income for 18 percent, private pensions for 7 percent, government pension for 6 percent and other for 5 percent (Figure 12–4). For the majority of Social Security recipients, however, it is the single most important source of income providing at least 50 percent of their total income.

Schulz points out that the aged are not a homogeneous group, and that to lump them all together has a tendency to make us view the entire group as if they were living under the same circumstances as the less fortunate members of the group. Obviously, the great majority of older Americans have incomes that place them above the poverty level. Most of them are secure enough economically to be able to maintain a desired style of life during their later years.

One often hears the argument that the family, and not government, should take care of its older members. This seems an unlikely prospect: Cox and others revealed that only 10 percent of older persons in their sample received benefits from family.

In 1972 Congress legislated a Supplemental Security Income program (SSI), which was to be administered by the Social Security Administration. This program provides a national minimum level of income for the aged, blind, and disabled. In 1982, the SSI guaranteed $284.30 monthly income ($3411.60 yearly) for individuals and $426.40 per month ($5116.80 yearly) for an elderly couple.

While a very small proportion of persons over age 65 work, for those that do their income is considerably higher than those that do not work. Harris reports that for families headed by a person 65 or older where there were no earners the median income was $3235, where there was one earner $6160, and where two or more family members had earned incomes the median was $10,157.

Figure 12–5

Source: Don Wright, *The Miami News.* Reprinted by permission.

Private pension programs are not as widespread nor as adequate a source of income for the current generation of retirees as they may be for future generations. As we observed in Chapter 9, most workers have to stay with a company throughout their entire career in order to receive the benefits. Also the company has to remain in business for the entire career of the worker. Any disturbances in either the worker's career or the company's business generally terminates the pension. Greenough and King found that private pensions were inaccessible to about 50 percent of the private workforce. The private pensions tend to be fixed permanently, with no compensation for inflationary factors, and they generally offer no coverage for the spouse after the husband's death.

Assets that older persons have may include such things as stocks and bonds, farmland, houses, and so on. For the great majority of older Americans with assets, homeownership is their only asset. Schulz speaks of housing as being a nonliquid "locked-in" asset.[7] The elderly cannot quickly turn equity in their homes into income for day-to-day use as they can with an interest in a business, or with stocks and bonds. On the other hand, the fact that many older Americans own their own homes and are thus living without any mortgage or rent payments means that they require less income than a younger person might need to maintain the same standard of living.

Table 12–5 indicates the relative amount of financial assets of the aged.[8] The table shows that 26 percent of the couples and 42 percent of the unrelated

Table 12–5   Aged[a] Financial Assets and Homeowner Equity, 1967[b]

ASSET AMOUNT	FINANCIAL ASSETS ONLY		EQUITY IN HOME	
	Couples	Unrelated Individuals	Couples[c]	Unrelated Individuals[c]
None	26	42	d	d
$1–999	17	19		
$1000–2999	15	11	13	18
$3000–4999	8	6		
$5000–9999	12	9	24	26
$10,000–19,999	11	7	40	39
$20,000 or more	13	5	23	17
Total Percent	100[e]	100	100	100

[a]Age 65 or older.
[b]Asset information does not include value of business and farm assets and equity in rental.
[c]Homeowners only.
[d]Not applicable.
[e]Totals may not add up to 100 due to rounding.

Source: James Schulz, *The Economics of Aging* (Belmont, CA: Wadsworth, 1980), p. 31. © 1980 by Wadsworth, Inc. Reprinted by permission of Wadsworth Publishing Company.

individuals have no assets. At the other extreme, only 13 percent of the couples and 5 percent of the unrelated individuals have $20,000 or more in assets.

There are two other factors that must be taken into account in considering the incomes of the elderly; these are in-kind income and tax breaks. In-kind income refers to a service or goods which older persons may purchase at a reduced price. Older persons are sometimes the recipients of goods and services provided by either the government or business community at a considerably reduced price. Schulz believes that subsidized government housing is the best example of an in-kind income, since one is allowed to pay a price for housing that is below the market value; one thus receives an in-kind service from the government. Schulz reports that there are 42 major federal programs benefiting the elderly over and above those providing direct money income. The largest single government expenditure is for health care. While the aged may have very low money incomes, they may have considerable in-kind incomes. Schulz believes that the special provision that permits persons over the age of 65 to double their personal tax exemption amount tends to help the higher-income elderly. Stanley Surrey has estimated that nearly half of the federal tax assistance goes to individuals with incomes above $10,000.

EFFECTS OF INFLATION

The economic problems associated with the U.S. population 65 and over are not necessarily different from those of the general population. The principal difference between the 65+ group and the general population is the vulnerability of the former to the effects of inflation. These can be much worse for those whose money incomes are relatively fixed than for those who remain in the work force earning supplemental money income that is geared to the inflation rate. Rising prices versus relatively fixed incomes means either a reduction in the standard of living or the selling of assets accumulated over the working years in order to maintain a given lifestyle. Without earned income to assist in offsetting the effects of rising prices, the retired must either reduce their standard of living or draw upon accumulated assets. Liquidation of accumulated assets is an especially difficult choice because of the specter of outliving one's income.

One of the best methods of measuring the effect of inflation on the purchasing power of the American consumer is the Consumer Price Index (CPI) which is presented monthly by the Bureau of Labor Statistics. The Index is calculated by determining how much it costs in a particular month to buy a market basket of goods and services that is representative of the buying pattern of consumers. This amount is then expressed in a ratio to what it would have cost to buy this same market basket of goods and services in the base period of 1967. This ratio is then multiplied by 100 to express the change in terms of percentage. Over 400 items are included in this analysis.[9]

Recently the inflation rate as measured by the CPI has been led by rising food prices, sharply increasing prices for energy, and a continuing escalation of prices for medical care. These three components of the CPI work a much greater hardship in the over-65 non-wage-earning population than on the general population. Higher food prices make maintenance of an adequate diet for those on relatively fixed incomes much more difficult. Rising energy costs have substantial effects on one's ability to live comfortably, especially for those Americans who live in areas subject to cold winters. Finally, and despite such programs as Medicare and Medicaid, increasing medical costs have been most devastating to those persons 65 years of age and older.

A 1974 Louis Harris and Associates survey of retirees in the United States brings into focus the difficulty faced by persons 65+ in trying to earn income. In 1974, 12 percent of the public over 65 were employed. The study further revealed that of the older public, about 4.4 million indicated that they did not retire by choice but were forced to retire. Although a majority of retired people 65 and over were not interested in work, over 3 in 10 (about 4 million) said that they would like to work.

The 1974 Harris study was reinforced by a Harris and Associates survey released in 1979. This study revealed that inflation (the first-quarter rate for 1979 being in excess of 10 percent) had reduced real income significantly for retired people. Of the respondents in the study, 34 percent indicated that the quality of their life had deteriorated since retirement. The concern over money replaced fear of crime and poor health as the major problem for retired people according to the study. Inflationary pressures were seen primarily responsible for the 46 percent in the survey that said they would prefer to be working.

The Harris study concluded that "the pressures of inflation are boosting retirement income needs and expectations." The determination and ability of both government and business programs to meet the needs and expectations of older Americans for adequate incomes remains in doubt.

Solutions to the problem of falling real income that confronts retirees are unfortunately limited. One set of solutions could be classified as internal—that is, the individual has control over his or her destiny by his or her own decisions on how he or she allocates his or her money income for purchases; the retiree sets his or her own priorities. The second set of solutions is external to the retiree—the individual is dependent on alternatives determined by an outside agency, such as government.

The impact of inflation has had a particularly devastating effect on the 65-and-older population because Social Security, regardless of what it was intended to do, has become the primary source of income for most older persons. In 1975 most elderly households received some form of Social Security payments; however, when the average Social Security payment is compared to the official poverty level, the inadequacy of these benefits is readily apparent. While the 1975 poverty level was $2791, the average Social Security beneficiaries received was $2461 for single persons. For a married couple the poverty level was $3232, while the average married couple received Social Security benefits in the amount of $4092 (Table 12–6).

Social Security benefits were increased by amendments to the Social Security law to assist in offsetting the effects of inflation. Benefits, beginning in July 1975, were geared to inflation by an "escalator" clause. In June of each year benefits are increased when the CPI shows an increase of 3 percent or more. The "escalator" was, of course, designed to compensate for rising price levels; however, the lag time of one year before benefits are adjusted never allows current payments to reflect current prices; in addition, the poverty-level income for the average Social Security beneficiary exacerbates the inflationary problem. Finally, it is Congress that decides what the cost-of-living increase shall be.

The problems created by inflation and the low incomes of many elderly persons have few solutions. An obvious solution would be either to slow or stop

Table 12–6 Comparison of Annual Social Security and Supplemental Security Income Benefits with Various Cost of Living Standards, 1975

	AVERAGE BENEFIT	POVERTY LEVEL FOR PERSONS 65+	LOWER BLS BUDGET	INTERMEDIATE BLS BUDGET
Retiree	$2,461	$2,791	$3,376	$4,526
Retiree and Spouse	4,092	3,232	4,501	6,465

Source: Charles Harris, *Fact Book on Aging* (Washington, D.C.: The National Council on the Aging, Inc., 1978), p. 58.

inflation or to increase Social Security benefits. The political difficulties confronting these governmental solutions would appear to make them presently less promising. Alternatively, solutions open to the elderly appear to be not very reliable. Entering the job market to supplement income may be either difficult or impossible because of either poor health, lack of skills, or discrimination by employers.

CONCLUSION

The great majority of older Americans find themselves living on incomes that are about half as large as those they were earning prior to retirement. Despite this, most of them initially believe that their income is enough for them to maintain their preretirement standard of living, for their families are raised and they usually own their homes. Many older Americans are therefore able to maintain their preretirement lifestyle during their early retirement years. However, for those who earned low incomes during their working years, retirement with its commensurate reduction of income often places them in a state of poverty. To reduce by half an already inadequate income can be catastrophic for the individual. Approximately 16 percent of older Americans find themselves in a state of poverty, and 25 percent find themselves in a state of near-poverty. Women are more likely to find themselves in a state of poverty than men, and blacks more than whites.

Whether or not persons believe that they have an adequate income at the time they retire, the longer they live, the less likely their income is to be adequate to meet their needs. Inflation is the major problem for older Americans. Older Americans, after retirement, are for the most part living on fixed incomes; as inflation keeps prices rising, the fixed incomes of the older persons buy less and less food, clothing, and shelter. Their medical expenses are likely to increase as they age, even without inflation. Old age brings for most Americans the increased probability of economic hardship.

While many older persons have economic assets in the form of homes and property, Social Security has for most of them become the economic mainstay of their budget. Congress, in its attempt to alleviate the economic woes of older Americans, has provided an escalator clause which allows Social Security payments to be increased whenever the Consumer Price Index shows an increase of more than 3 percent per year. This helps—but does not entirely solve—the problem of inflation, since Congress determines how much the increase will be, and the increases passed are sometimes lower than the rate of inflation.

While the incomes of older persons are considerably lower than those of the general population, they have made significant gains in purchasing power in the last twenty years. Allen and Brotman observed that while the Consumer Price Index rose by 145 percent from 1960 to 1979 the income of older families rose by 291 percent compared to a 259 percent increase for younger families. For older individuals the income in the same period rose by 343 percent compared to 278 percent increase for younger individuals. These improvements, as previously observed, have come about because of a multitude of factors including increased Social Security benefits, greater number of persons qualifying for Social Security benefits and an increasing number of retirees covered by private pension plans. While older persons will continue to have lower incomes than younger age groups they have made more rapid gains than their younger counterparts in their attempts to improve their standard of living. They are represented in Washington by a variety of interest groups and they are a large enough voting block to carry considerable political clout. One is led to believe that they are likely to continue to be successful in their attempts to improve their economic position in the society.

KEY TERMS

Consumer Price Index
Poverty Index
near-poverty threshold
liquid assets

nonliquid assets
Supplemental Security Income
inflation

SUGGESTED READINGS

ALLEN, CAROLE, AND HERMAN BROTMAN, *Chartbook on Aging.* Washington, D.C.: White House Conference on Aging, 1981.

BROTMAN, HERMAN B., "Income and Poverty in the Older Population in 1975," *The Gerontologist,* 17, no. 1 (1977), 23–26; quoting U.S. Bureau of the Census data.

COX, HAROLD, GURMEET SEKHON, AND CHARLES NORMAN, "Social Characteristics of the Elderly in Indiana," *Proceedings of the 1978 Indiana Academy of Social Sciences* (1978), pp. 186–97.

GRAD, SUSAN, AND KAREN E. FOSTER, *Income and the Population 65 and Older.* Washington, D.C.: Social Security Administration, 1976.

GREENOUGH, WILLIAM C., AND FRANCIS P. KING, *Pension Plans and Public Policy,* p. xi. New York: Columbia University Press, 1976.

HARRIS, CHARLES, *Fact Book on Aging: A Profile of America's Older Population.* Washington, D.C.: The National Council on the Aging, Inc., 1978.

HARRIS, LOUIS, AND ASSOCIATES, *The Myth and Reality of Aging in America* (2nd ed.). Washington, D.C.: The National Council on the Aging, Inc., 1975.

MANSFIELD, EDWIN, *Economics: Principles, Problems, Decisions* (3rd ed.), pp. 177–78. New York: W.W. Norton & Co., Inc., 1977.

SCHULZ, JAMES, *The Economics of Aging* (2nd ed.). Belmont, CA: Wadsworth, 1980.

SURREY, STANLEY, *Pathways to Tax Reform: The Concept of Tax Expenditures.* Cambridge, MA: Harvard University Press, 1973.

THOMPSON, GAYLE B., "Pension Coverage and Benefits: Findings from the Retirement History Study," *Social Security Bulletin,* 41 (February 1978), 3–17.

U.S. BUREAU OF THE CENSUS, "Consumer Income," *Current Population Reports,* Series P–60, no. 116. Washington, D.C.: U.S. Government Printing Office, 1978.

U.S. BUREAU OF THE CENSUS, "Demographic Aspects of Aging and the Older Population in the U.S.," *Current Population Reports,* Series P–23, no. 59. Washington, D.C.: U.S. Government Printing Office, 1976.

13
EXPLOITATION
OF THE AGED
Crimes, Confidence Games, and Frauds

When they go out—if they go out—they listen anxiously for the sound of footsteps hurrying near, and they eye every approaching stranger with suspicion. As they walk, some may clutch a police whistle in their hands. More often, especially after the sun sets, they stay at home, their world reduced to the confines of apartments that they turn into fortresses with locks and bars on every window and door. They are the elderly who live in the slums of the nation's major cities. Many are poor. White or black, they share a common fear—that they will be attacked, tortured or murdered by the teen-age hoodlums who have coolly singled out old people as the easiest marks in town. Except in a few cases, police statisticians do not have a separate category for crimes against the elderly. But law-enforcement officials across the nation are afraid that such crimes may be growing in number and becoming more vicious in nature.

"The Elderly: Prisoners of Fear"
Time, November 29, 1976

In the 1974 Harris survey, fear of crime ranked above health, money, and loneliness in a list of the major concerns of older Americans. Pope and Feyerherm and Malinchak have indicated that fear of crime is one of the major concerns of older Americans.[1]

Clements and Kleiman documented the fear of crime among the elderly and compared this with other age groups. While 52 percent of those respondents aged 65 and over said they were afraid of crime, only 41 percent of the under-65 group said so. A survey conducted by Erikson indicated that women are more likely to express fear of crime than are men. This may be a result of the fact that men are more reluctant to admit fear than women.[2] Kleiman and Clements reported that only 19 percent of all the males in a sample reported fear of crime. When broken down by age, however, 34 percent of the elderly men admitted to being afraid of crime.[3]

In examining race, Clements and Kleiman found that blacks are considerably more afraid of crime than are whites. While this was the case for all age categories, it was particularly strong among the aged. They found that whereas about 47 percent of the white elderly were afraid to walk alone in their neighborhoods at night, 69 percent of the black aged expressed the same fear.

Clements and Kleiman found that, among the elderly, poor people are more fearful of crime than are the more affluent. Fifty-one percent of those with incomes of less than $7000 per year expressed fear of crime in comparison to 43 percent of those with $7000 or more income.[4]

In comparing communities of different size, the residents of large cities tend to be more fearful of criminal victimization than are people in smaller towns and in rural areas. In large cities 76 percent of the elderly expressed fear of crime, compared to 68 percent in medium-size cities, 48 percent in suburbs, 43 percent in small towns, and 24 percent in rural areas.[5]

Elderly residents of cities of 50,000+ population show significantly greater fear of crime than do either younger persons or their counterparts in suburbs, small towns, or rural areas.

The picture, then, is quite clear concerning who is more fearful of crime. Older persons as a rule are considerably more afraid of crime than are any of the younger age groups. Women are much more likely to express a fear of crime than are men. Blacks are more fearful of crime than are whites. Older persons on incomes of less than $7000 are more fearful of crime than are those with incomes above that figure. Finally, residents of large cities are more fearful of crime than those living in suburbs, smaller cities, or rural areas. It would follow then that poor, black, older women living in large urban areas are likely to be the most fearful of crime.

While the data clearly indicate that older persons are more fearful of crime than are other age groups, the picture is not quite as clear when one attempts to determine whether this fear is justified. Many of the past studies have indicated that in fact older persons are least likely to be victimized. Others indicate that there are certain kinds of crimes in which the elderly are most likely to be victimized.

Cook, in examining statistics on criminal victimization, concluded that of all age groups, older persons are least likely to be victims of both personal and household crimes.[6] Table 13–1 indicates that the crime rate decreases with age across all age groups. For personal crimes, 15 older persons per 1000 were victims, whereas the rate was 98 per 1000 for persons aged 20–24 and 67 per 1000 for persons aged 25–34. A similar pattern is found for crimes against households (Table 13–2). Among the elderly, 55 per 1000 were victims as opposed to 140 per 1000 for 30–34 year olds and 114 per 1000 for 35–39 year olds. Tables 13–1 and 13–2 indicate that in reference to the nine classifications of crime, the elderly are significantly less likely to be victims than are other age groups.

Table 13–1 Crimes Against Persons by Age of Victim per 1000 Population

BOTH SEXES, AGE	TOTAL	RAPE	ROBBERY		ASSAULT		PERSONAL LARCENY
			With Injury	*Without*	*Aggravated*	*Simple*	
12–15	126.4	0.7	1.6	4.8	7.7	18.3	93.4
16–19	122.1	1.4	1.9	3.2	11.9	17.2	86.5
20–24	98.0	1.4	1.9	3.9	10.3	13.8	66.7
25–34	67.0	0.6	1.2	2.3	5.9	8.1	48.8
35–49	46.7	—	0.9	1.6	3.3	5.1	35.6
50–64	30.0	—	0.6	1.1	1.4	2.5	24.3
65 and over	15.1	—	1.0	1.5	0.8	1.1	10.6

Source: "Criminal Victimization in the United States, January–June, 1973: A National Crime Panel Survey Report." U.S. Department of Justice, Bureau of Justice Statistics.

Table 13–2 Crimes Against Households by Age of Household Head per 1000 Population

AGE	TOTAL CRIMES	BURGLARY	HOUSEHOLD LARCENY	MOTOR VEHICLE THEFT
12–19	236.6	106.0	105.4	25.3
20–34	140.9	56.9	71.0	13.0
35–49	114.0	46.4	58.4	9.3
50–64	83.1	35.9	40.4	6.9
65 and over	55.3	28.5	24.8	2.0

Source: "Criminal Victimization in the United States, January–June, 1973: A National Crime Panel Survey Report." U.S. Department of Justice, Bureau of Justice Statistics.

Other studies have come to different conclusions, however. Goldsmith and Thomas argue that the underreporting of crime by the elderly results in inaccurate projections when using standard police and FBI statistics.[7] Another problem in finding the true picture of crimes against older persons is the fact that many police departments do not routinely list the victim's age. Even when they list the victim's age, there will not be a uniform classification of crime in different cities. As Table 13–3 indicates, Miami delineates crimes against older persons but only includes the more serious assault cases classified as aggravated assaults. One would guess that most assaults against older persons are not aggravated assaults.

In order to determine the actual rate of criminal victimization in the nation's larger cities, given the problems of the standard police statistics and the number of crimes that go unreported, the Law Enforcement Assistance Administration conducted a research survey of criminal victimization in 26 cities. The

Table 13–3 Crimes Against the General
Population (Under 60) and the Elderly (60 years or
older)* for a Six-Month Period in Miami, Florida
(1976)

CRIME	GENERAL POPULATION	ELDERLY
Homicide	5	0
Rape	2	0
Robbery	81	53
Assault**	51	7
Burglary	912	364
Larceny	1,761	434
Auto Theft	145	34
Pick Pockets	116	99
Purse Snatch	87	64

*Approximately 59 percent of Miami Beach's permanent
residents are over age 60.
**Simple assaults not counted—only aggravated assaults or
worse.

Source: Adapted from John H. Tighe, "A Survey of Crimes
Against the Elderly," *The Police Chief* (February 1977),
p. 19.

data from this survey indicated that anywhere from one-half to two-thirds (depending on the type of crime) of all the crimes committed against victims of any
age group go unreported and that while this is true, older persons (65+) are
slightly more likely than are younger persons (12–64) to report victimization to
the police.

The LEAA survey which included both reported and unreported crimes
indicated that the two most frequent crimes committed against older persons are
robbery and personal larceny with contact (purse snatching and pocket picking).
(See Table 13–4.) The elderly rank highest of all age groups in terms of purse
snatching and are found the highest age group victimized in terms of personal
larceny with contact. If you lump all of the different crimes together, however,
the elderly have the lowest rate of victimization. Looking at the various crimes
individually, the elderly are most likely to be victims of theft. Ellen Hochstedler
reports that theft rather than violence constituted the greater part of the victimization of the elderly. Violence without theft was relatively rare for the elderly
victims.

The LEAA survey indicated a number of factors related to criminal victimization of the elderly that the more standard criminal statistics did not, such
as the following:

1. The rate of theft is higher for the elderly than for any other age group.
2. The poor inner-city elderly suffer from crime more often than do their
    non-inner-city counterparts.[9]

Table 13–4 Estimated Rates (per 100,000 Persons 12 Years of Age or Older) and Percent Distribution of Personal Victimization, by Type of Victimization and Age of Victim, Aggregate Data for 26 Cities, 1974, 1975

	AGE OF VICTIM				
	65 or Older	50 to 64	35 to 49	12 to 34	ESTIMATED TOTALS[a]
Population base	3,167,119	4,475,746	3,475,024	10,702,641	22,720,530
Rape	19	30	85	313	173
	0%	1%	2%	4%	3%
	(610)	(1,377)	(3,841)	(34,339)	(40,167)
Aggravated assault	288	560	957	2,265	1,402
	7%	12%	19%	26%	21%
	(9,303)	(25,489)	(42,601)	(247,583)	(324,977)
Simple assault	377	729	1,143	2,409	1,551
	9%	16%	22%	27%	24%
	(12,124)	(33,142)	(50,189)	(263,606)	(359,693)
Robbery	1,615	1,742	1,926	2,794	2,255
	40%	39%	38%	32%	34%
	(51,875)	(79,147)	(85,524)	(304,463)	(521,023)
Larceny with contact	1,752	1,442	1,050	999	1,201
	43%	32%	20%	11%	18%
	(56,488)	(65,524)	(46,792)	(109,278)	(278,093)
Estimated totals[a]	4,053	4,503	5,162	8,780	6,582
	100%	100%	100%	100%	100%
	(130,406)	(204,679)	(229,577)	(959,269)	(1,523,932)

[a]Categories may not sum to total due to rounding.

Source: Ellen Hochstedler, *Crime Against the Elderly in 26 Cities* (Albany, NY: Criminal Justice Research Center, 1981).

3. Income is negatively related (the lower the income the higher the incidence of crime) to crimes of violence but positively related (the higher the income the higher the incidence of crime) to crimes without violence. (Families with incomes less than $3000 are most likely to have been robbed and assaulted while families with incomes over $15,000 are most likely to have been victims of larceny.)

4. Blacks are more likely to be victimized than whites, especially in the case of robbery and assault rather than in the less harmful personal larceny cases.

The data at this point appears confusing. National crime statistics, such as those listed in Tables 13–1 and 13–2, indicate a considerably lower rate of criminal victimization of the elderly than for other age groups. Later studies done by the Law Enforcement Assistance Administration, which did not rely only on reported crimes but rather surveyed people living in the chosen neighborhoods and communities, found higher rates of theft and larceny with contact on older persons than on the general population. While the fear of crime among the elderly may be greater than the actual threat of the crime, this may in part be explained by the fact that the elderly are more likely to experience larceny with contact and be personally shoved around or assaulted while having a purse or billfold stolen; thus, the potential crime represents a threat to their personal safety. Moreover, the crimes are often committed in or near their homes. Cotton reports that the perpetuators of crimes against the elderly are most often males that live within ten blocks of the victim. According to Antunes and associates, this represents a penetration of one's personal life space and is therefore more threatening.[10] Also both personally and financially the elderly have few resources with which they can protect themselves or recover from the losses they might incur by being victimized. Therefore when the elderly are the victims of crime, the effect on their lives is likely to be more devastating than for other age groups. The conclusion would seem to be that the elderly are more likely to be personally assaulted in their own neighborhoods, which represents an encroachment on one's life space, and that their losses are more personally damaging since they have fewer resources to fall back on. Thus, their fears can be more easily understood even when the criminal statistics do not always indicate that they are justified. These fears are probably accentuated even further by the fact that many elderly persons live alone and are often somewhat isolated from neighborhood and community groups. Patterson reports that elderly who live alone fear crime more than those who do not live alone.[11] Fear is probably always more manageable when it is shared.

THE OLDER PERSON'S RESPONSE TO VICTIMIZATION

A critical question for people at any age in life is how one responds to a threat to person or property. Does the average person take precautions against being victimized before the actual incident occurs? Does one only after being victimized take steps to prevent oneself from being victimized? Rifai made a study of the response of persons to potential and actual victimization. She found that of the general population, regardless of whether they had been victims of crime, 25 percent of the males and 21 percent of the females indicated that some action had been taken to prevent themselves from being victimized. Of those persons who had been victims of crime, 42 percent of the males and 37 percent of the females had acted to make themselves more secure.[12] Thus, persons who have been victims of crime are somewhat more likely to take measures to prevent themselves from being victimized in the future.

As a rule, women are more likely to take precautions to prevent criminal victimization than are men, although there are some notable exceptions (Table 13–5). Women were more likely not to carry a purse or wallet when in public, to avoid going out at night, to add locks to doors and windows, and to have at-

Table 13–5 Responses Taken by Older Persons to Protect Themselves from Criminal Victimization

	MALE PERCENTAGE	FEMALE PERCENTAGE
Don't carry a wallet, money, or purse when out in public	9	12
Avoid going out at night	20	33
Carry a weapon	6	4
Add locks to doors and windows	31	34
Mark property with crime prevention identification	13	12
Attend a neighborhood crime prevention meeting	1	5
Keep lights on in the house when gone	20	20
Have a dog or alarm system	9	6

Source: Marlene Rifia, "The Response of the Older Adult to Criminal Victimization," *The Police Chief* (February 1977), pp. 32–34.

tended a neighborhood crime-prevention meeting. Men were more likely to carry a weapon, mark property with crime-prevention stickers, and have a dog or alarm system.

Rifia found that the four most common patterns of older persons in response to the threat of criminal victimization were

1. Not going out at night.
2. Adding locks to doors and windows.
3. Leaving some lights on at home when away.
4. Marking personal property with crime-prevention identification.[13]

Psychologists and anthropologists have for some time discussed the territorial behavior of animals. Their past research indicates that animals have a keen sense of territorial rights and will fight fiercely to protect their territory from other animals. Some gerontologists believe that creation of a sense of territory or neighborhood among older persons may reduce their fear of crime.

Patterson, in a study, divided respondents on the basis of whether or not they had a high sense of territoriality. He found that males who were highly territorial were markedly less fearful than males who were low on sense of territory. Females who were high on sense of territoriality were only slightly less fearful than females who were low on sense of territory. Thus the principle seems to hold stronger for males than for females.[14]

Homeowners who lived alone and who were low on territoriality were found in this study to be much more fearful than homeowners who lived alone and who were high on territoriality.[15] Concerning property loss and personal assault, those with a high sense of territoriality were significantly less fearful than those with a low sense of territoriality.[16] Those with a high sense of territory were much more likely to feel safe and secure in their homes and neighborhoods.

Older persons at some point may come to feel too weak to be able to exercise mastery and control of their environment. They become in the terms of the psychologists "field dependent" rather than "field independent." One would conclude that those older persons who are "field independent" and who feel themselves capable of managing their environment are much less likely to be afraid of crime or of becoming victimized than those who are "field dependent" and who do not feel in control of their environment. It may well be that the older one becomes, the more likely one is to shift from a "field independent" to a "field dependent" position, thereby becoming more fearful.

CONFIDENCE GAMES AND FRAUDS

Not only are the elderly often the victims of attack on persons and property but they also can fall prey to a variety of confidence games and frauds designed specifically to exploit them. Also, some business people exploit the emotionally vulnerable in order to make a profit. The elderly, who are frequently lonely, isolated, and fearful, then become the target.

The following are illustrations of a few of the most common techniques used in the various schemes to exploit older persons.

Example A

Mr. Smith, an elderly member of a respectable city neighborhood, is called and told that he will be given a free gift if he will merely provide information about purchasing patterns for a national survey that the caller claims to be conducting. Mr. Smith is asked whether he has made any major purchases recently; he responds that he has bought a new television in the last three months and a new couch in the last six months. Mr. Smith is then asked how the quality of these items compares with that of other home appliances and furniture. As the conversation progresses, Mr. Smith is gradually led into a discussion of most of the major items in his home. Some unique antiques owned by Mr. Smith as well as most of the routine furnishings are described. The caller then thanks Mr. Smith for his assistance and tells him that he will be delivering his free gifts and asks when he will be at home. Mr. Smith unsuspectingly tells the caller when he plans to be both at home *and away* for the next several days. The conversation ends cordially with the caller thanking Mr. Smith for his cooperation. By this ruse the criminal now knows the major items of value in Mr. Smith's home and when would be the most likely time to rob Mr. Smith's home without anyone being in the house. The criminal has successfully misrepresented himself and exploited his victim's trust.

Example B

In this case a Mr. Jones knocks on the door of Mr. Smith, flashes a badge, and identifies himself as an FBI agent. He carefully explains to Mr. Smith that the teller at the First National Bank, where Mr. Smith has his life savings, is suspected of stealing money from the bank. He asks Mr. Smith if he would be willing to help him catch the teller in the act of stealing money. Mr. Jones points out that this would be an act of public service—to the FBI, the bank, and the community. Mr. Smith is by now more than happy to assist the FBI in trapping the crooked bank teller. He is directed to go to the bank and withdraw all of his savings and then meet Mr. Jones outside the bank immediately after the withdrawal. He is asked not to discuss the matter with anyone for security reasons. Mr. Jones is waiting as Mr. Smith comes out of the bank with his life savings in hand. Mr. Jones takes the money from Mr. Smith, explaining that it will be used as evidence against the teller and assuring Mr. Smith that the money will be returned to his bank account in the next few days. The two part company exchanging cordial goodbyes and Mr. Smith has a feeling of pride in the good deed that he has performed.

There are also a variety of dishonest selling practices that are used to persuade older persons to buy products that they most often do not need. The following are two examples of such selling schemes.

Example C

The salesman shows up at Mr. Smith's door and offers him a reduction in price for aluminum siding on his house if he will allow the salesman to use his house as a model and bring potential clients to look at the siding. Mr. Smith agrees to the plan and is given a contract at a very reasonable price to have his house sided. The salesman then asks Mr. Smith to put new asphalt on his driveway in order to improve the looks of his home. He is given a very inexpensive price for the cost of the asphalt. Mr. Smith upon agreeing to this is quickly presented with a contract. Then Mr. Smith is told that the price will be further reduced if he pays cash for these jobs. Mr. Smith promptly produces the money, upon which the salesman leaves after informing Mr. Smith that his company's work crews will come by in the next few days to do the contracted work. The salesman leaves with Mr. Smith's money. The work crews never appear. Mr. Smith, in checking the telephone book, finds that there is no company with the name that he has on the contracts and realizes that he has been swindled.

Example D

In this case a person in a service truck from a plumbing and heating contractor appears at Mr. Smith's door and tells him that for a minimum charge of five dollars, he will inspect his furnace and heating system to make sure that everything is working before winter sets in. Mr. Smith notes that the price is most reasonable and promptly shows the man to the basement. The man then bangs on the furnace and pipes for about fifteen minutes to persuade Mr. Smith that he is doing his job. He next reappears upstairs and asks Mr. Smith to return to the basement with him. The furnace man shows Mr. Smith cracks in his furnace and tells him that the furnace is worn out and that if he doesn't have it replaced immediately, there is a distinct danger that it could burn down the house when fully heated. Mr. Smith is fearful of the danger to his home posed by the furnace and gladly agrees to sign a contract for the installation of a new furnace. Within a week the new furnace is brought to Mr. Smith's home and installed. Mr. Smith is pleased with the speed of the company in installing his new furnace. He brags to his neighbors about what a good company it is to do business with. What Mr. Smith does not know, and may never realize, is that any furnace after some use will have cracks in it and that he did not need a new one. The furnace salesman has played on Mr. Smith's fear for his home in order to sell him a furnace that he didn't need.

Nine out of ten victims of consumer fraud, it is believed, do not report it to police—they are either too embarrassed or feel that it would be of little value. Sadly, it is often true that the police cannot help, partly because although some of the practices are dishonest, they are not necessarily illegal. A law is currently being proposed that would prevent a victim from being forced to comply with the terms of a contract if it is canceled within seventy-two hours of signing. The main protection for the older person lies, however, in not allowing himself or herself to be rushed into signing a contract.

The Wisconsin Bankers Association has developed a customer's release form that advises the depositor of the dangers involved in withdrawing large amounts of money; it is, of course, designed to protect customers against various swindle schemes—something that would seem particularly helpful for older customers.

Kahana and others made a study attempting to determine the degree to which older persons felt themselves victims of crime in the private sector, in neighborhoods, and in the public sector. Victimization in the private sector was defined as rejection by friends and family, employment rejection, and problems as consumers in purchase of service or merchandise. Victimization in neighborhoods was defined as being victims of crime or living in undesirable neighborhoods. Victimization in the public sector was defined as problems with Social Security, taxes, the police, and the like.

The study indicated that 19 percent of the sample reported victimization in the private sector, 39 percent victimization in neighborhoods, and 12 percent victimization in the public sector. When probed further with questions regarding whether they thought that their victimization was related to age, approximately 30 percent of those reporting victimization in the private sector attributed it to age, as did 12 percent of those reporting neighborhood victimization, and 21 percent of those reporting victimization in the public sector. There is, then, a segment of those persons who are victimized in any of the three sectors

Box 13–1

This form is reprinted from the October, 1975, issue of the Bank Protection Bulletin with permission of the Insurance and Protective Division of the American Bankers Association. In utilizing this, or any other form, for senior citizens, be sure to use LARGE type to insure readability.

Customer release form

The Wisconsin Bankers Association says a customer release form may provide added protection for the bank and its customers against various swindle schemes, especially when older customers are the intended victims. WBA says this sample may be reproduced by banks without permission:

CAUTION

(You are presented with and asked to read and sign this as a courtesy to you. PLEASE READ AND CONSIDER IT CAREFULLY)

The following is to caution you with regard to your request for the lump-sum withdrawal of $_____ in cash from your account.

This bank does not conduct investigations or verifications of accounts by telephone. (Swindlers often use this method to gain information on accounts as well as the confidence of their victims.) Nor do police, FBI officials, bank regulatory authorities or bank officials conduct investigations by asking you to withdraw cash from your account for any reason.

Swindlers also often arrange to have you "find" or "help find" a wallet or other valuable. One way or another, they have you put up some amount of money to show your "good faith" — and then depart with the money.

If anyone has presented themselves to you as an FBI agent, bank examiner, police officer, detective or bank official, and requested any information about your account, *or asked you to withdraw any amount from your account,* whether to help them "catch someone" or to show "good faith," or for any other such reason, you are very possibly being swindled.

If any of these circumstances exist, please contact your local police department and have them investigate, *before* you withdraw your money. Remember, swindlers nearly always are friendly and have "honest" faces. They particularly tend to take advantage of older people.

I have read and understand the above statement and the bank has explained it to me. I insist upon the immediate withdrawal in cash.

The form should leave space at the bottom for the signatures of the customer, an officer and a teller.

who attribute their victimization to age. Thus not only do they fear victimization, but they often feel that they are being singled out because of their age.[17]

CONCLUSION

The data at this point are confusing concerning the criminal victimization of older persons. FBI and police statistics accumulated on a national or very broad basis tend to indicate that older persons are the victims of crime much less often than the general population. On the other hand, data gathered by LEAA in selected cities and neighborhoods across the country tend to indicate that older persons are more frequently the victims of certain kinds of crime (crimes involving direct personal contact between the victim and offender) than other age groups.

It is clear and irrefutable, however, that older persons are more fearful of crime than is any other age group. This may in part be explained by the fact that older persons often feel weak, vulnerable, and isolated. In a case of personal assault or attack, they feel unable to defend themselves. Where loss of money or property occurs, they are the group least likely to have additional resources that allow them to minimize the effect of the loss.

Goldsmith and Thomas list a series of reasons why they believe the elderly are more susceptible and vulnerable to criminal attack:

1. There is high incidence of reduced or low income among the elderly. Thus the impact of any loss of economic resources is relatively greater.
2. Older people are more likely to be victimized repeatedly, often the same crime and the same offender.
3. Older people are more likely to live alone. Social isolation increases vulnerability to crime.
4. Older people have diminished physical strength and stamina; hence, they are less able to defend themselves or to escape from threatening situations.
5. Older people are far more likely to suffer from physical ailments such as loss of hearing or sight, arthritis, and circulatory problems which increases their vulnerability.
6. Older people are physically more fragile and more easily hurt should they opt to defend themselves. For example, bones are more easily broken, and recovery is more difficult. Thus they are less likely to resist attackers.
7. Potential criminals are aware of the diminished physical capacity and the physical vulnerability of the elderly and thus are more likely to seek out an elderly target (whose aged status is easily visible).
8. There is a greater likelihood that older people will live in high-crime neighborhoods rather than in suburbia as a result of diminished income and of being rooted in central cities. Thus they find themselves in close

proximity to the groups most likely to victimize them—the unemployed, or teen-age dropouts.

9. The dates of receipt by mail of monthly pension and benefit checks (and hence the dates when older people are most likely to have cash on their person or in their dwelling) are widely known.

10. Dependency on walking or on public transportation is more usual among older people who, for physical, financial, or other reasons, are less likely to drive or own a private automobile.

11. There is evidence that older people are particularly susceptible to frauds and confidence games.

12. Older people have the highest rates of the crime of personal larceny with contact (theft or purse, wallet, or cash directly from the person of the victim, including attempted purse-snatching).

13. Awareness of increased vulnerability to criminal behavior has a chilling effect upon the freedom of movement of older Americans. Fear of criminal victimization causes self-imposed "house arrest" among older people, who may refuse to venture out of doors. Furthermore, even in those situations where the fear of being victimized may be somewhat exaggerated or unwarranted by local conditions, the effect on the older persons is just as severe as when the fears are justified.

14. Because of loss of status and decreased sense of personal efficacy associated in American culture with being old, older people may be less likely to process complaints through the criminal justice bureaucracy and to draw upon available community resources for protection and redress.[13]

In terms of what appear to be the determining factors in the fear of crime among the elderly, women were found to be more fearful than men, blacks more fearful than whites, inner-city dwellers more fearful than suburban or rural dwellers, and poor people more fearful than persons of middle or upper incomes. While the initial data indicate that older persons may be more fearful than the likelihood of their being victimized suggests, later refinements of police statistics seem to indicate that it is inner-city residents, women, blacks, and the poor who are most frequently the victims of crime. Thus, it is specifically those categories of old people who are most fearful of crime that are most frequently victimized. Perhaps there is greater justification for the older persons' fear than the earlier police statistics tended to indicate. Moreover, the elderly are most often victimized within a few blocks of their homes. This represents an invasion of their personal life space, which is more threatening to them.

In terms of alleviating fears and attempting to protect themselves from becoming the victims of crime, older persons most frequently stay in at night, put locks on doors and windows, leave the lights on in the house when away, and mark personal property. Staying in their own home at night in order to avoid being victimized becomes, in a sense, a form of house arrest for older persons.

A newly emerging phenomenon in the area of crime and the elderly is that of the older person as an offender and not a victim. Jim Le Beau, reporting on crimes committed by seniors, points out that in 1970, 6.6 percent of those 65 and older who were arrested were charged with serious crimes. In 1980, 17.6 percent of the seniors arrested were charged with serious crimes. Le Beau indicates that the increase in serious crimes (such as murder, robbery, arson, etc.) committed by seniors has increased steadily for the last ten years. Future researchers will undoubtedly delve into the causes for the increase of serious crimes committed by the nation's seniors.

KEY TERMS

field-independent persons
field-dependent persons

SUGGESTED READINGS

ANTUNES, GEORGE E., AND OTHERS, "Patterns of Personal Crime Against the Elderly," *The Gerontologist,* 17, no. 4 (1977), 321–27.

CLEMENTS, FRANK, AND MICHAEL KLEIMAN, "Fear of Crime Among the Aged," *The Gerontologist,* 16, no. 3 (1976), 207–10.

COOK, FAY LOMAX, "Criminal Victimization of the Elderly: A New National Problem," in *Victimization and Society,* ed. Emelio C. Viano. Washington, D.C.: Visage Press, 1976.

COTTON, LOU, *Elders in Rebellion.* New York: Doubleday Anchor, 1979.

ERIKSON, H., "The Polls: Fear of Violence and Crime," *Public Opinion Quarterly,* 38 (1974), 131–45.

GOLDSMITH, JACK, AND NOEL E. THOMAS, "Crimes Against the Elderly: A Continuing National Crisis," *Aging* (June-July 1974), pp. 230–37.

GOLDSMITH, JACK, "A Symposium on Crime and the Elderly," *The Police Chief* (February 1976), pp. 18-–0.

HARRIS, LOUIS, AND ASSOCIATES, *The Myth and Reality of Aging in America.* Washington, D.C.: The National Council on the Aging, Inc. 1975.

HINDELANG, MICHAEL, "Criminal Victimization in Eight American Cities," *Law Enforcement Assistance Administration* (1975), p. 377.

HOCHSTEDLER, ELLEN, *Crime Against the Elderly in 26 Cities.* Albany, N.Y.: Criminal Justice Research Center, 1981.

KAHANA, EVA, AND OTHERS, "Perspectives of Aged on Victimization, Ageism and Their Problems in Urban Society," *The Gerontologist,* 17, no. 2 (April 1977), 121–29.

LE BEAU, JAMES, "Increase in Serious Crimes by Seniors," *Terre Haute Tribune Star,* April 7, 1982, p. 3.

MALINCHAK, ALAN A., *Crime and Gerontology,* pp. 39–63. Englewood Cliffs, NJ: Prentice-Hall, 1980.

MALINCHAK, ALAN A., AND DOUGLAS WRIGHT, "The Scope of Elderly Victimization," *Aging,* nos. 281–282 (April 1978), 12–16.

PATTERSON, ARTHUR, "Territorial Behavior and the Fear of Crime in the Elderly," *The Police Chief* (February 1977), pp. 20–29.

POPE, CARL E., AND WILLIAM F. FEHARM, "A Review of Recent Trends: The Effects of Crime on the Elderly," *The Police Chief* (February 1976).

RIFIA, MARLENE A., "The Response of the Older Adult to Criminal Victimization," *The Police Chief* (February 1977), pp. 32–34.

TIGHE, JOHN H., "A Survey of Crimes Against the Elderly," *The Police Chief* (February 1977), p. 19.

14

POLITICS AND THE GOVERNMENT SERVICE DELIVERY SYSTEM

Precaution

I never dared be radical
when young
For fear it would
make me conservative
when old.

Robert Frost
The Poetry of Robert Frost

The demographic shifts in the number and percentage of our population comprised of persons 65 years and older was discussed in the earlier chapters of this text. These figures must be reiterated at this point because they leave direct implications regarding the potential political power of Americans 65 and older. Three million Americans in 1900 representing 4 percent of the population and widely distributed geographically across the country made few demands for public service and could easily be ignored by the politicians of the day. Twenty-five million Americans 65 and over in 1980, representing 11 percent of the population cannot so easily be ignored. This 11 percent of the population constitutes, moreover, approximately 20 percent of the electorate due to the fact that all those persons under the age of 18 do not vote.

While demographic predictions about what the percentage of those persons 65 and older will be in the year 2000 are risky at best, not even the most conservative of demographers predicts anything other than an even larger percentage of the population being in the older age group. A rapid upturn in the crude birth rate resulting in an unexpected increase in the number of young persons in the total population could alter these predictions. This seems unlikely, however, given the current trends of lower birth rates and the value of having small families shared by a large percentage of younger persons.

It seems likely, then, that in the foreseeable future, the 65-and-over age group is going to make up an ever-increasing number and percentage of the total population, and will make greater demands on government for services and expect allocation of greater shares of government resources. What must be remembered is that government never has enough resources to meet all the requests of its citizenry. Those requests which are met are usually in some way related to the group's exercise of political power.

POLITICAL PARTICIPATION

Political participation in one way or another connects the individual to the decision-making bodies of the country. Political participation includes such things as:

1. Holding opinions on the current issues facing the country.
2. Being an opinion leader and convincing others of your point of view.
3. Voting.
4. Joining political parties and movements.
5. Holding office.

Older people are slightly more likely than younger people to hold an opinion on an issue. Norval and Grimes found that the better educated and those actively involved in the community were more likely to hold an opinion than the less well educated or the uninvolved members of the community.[1]

Gubrium found that older persons were overrepresented among opinion leaders. Opinion leaders are those whom others turn to for advice on political matters. Young people are more prone to turn to older people for advice on political issues than to their own age group. While 22 percent of the general adult population have been identified as opinion leaders, 35 percent of the retired persons were so identified.[2]

The voting patterns of different age groups in the population have been fairly well established by past research. While younger people may talk at great length and with considerable emotion about political issues, older people are much more likely to turn out and vote when election time rolls around. Campbell reports that while only about 50 percent of the people in their early twenties vote, slightly more than 80 percent of those in their sixties vote and about 75 percent of those in their seventies vote. Moreover, Campbell argues that there is evidence that political involvement generally increases with age. Older people, he believes, are more interested in politics, they follow political activities in the media more closely and they participate more actively than younger people.[3]

Persons over 65 are split about equally between the two political parties with about 50 percent identifying as Democrats and about 50 percent identifying as Republicans. Since those under 60 are somewhat more likely to be Democrats, this has led some persons to conclude that there is a shift toward the more conservative Republican party in old age. This does not appear to be the case. Those now 65 and over were socialized with political attitudes and ideals before the New Deal. There were at that time about an equal number of Republicans and Democrats. Persons reared since the 1930s and the New Deal legislation are more likely to be Democrats than Republicans. One does not appear to shift parties as one ages. It may well be that a later cohort group of retirees, trained in their political beliefs during and after the 1930s will be more likely to be Democrats. Not only is there not a tendency to shift one's political party in old age but indeed the older one becomes, the more one becomes committed, partisan, and loyal to the party of choice.

Lane argues that insofar as voting is a conscious positive commitment of time and energy, older people, in direct contradiction to disengagement theory, display high political involvement and integration into society.[4]

There is much discussion concerning whether older voters are or are not likely to vote as a bloc for issues that they perceive to be in their best interest. In discussing this issue, Campbell argues that the most important general assertion which can be made is that there is no "aging vote." Campbell argues that elderly voters think more in terms of ethnicity, party, class and region when they come to the polls and rarely in terms of age.[5] Loether believes that age does not constitute a primary reference group because they are more likely to identify themselves with their families, their political parties, their churches, and their social groups.[6] Douglass, Cleveland, and Maddox report that only at the most immediate level, the family, did age enter at all as a significant determinant of political attitudes.[7]

While it may well be that the aged do not always or universally vote as a bloc and they do hold a variety of cross-cutting loyalties they do coalesce when they consider an issue vital to their interests. Loether did find that concentrations of voters in Miami, Florida, voted as a bloc when they felt their vested interests could be affected by the outcome of the election. Social Security, the Older Americans Act, and Medicare are examples of programs which were passed, at least in part, because of the strong support and endorsement of older Americans.

Political participation can include the individual's joining a political party in order to campaign for a party platform and candidates with favored political views, as well as joining a social movement whose goal it is to change society in one way or another.

One advantage that older persons have in either of these endeavors is ample amounts of free time. The middle-aged American who is torn between family, work, and community obligations frequently has little time left over for other kinds of commitments. Political participation, whether in political parties or social movements, requires large commitments of time and energy. Past research on social movements has indicated that the members tend to be young, unmarried, and frequently do not hold down full-time jobs. This means that they have the available time that social movements require.

Joining a political party and becoming active usually can be seen as a semicareer. Most loyal party members have joined in their early twenties and remained active throughout their adult lives. One wonders if at 65 persons who have not been active throughout their adult lives are likely to do so at this time. On the other hand, for those that have been active party members, they will now find that they have more time to become even more involved and therefore can exercise greater influence in political decisions.

Barrow and Smith argue that social movements don't just happen but rather are the combined results of social, economic, and historical events. Those who are affected in a negative or undesirable way usually join forces to change the situation demanding their rights and pointing out the injustices of the current arrangements. Barrow and Smith, in discussing the historical development of age-based social movements, state:

> This happened in the early 1900s when a large proportion of the aged were living in poverty. Retirement had increasingly become mandatory; yet pensions were not available which often left the aged with neither work nor money.[8]

This kind of deprivation which was being experienced by large numbers of the elderly led to the emergence of a social movement led by a retired physician, Dr. Townsend. The Townsend Plan called for paying, out of government funds, $200 a month into the hands of persons 60 and older with the requirement that the recipients retire from work and spend the money within thirty days. If put into practice it was felt by the backers to have two positive results. First, it would improve the economic conditions and status of older Americans and second, it would stimulate a depressed economy. Townsend Clubs sprang up across the country and at their peak in 1936 numbered more than 7000.

As with most social movements which have widespread appeal and backing, one of the two political parties incorporated the suggested changes into its party platform. Democratic New Deal legislation in 1935 enacted the Social Security Act which provided a pension for the elderly, thus undercutting the major thrust of the movement. There seems little doubt that the Townsend movement aided the passage of the Social Security Act.

The Townsend movement has been followed by other movements on behalf of older persons. George McLain in the 1940s led a California-based movement to improve the lives of older Americans. Kleyman notes that an interesting feature of all these movements was that they extracted great sums of money from the aged themselves. Kleyman describes the leaders of the movements as "pension panacea peddlers."[9] Social unrest, whether structured into a social movement or not, does most often bring about change. Prolonged social unrest among the elderly ultimately resulted in the passage of the Older Americans Act in 1965 and Medicare in 1966. While older persons have not shown any inclination to vote as a bloc except on local community issues, the causes addressed by any of the social movements on their behalf have most often been picked up and endorsed by one or both of the political parties. This almost guarantees legislation in behalf of older persons. The major advantage of the social movement seems to be to increase the public's awareness of the problem. Once political leaders become aware that there is widespread support for change it is very difficult for particular interest groups to block proposed legislation.

Gerontologists, in discussing the power of the older Americans movements, observe that they have yet to lose a major political campaign. The "gray lobby" has taken on the American Medical Association over Medicare, the large corporations over mandatory retirement, and taxpayers groups over Social Security, and defeated them all.

The 1970s have seen the emergence of the Gray Panthers movement led by Maggie Kuhn. Comprised of a loose coalition of young and old social activists, this group's major attacks have been on the AMA for its lack of attention and efforts to alleviate and solve the health problems of older Americans and the social structure and values which require older persons to disengage. Ragan and David believe that rather than social change, the focus of the Gray Panthers is more on alternative lifestyles for the aged.[10] Similar to other social movements on behalf of the aged, the major function of the Gray Panthers seems to be to raise the public consciousness of the problems of older Americans. They have at various times attacked compulsory retirement, advocated pension reform, and proposed the elimination of poverty.

The Gray Panther movement seems to be following on the heels of the civil rights movement and the women's liberation movement. These movements of the 1950s, 1960s and 1970s have one thing in common. They are all reflections of a new emphasis on the quality of life in America today. Black people in the civil rights movement were essentially saying, "We want an improvement in the quality of life for blacks. We want more jobs, opportunities for upward mobility, and a larger share of rewards that go with an affluent industrial economy." Similarly, the women's liberation movement was also a reflection of the quality of life demands expressed by a deprived group. The demands of the leaders of the movement were similar to those of the civil rights leaders. Women were demanding greater opportunities for employment and promotion, larger salaries, and protection from discrimination. Women, in essence, want a larger share of the rewards of the system and an improvement in the quality of their lives. In much the same fashion, the Gray Panther movement can be seen as one in which older persons are asking not to be discriminated against in employment, for improved pensions, and for a larger share of the nation's resources. In that way their demands can also be seen as an assertion of their rights for an improved quality of life.

There are a variety of more traditional organizations that are designed to pursue the best interests of older constituents. These include such organizations as the National Caucus of Black Aged, the National Council of Senior Citizens, the National Retired Teachers Association, and the National Association of Retired Federal Employees. While being more traditional and less militant than the social movements have been, these groups work systematically to improve the life of senior citizens, and because they are more widely accepted, probably have accomplished more. Like the other groups, one of their major functions is to keep the general public and the political leaders informed of the plight of older Americans.

Pratt believes the more traditional associations for older Americans have had greater success than the groups in the 1930s and 1940s due to the fact that they have had more financial support than solely membership dues. They had skilled and experienced leadership rather than the charismatic leadership of the 1930s and 1940s which relied solely on popular appeal; additionally, the political climate of the 1960s and 1970s has been more responsive to demands of older Americans.[11]

Most observers of the political power of the aged have concluded that it is not their power as a voting bloc which has brought about legislation and change but rather the fact that interest groups and the efforts of the more traditional associations of older Americans have brought their problems to the public attention. Hess states:

> If there is any political clout to be claimed for older Americans, my assessment at the moment is that this derives from those operating on behalf of the aged but who typically are not yet themselves elderly.[12]

As we pointed out in Chapter 1, demographers have traditionally thought of persons under 18 and over 65 as dependent for their goods and services on those between 19 and 64, who are in essence in the productive years. Cowgill maintains that the dependency ratio of the U.S. population has not changed dramatically since 1900 even with a dramatic increase in the 65+ group. Since the growing number of older Americans has been accompanied by a decline in the number and percentage of the population under 18, Cowgill argues that the percentage of the population defined as dependent has not increased but rather shifted. While maintaining about the same percentage of the population in the dependent category we now have fewer young people and more older persons.[13] There is one big difference, however, in terms of the demands on government. Whereas families consider it a moral obligation to look after their young, they do not consider it their obligation to necessarily look after their older family members.

Much of the legislation and governmental programs providing services to older Americans has come with the strong support and endorsement of middle-age voters who are anxious to shift the responsibility for older family members off of themselves and onto the government. Thus, younger family members and organized lobbying groups operating on behalf of older Americans are as much a factor in federal programs in their behalf as the efforts of the older persons themselves. Moreover, there is an ever-growing group of service providers, administrators, and scientists whose professional careers are dependent upon further programs and additional government resources for older Americans.

Most social movements that attempt to change society ultimately experience a backlash from elements of society that feel that the change will not be in their interest or that it is excessively costly. Whether the movements for older Americans will experience such a backlash remains to be seen.

There is no doubt that federal expenditures for older Americans have risen at alarmingly fast rates for many taxpayers. The cost of Social Security alone has risen from $36 billion in 1970 to $90 billion in 1976. Moreover, future increases are likely to be almost automatically mandated by Congress in order to keep the incomes of older persons somewhat abreast of the increasing costs due to inflation. Fischer maintains that the government spending has moved out of control of the president and federal administration in Washington and into the category of uncontrolled costs. Fischer describes the "graying" of the federal budget and the uncontrollable nature of the increases as the withering away of the ability to govern.[14]

The question that must be addressed by advocates for older Americans programs is at what point will taxpayers' lobbies and other groups come to believe that programs for older Americans are becoming too expensive and should, therefore, be curbed.

In terms of holding political office, older persons tend to be over-represented in Congress, the presidency, and the Supreme Court. Congressional and Senate subcommittees are usually chaired by the senior members of the committee. Because the Constitution does not permit anyone to be elected to the Senate until he or she is 35, and then when only the more senior members are likely to chair the committees and hold the more important posts, it is easy to see how the older senators exercise considerable power.

In 1974 the large number of new and younger congressmen loosened the hold of the older, experienced members on the committee chairs. The senior congressmen still exercise considerable power, however. Most presidents have been between the ages of 50–65 when elected. The first four presidents of the United States were 57 or older. While this is true, only two presidents ever entered office after the age of 65: William Henry Harrison and Ronald Reagan became president at 68. Several presidents have turned 65 while in office. The youngest two presidents have been Theodore Roosevelt at 42 and John Kennedy at 43. While most presidents are older, a youthful image of the president has become popular in the twentieth century.

The position of Supreme Court justice implies experience and wisdom. Those chosen have often been involved in the judicial system for some time and have served as judges in various courts. It is unlikely that a young lawyer would have had the opportunity for the kind of experiences presidents look for in appointing justices. In 1978 the youngest justice was 54, the oldest 72, and the average age was 65.5.

Thus while most often congressmen, senators, presidents, and Supreme Court justices have been in their middle or later years, the United States has not created a gerontocracy. A majority of these offices are still held by persons under the age of 65. A youthful image is a political asset even for older politicians and, even when politicians are old, old age does not appear to be the critical variable affecting their positions on the issues of the day.

STATUS INCONSISTENCY

Gubrium states that older persons' political attitudes can perhaps best be understood by assuming that many of them are experiencing status inconsistency.

Individuals at any age in life assume a variety of different roles in their various groups of which they are members. Each of these roles carries a status and the commensurate privileges that are assumed to go with that status. One may be the president of the Lions Club, which implies an important role and the accompanying status in the organization, while simultaneously being a junior salesman for a local construction firm. This latter role carries low status. Thus a person may have high status, power, and privilege in one group and low status, power, and privilege in another group simultaneously. The possession of discrepant ranks in various status hierarchies creates social and psychological strain. The stress generated by the holding of discrepant ranks in different groups in which an individual is a member causes the individual to adopt a course of action designed to bring his or her rank into balance. In other words, individuals are inclined to seek consistency in their rank and status in various disparate groups.

Hughes found that a combination of low racial or ethnic status (ascribed) and a high occupational and educational status (achieved) results in individuals who are most inclined to be liberal in political orientation.[15] Either consciously or unconsciously they apparently believe that change in the society would be good for them because it would result in a better alignment and balance between their current disparate statuses.

Gubrium uses the status inconsistency model to project some of the problems, frustrations, and stresses of old age. Age, he argues, should be considered an ascribed status hierarchy. He starts with the premise that being old in Western cultures is an unequivocably low status since youthfulness is highly valued.

Following Table 14–1, Gubrium argues that the profile of a person of higher socioeconomic status (achieved) who moves from Cell 1 to Cell 2 changes from a consistent to an inconsistent status. Those persons of a lower socioeconomic status (achieved) who move from Cell 3 to Cell 4 change from inconsistent to consistent status. Moving from Cell 1 to Cell 2 may be typical of the

Table 14–1   Status Inconsistency Model

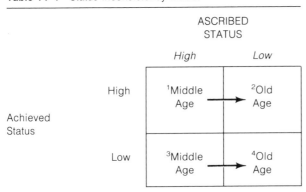

Source: Jaber F. Gubrium, *Time, Role and Self in Old Age* (New York: Human Sciences Press, 1976), p. 142. © 1976 by Human Sciences Press.

successful business executive who is forced to retire. Moving from Cell 3 to Cell 4 would seem to be more typical of the unskilled factory worker.[16]

Lenski observed that persons with low ascribed and high achieved status often see themselves as successful but victimized by the system. These individuals, he found, are likely to be liberal in political orientation and express strong desire for change which they feel would bring their discrepant statuses into balance. Thus persons of inconsistent status often respond to institutional barriers that block status equilibrium by generating pressures for change within the social structure.[17]

Gubrium argues that to compensate for his low status on the ascribed variable of age, the retired executive may continually remind his aged associates of his former rank and seek the deference that he was accorded at an earlier point in time.

What is not certain regarding older persons who are experiencing status inconsistency, is whether they would become liberal advocates of change in order to bring the discrepant statuses into balance as their younger counterparts do, or whether they might become increasingly conservative, seeking to return to the preretirement years when they experienced status consistency. Only future research will be able to answer these questions.

AGE AND POLITICAL CONSERVATISM

There is widespread belief that older persons tend to become more conservative and that the older one becomes, the more conservative one is likely to be. Young people, it is felt, have a low status and a low commitment to the current social order. They have little at stake and therefore can afford to be liberal advocates of change. Older persons, it is felt, distrust change because they hold valuable the things they currently have. The investments of a lifetime may be lost in radical changes of the system.

The past attitudes and voting records of older persons do not indicate consistently conservative patterns. Campbell found that older persons supported government programs for full employment and low-cost medical care, but did not support government programs to assure equal rights to blacks nor to build better schools.[18] It appears, then, that the degree of liberalism or conservatism found among older voters is more related to what they define as their vested interest rather than any lifelong drift in a liberal or conservative direction.

SOCIAL SERVICES FOR OLDER AMERICANS

The current generation of older Americans was born between 1890 and 1920. They were raised in a historical period in which only limited government services were available to individuals. Ogburn, a sociologist, coined the term "cultural lag" to refer to the fact that one part, section, or institution in a culture will change and thus require alterations and adjustments in other parts of the culture. Ogburn viewed the culture as functioning in much the same manner as a machine or clock. All the parts of the clock are interconnected and mechanically synchronized. For the clock to work, all the moving parts must turn at the right time, the right speed, and to the right degree. Ogburn states:

> The various parts of modern culture are not changing at the same rate, some parts are changing more rapidly than others; and that since there is a correlation and interdependence of parts a change in one part requires readjustments through changes in the various correlated parts of culture.[19]

The fact that it may take considerable time for the various elements of culture to catch up to a change in another part of the culture is referred to as a cultural lag.

Between 1850 and 1920 the Industrial Revolution was gradually changing the United States from an agricultural to an industrial nation. As an agricultural country the family was the unit of production and consumption. All family members worked collectively to accomplish whatever task needed to be accomplished, from building barns to planting corn. When the older members of the family were too old to work they were looked after by younger members. There were no government services offered to older Americans and none were desired. It would have been a threat to the feelings of self-sufficiency, independence, and usefulness of the individual to accept any government assistance. Welfare was considered appropriate for only the lazy and shiftless and should provide to the recipients barely enough for a minimum subsistence level of survival.

The Industrial Revolution moved work from home to factory, and ended the period in which families were the basic unit of production. Family members moved into different geographic locations and communities in order to meet labor demands of an industrial society. Thus dispersed families could no longer protect their members during times of crisis. There was a considerable lag between the Industrial Revolution in the United States, the passage of government assistance programs for older Americans, and the acceptance of these programs by the general public. The Social Security Act was not passed until 1935 and then it took a major economic depression to create enough public support for change to lead to its passage. This is the kind of cultural lag to which Ogburn refers.

The current generation of retired Americans was reared with values that were opposed to any kind of government assistance programs. They often do not utilize these programs when they are available to them because of their belief that acceptance of the program makes them welfare recipients.

Social Welfare

Lowry argues that there are four conceptualizations of social welfare today which include social welfare as a philosophy, a goal, an institution, and as a developing field.[20]

Social welfare as a philosophy is rooted in the Judeo-Christian ethic of one being his brother's keeper, according to Lowry. It implies that man's relationship to his fellow man be governed in such a way as to insure the well-being of everyone. Thus social welfare is a means of fulfilling one's philosophical view of life.

When society views welfare as a goal it seeks to promote the best interests of both the individual and the larger group. Having large numbers of persons starving, unemployed, and improperly housed can easily be seen as not good for the individual as well as a source of potential ferment and revolution which could seek to overturn the current social order. Therefore, it is not in the best interest of the larger society. Thus, according to Lowry, social welfare seen as a goal seeks to promote the general well-being of all people and simultaneously guard its own survival.

Wilensky and Lebeaux outline what they believe to be the five characteristics of social welfare as an institution:

1. Formal organization
2. Social sponsorship
3. Absence of the profit motive
4. An integrative rather than a segmented view of human needs
5. Direct concern with human consumption[21]

A formal organization which routinely administers welfare programs implies that regardless of which political party is in power or what the state of the economy is, the program continues and citizens continue to receive the services. Thus the program is permanent. Social sponsorship of the program implies that at least a segment of the general public believes that the program is useful and therefore gives continued support to the program. The absence of the profit motive takes the program out of the sphere of business and places it under an established community or government director or supervisor. The integrated view of human needs implies a total picture of what people must have to lead normal lives and some selection on the part of professionals in the field as to which services are most needed and useful to the client. The main concern is for all of the individual's needs and how they can most adequately be met. Meeting human consumption needs of the client is the primary goal.

There are, moreover, residual and institutional views of social welfare. The residual view maintains that social welfare should come into play only when the normal structure of supply and of family support break down. Then, and only then, should the government provide the service. The institutional concept sees government services as normal, expected, and routine functions of modern society and not merely a stopgap emergency measure. The Social Security pension system reflects an institutional approach to government services since all persons receive this at a given age. The means test in the Medicaid program reflects the residual motive of social welfare in that it is only a stopgap measure for the less fortunate.

The "developing field" view of government assistance programs sees them as enhancing the development of a community and a society. Government assistance is seen as a part of the overall economic and social development effort of the community. Thus, government agencies are expected to prevent, alleviate, or solve social problems, according to Lowry.

It is probably accurate to say that most older Americans believe government services should have a residual philosophic orientation. Those in need should be provided for as a result of a philosophic compassion for one's fellow man, but the need should not be constant and individuals for the most part should look after themselves. Government planners and civil service employees are more likely to hold an institutional or developmental view which maintains that government services should be routinely provided to those in need. The planning, implementation, and coordination of government tasks should require a full-time and not intermittent effort by civil servants. This discrepancy often places the providers of government programs in the position of selling the programs to older Americans. Thus, they often are cast in the role of creating the need for the program and then implementing the program to serve the need.

There is no doubt, however, that older persons have greater need for government services than any other age group in the population. They are at a time in their lives when numerous adjustments must be made to their conditions of declining health and altered lifestyle, and when many of their resources are shrinking. Moreover, they have practically no place to turn to for additional resources during a time of crisis.

Historical Development of Government Services for the Aged

The first major federal legislation which specifically addressed the problems of older Americans was the Social Security Act of 1935. Congress passed this law with the intention that Social Security would provide a supplemental income that could be combined with savings, investments, and other income to make an adequate level of retirement income for qualified older Americans. Social Security, however, has become the major source of income for most older Americans since many of them have no additional savings, investments, or other income. Originally the Social Security Act established the retirement age of 65, which has generally been adopted by business, industry, religious, and government agencies as the age of retirement. In 1978 legislation was passed allowing persons to work to age 70 before mandatory retirement policies could be imposed. The long-range direction has been, however, for older persons to retire prior to age 70. Later amendments to the Social Security Act provided Old Age Insurance, Medicare, and reduced the age of eligible applicants.

The next major effort by government to confront the problems of older Americans came in 1950, when the first National Conference on Aging was held. Sponsored by the Federal Security Agency, this conference attracted participants from a number of private and federal agencies as well as representatives from the state and federal government. It led to the establishment of the first Federal Administrative Committee on Aging and Geriatrics in 1951. The Geriatric Committee was placed under the authority of the Department of Health, Education, and Welfare. The committee functioned primarily to create nationwide awareness of the problems of older Americans and the need for services.

The first White House Conference on Aging was held in 1961. The critical issue of the conference was medical problems of the elderly. Medicare was brought forth by this conference as the solution to this problem. While being basically an exploratory and information-gathering conference, it did raise and carefully examine the need for a federal agency on aging.

In 1963, the Office on Aging was established by transferring the functions of the Special Staff on Aging from the Welfare Administration to this new and separate office. The role of this office was the collection of social welfare programs under a unified authority. One question which arose in the development of programs was whether needed services for older Americans should be provided through comprehensive programs designed to aid people of all ages, or whether separate programs should be developed specifically and solely to aid older Americans. Congress was convinced that older Americans would always be overlooked in programs designed for all age groups. The Older Americans Act of 1965 was formulated to insure that all persons over 60 would have programs tailored specifically to their needs, and established the following statutory entitlements to help reach that goal:

> *Title I:* Committed the government to assist the elderly in securing full and equal opportunity in such areas as income, housing, health care, and employment.
>
> *Title II:* Created the Administration on Aging.
>
> *Title III:* Provided grants for community planning services and training.
>
> *Title IV:* Funded research and demonstration projects to study the status of the elderly and to develop approaches to improving their living conditions.
>
> *Title V:* Provided funds for training persons employed or to be employed in programs assisting older Americans.

In 1967, the amendments to the Older Americans Act extended existing grants and contract authorities under Title III, IV, and V and increased funding for the various titles.

In 1969, Congressional amendments authorized additional funds under Title III for areawide model projects. Title VI was added, creating the National Older Americans Volunteer Program. In 1971, control of Title VI was transferred to Action, another federal agency. In 1973, Title VI was repealed.

In 1971, the second White House Conference on Aging recommended the establishment of a network of federal, state, and local planning and advocacy agencies to influence the major service providers to provide better services for the elderly. It also recommended the development of a wide range of services to meet specific identifiable needs of older persons.

In 1972, amendments to the Older Americans Act created Title VII, which provided funds for nationwide projects to meet nutritional needs of the aged.

In 1973, the Older Americans Comprehensive Amendments effected the following five changes in existing legislation:

1. Created a national clearinghouse on aging and a Federal Council on Aging under Title II.
2. Enabled State and Area Agencies on Aging to develop comprehensive service programs under Title III.
3. Provided additional monies for multidisciplinary gerontology centers by combining Titles IV and V.
4. Established multipurpose senior centers under Title V.
5. Provided for community service employment for older Americans under Title IX.

In 1974, the Social Service Amendments established Title XX of the Social Security Act. While being directed toward the needs of all age groups, this entitlement included some programs directed specifically toward needs of the elderly. For example, Title XX funds can be used for protective services for adults, housekeeping and homemaker service assistance programs, housing improvement programs, preventive services, transportation, information and referral services.

The 1978 amendments to the Older Americans Act:

1. Required states to develop a comprehensive and coordinated service delivery system for older Americans.
2. Required states to create a sole state agency on aging in order to qualify for funds.
3. Mandated three-year plans from each area agency on aging.
4. Expanded the funds available for the development of multipurpose senior centers.

Programs Serving Older Americans

The programs serving older Americans are numerous, and funded by government, religion, and the private sector of the economy. The following is a brief description of some of the more well-established programs.

RETIRED SENIOR VOLUNTEER PROGRAM (RSVP). The Retired Senior Volunteer Program was designed to solicit the support of anyone 60 and older who wants to use his or her experience and talents to serve or improve the community. Seven hundred RSVP projects are located across the country employing more than 50,000 senior volunteers. All kinds of activities are pursued by the volunteers; they serve in schools, libraries, correctional institutions, hospitals, nursing homes, telephone reassurance programs, government agencies, and more. The volunteers in this program receive no pay; however, they are reimbursed for the cost of their transportation to and from their volunteer stations and also the cost of a meal if they are volunteering during a meal period.

FOSTER GRANDPARENT PROGRAM. The Foster Grandparent Program is a double-barreled program designed to assist both low-income elderly and disadvantaged children. Low-income elderly are paid to spend a prescribed amount of time each week working in the public and private schools with disadvantaged youngsters. Normally they work 20 hours a week providing individual attention, companionship, advice, and counsel to this group of young people who need special attention. These elderly give of their experiences and talents to a group of children who otherwise might not receive this extra support in the regular school setting. The foster grandparents often assist with homework, provide advice about problems, and assist in speech and physical therapy. This program has proved meaningful for both the older persons serving and the children being served.

SENIOR COMPANION PROGRAM.   The Senior Companion Program employs low-income older persons to assist other older persons in need. The sick, the bedridden, the very old, and the infirm are often helped by the senior companions. Companionship, concern, housekeeping, cooking, letter writing, and bill paying are just a few of the varied activities taken up by the senior companions. This program is designed to help older persons stay in their homes longer, thus delaying the more expensive institutionalization.

FRIENDLY VISITOR PROGRAM.   Title XX provides for a Friendly Visitor Program which matches up a volunteer visitor with a lonely, isolated, elderly person. The visitor meets with the elderly on a frequent basis, providing friendship and a helping hand with personal or household problems. The visitor can write letters, take small gifts, run errands, or just give the senior someone to talk with. If a person is interested in giving of their time but unable to go visit someone, they can act as a telephone visitor by making calls to an older person. This kind of visitor still gives the older person someone to talk to and prevents prolonged periods of isolation that might otherwise be endured. The only reimbursement offered to the friendly visitor is transportation costs.

SENIOR COMMUNITY SERVICE EMPLOYMENT PROGRAM (SCSEP).   The Senior Community Service Employment Program is funded by the Department of Labor. Its goal is to provide employment for economically disadvantaged persons who are 55 years of age and older. The seniors are paid for part-time community jobs at about minimum wage. Participants often work in parks, hospitals, senior centers, schools, day care centers. Participants receive an annual physical exam, on-the-job training and related services. "Green Thumb" is a branch of the program involved in conservation and restoration projects in rural areas. Green Thumb workers can earn up to $1600 per year.

SENIOR EMPLOYMENT SERVICE.   In 1975 Congress passed a Title V older workers' program. This program subsidizes public and private nonprofit organizations to hire unemployed, low-income aged for part-time work.

NUTRITION PROGRAM.   The Older Americans Act provides money to establish and operate programs serving meals to senior citizens. This program provides nutritious low-cost lunches for area senior citizens. These are usually served Monday through Friday at local neighborhood sites throughout the county. Participants must be 60 years of age or older (or a person is eligible if they are under 60 but their spouse is over 60). Home-delivered meals are available on a limited basis. The site of the lunch program is also often a location for after-lunch activities such as bingo and crafts. Not only does the program provide a hot noon meal but it provides companionship to many who would otherwise eat alone. People who eat alone or cook for only one do not get as hungry or eat as well as the ones who eat in a setting like the congregate dining sites. Eating is a social as well as physiological event.

No set price is charged. The seniors, however, are encouraged to make a donation. The amount of the donation is left up to the senior and ranges from 5¢ per meal to $1.50 per meal. Even though donations are encouraged, no one is left out of the program due to an inability to pay.

TRANSPORTATION. Area agencies can use Title III money of the Older Americans Act to either provide transportation by a van service, or contract with a local taxi company to provide transportation at a discount rate to senior citizens.

Federal funds pay for the cost of leasing or buying a van or vans and for the driver's salary in the senior transportation programs. No set price is charged although donations are encouraged to cover the cost of the gasoline.

This service gives the seniors door-to-door transportation to their doctor's office, supermarket, or to take care of personal business. The van services small communities in outlying areas as well as the urban districts.

When a contract is made with a taxi company, the discount coupon method is used. The service is run similarly, as far as places the seniors are taken and the opportunity for door-to-door service. However, the payment for the service is different. Coupon booklets can be purchased by the senior citizens to hire the cab at a discount rate. For example, they would receive two dollars worth of coupons for one dollar. The goal of both programs is to assist the elderly in their attempts to remain independent.

MULTIPURPOSE CENTERS. The multipurpose centers are designed to provide a central location where social, recreational, educational, and nutritional services can be brought to meet the needs of the senior citizens. The centers may also be designed to serve as an Information and Referral Center for each of the counties in which they are located. Senior citizens are able to obtain vital information and needed referrals from a central location in their own county. The center director also refers participants of the center to an outreach program if he or she feels they are in need of further assistance. Activities that a person can participate in at the center include such things as arts and crafts, physical fitness, kitchen bands, field trips, and health screenings.

The goal of the multipurpose senior centers is to provide a central location where senior citizens can learn, grow, relax, be creative, and socialize with other people.

DAY CARE CENTERS. Title XX provides funds for the establishment of senior day care centers. Many older persons are living in the homes of their adult children and receive the kind of attention and support they need from their children during the nonworking hours. If they can be placed in a day care center during the normal workday it often means at some point that they can be kept out of retirement homes, hospitals, and nursing homes during their last few years. They are brought to the day care centers by their children as the children leave for work in the morning and picked up by their children as they return from work in the evening. The day care centers usually employ a nurse, who can give the older person any needed medication, do such things as periodic blood pressure checks, and help with the common problems of the elderly.

Other staff members at the day care center plan activities, crafts, and field trips for the clients. Many community service projects are performed by the clients such as tray favors for the hospitals and bandage folding for the Red Cross. This not only makes the elderly person feel useful and involved, but makes the community aware of the day care center.

INFORMATION AND REFERRAL.   The Information and Referral Program is the link between the aging person and the aging programs. This program provides information to the seniors and acts as a referral agency to help the seniors know where or who to contact in order to meet their needs. Information is given out on every subject from Social Security insurance, to who to contact to have yardwork done and what to do if they run out of fuel. It is much easier to educate the staff of the I & R program and let them give out information than to try to educate the public on every number and agency name and service that they might ever need.

Most I & R programs distribute booklets to the elderly that include regularly called numbers and emergency numbers for their area. These books are free for the asking and are often printed in large print to make reading easier for older people.

In programs where several counties are involved, a toll-free number to the I & R program is used to make it convenient for the elderly to gain information. Elderly people would be less apt to call for information if they would have to go through an operator or pay for the call on their limited income.

PROTECTIVE CARE.   This program provides for the protection of the elderly persons who are unable to protect their own interests, which may result in physical or mental injury, neglect, inadequate food or shelter, or loss of resources. The program is designed to provide assistance and intervention for cases of suspected or actual neglect or abuse or health problems which seriously disrupt the living situations of older Americans.

OMBUDSMAN.   The Older Americans Act also provides funds for the establishment of an Ombudsman Program. The Ombudsman acts as a liaison between a nursing home administrator and the nursing home residents and their families. The Ombudsman's duty is to investigate any problems or complaints reported to him or her involving the residents. These problems include such things as mistreatment of the patients, poor dietary procedures, or questionable acts carried out by the home's staff.

In most cases that are handled by the Ombudsman, the home's administrator is very cooperative in working out the problem; however, it may be necessary for the Ombudsman to seek legal assistance for the nursing home residents.

PERSONAL CARE ASSESSMENT. The basic goal of the personal care assessment program is to locate, assess, and evaluate the needs of the elderly. After the assessment has been made the PCA worker then assists the older persons in solving their problems by referring them to the appropriate social service providers.

Funded by Title XX, this program was designed to assist the elderly in remaining self-sufficient for as long as possible.

Referrals come to the personal care assessor from many sources: welfare departments, township trustees, hospitals, churches, interested neighbors; sometimes even the person needing the help will call the office.

This program and the I & R program work hand in hand to refer the elderly to the agency that can best meet their needs.

HANDYMAN AND HOMEMAKER SERVICES FOR THE ELDERLY. Often older persons because of poor health are no longer able to fix leaking roofs, sagging drainpipes, and broken windows. The cost of hiring someone to do these chores can often become excessive and can lead the older person to decide to give up his or her home. To alleviate this problem, the Handyman and Homemaker Services have been funded, providing services for persons over the age of 60 who need such services. The handyman can repair broken windows, install and remove storm windows, make plumbing repairs, do light yardwork, repair leaking roofs, and generally maintain the older person's home.

The homemakers try to maintain the basic household needs of older persons. They do light housework, laundry, wash windows, pay bills, and run errands for the older person. This service also gives the elderly person someone to look forward to seeing. Many close relationships have come about between homemaker and client.

MEDICARE. Medicare was provided by Congress to help alleviate some of the costs of medical expenses incurred by older Americans. Medicare covers about 66 percent of short-term hospital bills. Most persons on Social Security pay no premiums for Medicare. The second part of the program is a major medical insurance for which the individual pays a fee of $8.70 per month. This covers the cost of the necessary doctors' services and additional outpatient services.

As a general rule medical care is designed to handle acute conditions but not chronic ones. Unfortunately, many of the problems of older Americans are chronic. Medicare was designed to help pay for services that are reasonable and necessary but not those that are custodial in nature.

Medicare covers

1. A semiprivate room (2 to 4 beds in a room)
2. All meals, including special diets
3. Regular nursing services
4. Costs of special care units, such as an intensive care unit
5. Drugs furnished by the hospital
6. Lab tests included in the hospital bill
7. X-rays and other radiology services, including radiation therapy, billed by the hospital
8. Medical supplies such as casts, surgical dressings, and splints
9. Use of appliances, such as wheelchair
10. Operating and recovery room costs
11. Rehabilitation services, such as physical therapy, occupational therapy, and speech pathology services

Medicare does not cover

1. Personal convenience items that you request, such as television, radio, or telephone in your room
2. Private-duty nurses
3. Any extra charges for a private room, unless you need it for medical reasons
4. The first 3 pints of blood you receive in a benefit period[22]

In addition, Medicare does not cover acupuncture, Christian Science practitioners' services, cosmetic surgery, dental care, drugs or medicines the person buys without a prescription, eyeglasses, eye examinations, nursing care on a full-time basis in the home, and physical examinations that are routine in nature.

It is easy to understand why critics of Medicare maintain that it covers only those problems of an acute or crisis nature regarding the older person's health and ignores any aspect of preventive medicine since routine checkups are not covered.

Low-income elderly can, if they qualify, obtain Medicaid which pays for several services not covered by Medicare. These services include eyeglasses, dental care, prescribed drugs, and long-term nursing home care.

LEGAL SERVICES.   Older persons are at a time in their lives in which they are more likely than any other age group to need the advice of a lawyer. They often experience the death of a spouse and the problems involved in settling an estate. They themselves must plan for the distribution of their property upon their death. They are likely to need to know how to claim their legitimate retirement benefits, to cash in insurance policies, to invest savings accumulated in an insurance program, and may need a myriad of other legal questions answered.

Illustrations of Programs

Often the description of government services provided to any group of persons leaves the reader with questions concerning the necessity of the programs and the value that they have for the clients. The following cases were given by the social service providers in Area #7 of West Central Indiana. They provide some idea of the need for the program as well as the services rendered.

CASE 1

Dovie lives on a rural route in an agricultural county. The county seat has a population of approximately 10,000. She was assessed to need a Friendly Visitor. Dovie is in very poor health and almost blind. Her visitor, Mrs. P., came to visit on a July afternoon and this is what she wrote in her visitor's log:

> Called her the night before, and she told me about her leg and back. I went to the drugstore and got her a tube of Mobisyl Creme and took it to her to rub the affected parts of her body. I also took her some homemade sausage. I called her the next evening and she told me she slept "like a log" and didn't get up until eight o'clock the next morning. She said it really helped her. She even got out in the yard and pulled weeds from her flowers. Said her leg didn't even hurt to walk on it. She liked her sausage also. Now, she is telling everyone she talks to about the Mobisyl Creme because it helped her so much. I am so glad she got relief. Dr. Jones is my doctor and he said it is the only thing he has found that helps *him*. Try it, if you have aches, pains, or sore places. Dovie wanted to pay me for it, but I refused. I told her "that was my good deed for the day."[23]

CASE 2

Early one morning I received a call from the Sullivan County Senior Citizen Center informing me that an elderly lady in Sullivan was having difficulty in obtaining home repairs. I had a difficult time finding her home due to the fact that the front porch had collapsed and the remainder of the house appeared unfit for human life. I asked a neighbor, who directed me to this home, which was the most dilapidated abode I had seen since I have been connected with aging programs. No one was home, except for 10 to 15 cats that were climbing in and out of a couple of broken windows. Since the front porch was unsafe, I went to the back door to meet the lady. The back porch was not much better than the front porch. The floorboards were rotten and in places you could see through to the ground. As I rounded to the front of the building, I saw coming down a side street an elderly crippled lady pushing a grocery cart with a couple of sacks in it.

I asked if I might be of assistance to her and if she was Ms. Y. She said she was and she accepted my offer to help. We entered the back door. The odor from the cats was overbearing. Upon entering the living room I saw sunlight streaming through holes in the roof a foot square. How, I wondered, could this lady have survived the severe winters we'd been having?

Our handyman program obviously could not handle a project of such magnitude. However, in concert with other sources of assistance I felt that maybe the network of services could handle the problem.

After returning to the office, I contacted our personal care assessor and asked that he contact the Farmer's Home Administration. They can provide interest-free grants of up to $5000.00 to eligible senior citizens. This lady only received Supplemental Security Income—approximately $190.00 a month. There was no question of her eligibility for an FHA grant. However, the FHA decided that her home was not worth investing the money in. Without the assistance of the FHA, our handyman program and the winterization program could do nothing. Within 3 months the house was condemned and the lady was placed in a nursing home. I am certain that if she had a home which was livable, and our homemaker service to help with transportation and housework, this lady could have continued to live independently.[24]

CASE 3

Because of a winter snow storm only two staff members could make it into the office. Midmorning I received an anonymous phone call from a nurse at one of our local hospitals stating her concern for an elderly lady they had treated in the emergency room the night before.

This lady had been brought in by ambulance with a cut on her head. Someone had called the ambulance when they saw her laying in the road. She had been treated and released to the care of her guardian. The nurse was not concerned with the cut but during the treatment Gladys said many things that the nurse couldn't block out of her mind. The nurse reported that Gladys had stated she was hungry, that her guardian would not let her keep food in her own house but had to walk up a hill a quarter of a mile to get her meals at the guardian's house. This explained why she was going up the road in such bad weather.

Gladys was really bundled up explaining to the nurse that she had burnt almost all of her coal and it would last longer if she didn't keep it so warm in her house. But she just had to get home because of her dog, Tobey, was all alone.

After getting Gladys' approximate address from the nurse, another staff member and I drove the 10 miles out of town to the post office thinking the postman might be familar with the situation. We were lucky enough to catch the postman there and he drove us to Gladys' house.

We walked back from the road and found an old shack, the elderly lady, and Tobey. The lady was out combing the ground to find small pieces of coal to burn in the stove. She was very glad to see someone and immediately invited us in. The windows of the shack were covered with cardboard, the pipes of the coal burning stove were burnt out and open flames were exposed. The furniture of the house was scarce: a bed, a table, a kitchen chair and the remains of a dresser. The other part of the dresser had been chopped up and used to burn in the stove. The walls of the shack were covered with tar paper; however, there were cracks in the walls where the paper had fallen off. The only food we found in the house were two half-rotten potatoes.

She was very fearful about telling us anything about her guardians, apparently they had mistreated her when she complained about her situation. I could tell the lady was underfed and neglected. We told Gladys we would help her and not to worry about her guardians anymore.

We went to a phone, contacted her doctor, and he agreed to admit her to the hospital because of malnutrition. We went back to get Gladys and to meet the guardian.

When we arrived at the guardian's house we were met at the back door by at least 15 dogs all on the inside of the house. It wasn't until we were asked in did we see the chickens that were also inside. After introducing ourselves and explaining why we were there, the guardian became very defensive. When we said we were taking Gladys with us to the hospital, the guardian said she would sue our agency and us personally for taking Gladys without her consent. The guardian also told us Gladys had no relatives and she was appointed guardian because Gladys was mentally not able to care for her own affairs.

When Gladys left with us to go to the hospital, she padlocked the shack door and trusted me to keep her key. Her whole life's memories of her childhood and her late husband were stored there. Should anything happen to her, she asked me to care for her most valued possessions.

After getting Gladys settled for the weekend, we had at least until Monday morning to decide what to do next. On Monday we checked birth certificates and marriage licenses and found that Gladys had a niece living in a town about 120 miles away. When calling the niece we found Gladys had a living sister, too, and they had always been concerned about this situation but were scared of her guardian.

When the guardian realized that she was really likely to have legal problems herself for receiving Gladys' Social Security checks and not spending it on her, she decided not to sue us but just to bow out of the case as soon and as quietly as she could.

I worked with the niece, who agreed to have Gladys come to live with her and to take care of whatever needed to be done. After one week in the hospital, Gladys was released to go live with her niece. However, she had no clothes because hers had been destroyed upon admission and the ones in her home were very dirty.

Our office asked for donations and finally got her ready to go. Thinking we were on the home stretch we sighed with relief, when we realized Gladys had no transportation to get to her new home. As you can probably guess, I drove her to meet her family, making only one stop on the way. We went by Gladys' old shack to pick up the possessions that she had locked up and Tobey, her pet dog.

Upon arriving at Gladys' new home, it was good to see a family anxiously awaiting a new member. The family accepted Gladys and Tobey with open arms.

That's been 3 years ago and I still hear from Gladys and her family. Her sister has since died but Gladys still stays with her niece and lives a happy life.[25]

CASE 4

A minister called our office one morning and gave us the name and address of a man that walked into his church the night before. He said the man was very hard of hearing and was in need of help!

We went to see George and found that he lived in an upstairs apartment in a very run-down house. When we got there the apartment door had a padlock on it and a very nosey neighbor said they had seen him leave a couple of hours ago. We later found out that George had walked about ten blocks in several inches of snow carrying the battery from his car. After leaving the battery at a garage, he walked the ten blocks back in the bitter cold snowy weather.

We went back that afternoon and found George at home. As we walked up the steps of the dark apartment building, several doors opened to see who was coming and what we wanted. We pounded on the apartment door and introduced ourselves to George. He was so hard of hearing we had to talk loudly, however, he kept putting his hand to his mouth to give us the quiet sign because he didn't want the neighbors to hear his business through the paper-thin walls. I suggested we communicate by writing and that's when he told me he could neither read or write.

He said that he had appeared in court the day before because the lady that took care of the apartments wanted him out. They didn't like him, he said, and since they couldn't steal what they wanted from him they would just kick him out. I'm sure there were two sides to this, but right now our only concern was this elderly gentleman. Even though he had gone to court, he said he didn't know what had gone on because he couldn't hear the judge so he was scared as to what would happen next. I gave him my card and said if he needed anything, someone could either dial the number for him or give him directions to the office. In the meantime, I told him I would find out what happened in court and get back with him. The judge was out of his office until the next morning so I could only hope nothing would happen the rest of the day.

The next morning there stood George in front of my office door before 8:00 A.M. He said the police had come at midnight the night before and evicted him from his apartment and took him to the Light House Mission to spend the night. The eviction notice said he would be given three days to remove his belongings and he would have to get the key from the lady who took care of the apartments whenever he wanted to get in and pack. Where do you put a low-income elderly man and three rooms of junk in only three short days? And if we had a place, how would we move him?

After begging the judge and the landlord, they jointly agreed to extend the time to a week so we could breathe a little easier. The Light House Mission helped us a lot by providing George a place to eat and sleep until we found an apartment. The Housing Authority worked with us to speed up a Section 8 Application and it was up to me to find an apartment and a landlord who would accept a Section 8 applicant (Section 8 is a program which subsidizes a person's rent if they meet the income guidelines). After a couple of days and evenings of apartment looking, we finally found a satisfactory place. By this time we only had two days to move so we couldn't waste any time. The apartment chosen was close to a grocery store and laundromat. As soon as we got him moved in we would teach him how to use a washing machine.

Friday was moving day and it was the project of our total staff. We got a truck, a roll of trash bags, and off to George's we went. I tried to explain to him that time was running out, the new apartment was a lot smaller and there is no way we could or would move all that stuff. We filled 27 trash bags with all kinds of things from old clothes to dead dried-up flowers. Much against his better judgment he closed his eyes, protested under his breath, and let us throw away whatever we felt had to go.

We got to the new apartment, hung some pictures, put clean sheets on the bed and halfway unpacked to make him feel at home. We left George on a Friday night to let him get settled and enjoy his new place.

I spent the weekend calling people I knew to get some donated towels, sheets, dishes, and his size clothing. On Monday morning I was off again to George's new apartment, to take these things and to see if he had survived the move and the weekend.

He was pleased with his new home and things I had brought to him, but he asked if I could do just one more favor. George and I went and picked up his car battery and he got his car running.

We set up the homemaker service and they taught George to use the laundromat and how to keep his house a little cleaner.

George was upset that so much of his stuff was thrown away, but finally realized it had to be done.

That was about a year ago and George still lives in that same apartment but he seems a little happier now. He met the elderly lady in the front apartment and they have started a courtship. Whether it does or does not turn into a more serious relationship, temporarily they are enjoying each other's company.[26]

FUTURE DIRECTIONS OF SERVICE PROGRAMS FOR THE AGED

The 1981 White House Conference on Aging was surrounded with controversy and probably will be the least fruitful conference in terms of promoting the interest of older Americans through federal legislation and program support. The major difference between the 1981 Conference and the other White House Conferences on Aging was the attitude of the president and the party currently in power in Washington. Until 1981 all the previous conferences had received a sympathetic ear from the president and the party in power. The 1981 conference, however, found a president who was committed to a program of curbing inflation by reducing government spending. The reduction of government spending was to be done primarily by reducing social service and entitlement programs. Thus, while the delegates to the 1981 White House Conference on Aging asked for increases in government services for older Americans, the Reagan administration was committed to curbing any further expansion of these programs.

This impasse between advisory committee of the 1981 White House Conference and the administration became apparent even before the delegates to the conference assembled. Laurie Soriano, in the *Gray Panther Network*, pointed out how minute changes in conference rules and in the selection of committee leaders imposed by the administration would have the effect of bringing the committees more under the control of the committee leaders and restricting democratic discussions by the committee members since no subcommittees were to be formed. Soriano argued that the input of the individual delegates would be reduced and would be more at the mercy of the interpretation of the chairperson of the committee.

Regardless of the controversy surrounding the structure of the 1981 White House Conference on Aging, it was held and the committees did produce 668 separate recommendations. While it would be impossible to list and discuss all of these recommendations, a few of the more important issues can be identified. The two most urgent priorities in the minds of the delegates were the maintenance of the current Social Security benefits and the expansion of health insurance benefits for older Americans.

While maintaining current Social Security benefits was agreed upon by all the delegates, they did disagree on how this was to be done. The recommendation of one committee was for Congress not to use the general revenues to shore up the depleted Social Security funds. The recommendation of another committee was for Congress to use the general revenue funds to shore up the depleted Social Security funds.

In terms of the delegates' demands for increased health insurance benefits, the committee recommendations emphasized

1. the need to develop a comprehensive long-term care system, to include an array of home-based services
2. the need for Medicare coverage to include preventive care and health maintenance (in addition to the current coverages)
3. the need to protect the rights of the institutionalized aged through such mechanisms as a patients' bill of rights, ambulance service, and advocacy councils.

The political effect of the 1981 White House Conference on Aging would seem to have been to educate congressmen, senators, and the President of the inadvisability of considering reducing Social Security benefits no matter how great the temptation. On the other hand, it seems unlikely that there will be any expansion of the health insurance program in the near future.

While the early 1980s have seen a curbing of the expansion of federally funded social service programs for older Americans, one wonders if this is a temporary or permanent phenomenon. The best educated guess, given the needs of older Americans and the numbers of voters they represent, is that ultimately there will be an expansion of the programs. This expansion may be some time in coming, however.

In terms of critique of the current government service programs for older Americans it would seem that Estes has been most critical. Employing a conflict perspective, Estes argues that the current programs are shortsighted and piecemeal attempts to enhance the social activities and life satisfaction of older persons while ignoring the larger economic, political, and social conditions that determine the quality of their lives. Moreover, she believes the current programs stigmatize the elderly as sick, feeble, dependent, and the cause of their own problems.[27] Estes sees four major problem areas with the current service delivery programs:

1. The aged are economically prevented from creating their own choices and options and must depend on service providers for minimum assistance and quickly learn to be submissive in order to receive the service.
2. The policies that provide for jurisdictional expansion of service providers and middle-level bureaucrats are likely to increase the general public's dependence on the service.
3. Service strategies in general and those for the aged in particular tend to stigmatize their clients as recipients in need, creating the impression that they have somehow failed to assume responsibility for their lives.
4. Service approaches are likely to inhibit thinking about problems of the aged as related to or concomitant with larger social and economic conditions.[28]

While Estes's analysis is perceptive and insightful, it, in essence, demands a restructuring of the entire social service delivery system in order to improve the power position and thereby social status of the elderly. Short of a revolution, societies have not been known to completely restructure any of their institutions in order to improve the social standing of a particular group. This drastic a shift in the current social service delivery seems unlikely at the present time.

CONCLUSION

The fact that in the 1980s persons 65 and above comprised 11 percent of the population and 20 percent of the voters has resulted in a great deal of interest in and deference accorded to their wishes among political candidates. This interest, while understandable, may not be entirely deserved. The current group of retirees are about equally divided between the Democratic and Republican parties and are the least likely group to abandon their party because of a particular issue.

In terms of political participation older persons appear to be the most active of any age group. They follow news about political issues regularly, are more likely than other age groups to hold an opinion on a particular issue, and are disproportionately represented among opinion leaders. They vote more regularly than other age groups. Most of them are long-standing party members. While the United States does not have a gerontocracy, most of the Congress and many presidents have been middle- or old-aged. The Supreme Court, which does not require justices to retire, tends to be comprised of several persons beyond the age of 65. Older political figures, however, tend to vote more on the issues as a result of political beliefs and ideologies rather than on the basis of their age.

Older Americans tend to vote more along social class lines based on what they believe to be the best interest of their particular socioeconomic group. They are not a homogeneous group and apparently have not formed a pervasive subculture. They represent the views of their different class backgrounds, ethnic, racial, and religious identities. They vote as a bloc only when they feel that the issue is directly related to the interest of their age group. When they do solidly back legislation which addresses an issue they consider important, they are most often successful. A few examples of their successful efforts include: Congress changing the mandatory retirement age from 65 to 70 (something large corporations and universities clearly did not want); the passage of a Medicare program, which was opposed by the American Medical Association; the increasing of Social Security benefits, which some taxpayer groups did not want; and through the Older Americans Act, a whole multitude of services for older Americans, which those opposed to large government and a growing federal bureaucracy clearly did not want.

It should be pointed out, however, that these sweeping changes in legislation which favored older Americans seem to have resulted in part from the fact that a variety of different organizations and associations brought the problems of the elderly to the public's and political leaders' attention, that middle-age voters wanted to shift the responsibilities for aging family members off of themselves and onto the government, and that both big business and the labor unions have wanted to encourage older workers to retire early.

The costs of the social service programs for older Americans have risen dramatically in the last decade and one wonders if there will be a backlash among younger age groups to the ever-growing national resources allocated on behalf of the elderly. At the present time there seems to be general support for the programs among all age groups and a reversal of the trend does not appear imminent.

KEY TERMS

Townsend movement   status inconsistency
Gray Panthers   cultural lag

SUGGESTED READINGS

BARROW, GEORGIA M., AND PATRICIA A. SMITH, *Age, Ageism, and Society,* pp. 355–59. St. Paul, Minn.: West, 1979.

CAMPBELL, A., "Political Through the Life Cycle," *The Gerontologist,* 11 (1971), pp. 112–17.

CAMPBELL, A., "Social and Psychological Determinants of Voting Behavior," in *Politics and Age,* eds. W. Donahue and Clark Tibbitts, p. 92. Ann Arbor: The University of Michigan Press, 1962.

COWGILL, DONALD, "Critical Problems of Aging." Lecture given at Indiana State University Workshop, June 1977.

DOUGLAS, ELIZABETH B., WILLIAM P. CLEVELAND, AND GEORGE L. MADDOX. "Political Attitudes, Age and Aging: A Cohort Analysis of Archival Data," *Journal of Gerontology,* 26 (1976), 666–75.

ESTES, CARROLL, *The Aging Enterprise,* pp. 221–24. San Francisco: Jossey-Bass, 1979.

FISCHER, DAVID HACKETT, "The Politics of Aging in America: A Short History," *The Journal of the Institute for Socioeconomic Studies,* 4, no. 2 (1979), 51–66.

GLENN, NORVAL D., AND MICHAEL GRIMES, "Aging, Voting and Political Interest," *American Sociological Review,* 33, no. 4 (1968), 563–75.

GUBRIUM, JABER F., *Time, Roles and Self in Old Age,* p. 142. New York: Human Sciences Press, 1976.

Health, Education, and Welfare Publication No. (SSA) 78-10050, p. 13. Washington, D.C.: U.S. Government Printing Office, 1977.

HESS, BETH B., "The Politics of Aging," *Society,* 15, no. 5 (July-August 1978), 22–23.

HUGHES, E. C., "Dilemmas and Contradictions of Status," *American Journal of Sociology,* 50 (1944–45), 353.

JACKSON, E., "Status Consistency and Symptoms of Stress," *American Sociological Review,* 27 (1962), 469.

KLEYMAN, PAUL, *Senior Power: Growing Old Rebelliously.* San Francisco: Glide Publications, 1974.

LANE, R. E., *Political Life.* New York: Free Press, 1959.

LENSKI, G., "Status Crystallization: A Non-Vertical Dimension of Social Status," *American Sociological Review,* 19 (1954), 204.

LOETHER, HERMAN J., *Problems of Aging,* pp. 155–56. Belmont, CA: Dickenson, 1967.

LOWRY, LOUIS, "Social Welfare and the Aging," in *Social Problems of the Aging,* ed. Mildred Seltzer and others, pp. 300–314. New York: Wadsworth, 1978.

OGBURN, WILLIAM F., *Social Change,* pp. 200–201. New York: B. W. Heubsch, 1922.

PRATT, HENRY J., "Old Age Associations and National Politics," *Annals of American Academy of Political and Social Sciences* (September 1974), pp. 106–19.

RAGAN, PAULINE, AND JAMES DOWD, "The Emerging Political Consciousness of the Aged: A Generational Interpretation," *Journal of Social Issues*, 3, no. 3 (1977), 137–50.

SORIANO, LAURIE, "White House Conference: A Political Rodeo," *Gray Panther Network* (November/December 1981), p. 1.

WILENSKY, H. L., AND C. N. LEBEAUX, *Industrial Society and Social Welfare* (2nd ed.). New York: Free Press, 1966.

15

AGING AND THE AGED
Future Prospects and Issues

The golden age is before, not behind us.

C. H. Saint Simon
Emerson Uncollected Lectures: Resources

Often the most learned, wise, and scholarly persons appear foolish when making long-range predictions about the future. This is particularly true if their predictions are widely known by others and they are examined over any prolonged period of time. The hazards of prediction are based on the fact that there are a large number of interrelated and interconnected variables that must be taken into account in making any future projections. Each of these variables can move in a variety of different directions and, therefore, none are entirely predictable. Thus, when one makes predictions about the future he or she is making them on the basis of expected changes in a large number of interrelated variables each of which is somewhat unpredictable. Since no one can perfectly predict changes over time in any of these variables, to predict how the entire group is going to be altered is even more hazardous.

After recognizing the often imprecise and foolhardy nature of predictions most authors of textbooks reveal themselves to be more bold than wise and attempt in a concluding chapter of a text to make some educated guesses regarding the future of the given subject matter or discipline. This author is no different than his predecessors.

Since predictions cannot immediately be reality tested, they often range between extremes. Kahn and Wiener have painted a picture of Utopia by the year 2000. They see technical innovations resulting in permanent undersea colonies, large-scale desalinization of sea water, genetic control of plants and animals, as well as new drugs which will aid memory and learning. Others, however, paint a gloomy picture of the future which includes population explosions resulting in overpopulation in which energy and food sources are depleted and "rich" and "poor" nations will battle for control of the remaining resources.

The problem of the future of aging can be seen from two perspectives: one from the point of view of the individual experiencing old age; the other from the point of view of the scientist studying the aging process. Thus, what life will be like for the 65-year-old and older group of persons in the year 2000 and what the critical issues and research questions will be for gerontologists studying the problems of aging in the year 2000 or beyond are two different questions. Both for the individual arriving at the later years and the scientists studying gerontology, the future can be seen in both optimistic and pessimistic terms. Instead of discussing either the glorious golden years or the gloom and doom of the future, a range of variables from family to health, from retirement to theories of aging, will be discussed separately to determine possible future developments and issues.

GERONTOLOGY: THE FUTURE OF THE DISCIPLINE

Gerontology is a discipline whose time has arrived. The increasing public awareness of the problems of aging has resulted in pressure for political action, government services, scientific research, and practical solutions to those problems. Gerontology seems to be a discipline in ferment and perhaps one that is at the threshold of new discoveries and knowledge. The result is that gerontology is an exciting place to be as a scientist. There is much fertile soil for new research in the discipline that needs to be carefully cultivated by persons in the field.

The discipline has commanded and probably will continue to command the interests of scientists from a variety of different subject areas. Biology, psychology, sociology, economics, political science, and psychiatry will be actively involved in conducting research in the field. The interdisciplinary nature of the field is likely to result in considerable cross-fertilization of ideas from the various subject areas. Theoretical perspectives developed by sociologists may prove useful to psychologists, or the perspective of the biologists may be incorporated into the human developmental theories of both the psychologists and the sociologists. The future directions and developments of new knowledge in the field should prove interesting as scientists attempt to synthesize and integrate information coming from a variety of different subject matters and theoretical perspectives.

The press to solve immediate problems of older persons in the past has resulted in research and findings which produce immediate results but may not be well-grounded theoretically. Over time the discipline is likely to become much more scientifically sophisticated. Undoubtedly, the future holds much in the way of theoretical developments that address the subject matter of human development and aging.

While the future of the gerontology discipline certainly appears promising, there may simultaneously be problems. Much is expected of the discipline by the public, politicians, and government planners. Public attention and sensitivity to the aging process and the related problems have led leaders to expect a great deal in the way of new discoveries and expert advice on the resolution of the problems. Will the gerontologists be able to live up to the expectations currently being placed on them? Only time will tell. It is certainly fair to say that never has any academic discipline been placed more in the limelight of public attention and scrutiny.

In examining what we really know about aging, Bosco and Porcino outlined a number of paradoxes of the field:

1. That while medical doctors spend about 60 percent of their time with 40 percent of their patients who are over 65, geriatrics, as a branch of medicine, has been extremely slow in developing in the United States. They point out that in a congressional survey of all medical schools only 15 out of 20,000 faculty members identified aging as their specialty. Health needs of the elderly, it is felt, are often viewed as not worth the bother in medical schools.

2. The belief that older persons have been abandoned by their families appears not to be true. Often older family members move near their adult children during their retirement years and interact with them frequently. Moreover, a higher percent of the sick elderly live with a family member rather than in a nursing home. While this is true it is also the case that there is a strong sentiment among the general population to shift the responsibility for aging family members off of themselves and onto the government.

3. Retirement is not a dreaded evil feared universally by older persons. A high proportion of older persons look forward to this stage of life and when retired become involved in a variety of creative activities.

4. Romance, love, and sexual fulfillment are not the exclusive province of the young. People 65 and older can and do maintain intimate personal relationships, fall in love, marry, and remain sexually active.

5. Old people are not sick and feeble. While older people do suffer more frequently from chronic health problems, most of these are not debilitating and many are no more serious than short sight and hay fever.

6. Older people are not often senile. Older persons are often misdiagnosed as senile when they are in fact suffering from depression or a treatable physical disorder.

7. Government services are not so tied up with bureaucratic red tape that most older persons don't want to become involved. In reality most government services do not involve a means tests and are relatively accessible for both the economically advantaged and disadvantaged older persons. While many older persons choose not to participate, this choice is rarely related to the red tape involved.

8. While the goal of the gerontologist and the service providers is to help the old remain independent and self-sufficient members of the community, transportation, shopping centers, public buildings and most community activities are structured for the healthy young adult.[1]

Undoubtedly as knowledge in gerontology becomes more widely distributed and the public more informed and sophisticated in their understanding of the aging process, many of these paradoxes will disappear.

THEORIES OF AGING

Initially the theories of aging were narrowly focused and philosophical in nature, thus, successful aging was best accomplished through disengagement, activity, continuity of life styles, and so on. These approaches sensitized persons to the problems of later life and instructed them as to how to best adjust. While they were therapeutic in nature, they were very narrow in focus.

Later theories emphasize the developmental process of life and are broader based, thereby connecting the individual to the larger social system and describing the relation of the individual's adjustment patterns to the norms, roles, and institutions of the society. Stratification and symbolic interaction are two of these more recent theoretical developments which fit this pattern. The age stratification approach looks at the relative positions of different age groups and examines the possibility of conflict over scarce resources and the more prestigious roles in the social system. Intergenerational conflict, strain, and tension can be easily examined from this theoretical basis. Moreover, one can expect changing attitudes and values as one's age and thereby position in the social system changes over time. While age does have a leveling effect, Ward observes that the aging experience differs for men and women, blacks and whites, blue-collar and white-collar workers. These differences cannot entirely be accounted for in the age stratification approach.

Subgroup and subcultural experiences in the aging process could perhaps best be explained by the symbolic interaction approach. Symbolic interactionists maintain that in order to truly understand the aging experience we must be able to take the role of the other. We must be able to figuratively put ourselves in the shoes of the aging person and view the aging process from his or her point of view. This approach would help us to better understand differences in the aging experience for men and women, blacks and whites, rich and poor, since each of these groups are confronting the aging experiences from a different perspective. Role losses such as retirement, moves to the Sun Belt, declining health, and a variety of other factors can be seen from this perspective to alter the social world and status of the older persons and thereby both how they are treated by significant others and how they in turn are expected to respond to these others in interpersonal relations. Deprived of past social groups' identities and roles, the older person does have the opportunity to adopt new roles, reference groups, and lifestyles. Depending on the reaction of the older person, the retirement years, according to Ward, can bring new opportunities, personal growth and development, or stress, maladjustment, and unhappiness.

Both age stratification and symbolic interaction as theoretical approaches to the aging process recognize that one cannot understand the experiences of the later years without understanding what occurred before. Aging is viewed as a developmental process encompassing the entire life cycle. Ward observes:

> One cannot understand aging as a developmental period without looking at the whole of the life cycle, retirement without looking at work, widowhood without looking at marriage.[2]

Thus, the more recent theoretical thrusts of the discipline seem to be broader based and attempt to understand the aging experience in light of the entire life cycle and the particular society in which the experience took place. The bias of this text has been in the direction of symbolic interaction but undoubtedly age stratification and other as-yet-undiscovered theoretical approaches to the aging experience will all lead to a better understanding of the aging process and intriguing new research questions.

While many of the unanswered questions in gerontology will be addressed in the traditional cross-sectional studies, which examine attitudes and behavior at one point in time, the longitudinal studies that follow a particular sample of cohorts over time offer the greatest promise for explaining the developmental processes in the aging experience. Unfortunately, longitudinal studies require extreme dedication and patience on the part of the researcher. To systematically study a sample of cohorts for the next 10, 20, 30, or 40 years requires a very highly motivated scientist who can delay the rewards of scientific recognition and accomplishment over long periods of his or her career. Few scientists have that degree of dedication and patience. Moreover, few funding agencies are willing to invest in such long-range projects. Nevertheless, the longitudinal studies offer the greatest hope for resolving many of the unanswered questions in gerontology.

HEALTH

Life span is not likely to be changed by the year 2000 or 2010, but life expectancy will. Neugarten and Havighurst report that it was the consensus of a panel of medical specialists that medical discoveries would extend life expectancy from five to ten years by the year 2000.[3] Life span refers to the maximum number of years it is possible for Homo Sapiens to survive. This currently appears to be somewhere between 110 and 120 and is not likely to change in the near future. What we will see is a larger proportion of the total population living well into their eighties and remaining in good health throughout most of their later years. This will have the effect of extending life expectancy at birth.

Medical research will undoubtedly continue on its course of examining the internal biological and organic changes that accompany the aging process.

Research on cell division, the immune system, and the deterioration of the body's vital organs will undoubtedly lead to medical breakthroughs in the control of cancer and heart disease. Any major breakthrough which allows medicine to gain greater control over the body chemistry of the older persons will undoubtedly extend their lives. Hendricks and Hendricks report:

> Already extensive research is underway to investigate basic immunological systems perhaps involved in aging and the disruption of the body's processes which enable it to discriminate between inherent and foreign elements.[4]

The body's ability to distinguish between internal and external threats could lead to control of the crippling diseases, such as arthritis, in which the body reacts against itself.

The recognition in recent years that life expectancy can be affected by such things as housing, nutrition, sanitation, smoking, and alcoholism has led to a discussion of both preventive medicine and holistic medicine. What we have now is a better-educated and better-informed adult population concerning health problems. A sizeable segment of the adult population are both knowledgeable and concerned about their health. This group have stopped smoking, developed a pattern of regular exercise, watch their diet, and adopt a maintenance and preventive attitude about health care. Jogging, handball, tennis, and a great variety of sports are participated in regularly by the ever-larger segment of the adult population. These are the people that will be entering their older years in the twenty-first century and one can expect that they will be a healthier group of older persons than the current generation of retirees. Moreover, they will be more knowledgeable about potential health problems and will have adopted a lifestyle conducive to good health.

Nelson, reporting on the predictions of a futurologist regarding biofeedback, points out that the individual himself or herself may learn through conscious effort and meditation to control the body's internal chemistry. In the animal world stress triggers an internal biological reaction which allows the frightened animal to run farther and faster as he or she attempts to flee danger. Once the burst of energy is expended, the animal usually escapes the danger and is able to return to a state of relaxation. Stress in humans is often produced not by attacks on life but rather by competition and conflict in families, in work, and the community. Tension in human life is most often a result of conflict with significant others in the individual's environment. Modern society requires the individual, rather than fleeing threat, to remain outwardly calm and appear to be rational in reaction to whatever may have produced the stress. Thus, the individual's blood pressure rises, the heart pumps faster, the body's chemistry is altered and there is not an immediately socially acceptable way to relieve this tension. Moreover, people, with their acquisition of language, have the ability to rethink the stressful situation, to relive the insult over and over again in the mind, thus recreating the stress many times over. Students of stress believe that if people are capable of creating stress by their own thoughts, by remembering the past insults and anxiety-arousing situations, they should equally well be able to recognize stress, alter the thought process, and produce relaxation. Thus an individual may learn to recognize the symptoms of rising blood pressure and through his or her own actions and thoughts lower the blood pressure. Researchers have not really begun to investigate this kind of biofeedback. Once this model of biological control is carefully examined it could lead to a variety of alterations in behavior patterns, lifestyles, and mechanisms of self-control that few of us can currently imagine.

Regardless of which of the several directions medical research is now going, the result is fairly predictable. There will be a stronger and healthier life for an ever-increasing proportion of the adult population. We may be entering a period in which most Americans can expect to live in good health well into their eighties.

Tobin sees three forms of future health services becoming more prevalent. First, community-based organizations which are developing to provide a range of health services to the elderly in order to delay institutionalization; second, small local nursing facilities to care for the elderly who need constant care. Tobin believes the smaller institutions can provide more personal care. Third, hospices will be established to care for and help the dying person, and to provide counseling for their families. Neighborhood health services and hospices may well become more common in the future, but small nursing homes are highly unlikely. A series of federal regulations requiring fire escapes, sprinkler systems, recreational therapists, just to name a few, while being well-intended, have had the effect of putting small nursing homes out of business since the regulations have made them too expensive to operate. The result is large nursing homes that are economically feasible and which will, undoubtedly, become the most common form of health service for those persons requiring institutionalization in the future.

RETIREMENT INCOME

While current retirees earn approximately one-half of what their income was when they were working, the future looks somewhat brighter for forthcoming generations of retirees.

First, private pension and insurance programs have become more common and widespread and, therefore in the future will cover a larger proportion of retirees. Hendricks and Hendricks observed that the more than 5 million private pension plans in existence in 1975 covered 35 million workers, representing almost half the full-time workers in the country. An additional 40 million workers are either self-employed or employed where pension plans are not available. They believe that those covered by private pension programs will increase and the programs will become more solvent as a result of the Employee Retirement Security Act of 1974 (ERISA). This law encourages the establishment of private pension programs and insures the benefits of workers in the private pension programs. Eligibility for existing plans must be determined by age 25 and grant the employee the right to half of the benefits after ten years of service and an additional 10 percent for each year thereafter. This law also imposes restrictions on the investments and actions of trust officers for private pensions thus insuring the soundness of the programs. Simultaneously the government established the Individual Retirement Account (IRA) which enabled those wanting to supplement Social Security to set aside 15 percent of their income in an annual tax-sheltered annuity. The IRA constitutes an income reduction in which no taxes are paid on either the amount set aside or on the accumulated interest.[5] As was mentioned in Chapter 10, Social Security benefits, while lagging somewhat behind inflation, can be adjusted periodically by Congress to stay abreast of inflation.

All of the above factors are likely to increase the retirement incomes of older persons. In addition, American workers are becoming increasingly aware of the problems of retirement income and this more frequently becomes an item for collective bargaining during contract negotiations. Thus, it seems clear that an ever-increasing proportion of future retirees will be covered by more than just their Social Security benefits and that their overall retirement income should rise.

Some would argue that Social Security will have to keep increasing the tax rate on the American workers to pay the benefits earned by an ever-increasing older population. By the year 2030 it has been estimated there will be one Social Security beneficiary for every two workers paying Social Security taxes instead of the current one beneficiary for every three workers. At some point many political analysts have predicted a tax revolt which would set the adult working population against the elderly. This does not seem likely, however, for two reasons: First, the adult population will themselves anticipate their own retirement and not want to see Social Security benefits attacked; second, most of them would prefer to see their older relatives receive Social Security benefits rather than be individually responsible for them economically. In short, a taxpayers' revolt against Social Security seems unlikely.

Moreover, it seems unlikely that Congress is going to do anything other than support the Social Security program since such a large group of voters are dependent on it for their economic survival. One questions whether Congress will even raise the age at which one can draw benefits in order to make the program more economically solvent since this would be so unpopular with older voters. Neugarten has predicted that by the year 2000 demand for older workers may increase as a result of demographic trends and the fact that fewer young people will be entering the work force. In all probability some older workers may choose to work longer before retiring but it is unlikely that they will be forced to do so by Congress changing the retirement age.

Most observers expect that the number of older persons with income below the poverty line will decrease by the year 2000 and that the overall incomes of retirees will have increased by that time. Schulz predicts an increase in retirement incomes due to the "demographic turnover"—that is, every day a large number of persons enter the 65 age group and a large number over 65 die. Those who die are usually poorer than those who have just become members of the aged population. The new aged often retire on pension incomes considerably higher than the previous generation of retirees.

FAMILY

As was pointed out in Chapter 8, approximately two-thirds of all aged persons are husband-wife couples living alone, most of whom maintain their own household. These couples have for the most part had one-fourth of their married life to live after the last child left home. Legitimate topics for future research on the family will undoubtedly include adjustment patterns of widows and widowers, second marriages, and alternative family forms during later life.

While the typical elderly couple today have often enjoyed a long-standing marriage lasting 30 or 40 years, some have projected that the high divorce rate, the greater tolerance of and acceptance of divorce, as well as more casual attitudes toward cohabitation, might result in many older persons in the future not being married. The Population Reference Bureau's article in *Inter-Change* does not indicate that this will be the case, however. There is evidence that the divorce rate has reached its peak and may even decline during the next few years. This seems to be related to the fact that fewer marriages are occurring among the very young and other groups which in the past traditionally have been known to have high divorce rates. Census Bureau data indicates that fewer Americans, especially women, are marrying in their teens and that couples are having fewer children and delaying the birth of their first child. All of these trends tend to improve the economic position of the family which is a positive factor contributing to marital stability.[6] Simultaneously there will be fewer families broken up because of the death of a spouse.

Clayton and Voss have suggested that "living together," along with delayed marriages, will lead to a more careful selection of a spouse and thus to a more enduring marriage in terms of the survival rate of the marriage. Table 15–1 illustrates the pattern of survival rates for marriage projected by Clayton and Voss.

Thus, it may well be expected that probably just about as many couples arriving at age 65 in the twenty-first century will have lived together for a considerable proportion of their adult life as those now 65. They will probably have married a few years later than their parents and grandparents did and have had fewer children. Most of them, however, will have experienced marital stability throughout most of their adult lives.

Table 15–1   How Long Do Marriages Last?

WEDDING ANNIVERSARY, FIRST MARRIAGE	CHANCES OF REACHING THE ANNIVERSARY
5th	5 of every 6
10th	4 of every 5
20th	3 of every 4
30th	2 of every 3
35th	1 of every 2
40th	2 of every 5
45th	1 of every 3
50th	1 of every 5
55th	1 of every 10
60th	1 of every 20
65th	1 of every 50
70th	1 of every 100

Source: Richard R. Clayton and Harwin L. Voss, "Shacking Up: Cohabitation in the 1970s," *Journal of Marriage and the Family,* 39, no. 2 (May 1977), 273–83. Copyright 1977 by the National Council on Family Relations. Reprinted by permission.

Projections about the sex ratio in the year 2000 or 2010 are less consistent and depend on the point of view of the person making the projection. Bosco and Porcino report:

> The elderly population of the future will be mostly female, and many of them will be widows. Of those 65 and older, there are now 69 males for every 100 females; whereas, 400 years ago the ratio was about even. By the year 2000, there will be an estimated 65 males for every 100 females of the same age.[7]

As pointed out in this text, there is evidence that at conception more boys are conceived than girls; during the nine months of pregnancy, during childbirth, and at every age in life thereafter, boys are more likely to die than girls. The result has been that the older the age of a group of cohorts become, the more imbalanced the sex ratio becomes in favor of women. Moreover, each new medical discovery has so far ended up saving more women's lives than men's and the gap in the life expectancy of the two groups widens. Thus, it is easy to understand the reasons for Bosco and Porcino's projections.

There is, however, a counterargument being made by the students of the feminist movement and the family. They argue that as women enter careers and strive for success and upward mobility with the same vigor that men have in the past that they will experience the same physiological stresses and strains and thereby come to approximate the male in terms of the frequency of ulcers, heart attacks, and other stress-related illnesses and deaths. The result should be a narrowing of the gap in life expectancy between men and women and the narrowing of the differences in the number of men and women in the 65-and-over group. Projections, as stated earlier, are always hazardous, and determining who is most correct in terms of the above projections is difficult. One wonders, however, if the differences in the life expectancies of men and women have not peaked and that in the future one might expect to see a narrowing of the gap.

The best-educated guesses about the older family in the twenty-first century might conclude that the older couples will have life experiences in which both husbands and wives have been involved in occupational pursuits throughout most of their married life. They will have had small families of two or three children at most and will have more than one-fourth of their married life to live after the last child leaves home. They will have had a marriage based on companionship and a sharing of childrearing and household chores rather than on a complicated division of labor. They will have experienced more adequate and stable incomes during their adult years as a result of both partners working. Similarly, their retirement incomes will be more secure since they will be able to depend on two separate retirement incomes rather than one. Inevitably, one of the marital partners will precede the other in death and it will be crucial to the remaining partner that a proportion of the deceased partner's retirement income be transferred. While two cannot live as cheaply as one, they can collectively live cheaper than two. Rent, utilities, heat, and other bills continue whether there is one or two persons living in the household. The retirement couples of the twenty-first century will probably enjoy their retirement more and have more common interests during the retirement years. Having lived throughout most of their adult life in a marriage in which household duties as well as recreation and leisure interests were shared on a companionship basis rather than as a division of labor based primarily on sex, the future retirement couples should have many more common interests and shared values on which to build their retirement lives.

RESIDENTIAL LOCATION

In terms of migration patterns and shifts of the population, the elderly have in the past been the group least prone to move. Earlier, they were disproportionately represented in the older rural areas, then they were left in the zones immediately surrounding the inner city as their younger counterparts moved to the suburbs. The next projected concentrations of the elderly might be in the suburbs as the current population in the suburbs ages and their younger counterparts move to alternative residential locations. The relatively low crime rates and less expensive living costs of small towns across the country will probably continue to be attractive to many older persons. Therefore, we would expect small towns in rural areas also to have disproportionately larger numbers of older persons residing there.

The future generation of retirees will probably be even more likely than the past generation to move to the Sun Belt. First, their incomes are going to be better as retirement programs become more widespread and their benefits more secure. Second, as was just observed, there will be more couples with two retirement incomes. Given adequate incomes more older persons will have more freedom to choose where they would like to live rather than being forced to live in their present location because they cannot afford to do anything else. Undoubtedly, many will choose to live a part or all of their retirement years in the warmer climates. Some older persons will follow the common pattern of wintering in Florida, Arizona, or California and spending their summers in other states in which their children are currently located, thus maintaining viable family relations. Others will choose to reside permanently in the southern states, visiting their children periodically during vacations.

In all probability what one will find is that if the incomes of the retirement couples improve, then their choices of residential location and lifestyle will become more diverse. Guaranteed adequate resources, they will become much like other age groups in which values and personal choice lead them in a variety of different directions. Economic deprivation often leaves few choices available to the current population of older Americans and they tend to cling to their current homes and residential locations regardless of their appropriateness.

POSTINDUSTRIAL SOCIETY

Everett Hughes, Daniel Bell, and other social scientists have speculated on what life will be like in postindustrial society. The consensus of the social scientists seems to be that the postindustrial period will see a shift away from expansion in manufacturing and industry to the expansion of social services, entertainment, athletics, and recreation and leisure enterprises. The basic argument of the social scientists is that as the industrial development of a nation peaks and as an ever-efficient manufacturing technology emerges, less of the population will be required to produce the nation's goods. This will make surpluses of manpower available; the service occupations, the entertainment industry, and industries catering to recreation and leisure activities will develop. Bell believes that postindustrial society may be characterized by a new elite based on professional expertise. He observes that the number of scientists and engineers doubled from 1900 to 1975 and predicts that by the year 2000 the technical and professional class will be the largest occupational group in the country. It will, he argues, form a pool of experts that government and industry can use to plan and organize for the future. The result is expected to be a tremendous growth of government employment and the expansion of social services. Simultaneously the reduced working hours, the advent of a four-day work week, and related trends will result in larger amounts of free time for the average citizen. This will mean greater opportunity for entertainment, athletic events, recreation and leisure pursuits as well as opportunity for education and cultural enrichment. Colleges and universities are more likely to find their student bodies comprised of all age groups rather than just 18- to 25-year-olds, as the adult population has more free time to pursue its own interests and personal development.

VALUES

The values of the postindustrial period are expected to be slightly different among the general public from what we know today; it is thought that there will be a movement away from the "Protestant ethic" and toward emphasis on the "quality of life," including considerable emphasis on individuality, self-expression, and personal development. There will be somewhat less pressure to shape oneself to fit the demands of industry by developing a narrow occupational skill. There may well emerge in the postindustrial period the belief that everyone should be guaranteed the right to work and that a job should be shaped to fit the individual as much as the individual shaped to fit the job.

According to Rapoport and Rapoport, values of achievement, productivity, and independence may seem less important in the postindustrial period, being replaced by such values as the importance of congeniality, concern for the meaning of life, and the cultivation of satisfying human relationships. Eric Trist argues that the postindustrial period will be marked by value shifts from achievement to self-actualization, from self-control to self-expression, from independence to interdependence.

If the values of the twenty-first century shift along the lines suggested by the social scientists, we should expect an improvement in the status of older persons. Less emphasis on achievement and productivity, in which the young are always viewed as having the greatest potential for development, and greater concern with interpersonal relationships and the meaning and quality of life, in which the old may have the distinct advantage of breadth of past experience and wisdom accumulated over a lifetime, should improve the status of older persons. Butler argues that the "loosening up of life," in which we are not locked into lifelong careers and bound by decisions made early in life, may greatly benefit those in the middle and later years. Time for recreation and leisure activities throughout the entire life cycle is to be expected. For many, the opportunity of second and third careers in later life will become more common.

WORK AND LEISURE

As greater flexibility in work and leisure patterns emerges and there is greater flexibility in lifestyles, one would expect people to enter and exit from formal educational programs at different phases of the life cycle. Adults may be retrained after deciding to change careers in midlife. Sarason has written a book depicting the variety of midlife career changes experienced by a number of persons in very diverse occupations. Sarason asserts that the major reason for the frequent midcareer changes is one of self-expression: The individual over time comes to realize that the manner in which he or she is required to present himself or herself in his or her current occupation is inconsistent with his or her innermost view of self. The individual thus changes jobs in order to assume a role in which his or her best self-image can be presented. Sarason's hypothesis is consistent with the symbolic interactionist view of personality development. To the degree that this pattern becomes more widespread, we would expect a greater number of the adult population to change careers more frequently and to enter formal educational training programs at different phases of the life cycle. This may make formal education a lifelong experience rather than the exclusive privilege of the young. Thus, older persons might be more inclined to return to colleges and universities after retiring as a means of cultural enrichment rather than for career preparation. The amount of time available to the individual for recreational and leisure pursuits will undoubtedly grow.

POWER

If the trend of low birthrates that has prevailed for the last two decades continues, we can expect the mean age of the population to move upward and for the 65+ group to make up an even larger percentage of the total population. Instead of middle-aged persons maintaining a concentration of power in the society, we might expect middle-aged and older persons to share power in the social system. We have already seen the law requiring people to retire at 65 changed to age 70. Ultimately, there will undoubtedly be cases brought to court claiming reverse age discrimination in employment. One might expect that more semiprofessional and professional employees in the future will choose to work beyond the age of 65. These two groups in particular have been found to find greater satisfaction and meaning in their work than have many of the blue-collar workers. If they do work beyond age 65, these persons will often be found in key organizational positions, exercising considerable authority in decision making. In short, the power now concentrated in the hands of middle-aged adults may shift in the direction of older adults.

DEATH

Traditional attitudes and values surrounding death may be more challenged in the future than any other of the social system's cherished beliefs. The ability of medical technologists to maintain and prolong life even if only in near-vegetable condition will ultimately force society to address the issue of humankind's apparent control over life and death. One does not like to think of oneself as deciding either individually or for loved ones when the proper time to die shall be. We have generally viewed self-determination of death as suicide and maintained that suicide is an act of desperation or cowardice. In the future our values may shift so that we come to believe that if life is maintained only by medical technology and there is no hope for an improvement in the condition, it is a person's right to choose to die. Euthanasia may be more acceptable in the next century than it is presently.

GOVERNMENT SERVICES

While there may be temporary setbacks and reversals, the long-range trend will be to increase government services for older Americans. This group will clearly be a large voting bloc capable of keeping political leaders informed of their more pressing problems. The political process in the United States tends to be strongly influenced by special-interest groups. Political leaders, faced with organized groups composed of older Americans, will no doubt look with favor on legislation that would improve the welfare of this group of citizens. Cox and Sekhon asked a sample of old, rural, and low-income Americans to rank their most pressing needs. These were perceived to be

1. Adequate income
2. Concern about physical health
3. Energy (fuel, gas, electric)
4. Transportation
5. Nutrition
6. National health insurance

Having a rural sample rank national health insurance as important to them when it is usually identified as a clearly liberal cause is somewhat surprising; rural Americans have generally been thought to be the most conservative politically. Apparently they are willing to endorse liberal programs that they believe will bring much-needed assistance to them. The results suggest that in both rural and urban America there will be growing pressure for an increasing number and variety of service programs for older Americans.

Finally, as we have already noted, older Americans in the future can be expected to be reasonably healthy into their eighties and to have greater economic security than the previous generation of older persons. The result will be more diverse and heterogeneous lifestyles for the future retirees. Their increasing resources will allow them to choose more freely among geographic locations, housing, neighborhoods, communities, and social groups with which they would like to identify. In short, it would appear that future generations of older persons will have brighter prospects than the past generations for a healthy and productive later life, with greater freedom to choose among a wide range of lifestyles, roles, and activities in which to engage, and more economic resources to support themselves in their chosen way of life.

KEY TERMS

biofeedback	tax-sheltered annuity
holistic medicine	sex ratio
futurologist	cohabitation
demographic turnover	euthanasia

SUGGESTED READINGS

BELL, DANIEL, *The Coming of Post-Industrial Society.* New York: Basic Books, 1973.

BOSCO, ANTOINETTE, AND JANE PORCINO, *What Do We Really Know About Aging.* Albany: State University of New York, 1977.

BUTLER, ROBERT, *Why Survive? Being Old in America.* New York: Harper and Row, Pub., 1975.

CLAYTON, RICHARD R., AND HARWIN L. VOSS, "Shacking Up: Cohabitation in the 1970s," *Journal of Marriage and the Family,* 39, no. 2 (May 1977), 273–83.

COX, HAROLD, AND GURMEET SEKHON, *Statistical Report 1981 White House Conference: Prioritizing the Needs of the Rural Elderly.* Washington, D.C.: National Green Thumb, 1981.

HENDRICKS, JON, AND C. DAVIS HENDRICKS, *Aging in Mass Society.* Cambridge, MA: Winthrop, 1977.

HUGHES, EVERETT, *Men and Their Work.* New York: Free Press, 1964.

KAHN, HERMAN, AND ANTHONY WIENER, "The Next Thirty-Three Years: A Framework for Speculation," in *Toward the Year 2000: Work in Progress,* ed. Daniel Bell. Boston: Houghton Mifflin, 1968.

NELSON, CHARLES, "Holistic Medicine." Lecture at Futures Forum, Indiana State University, 1981.

NEUGARTEN, BERNICE, "The Future and the Young-Old," *The Gerontologist,* 15, no. 1 (1975), p. 7.

NEUGARTEN, BERNICE, AND ROBERT HAVIGHURST, eds., "Extending the Human Life Span," *Social Policy and Social Ethics.* Washington, D.C.: U.S. Government Printing Office, 1977.

Population Reference Bureau, Inc., Inter-Change, Population Educators Newsletter (ISSN: 0047–0465), 7, no. 1 (January 1978), 2.

RAPOPORT, RHONA, AND ROBERT RAPOPORT, *Leisure and the Family Life Cycle.* London: Routledge and Kegan Paul, 1975.

SARASON, SEYMOUR, *Work, Aging and Social Change: Professionals and the One Life–One Career Imperative.* New York: Free Press, 1977.

SCHULZ, JAMES A., *The Economics of Aging,* pp. 179–80. New York: Wadsworth, 1980.

TIRST, ERIC, "Toward a Post-Industrial Culture," in *Handbook of Work, Organization and Society,* ed. Robert Dubin. Skokie, IL: Rand McNally, 1976.

TOBIN, SHELDON S., "Social and Health Services for the Future Aged," *The Gerontologist,* 15, no. 1, pt. 2 (1975), 32–37.

WARD, RUSSELL, *The Aging Experience.* New York: J. B. Lippincott, 1979.

NOTES

CHAPTER 1

1. For demographic trends see: L. A. Epstein, and J. H. Murray, "The Aged Population of the United Stated," *Research Report No. 19* (Washington, D. C.: Office of Research and Statistics, Social Security Administration, U.S. Department of Health, Education and Welfare, the Government Printing Office, 1967), p. 967.
2. Carole Allen and Herman Brotman, *Chartbook on Aging in America* (Washington, D.C.: Administration on Aging, 1981), p. 6.
3. Ibid., p. 8.
4. George Maddox, lecture given at Indiana State University, May 1982.
5. Antoinette Bosco and Jane Porcino, *What Do We Really Know About Aging* (State University of New York at Stony Brook, 1977).
6. Allen and Brotman, p. 14.
7. J. Botwinick and L. W. Thompson, "Individual Differences in Reaction Time in Relation to Age," *Journal of Genetic Psychology*, 112 (1968), 73–75.
8. Leslie Libow, "Medical Problems of Older People" in *What Do We Really Know About Aging*, eds. Antoinette Bosco and Jane Porcino (State University of New York at Stony Brook, 1977), pp. 14–20.
9. Herbert S. Parnes, *A Longitudinal Study of Men, Work, and Retirement* (Cambridge, Mass.: MIT Press, 1981), p. 27.
10. Ibid., pp. 93–131.
11. Richard Kalish, *Late Adulthood: Perspectives on Human Development* (Monterey, CA: Brooks/Cole, 1975), p. 2.

CHAPTER 2

1. Douglas Kimmel, *Adulthood and Aging* (New York: John Wiley, 1974), p. 27.
2. R. A. Kalish, "Of Social Values and the Dying: A Defense of Disengagement," *The Family Coordinator,* 21 (1972).
3. Robert J. Havighurst, "Successful Aging," in *Processes of Aging*, eds. Richard H. Williams, Clark Tibbitts, Wilma Donahue (New York: Lieber-Atherton, 1963), p. 299.
4. Fred Cottrell and Robert C. Atchley, *Retired Women: A Preliminary Report* (Oxford, Ohio: Scripps Foundation, 1969).
5. Sigmund Freud, *An Outline of Psychoanalysis* (New York: W. W. Norton and Co., Inc., 1949), pp. 14–37.
6. Ibid., p. 17.
7. Ibid., p. 37.
8. Erik Erikson, *Childhood and Society* (New York: W. W. Norton and Co., Inc., 1964), pp. 219–31.

9. Gordon F. Streib, "Are the Aged a Minority Group?" in *Middle Age and Aging*, ed. Bernice Neugarten (Chicago: The University of Chicago Press, 1968).

10. James J. Dowd, "Aging as Exchange: A Preface to Theory," *Journal of Gerontology*, 30 (1975), 584–94.

11. Ibid., pp. 584–94.

12. Joseph Kuypers and Vern Bengtson, "Competence and Social Breakdown: A Social-Psychological View of Aging," *Human Development*, 16, no. 2 (1974), 37–49.

CHAPTER 3

1. R. Thomlinson, *Population Dynamics: Cause and Consequences of World Demographic Change* (New York: Random House, 1965), pp. 75–78.

2. Shelburne Cook, "Aging of and in Populations," in *Developmental Physiology and Aging*, ed. P. S. Timiras (New York: Macmillan, 1972), p. 595.

3. S. F. Cook, "Survivorship in Aboriginal Populations," *Human Biology*, 19, no. 2 (1947), 83–89.

4. J. C. Russel, *British Medieval Population* (Albuquerque: University of New Mexico Press, 1948), p. 24.

5. David H. Fischer, *Growing Old in America* (New York: Oxford University Press, 1978), p. 6.

6. A. R. Holmberg, *Nomads of the Long Bow* (Garden City, N.Y.: Natural History Press, 1969), pp. 224–25.

7. William H. Watson and Robert S. Maxwell, *Human Aging and Dying: A Study of Sociocultural Gerontology* (New York: St. Martin's Press, 1977), pp. 26–29.

8. Ibid., p. 17.

9. Erving Goffman, *The Presentation of Self in Everyday Life* (Garden City, N.Y.: Doubleday, 1959), p. 70.

10. H. W. Elliott, *Our Arctic Province: Alaska and the Sea Islands* (New York: Scribner's, 1886) pp. 170–71.

11. Watson and Maxwell, *Human Aging and Dying*, p. 20.

12. Sula Benet, "Why They Live to be 100 or Even Older in Abkasia," *The New York Times Magazine*, December 26, 1971, p. 28. © 1971 by The New York Times Company. Reprinted by permission. Some have questioned the authenticity of the ages given by the Abkasians.

13. Ibid., p. 29.

14. Ibid., p. 31.

15. Donald Cowgill and Lowell Holmes, eds., *Aging and Modernization* (New York: Appleton-Century-Crofts, 1972), p. 320.

16. Ibid., p. 17.

17. Ibid., p. 19.

19. Ibid., p. 23.

CHAPTER 4

1. B. L. Strehler, *Time, Cells, and Aging* (New York: Academic Press, 1977), p. 11.

2. Marion J. Lamb, *Biology of Aging* (New York: John Wiley, 1977), p. 3.

3. Ibid., p. 4.

4. Adrian Verwoerdt, "Biological Characteristics of the Elderly," in *Foundations of Practical Gerontology,* eds. Rosamonde Ramsay Boyd and Charles G. Oakes (Columbia: University of South Carolina Press, 1973), pp. 51–57. Copyright © 1969 and 1973 by the University of South Carolina Press. Paraphrased by permission of the University of South Carolina Press.

5. Strehler, *Time, Cells, and Aging,* p. 106.

6. Charles S. Harris, *Fact Book on Aging: A Profile of America's Older Population* (Washington, D.C.: The National Council on Aging, 1978), p. 105.

7. Ibid., p. 109.

8. Robert Butler, "Why Survive? Being Old in America" in *The Unfilled Prescription* (New York: Harper & Row, Pub., 1975), pp. 174–224.

9. Ibid., p. 177.

10. Harris, *Fact Book,* p. 111.

11. Butler, "Why Survive," p. 179.

12. Lamb, *Biology of Aging,* p. 21.

13. Lamb, *Biology of Aging,* pp. 117–18.

14. Marcella Weiner, Albert Brok, and Alvin Snadowsky, *Working with the Aged* (Englewood Cliffs, NJ: Prentice-Hall, 1978), p. 13.

15. B. L. Neugarten, R. J. Havighurst, and S. S. Tobin, "Personality and Patterns of Aging," in *Middle Age and Aging,* ed. B. L. Neugarten (Chicago: University of Chicago Press, 1968).

16. L. Hayflick, "Why Grow Old," *The Stanford Magazine* (1975), pp. 36–43.

17. E. L. Bierman and W. R. Hazzard, "Biology of Aging" in *The Biological Ages of Man from Conception through Old Age,* eds. D. W. Smith and E. L. Bierman (Philadelphia: Saunders, 1973), p. 34.

18. Lamb, *Biology of Aging,* p. 156.

19. Marjorie F. Lowenthal, "Social Isolation and Mental Illness in Old Age," *American Sociological Review,* 29 (1964), 54–70.

20. P. Sainsbury, "Suicide and Depression" in *Recent Development in Affective Disorders,* eds. Coppen and Walk, British Journal of Psychiatry Special Publications, no. 2 (1968), p. 8.

21. A. Foner and M. Riley, *Aging and Society, Vol. I: An Inventory of Research Findings* (New York: Russell Sage, 1968), pp. 382–83.

22. David Cousert, "Symbolic Interactionist Approach to Attitudes of Older People Toward Psychiatrists Versus Medical Doctors" (unpublished paper, Indiana State University, 1977).

23. Talcott Parsons, *The Social System* (New York: Free Press, 1951), pp. 436–37.

24. Harris, *Fact Book,* p. 12.

CHAPTER 5

1. Daniel J. Levinson and others, "Stages of Adulthood" in *Socialization and the Life Cycle,* ed. Rose Arnold (New York: St. Martin's, 1979), pp. 279–93.

2. Vern L. Bengtson, *The Social Psychology of Aging* (Indianapolis: Bobbs-Merrill, 1973), pp. 9–10.

3. Bernice Neugarten, *Middle Age and Aging* (Chicago: The University of Chicago Press, 1968), p. 137.

5. James E. Birren, "Psychological Aspects of Aging: Intellectual Functioning," *Gerontologist* (1968), pp. 16–19.

6. Ibid., p. 17.

7. R. E. Conestrari, "Research in Learning," *The Gerontologist,* 7, no. 2, pt. 2 (1967), 65.

8. Richard A. Kalish, *Late Adulthood: Perspectives on Human Development* (Monterey, CA: Brooks/Cole, 1975), p. 40.

9. Kalish, *Late Adulthood*, p. 46.

10. Douglas Kimmel, *Adulthood and Aging* (New York: John Wiley, 1974), pp. 300–305.

11. Carl G. Jung, "The Stages of Life," trans. R. F. C. Hull, in *The Portable Jung*, ed. Joseph Campbell (New York: Viking, 1971).

12. M. W. Riley and A. Foner, *Aging and Society, Volume I: Inventory of Research Findings* (New York: Russell Sage, 1968), p. 63.

13. Kalish, *Late Adulthood*, p. 57.

14. Bernice L. Neugarten, Robert J. Havighurst, and Sheldon S. Tobin, "The Measurement of Life Satisfaction," *Journal of Gerontology*, 16, no. 134–143 (1961), 168–74.

15. M. Clark and B. C. Anderson, *Culture and Aging* (Springfield, Ill.: Chas. C Thomas, 1967), pp. 232–33.

16. C. Buhler, "Old Age and Fulfillment of Life with Consideration of the Use of Time in Old Age," *Acta Psychologica*, 19 (1961), 126–48.

17. Kalish, *Late Adulthood*, p. 65.

18. M. Fried, *Social Differences in Mental Poverty and Health*, eds. S. J. Rosa, A. Antonovska, K. Zola (Cambridge, MA: Harvard University Press, 1969).

19. Robert Butler and Myrna Lewis, *Aging and Mental Health: Positive Psychosocial Approaches* (St. Louis: C. V. Mosby, 1973), p. 115; and Herman B. Brotman, "Who are the Aging?" in *Mental Illness in Later Life*, eds. Edward W. Busse and Eric Pfeiffer (Washington, D.C.: American Psychiatric Association, 1973), p. 36.

20. Carole Allen and Herman Brotman, *Chartbook on Aging in America* (Washington, D.C.: White House Conference on Aging, 1981), p. 90.

21. Charles Harris, *Fact Book on Aging* (Washington, D. C.: The National Council on Aging, 1978), p. 150.

22. Lawrence Krupka and Arthur Vener, "Hazards of Drug Use Among the Elderly," *The Gerontologist*, 19, no. 1 (1979), 90.

23. Phyllis K. Snyder and Ann Way, "Alcoholism and The Elderly," *Aging* (January-February 1979), p. 10.

24. Margaret Bailey, Paul W. Haberman, and Harold Alksne, "The Epidemiology of Alcoholism in an Urban Residential Area," *Quarterly Journal Studies of Alcohol*, 26 (1965), 13.

CHAPTER 6

1. Richard A. Kalish, *Late Adulthood: Perspectives on Human Development* (Monterey, CA: Brooks/Cole, 1975), p. 47.

2. David A. Goslon, *Handbook of Socialization Theory and Research* (Skokie, Ill.: Rand McNally, 1969), p. 6.

3. Harold Cox and Albert Bhak, "Determinants of Age Based Residential Segregation," *Sociological Symposium*, no. 29 (Winter 1980), 27–41.

4. Bernard S. Phillips, "A Role Theory Approach to Adjustment in Old Age," *American Sociological Review*, 22 (1957), 213.

5. Ibid., p. 215.

6. Ibid., p. 216.

7. Ibid., p. 214.

8. S. Reichard, F. Livson, and P. G. Peterson, *Aging and Personality: A Study of 87 Older Men* (New York: John Wiley, 1962).

9. Bill D. Bell, "Role Set Orientations and Life Satisfaction: A New Look at an Old Theory," *Time, Roles and Self in Old Age*, ed. Jaber F. Gubrium (New York: Human Sciences Press, 1976), pp. 148–64.

10. Douglas C. Kimmel, *Adulthood and Aging* (New York: John Wiley, 1974), p. 313.

11. Jaber F. Gubrium, *Time, Roles and Self in Old Age* (New York: Human Sciences Press, 1976), p. 113.

12. Bernice J. Neugarten, Joan W. Moore, and John C. Lowe, "Age Norms, Age Constraints, and Age Socialization," *American Journal of Sociology*, 70 (1965), 710–717.

13. Kathy Serock and others, "As Children See Old Folks," in *Focus: Aging*, ed. Harold Cox (Guilford, CT: Dushkin, 1978), pp. 102–103.

14. Louis Harris and Associates, *The Myth and Reality of Aging in America* (Washington, D.C.: The National Council on the Aging, Inc., 1975).

15. H. L. Wilensky and H. Edwards, "The Skidder: Ideological Adjustments of Downward Mobile Workers," *American Sociological Review*, 24 (1959), 215–31.

16. Thomas Tissue, "Downward Mobility in Old Age," in *Socialization and Life Cycle*, ed. Peter J. Rose (New York: St. Martin's Press, 1979), p. 356.

17. Ibid., p. 362.

CHAPTER 7

1. Stanley D. Eitzen, *Social Problems* (Boston, MA: Allyn & Bacon, 1980), pp. 123–24.

2. Jacquelyne Jackson, *Minorities and Aging* (Belmont, CA: Wadsworth, 1980), p. 4.

3. Gordon F. Streib, "Are the Aged a Minority Group," in *Middle Age and Aging*, ed. Bernice Neugarten (Chicago: University of Chicago Press, 1968), pp. 34–35.

4. U.S. Bureau of the Census, *Current Population Survey* (unpublished data, March 1978).

5. Ibid.

6. Federal Council on Aging, *Policy Issues Concerning the Elderly Minorities* (Washington, D.C.: HHS Publication, no. 80-20670, 1979).

7. Andre Hammonds, "Poverty and Older Black Americans: A Demographic Portrait" (unpublished paper, 1980).

8. National Advisory and Resource Committee, *Pacific/Asian Elderly Research Project* (Special Services for Group Inc., May 1978).

9. U.S. Bureau of the Census, "Household and Family Characteristics," *Current Population Reports*, no. 340, Table 3 (March 1978), p. 20.

10. Ibid.

11. U.S. Bureau of the Census, *Current Population Survey*.

12. Karen C. Ishizuke and others, *The Elderly Japanese, Latino, Black, Chinese, Quamanian* (San Diego: Center on Aging, San Diego State University, 1978), p. 57.

13. Donce Yee, "The Older Chinese" (statement presented at the San Francisco Meeting on the Minority Elderly, June 1979).

14. Federal Council on Aging, *Policy Issues*, p. 32.

15. Ibid.

16. U.S. Bureau of the Census, *Current Population Survey*.

17. Federal Council on Aging, *Policy Issues*, p. 32.

18. Ibid., p. 23.

19. U.S. Department of Health, Education and Welfare, Administration on Aging, "The Older Black Population," *Statistical Reports on Older Americans*, no. 5 (Washington, D.C.: HEW, 1978).

20. Federal Council on Aging, *Policy Issues*, p. 26.

21. National Advisory Resource Committee, *Pacific/Asian Elderly Research Project*.

22. Federal Council on Aging, *Policy Issues*, p. 33.

23. U.S. Bureau of the Census, *Current Population Survey*.

24. National Advisory and Research Committee, *Pacific/Asian Elderly Research Project*, p. 57.

25. Jackson, *Minorities and Aging*, p. 35.

26. Irving Rosow, "Status and Role Change Through the Life Span," in *Handbook on Aging and the Social Sciences*, ed. Robert H. Binstock and Ethel Shanas (New York: Van Nostrand Reinhold, 1976), p. 462.

27. Ibid., p. 465.

28. Ibid., p. 466.

29. Jackson, *Minorities and Aging*, pp. 121–22.

30. Federal Council on Aging, *Policy Issues*, pp. 39–40.

31. Ibid., p. 42.

32. Gossie Harold Hudson, "Some Special Problems of Older Americans," *Crisis Magazine*, (March 1976).

33. F. L. K. Hsu, *The Challenge of the American Dream: The Chinese in the United States* (Belmont, CA: Wadsworth, 1971).

34. Richard A. Kalish and Sharon Moriwaki, "The World of the Elderly Asian American," *Journal of Social Issues*, 29, no. 2 (1973), 192–93.

35. Ibid., p. 193.

36. Ibid., p. 195.

37. Ibid., pp. 201–202.

38. U.S. Department of Health, Education and Welfare, Public Health Service, Office of the Surgeon General, Division of Public Health Methods, *Health Service for the American Indians*, (Washington, D.C.: U.S. Public Health Service Publication No. 531, 1957), p. 10.

39. Jerrod Levy, "The Older American Indian," in *Older Rural Americans*, ed. E. Grant Youmans (Louisville: Univeristy of Kentucky Press, 1967), p. 224.

40. Ibid., p. 226.

41. E. A. Kennard, "Hopi Reactions to Death," *American Anthropologist*, 39 (1937), 494.

42. John C. Ewers, "The Hore in Blackfoot Indian Culture," *Bureau of American Ethnology Bulletin*, 159 (1955), 243.

43. Levy, "The Older American Indian," p. 231.

44. Ibid., pp. 231–32.

CHAPTER 8

1. Paul H. Glasser and Lois N. Glasser, "Role Reversal and Conflict Between Aged Parents and Their Children," *Marriage and Family Living*, 24 (1962), 46–51.

2. Bert N. Adams, *The Family: A Sociological Interpretation* (Skokie, Ill.: Rand McNally, 1975), p. 301.

3. Peter C. Pineo, "Disenchantment in the Later Years of Marriage," *Marriage and Family Living*, 23 (1961), 9–10.

4. William H. Masters and Virginia E. Johnson, *Human Sexual Response* (Boston, MA: Little, Brown, 1966), p. 264.

5. William Masters and Virginia E. Johnson, *Human Sexual Inadequacy* (Boston, MA: Little, Brown, 1970), p. 247.

6. Masters and Johnson, *Human Sexual Response*, p. 269.

7. Ibid., p. 264.

8. Aaron Lipman, "Role Conceptions of Couples in Retirement," in *Social and Psychological Aspects of Aging*, ed. Clark Tibbitts and Wilma Donahue (New York: Columbia University Press, 1962), pp. 475–85.

9. Marvin R. Koller, *Families: A Multigenerational Approach* (New York: McGraw-Hill, 1974), p. 5.

10. Eugene Litwak, "The Use of Extended Family Groups in the Achievement of Social Goals: Some Policy Implications," *Social Problems,* 7 (Winter 1959–60), 177–87.

11. Lillian E. Troll, Sheila J. Muller, and Robert C. Atchley, *Families in Later Life* (Belmont, CA: Wadsworth, 1979), p. 104.

12. Ibid., p. 104.

13. Ethel Shanas and Gordon Streib, *Social Structure and the Family: Generational Relations* (Englewood Cliffs, N.J.: Prentice-Hall, 1965), p. 80.

14. Marvin B. Sussman and Morris W. Stroud, *Studies in Chronic Illness and the Family* (unpublished paper, Western Reserve University and Highland View Hospital, 1959–1964), pp. 1–25.

15. Peter Townsend, "The Emergence of Four-Generation Family in Industrial Society," *Proceedings of the 7th International Congress of Gerontology, Vienna,* 8 (1966), 555–58.

16. Ivan F. Nye and Felix Berardo, *The Family: Its Structure and Interaction* (New York: Macmillan, 1973), pp. 533–63.

17. Jessie Bernard, *Remarriage* (New York: Dryden, 1956), p. 345.

18. Walter C. McKain, *Retirement Marriage* (Storrs: University of Connecticut, 1969), pp. 132–34.

19. Ibid.

CHAPTER 9

1. Robert Dubin, "Industrial Workers' Worlds: A Study of the 'Central Life Interests' of Industrial Workers," *Social Problems,* 3 (January 1956), 131–142.

2. R. K. Merton, L. Broom, and L. S. Cottrell, eds. "The Study of Occupation," in *Sociology Today* (New York: Harper and Row, Pub., 1965), p. 445.

3. Richard Hall, *Occupations and the Social Structure* (Englewood Cliffs, NJ: Prentice-Hall, 1975), p. 6.

4. Clifton Bryant, *The Social Dimensions of Work* (Englewood Cliffs, NJ: Prentice-Hall, Inc., 1972), p. 33.

5. Delbert Miller and William Form, *Industrial Sociology* (New York: Harper and Row, Pub., 1969), pp. 541–45.

6. Adriano Tilgher, *Work: What It Has Meant to Men Through the Ages,* trans. Dorothy Fisher (New York: Harcourt Brace Jovanovich, Inc., 1930).

7. Ibid.

8. Nancy Morse, and R. S. Weiss, "The Function and Meaning of Work and the Job," *American Sociological Review,* 20, no. 2 (April 1955), 192.

9. For a further discussion see Max Weber, *The Protestant Ethic and The Spirit of Capitalism,* trans. Talcott Parsons (London: George Allen & Unwin, 1935), pp. 35–198.

10. Nancy Vanlue (unpublished master's thesis, Indiana State University, 1974).

11. Victor Vroom, *Work and Motivation* (New York: John Wiley, 1964), p. 32.

12. S. DeGrazia, *Of Time, Work and Leisure* (New York: Twentieth Century Fund, 1962), p. 90.

13. Ronald M. Pavalko, *Sociology of Occupations and Professions* (Itasca, Ill.: F. E. Peacock Publishers, 1971).

14. DeGrazia, *Of Time, Work and Leisure.*

15. Harold L. Wilensky, "Professionalization of Everyone," *American Socological Review,* 70 (April 1964), 137–138.

16. J. Dumazediers, *Towards a Society of Leisure* (London: Collier-Macmillan, 1967), and *Lo Spettacalo* (London: Collier-Macmillan, 1972).

17. J. T. Haworth and M. A. Smith, *Work and Leisure* (Princeton, NJ: Princeton Book Company, 1975).

18. Carole Allen and Herman Brotman, *Chartbook on Aging in America* (Washington, D.C.: Administration on Aging, 1981), p. 40.

19. Robert Atchley, *The Sociology of Retirement* (Cambridge, MA: Schenkman, 1976).

20. Kurt W. Back and Carleton S. Guptill, "Retirement and Self Rating," in *Social Aspects of Aging*, eds. Ida J. Simpson and John C. McKinney (Durham, NC: Duke University Press, 1966), p. 129.

21. Robert Atchley, *The Social Forces in Later Life* (Belmont, CA: Wadsworth, 1977).

22. Sheldon Stryker, "Symbolic Interaction as an Approach to Family Research," *Marriage and Family Living, 21* (1959), 111–19.

23. Alton Johnson, Christopher Forrest, and Frank Sammartino, "Mandatory Retirement," in *Monographs on Aging*, no. 1 (Madison: University of Wisconsin, Faye McBeath Institute on Aging and Adult Life, 1979), pp. 18–19.

24. Ibid., p. 19.

CHAPTER 10

1. G. D. Hansen, "Meeting Housing Challenges, Involvement: The Elderly In Housing Issues," in *Proceedings of the Fifth Annual Meeting, American Association of Housing Educators* (Lincoln: University of Nebraska Press, 1971).

2. Charles Harris, *Fact Book on Aging: A Profile of America's Older Population* (Washington, D.C.: The National Council on the Aging, Inc., 1978), p. 185.

3. Ibid.

4. J. E. Montgomery, "Social Characteristics of the Aged in a Small Pennsylvania Community: State College, PA," *College of Home Economics Research Publication*, no. 233 (State College: The Pennsylvania State University, 1965).

5. E. Fromm, *The Art of Loving* (New York: Bantam, 1963).

6. Richard A. Kalish, *Late Adulthood Perspectives on Human Development* (Monterey, CA: Brooks/Cole, 1975), p. 97.

7. R. P. McKenzie, "Spatial Distance and Community Organization Patterns," *Social Forces, 5* (June 1927), 623–38; Robert E. Park, *Human Communities* (New York: Free Press, 1952); E. O. Laumann, *Prestige and Association in an Urban Community* (Indianapolis, IN: Bobbs-Merrill, 1966).

8. Otis D. Duncan and Beverly Duncan, "Residential Distribution and Occupational Stratification," *American Journal of Sociology, 60* (March 1955), 498–503.

9. A. S. Feldman and C. Tilly, "The Interaction of Social and Physical Space," *American Sociological Review, 25* (December 1960), 877–84.

10. Richard P. Coleman and Bernice L. Neugarten, *Social Status in the City* (San Francisco: Jossey-Bass, 1971).

11. S. N. Eisenstadt, *From Generation to Generation: Age Groups and Social Structure* (New York: Free Press, 1956).

12. Frances Carp, "Life Style and Location Within the City," *The Gerontologist, 15* (February 1975), 27–34.

13. Edward Steinfeld, James Duncan, and Paul Cardell, "Toward a Responsive Environment: The Psychosocial Effects of Inaccessibility," in *Barrier Free Environments*, ed. Michael Bednar (Stroudsburg, PA: Dowden, Hutchinson, and Ross, 1977).

14. Kalish, *Late Adulthood*, p. 255.

15. F. M. Carp, *A Future for the Aged: Residents of Victoria Plaza, Austin* (Austin: The University of Texas Press, 1966).

16. Irving Rosow, *Social Integration of the Aged* (New York: Free Press, 1967).

17. Powell Lawton, "Social Ecology and the Health of Older People," in *Aging in America: Readings in Social Gerontology*, eds. Cary S. Kart and Barbara B. Manard (Sherman Oaks, CA: Alfred Publishing, 1976).

18. G. L. Bultena and V. Wood, "The American Retirement Community: Bane or Blessing?" *Journal of Gerontology,* 24 (1969), 209–17.

19. Lawton, "Social Ecology," p. 317.

20. Victor Regnier, "Neighborhood Planning for the Urban Elderly," in *Aging,* eds. Diana S. Woodruff and James E. Birren (Belmont, CA: Wadsworth, 1975), p. 303.

21. James A. Peterson and Culi E. Larson, "Socio-Psychological Factors in Selecting Retirement Housing" (revised version of a paper read at the Research Conference on Patterns of Living and Housing of Middle Age and Older People, Washington, D.C., March 1956), pp. 8–9.

22. Bultena and Wood, "The American Retirement Community."

23. G. C. Hoyt, "The Life of the Retired in a Trailer Park," *American Journal of Sociology,* 59 (1954), 361–70.

24. Harris, *Fact Book,* p. 183.

25. Ibid., p. 185.

26. Ibid., pp. 192–93.

27. Irving Rosow, "Patterns of Living and Housing of Middle-Aged and Older People," in *Proceedings of Research Conference* (Washington, D.C.: U.S. Department of Health, Education and Welfare, 1965), pp. 47–57.

28. Ibid., p. 51.

29. Ibid., p. 56.

30. Ibid., p. 55.

31. L. E. Gottesman, C. E. Quarterman, and G. M. Colin, "Psychosocial Treatment of the Aged," in *The Psychology of Adult Development and Aging,* eds. C. Eisdorfer and M. Lawton (Washington, D.C.: American Psychological Association, 1973), p. 56.

32. E. Goffman, *Asylums* (New York: Anchor, 1961), p. 1.

33. J. Zusman, "Some Explanations of the Changing Appearance of Psychiatric Patients," *International Journal of Psychiatry,* 4 (1967), 216–37.

34. Marcella B. Weiner, Albert J. Brok, and Alvin M. Sandowsky, *Working with the Aged* (Englewood Cliffs, NJ: Prentice-Hall, 1978), p. 38.

35. Kalish, *Late Adulthood,* p. 110.

36. Max Weber, *The Theory of Social and Economic Organization,* trans. A. M. Henderson and Talcott Parsons, ed. Talcott Parsons (New York: Free Press, 1940), p. 38.

37. James D. Thompson, *Organizations in Action* (New York: McGraw-Hill, 1967), pp. 4–7.

38. Ronald G. Corwin, *Militant Professionalism* (New York: Appleton-Century-Crofts, 1970), p. 63.

39. Kalish, *Late Adulthood,* p. 100.

40. John C. Briggs, "Ecology as Gerontology," *The Gerontologist,* 8, no. 2 (1968), 78–79.

41. M. A. Lieberman, "The Relationship of Mortality Rates to Entrance to a Home for the Aged," *Geriatrics,* 16 (1961), 515–19.

42. Jerry H. Borup, Daniel Gallego, and Pamela G. Hefferman, "Relocation and Its Effect on Mortality," *The Gerontologist,* 19, no. 2 (1979), 135–40.

43. Ibid.

CHAPTER 11

1. Epicurus, quoted in *The Great Quotations,* ed. George Seldes (New York: Simon and Schuster, 1967), p. 252.

2. Robert Blauner, "Death and Social Structure," *Psychiatry,* 29 (1966), 378–94. Blauner has a long footnote concerning the source of his statistics. See also Krzywicki, *Primitive Society,* pp. 148, 271; T. E. Smith, "The Cocos-Keeling Islands: A Demographic Laboratory," *Population Studies,* 14 (1960), 94–130.

3. Blauner, "Death and Social Structure," p. 531.

4. Robert Herty, "The Collective Representation of Death," in *Death and the Right Hand,* trans. Rodney & Claudia Needham (Aberdeen: Cohen and West, 1960), pp. 84–86.

5. Bronislaw Malinowski, *Magic, Science, and Religion and Other Essays* (New York: Free Press, 1948), p. 29.

6. C. Wahl, "The Fear of Death," in *The Meaning of Death,* ed. Herman Feifel (New York: McGraw-Hill, 1959), p. 26.

7. Harold Cox, "Mourning Populations: Some Considerations of Historically Comparable Assassinations," *Death Education,* 4, no. 2 (Summer 1980), 125–38.

8. Wayne Sage, "Choosing the Good Death," in *Focus: Aging,* ed. Harold Cox (Guilford, CT: Dushkin Publishing Group, Inc., 1978), pp. 188–194.

9. Victor W. Marshall, "Socialization for Impending Death in a Retirement Village," *American Journal of Sociology,* 80 (1975), 1125.

10. Ibid., p. 1127.

11. Ibid., pp. 1127–8.

12. Quote in Oedipus Coloneau, lines 1224–6, in *Death: Current Perspectives,* ed. Edwin S. Schneidman (Palo Alto, CA: Mayfield, 1976).

13. Arnold Toynbee and others, "Man's Concern with Death," in *Death: Current Perspectives,* ed. Edwin Schneidman (Palo Alto, CA: Mayfield, 1976), p. 19.

14. John A. Behnke and Sissela Bak, eds., *The Dilemma of Euthanasia* (Garden City, NY: Anchor Press, 1975).

15. Marshall, "Socialization," p. 1138.

16. Avery Weisman, "Fallacies about Dying Patients," in *Death: Current Perspectives,* ed. Edwin S. Schneidman (Palo Alto, CA: Mayfield, 1976), pp. 439–40.

17. Howard Becker, "The Sorrow of Bereavement," *Journal of Abnormal and Social Psychology,* 27 (1933), p. 399.

18. W. M. Lamers, "Funerals are Good for People—M.D.'s Included," *Medical Economics,* 46 (June 24, 1969), 104–107.

19. K. C. Aldrich, "Some Dynamics of Anticipatory Grief," in *Anticipatory Grief,* ed. B. Schoenberg and others (New York: Columbia University Press, 1914), p. 5.

CHAPTER 12

1. Harold Cox, Gurmeet Sekhon, and Charles Norman, "Social Characteristics of the Elderly in Indiana," *Proceedings of the 1978 Indiana Academy of Social Sciences* (1978), pp. 186–97.

2. U.S. Bureau of the Census, "Demographic Aspects of Aging and the Older Population in the U.S.," *Current Population Reports,* series P–23, no. 59 (May 1976), p. 52.

3. Herman B. Brotman, "Income and Poverty in the Older Population in 1975," *The Gerontologist,* 17, no. 1 (1977), 24. Quoting U.S. Bureau of the Census data.

4. Carole Allen and Herman Brotman, *Chartbook on Aging* (Washington, D.C.: White House Conference on Aging, 1981), p. 54.

5. James Schulz, *The Economics of Aging,* 2nd ed. (Belmont, CA: Wadsworth, 1980), p. 37.

6. Ibid., p. 28.

7. Ibid., p. 29.

8. Ibid., p. 31.

9. Edwin Mansfield, *Economics: Principles, Problems, Decisions,* 3rd ed. (New York: W. W. Norton & Co., Inc., 1977), pp. 177–78.

CHAPTER 13

1. See Louis Harris and Associates, *The Myth and Realities of Aging in America* (Washington, D.C.: The National Council on the Aging, Inc., 1975); Carl E. Pope and William F. Feyherm, "A Review of Recent Trends: The Effects of Crime on the Elderly," *The Police Chief* (February 1976); Alan A. Malinchak, *Crime and Gerontology* (Englewood Cliffs, NJ: Prentice-Hall, 1980).

2. H. Erskine, "The Polls: Fear of Violence and Crime," *Public Opinion Quarterly*, 38 (1974), 131–45.

3. Frank Clemente, and Michael Kleiman, "Fear of Crime Among the Aged," *The Gerontologist*, 16, no. 3 (1976), 207–208.

4. Ibid., p. 309.

5. Erskine, "The Polls," p. 144.

6. Fay Loma Cook, "Criminal Victimization of the Elderly: A New National Problem," in *Victimization and Society*, ed. Emelio C. Viano (Washington, D.C.: Visage Press, 1976).

7. Jack Goldsmith and Noel F. Thomas, "Crimes Against The Elderly: A Continuing National Crisis," *Aging* (June-July 1974), p. 11.

8. Michael Hindelang, "Criminal Victimization in Eight American Cities," *Law Enforcement Assistance Administration* (1975), p. 377.

9. Alan A. Malinchak and Douglas Wright, "The Scope of Elderly Victimization," *Aging*, nos. 281–82 (April 1978), 12–16.

10. George E. Antunes and others, "Patterns of Personal Crime Against the Elderly," *Gerontology*, 17, no. 4 (1977), 321–27.

11. Arthur Patterson, "Territorial Behavior and the Fear of Crime in the Elderly," *The Police Chief* (February 1977), pp. 26–29.

12. Marlene A. Rifia, "The Response of the Older Adult to Criminal Victimization," *The Police Chief* (February 1977), pp. 32–34.

13. Ibid., p. 33.

14. Patterson, "Territorial Behavior," p. 27.

15. Ibid., p. 27.

16. Ibid., p. 28.

17. Eva Kahana and others, "Perspectives of Aged on Victimization, Ageism, and Their Problems in Urban Society," *The Gerontologist*, 17, no. 2 (April 1977), 121–29.

CHAPTER 14

1. Glenn D. Norval and Michael Grimes, "Aging, Voting, and Political Interest," *American Sociological Review*, 33 (1978), 563–75.

2. Jaber F. Gubrium, *Times, Roles and Self in Old Age* (New York: Human Sciences Press, 1976), p. 142.

3. A. Campbell, "Social and Psychological Determinants of Voting Behavior," in *Politics and Age*, eds. W. Donahue and Clark Tibbitts (Ann Arbor: The University of Michigan Press, 1962), p. 92.

4. R. E. Lane, *Political Life* (New York: Free Press, 1959).

5. A. Campbell, "Politics Through the Life Cycle," *The Gerontologist* (1971), pp. 112–17.

6. Herman J. Loether, *Problems of Aging* (Belmont, CA: Dickerson, 1967), pp. 155–56.

7. Elizabeth B. Douglas, William P. Cleveland, and George Maddox, "Political Attitudes, Age, and Aging: A Cohort Analysis of Archival Data," *Journal of Gerontology*, 74, no. 26 (1976), pp. 666–73.

8. Georgia M. Barrow and Patricia A. Smith, *Age, Ageism, and Society* (St. Paul, Minn.: West, 1979), p. 356.

9. Paul Kleyman, *Senior Power: Growing Old Rebelliously* (San Francisco: Glide Publications, 1974).

10. Pauline Ragan and James Dowd, "The Emerging Political Consciousness of the Aged: A Generational Interpretation," *Journal of Social Issues*, 3, no. 3 (1977), 137–50.

11. Henry J. Pratt, "Old Age Associations in National Politics," *Annals of American Academy of Political and Social Sciences* (September 1974), pp. 106–19.

12. Beth B. Hess, "The Politics of Aging," *Society*, 15, no. 5 (July–August 1978), 23.

13. Donald Cowgill, "Critical Problems of Aging" (Lecture given at Indiana State University Workshop, June 1977).

14. David Hackett Fischer, "The Politics of Aging in America: A Short History," *The Journal of the Institute for Socioeconomic Studies*, 3, no. 2 (1979), 64.

15. E. C. Hughes, "Dilemmas and Contradictions of Status," *American Journal of Sociology*, 50 (1944–45), 353; E. Jackson, "Status Consistency and Symptoms of Stress," *American Sociological Review*, 27 (1962), 469.

16. Gubrium, *Time, Roles, and Self*, pp. 128–30.

17. G. Lenski, "Status Crystallization: A Non-Vertical Dimension of Social Status," *American Sociological Review* (1954), p. 204.

18. Campbell, "Social and Psychological Determinants of Voting Behavior," p. 152.

19. William F. Ogburn, *Social Change* (New York: B. W. Heubsch, 1922), pp. 200–201.

20. Louis Lowry, "Social Welfare and the Aging," in *Social Problems of the Aging*, ed. Mildred Seltzer and others (New York: Wadsworth, 1978), pp. 300–314.

21. H. L. Wilensky and C. N. Lebeaux, *Industrial Society and Social Welfare*, 2nd ed. (New York: Free Press, 1966).

22. HEW Publication No. (SSA) 78–10050 (Washington, D.C.: U.S. Congressional Budget Office, 1977), p. 13.

23. Case cited by Jane Royse, Director of Transportation, Program Area #7, Agency on Aging, Terre Haute, IN. Reprinted by permission.

24. Case cited by Rick Jimison, Director of Area #7, Agency on Aging Homemaker and Handyman Services, Terre Haute, IN. Reprinted by permission.

25. Jane Royse, as cited above.

26. Rick Jimison, as cited above.

27. Carroll Estes, *The Aging Enterprise* (San Francisco: Jossey-Bass, 1979), pp. 221–24.

28. Ibid., pp. 241–45.

CHAPTER 15

1. Antoinette Bosco and Jane Porcino, *What Do We Really Know About Aging* (Albany: State University of New York, 1977), pp. 75–78.

2. Russell Ward, *The Aging Experience* (New York: J. B. Lippincott, 1979), p. 502.

3. Bernice Neugarten and Robert Havighurst, eds., *Extending the Human Life Span: Social Policy and Social Ethics* (Washington, D.C.: U.S. Government Printing Office, 1977).

4. Jon Hendricks and C. Davis Hendricks, *Aging in Mass Society* (Cambridge, MA: Winthrop, 1977), p. 387.

5. Ibid., pp. 396–97.

6. Population Reference Bureau, Inc., *Inter-Change, Population Educators Newsletter* (ISSN: 0047–0465), 7, no. 1 (January 1978), 2.

7. Bosco and Porcino, *What Do We Really Know About Aging*, p. 77.

INDEX